Y0-BDV-784

Contributions to Management Science

Daniel O. Klier

Managing Diversified Portfolios

What Multi-Business Firms Can Learn from Private Equity

Physica-Verlag

A Springer Company

Daniel O. Klier
daniel.klier@alumni.unisg.ch

Dissertation, Technical University of Dortmund, 2008

ISBN: 978-3-7908-2172-7 e-ISBN: 978-3-7908-2173-4
DOI: 10.1007/978-3-7908-2173-4

Springer Series in Contributions to Management Science ISSN 1431-1941

Library of Congress Control Number: 2009921234

Cover design: SPi Publisher Services

Printed on acid-free paper

Springer is part of Springer Science+Business Media (www.springer.com)

Foreword

There has been a long tradition of research on the relation between diversification and performance of public corporations in the strategy and finance fields. As for private equity portfolios, research on this matter is rather scarce. From a theoretical as well as from a practical perspective, however, it is interesting to know more about the relation between private equity portfolio diversification and performance, how private equity firms manage their portfolios, and what public companies can learn from private equity firms. These are the research questions which are addressed in Daniel Klier's research.

In order to answer these questions, the author uses a two-tier research design. As a first step, he compares the diversification-performance link of public corporations and private equity firms. With respect to the private equity sample and the operationalization of the relevant variables, the study is highly innovative in terms of generating the PE sample from databases like Preqin and Dealogic, constructing a diversification measure from transaction data, and developing comparable performance measures for private equity firms as well as traditional multi-business firms.

As the second step, which is exploratory in nature, the author explores management models of PE firms. The sample of 20 US and Europe-based private equity firms is unique and of high quality, because the author succeeded in getting in-depth interviews with top decision makers of PE firms. The exploratory study extracts three clusters of management models that PE firms are using, and their relation to performance.

Beyond its high academic standards and its significant contribution to the empirical knowledge on the diversification-performance link in PE firms, the study provides important lessons for private equity managers, investors and corporate managers with regard to choosing the right portfolio strategy and the right management model.

For these reasons, the study is highly relevant to practitioners as well as to academics in the field of strategy and finance. Therefore, the study deserves wide attention in the academic and in the business world.

Professor Dr. Martin K. Welge

Acknowledgements

The research theme "managing diversified portfolios – what multi-business firms can learn from private equity" provided me with an exceptional opportunity to combine some of my strongest interests in my dissertation. Diversification, conglomerates, and corporate strategy sparked my interest early on in my academic and professional path and let me through my studies at the University of St. Gallen and my career at McKinsey & Company. Corporate finance, on the other hand, has always provided me with a counterbalance to strategic insight and has given me the ability to properly evaluate strategic initiatives from an investor perspective. Private equity combines both elements and resembles at the same time a highly innovative form of ownership and management that so far has found only limited consideration in academic research. Fascinated by this phenomenon and motivated by the increasing importance of private equity as an asset class and public matter, this dissertation has been an academically, professionally, and privately enriching experience that has only been possible with the support and contribution from many sides.

First of all, my thanks go to my doctoral advisor Professor Dr. Martin K. Welge. Not only was he able to provide me with excellent guidance through the world of strategic management, he also granted me the right level of academic freedom together with targeted intervention whenever necessary. I appreciate his strong commitment to my research, his continuing willingness to offer advice, as well as the pleasant and encouraging work atmosphere he created. I would also like to express great gratitude to Professor Dr. Peter Witt and Professor Dr. Wolfgang Leininger for their support and valued input.

I further owe great thanks to Professor Kathryn R. Harrigan, who welcomed me as my academic advisor at Columbia Business School in New York. The regular and intense exchange of ideas with her in early-morning sessions gave me the opportunity to challenge my own thinking and improve the quality of my research. I am also indebted to Professor Malia F. Mason at Columbia Business School for her methodological support and openness about her experiences in empirical research as well as Professor Laura B. Resnikoff, Director of Columbia's Private Equity program, for sharing her thoughts about private equity.

This dissertation would not have been feasible without the willingness of investment professionals in leading private equity firms in the United States and Europe to reveal information about their management models that are generally undisclosed to the public. I highly value the time spent by private equity professionals to support this research and the ability to gain such privileged insights into the investment and management philosophy as well as value creation levers of private equity investors.

I moreover owe sincere gratitude to my employer McKinsey & Company for the opportunity to write this dissertation and their financial and intellectual support during this time. I would like to thank Dr. Markus Boehme, Dr. Philipp Haerle, and Conor F. Kehoe for their contributions during the definition of my research question as well as Andreas Beroutsos and Aly Jeddy for challenging my findings in intellectually engaging discussions during my stay in New York. I owe further recognition to the outstanding support received from McKinsey colleagues around the world and to the great office communities in Berlin and New York.

Finally, I would like to thank those people, who made my time during this dissertation a wonderful experience. My friends in Europe and New York made this period of academic challenges a highly enjoyable time. My parents gave me everything I needed to get to this point in my life and always believed in me. And last but not least, my girlfriend Friderike, who showed great encouragement and patience and walked with me along the ups and downs of my academic adventures.

Berlin, January 2009 Daniel O. Klier

Contents

Abbreviations

AIM	Alternative Investment Market
ARD	American Research and Development Corporation
BSD	Broad spectrum diversification
CAPM	Capital asset pricing model
CD&R	Clayton, Dubilier & Rice
CEO	Chief executive officer
CFO	Chief financial officer
COO	Chief operating officer
DR	Related diversification
DT	Total diversification
DU	Unrelated diversification
EBIT	Earnings before interest and taxes
EBITDA	Earnings before interest, tax, depreciation and amortization
EU	European Union
E.U.	European Union
EUR	European currency Euro
EVCA	European Private Equity and Venture Capital Association
GSB	Graduate School of Business, Columbia University
GP	General partner
HBS	Harvard Business School, Harvard University
IPO	Initial public offering
IRR	Internal rate of return
KKR	Kohlberg Kravis Roberts & Co.
LBO	Leveraged buyout
LEPP	Leveraged equity purchase plan
LP	Limited partner
M&A	Mergers and acquisitions
MBI	Management buyin

MBO	Management buyout
MIRR	Modified internal rate of return
NASDAQ	National Association of Securities Dealers Automated Quotations
NAV	Net asset value
NPV	Net present value
NSD	Narrow spectrum diversification
NVCA	American National Venture Capital Association
NYSE	New York Stock Exchange
PE	Private equity
P/E ratio	Price/earnings ratio
R&D	Research and development
PIPE	Private investment in public equity
RoA	Return on assets
RoE	Return on equity
RoS	Return on sales
S&P	Standard and Poor's
SBIC	Small business investment company
SIC	Standard industrial classification system
TSR	Total return to shareholder
UK	United Kingdom
U.K.	United Kingdom
US	United States
U.S.	United States
USD	United States currency U.S. Dollar
VC	Venture capital
WACC	Weighted averaged cost of capital

List of Figures

List of Tables

Chapter 1
Introduction

The rise of the new conglomerates
Paul O'Keeffe, BBC

There have been two trends dominating the shape of the corporate landscape in the past decade: On the one hand, large publicly listed corporations have been urged by investors to focus their activities and divest unrelated businesses blaming diversification of the corporate business portfolio for performance deficits when compared to single-business benchmarks. On the other hand, private equity firms have been experiencing tremendous growth rates with a single value proposition to its investors – superior return – disregarding and even taking advantage of focus movements of corporations.

On the side of public corporations, there has hardly been any topic as high on a CEO's agenda as the level of diversification and scope of businesses the company is active in. After decades of conglomerate merger activity and dominance of broadly diversified companies, an increasing professionalism of capital markets and their investors has led to pressure on unrelated multi-business firms. Diversified firms are blamed for cross-subsidizing negative NPV projects, destroying value instead of realizing synergies with their corporate centers, as well as less robust incentive, performance management, and control mechanisms than single-business firms (Koltes, 2005; Smolka, 2006). Markets are therefore quicker than ever to discount the valuations of diversified companies.

While traditional conglomerates face increasing headwind, the private equity industry and more specifically the leveraged buyout part of the industry is experiencing strong and – despite recent woes in the credit market – ongoing growth with average increases of the industry's annual investment volume of almost 30%. This development spiraled to US$ 734 billion of announced global deal volume in 2006 (Capital, 2007) making the private equity industry responsible for 20% of all M&A activity (Stocker, 2007). Interestingly, only few of the world's dominating private equity firms of the nature of KKR, Blackstone, the Texas Pacific Group or Permira are positioning themselves as specialists in a specific industry, and by now most firms are owners and managers of broadly diversified portfolios as Jon Moulton, head of Alchemy in London, clearly positions his industry: "We are the people who run the

D.O. Klier, *Managing Diversified Portfolios*,
DOI: 10.1007/978-3-7908-2173-4_1, © 2009 Physica-Verlag Heidelberg

new conglomerates" (Jon Moulton in O'Keeffe, 2005). And indeed, there are numerous parallels between the old conglomerates and private equity firms; both would claim for themselves that they can provide their businesses with superior management skills, both would also say that they have a better grip on the financials of each business and both would most certainly say that they know when to buy and when to divest a business (Jackson, 2006). Ironically, however, many of today's private equity acquisitions are in fact businesses divested by former industrial conglomerates striving to bring focus into their portfolios and finding their place in the diversified portfolio of one of the numerous LBO firms screening the market for attractive targets.

1.1 Research Motivation

This dissertation has been motivated by two key elements: (1) the practical relevance of these two trends in recent economic developments and their power to further shape the corporate landscape and (2) the theoretical relevance of these phenomena due to the unbalanced coverage of diversification effects as well as management models of multi-business firms, on the one side, and private equity firms, on the other side, in academic literature.

1.1.1 Practical Relevance

Both trends, the discussion about corporate diversification and the success of private equity LBO funds, have had a significant impact on strategic directions of today's corporations and will continue to do so.

On the side of publicly listed corporations, the last decades have been marked by pressure on diversified firms. CEOs, however, know that no matter how focused their firms are, diversification will eventually be necessary to generate new growth and redeploy the firms' capital (Harper & Viguerie, 2002b). New concepts such as related diversification around a core competence are currently finding interest with large corporations thriving for new growth (Varanasi, 2005). A recent example for this movement is the acquisition of U.S. based Engelhard by BASF. Although the product is new to the chemical giant, it allows the firm to position itself better as leading supplier of a broad spectrum of products for the automotive industry (Froendhoff, 2006). Similar transactions and strategic concepts will follow to justify management's decisions to generate growth through diversification and will keep alive the discussion about the influence of diversification on valuation and performance as well as the most appropriate management techniques.

At the same time, corporations will increasingly wonder how private equity firms generate value out of assets their former owners have divested – often due to performance deficits and lack of strategic opportunities. By now, first transactions such as the takeover of Corus, an Anglo-Dutch steelmaker, by the Indian conglomerate Tata are found to have private equity structures with high leverage and non-recourse financing to the parent company (Jackson, 2006). Another example is the German media giant Bertelsmann, that recently announced the setup of a 500 million investment vehicle in cooperation with the private equity arms of Citigroup and Morgan Stanley to give the company access to a broad spectrum of innovative business models (Financial Times Deutschland, 2007). In a next step, managers of public corporations will also need to wonder how private equity firms actually manage their portfolios and what lessons can be drawn for their businesses.

Private equity, on the other side, is experiencing almost unrivaled growth in investor demand. The contributions of investors are – despite the current turbulences on the world's debt markets – expected to more than double by 2010 allowing private equity firms to take on even larger targets than today. There are already increasing rumors that there have been repeated attempts to take over large caps such as Vivendi, Continental, or Tui and move out of the mid-market segment or the acquisition of divested business units of diversified firms respectively (Guerrera & Politi, 2007). This move is supported by the augmenting cooperation between PE firms by pooling funds for single transactions, so-called club deals (Capital, 2007; Koehler & Koenen, 2007).

This success story of the PE industry is largely driven by broadly diversified companies such as Blackstone with investments in media, automotive suppliers, waste managers, real estate and several other unrelated businesses or the Texas Pacific Group that owns among others the fast food chain Burger King as well as the motorcycle producer Ducati and several airlines (Haimann & Osadnik, 2006). So far, little worry has spread about the potential negative impact of diversification on the performance of private equity firms and their funds. Based on the experience drawn from stock market listed corporations, however, similar discussions about the need to focus could eventually be on the agenda of the PE industry. A first taste of this was given by Klaus Zumwinkel, former CEO of Deutsche Post, in a recent interview in a German business publication openly questioning the ability of private equity firms to manage diversification any better than multi-business firms (Zumwinkel in Boehmer & Ruess, 2006).

Furthermore, there is little transparency about the way private equity firms manage their investment portfolios and what could be described as key success factors of this industry – not only from outside the PE scope but also within the industry. Yet rising competition and a commoditization of the private equity industry will put increasing spotlight on the importance of an active management of a firm's investment portfolio (Harper & Schneider, 2004). The days when pure financial engineering dominated the value generation during a transaction finally seem to be over (Jackson, 2006) and will require PE firms to look for management best practices to maximize value creation.

1.1.2 Theoretical Relevance

When trying to find these trends in academic literature, results are mixed. There has been intensive research investigating the influence of diversification on the valuation and performance of publicly listed companies as well as the different management styles used by multi-business firms to justify their existence. When looking on the private equity side, however, research about the influence of diversification on the performance of a private equity firm's funds as well as the management methods applied to PE investment portfolios is scarce.

Academic research has been on and off the question of how diversified firms are valued and perform compared to single-business counterparts since the 1960s with influential contributions such as Gort (1962), Rumelt (1974, 1982), Montgomery (1982, 1985), Berger and Ofek (1995), Lang and Stulz (1994) and many others. The topic has again sparked particular interest in recent years as more and more diversified firms in Europe and Asia see pressure similar to what happened in the U.S. during the 1980s forcing corporations to focus on core businesses (e.g. see Chakrabarti, Singh, & Mahmood, 2007; Nicolai & Thomas, 2006).

Academics have also been intensely investigating the question of how management deals and should deal with diversified portfolios ranging from the role of the corporate center to the interaction with individual business units and the overall strategic management of the business portfolio. These areas have drawn the attention of similarly well-known researchers and brought forward seminal studies such as, among many others, Campbell and Goold (1995a, 1995b, 1998, 1999), Prahalad and Hamel (1989, 1990), Prahalad and Bettis (1986, 1995), as well as Eisenhardt together with colleagues (1992, 1999).

On the private equity front on the other hand, most of the influential literature was published during the late 1980s and early 1990s, when the buyout phenomenon for the first time became a matter of public and academic interest. Only the recent steep rise in LBO transactions has brought the topic prominently back onto researchers' agendas. So far, however, research has centered on the relevance of private equity as an asset class for investors, methodologies to compare private equity performance to public market benchmarks, and the value creation techniques on a single transaction level. The ongoing creation of private equity research centers as well as increasing interest of researchers from finance and strategic management research have allowed substantial light to be shed into these areas of research with important contributions, among others, by Kaplan (Andrade & Kaplan, 1998; Kaplan, 1989, 1991; Kaplan & Schoar, 2004), Lerner (Lerner, 1995; Lerner & Hardymon, 2002; Lerner, Sorensen, & Strömberg, 2008), Gottschalg (Gottschalg & Meier, 2005; Gottschalg, Phalippou, & Zollo, 2004) as well as Ljungqvist and Richardson (2003a, 2003b). The question of how diversification affects the performance of private equity firms and how private equity players manage the diversified portfolios of their funds, however, has found only very limited representation in academic research.

Taking it even one step further, there is a substantial gap in academic research bringing the two sides of the medal together assessing what causes the observed similarities or differences in valuation and performance of publicly listed corporations and private equity firms in correlation with the degree of diversification of their business portfolios. It furthermore signals significant research headroom to understand and assess what multi-business firms can learn from private equity management styles and how applicable these techniques are to the world of stock-listed companies.

1.2 Research Objective

Based on these practical and theoretical observations, there is considerable interest from practitioners – in particular managers of diversified corporations – as well as academic researchers to approach the overall research questions of this study: "Managing diversified portfolios – what multi-business firms can learn from private equity". In order to approach this question, the research can be broken down into two key objectives: (1) the investigation of the influence of diversification on the performance of private equity and a comparison with public corporations as well as (2) the investigation of the key success factors of private equity firms in managing diversified portfolios.

This dissertation is generally oriented at the strategic management discipline of academic research but will draw on insights and techniques of the corporate finance discipline as required.

1.2.1 Diversification and Performance

The first part of the empirical analysis aims at researching the impact of diversification on the performance of private equity portfolios and comparing these results with the relationship of diversification and performance in publicly listed corporations. In other words, the objective of this analysis is to determine "whether private equity firms really have the ability to deliver higher returns independent of the degree of diversification and can therefore function as a role model for public corporations". Consequently, this part of the research is supposed to address the following research questions:

(1) *Performance – private equity vs. public corporations*: Does private equity generally show a stronger performance than investments in publicly listed corporations?
(2) *Diversification and performance in private equity*: Does private equity experience a performance difference between business portfolios with a clear industry focus and diversified portfolios? Are there specific clusters such as focused, related-diversified, unrelated-diversified that show significant performance differences?
(3) *Diversification and Performance – private equity vs. public corporations*: Do private equity and publicly listed corporations experience a comparable relationship between the performance of business portfolios with a clear industry focus and diversified portfolios? Are there comparable performance clusters between private equity and public corporations?

While the research field of diversification in the private equity industry is fairly uncovered, the methodology to investigate comparable questions long exists. The large number of publications regarding the influence of diversification on valuation and performance within public corporations has produced a set of methodologies that have been tested and widely approved as effective for the quantitative investigation of the relationship between diversification and valuation as well as performance. This research will therefore apply existing and reliable methodologies with the required adjustments for the private equity industry. It will furthermore concentrate on the correlation of diversification with performance rather than valuation as these metrics are most accessible and comparable between private equity firms and public corporations.[1]

1.2.2 *Managing Diversified Portfolios*

The second element of the empirical research of this study aims at investigating the key success factors of private equity in the management of diversified business portfolios. It therefore addresses the question "what are the practices that enable private equity to manage diversified investment portfolios" and "what should public corporations pay further attention to" from a comprehensive perspective of the overall private equity management model. The study is intended to examine the activities a general manager in a multi-business firm's holding would be engaging in to create value to the overall portfolio, the so-called parenting advantage (Campbell, Goold, & Alexander, 1995a, 1995b). It therefore addresses questions of the following kind:

(1) *Governance model*: How does the 'corporate center' interact with the individual portfolio companies of the private equity firm? What kind of performance metrics are required by the center? How autonomous are individual portfolio companies in decision making? How are incentive systems installed to improve the alignment between private equity partnership and portfolio companies?
(2) *Availability of center functions and resources*: What role does the corporate center play in a private equity firm? What services does the corporate center provide? How are 'corporate resources' coordinated within the private equity firm?
(3) *Leverage of competences and resources*: Do private equity firms attempt to leverage competences and resources across different portfolio companies of the firm and if so, what mechanism do they apply?
(4) *Portfolio management*: How do private equity firms manage the overall investment portfolio of the firm? How does active and strategic portfolio management look like in a private equity firm?

---

[1] A more detailed description of the diversification and performance measures applied in this study will be provided in the introduction of the empirical methodology in Section 5.2.

Thus, the study will not explore the value creation techniques on the level of individual transactions and portfolio companies of a private equity firm or what would be comparable to the job of the manager of individual business units in a multi-business firm but instead focuses on the value creation opportunities from a holding and shareholder perspective.

As an outlook for further academic research, this paper is moreover supposed to lay the foundation to quantitatively test the propositions derived regarding the key success factors of private equity and to evaluate the applicability of the private equity management model in traditional multi-business firms.

1.3 Structure of Dissertation

This study is structured in seven chapters as outlined in Fig. 1.1. The structure is supposed to establish a joint starting position for the reader followed by empirical analyses, which are divided into two sections, addressing the two different research objectives in one empirical chapter each. These chapters present the approach and the results of the study and are completed by a final chapter for conclusions and outlook.

To establish the joint starting position of the study, the paper outlines an overview of academic theories and literature about diversification in public corporations including key definitions and a general overview of academic contributions in this

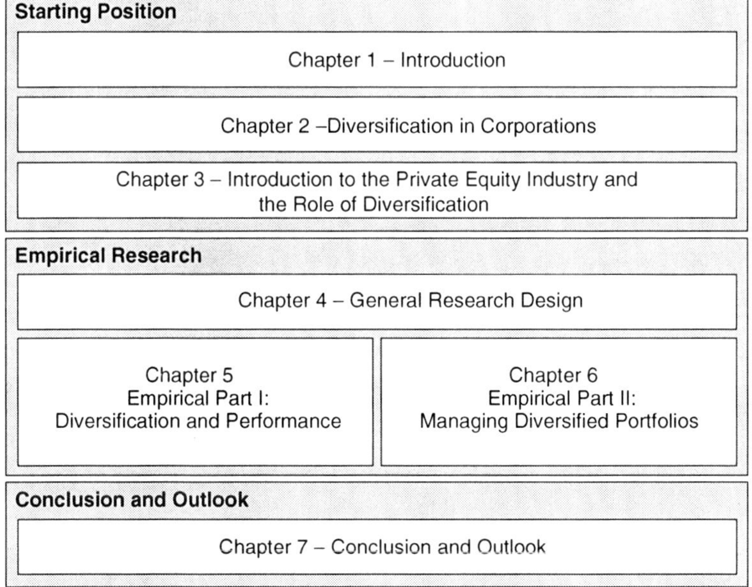

Fig. 1.1 Structure of dissertation

particular area of research. It is followed by two detailed sections regarding the focus areas of this research: the relationship between diversification and performance as well as the different academic views about the management approaches to diversified portfolios (Chap. 2). It furthermore gives an introduction into the private equity industry including a detailed definition of all parts of private equity relevant for this study as well as an overview of the historic developments and current trends of the industry. It also outlines the value creation techniques of private equity firms and reviews the scarce academic literature concerning diversification in private equity (Chap. 3).

After an introduction of the general research design (Chap. 4), the paper is divided into two empirical sections, one for each research objective. The first part (Chap. 5) outlines the study's hypotheses, explains the detailed methodology to generate insights about the correlation of diversification and performance and portrays as well as discusses the empirical results. The second part (Chap. 6) of the empirical research displays the detailed methodology and results of the research concerning the key success factors of private equity in managing diversified portfolios and develops propositions about the applicability of the private equity management model in traditional multi-business firms. Consequently, the paper closes with conclusions and outlook for practitioners and academic researchers (Chap. 7).

Chapter 2
Diversification in Corporations

The wheel of fashion has moved virtually full circle from the days of specialization through the heyday of conglomerates to the advice of sticking to the knitting

Richard Reed, Georg Luffmann, Strategic Management Journal

Diversification in – mostly public – corporations has been subject to academic research for decades and has found its place in academic literature in multiple disciplines. Along with such concepts as synergies, distinctive competences, and generic strategies, the diversification theme is furthermore commonly acknowledged as one of the key drivers of the strategic management discipline (Ramanujam & Varadarajan, 1989: 523). This chapter is supposed to (a) establish an understanding of the definition of diversification used in academic literature, (b) give a summary of the different streams of research including a general overview of different research areas and the key learnings from predominant research and leading publications as well as (c) provide a detailed analysis of relevant theories and literature in the two focus areas and research objectives of this dissertation – "Diversification and Performance" and "Managing Diversified Portfolios".

This chapter should therefore establish the starting position of academic thinking about diversification in corporations and lay the foundation for the further investigation of diversification in private equity and its influence on performance as well as the key success factors of PE firms in managing diversified portfolios.

2.1 Definition of Diversification

"As a topic of research, diversification has a rich tradition" (Ramanujam & Varadarajan, 1989: 523). Along with the intense academic coverage of the concept of diversification, researchers have produced various definitions of diversification. Indicators of diversification range from the entrance of an existing firm into new products over the use of new resources to the way into new markets (Pitts & Hopkins, 1982; Varanasi, 2005). Gort (1962), as one of the first, defined diversification in terms of the concept

D.O. Klier, *Managing Diversified Portfolios*,
DOI: 10.1007/978-3-7908-2173-4_2, © 2009 Physica-Verlag Heidelberg

of "heterogeneity of output" which is found in similar shape in Bettis (1981), Bettis and Hall (1982), and Bettis and Mahajan (1985) or Montgomery (1982, 1985), Montgomery and Wernerfelt (1988) who define diversification in terms of the reported industry classification. The lack of numerous publications to clearly state their definition of diversification has been acknowledged as a significant shortcoming in creating comparable research results and has evoked the call for an explicit definition in each study (Briglauer, 2000). Generally, diversification has been defined from two directions – a process-view of diversification as well as a status-view, so-called "diversity" – each bringing forward a fairly distinct area of academic research (Beckmann, 2006: 15; Simmonds, 1990: 400–401).

2.1.1 Diversification as Process

Diversification as process defines the activities of firms to enter new product-market combinations as defined by Ansoff (1958) and Rumelt (1974). The process of diversification thereby is the primary interest of researchers. It covers the decision process of firms determining why a firm should diversify into new businesses. It furthermore comprises the decision in which direction a firm should diversify as well as the selection of the appropriate mode of diversification, i.e., by internal development or via acquisitions on the external market (e.g., see Lamont & Anderson, 1985; Yip, 1982). From this perspective, simple product line extensions that are not accompanied by changes in the administrative linkage mechanisms do not qualify as diversification (Ramanujam & Varadarajan, 1989: 525–526). This definition of diversification has been adapted by numerous researchers providing insights on different steps of this decision process. An overview of the key contributions within this definition will be provided in Sect. 2.2.3 "Entry into New Businesses" of this chapter.

2.1.2 Diversification as Status

The status of diversification or "diversity" on the other hand focuses on the degree of diversification across different products and rarely different markets or resources, whereby a product is defined as a good or service that passes between a supplier and its customers.[1] This approach then considers each product or product type to be a separate business (Pitts & Hopkins, 1982: 621). Overall, three major categories of diversity can be found in academic literature laying the basis for most studies: focused businesses,

[1]The definition of diversity based on products has taken the dominant share within academic literature. Pitts and Hopkins (1982) explain this dominance by the availability of objective data about firm products in the form of SIC codes while data about required and available resources and market characteristics are difficult to measure and highly subjective.

related diversified businesses and unrelated diversified businesses (e.g., see Hall & St. John, 1994; Markides, 1995; Montgomery, 1982; Palepu, 1985; Varanasi, 2005).

(1) *Focused businesses*: Focused firms are generally characterized by their commitment to a discrete single product
(2) *Related diversified businesses*: Related diversification occurs when a company manufactures products using a common production facility or a technology which is already being used within the company. The joint use of identical distribution or other marketing systems as well as the vertical integration, e.g., of successive stages of production into a common unit, also characterize related diversification
(3) *Unrelated diversified businesses*: Unrelated diversification occurs when a company produces goods or services, which are not related production-, technology- or market-wise.

Based on these categories, researchers have developed various sub-categories such as Rumelt's ten strategic categories (Bettis, 1981; Bettis & Hall, 1982; Grant & Jammine, 1988; Rumelt, 1974, 1982) or have narrowed their studies to two broad clusters "focused vs. diversified" (Berger & Ofek, 1995; Lang & Stulz, 1994; Mansi & Reeb, 2002). However, the overall consensus – specifically in recent publications – confirms the relevance and practicability of this three category system (Hall & St. John, 1994; Harper & Viguerie, 2002a; Markides, 1995; Palepu, 1985; Varanasi, 2005). A more detailed overview of the different diversification measures used in academic research will be provided in Sect. 2.3 "Diversification and Performance".[2]

This study employs the status-view of diversification as primary definition criteria and thereby focuses on the product dimension of diversification. It uses the widely accepted three category classification of diversification – focused, related-diversified and unrelated-diversified – for its empirical investigation. The precise implementation of this definition for the empirical research of this dissertation will be provided during the methodological introduction of empirical part I (Sect. 5.2).

2.2 Overview of Academic Research on Corporate Diversification

The phenomenon of corporate diversification has sparked the interest of researchers from numerous directions and has created a large amount of literature shedding light on different areas of this field of interest. Besides a "General Overview of Academic Research", this section of the literature review is structured along the main research directions "Motives for Diversification", "Entry into New Businesses",

[2]The term 'conglomerate' is commonly used as a synonym for unrelated-diversified firms, mostly used in media and commercially-oriented publications while academia generally uses the term 'unrelated-diversified'. The term 'multi-business firm' is a synonym for related- and unrelated-diversified firms used to group all diversified firms together when contrasted to focused/single-business firms.

"Structure of Multi-business Firms", "Management of Multi-business Firms" and "Influence of Diversification on Financial Performance".

2.2.1 General Overview of Academic Research

The topic "diversification" has sparked the interest of business historians, economists as well as researchers in the areas of, among others, strategic management, industrial organization, finance, marketing, and law. Although a broad spectrum of research has covered corporate diversification since the late 1950s, little has been done so far to structure the overall field of research. The most comprehensive and most acknowledged contributions have been written by Ramanujam and Varadarajan (1989) and Goold and Luchs (1993) – the former attempting to structure the field by areas of research, the latter leading through the literature chronologically linking academic contributions to economic developments.

Ramanujam and Varadarajan (1989) identify 11 themes of research as presented in Fig. 2.1, whereby four of the themes (box 1–3 and box 11) represent "generic" concepts of strategic management and 7 themes are specific to the topic of diversification (boxes 4–10). They furthermore allocate research publications along the

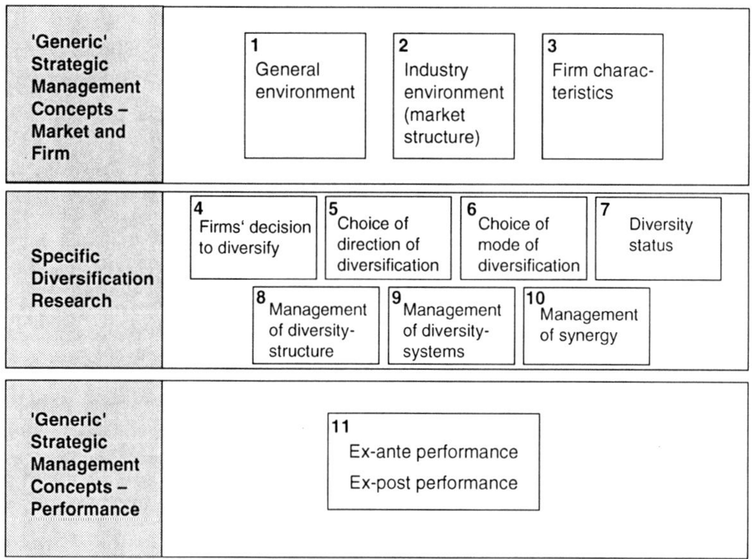

Fig. 2.1 Themes and linkages of diversification research based on Ramanujam and Varadarajan (1989)

linkages between these themes to create a complex but highly comprehensive framework to allow the structuring of a wide field of diversification research.[3]

The central research clusters of this model are largely oriented on the process of diversification a company would undergo starting with the decision to diversify and its motive to do so (box 4) over the direction (box 5), mode of diversification (box 6), and status of diversification (box 7) to the management approach to govern a diversified business portfolio (boxes 8–10).

A similar structure – although not as explicit – can be found in Dundas and Richardson (1982) who describe the implementation of the unrelated product strategy by classifying motives and requirements to pursue diversification, the mode and direction of diversification as well as the structure and management of a diversified business portfolio. A similar approach to organize existing research can also be found in Prahalad's and Bettis' research efforts (Bettis & Prahalad, 1995; Prahalad & Bettis, 1986) resulting in the so-called dominant logic of diversified firms.

Goold and Luchs (1993), on the other hand, take the reader through the historic developments of diversification research and explain how academic concepts are interlinked with economic changes as highlighted in Fig. 2.2.

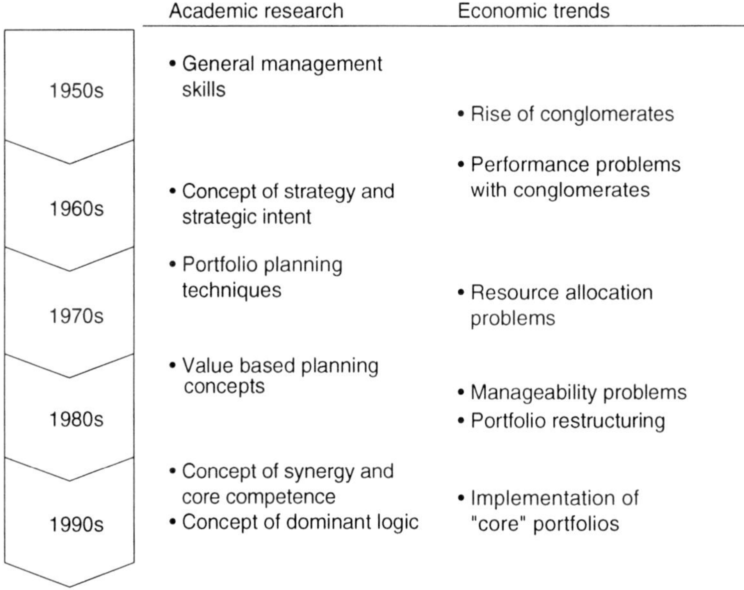

Fig. 2.2 Evolution of thinking on corporate strategy and diversification based on Goold and Luchs (1993)

[3]Ramanujam and Varadarajan's contribution provides a very detailed overview of relevant literature originated between 1962 and the end of the 1980s. The granular structure furthermore allows to cluster most publications of more recent research.

The paper largely concentrates on the different aspects of managing a multi-business firm and excludes such research areas as the influence of diversification on performance. It, however, provides valuable insights in the motives and techniques of conglomerates as well as academics, while at the same time providing a broad overview of relevant literature. It starts with the evolution of the theory of general management skills in the 1950s and the rise of conglomerates. It then displays the ideas of portfolio management in the 1970 and the close link to the resource allocation problems and manageability problems of diversified firms during these years. It closes with the idea of core competences and dominant logic of the 1990s, which finds a corresponding trend in the move towards core portfolios by leading multi-business firms.

Based on these contributions, the following sections of this review of academic theories and empirical results are structured along five clusters resembling a streamlined version of the framework provided by Ramanujam and Varadarajan (1989). The structure along the five themes "Motives for Diversification", "Entry into New Businesses", "Structure of Multi-Business Firms", "Management of Multi-Business Firms", and "Influence of Diversification on Financial Performance" as presented in Fig. 2.3 allows an inclusive while concise overview of relevant academic literature in the following sections. The themes "Diversification and Performance" and "Managing Diversified Portfolios" as most relevant areas for this dissertation will subsequently be regarded in further detail in Sects. 2.3 and 2.4.

2.2.2 *Motives for Diversification*

Diversification has been going through turbulent times, but it has never vanished from a CEO's agenda. Driven by external requirements from investors such as the

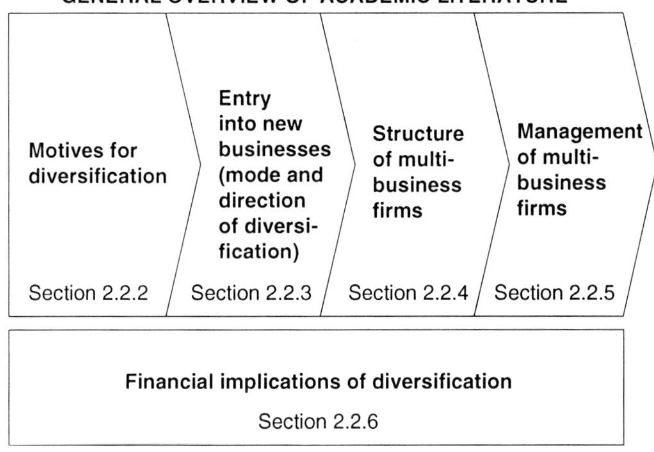

Fig. 2.3 General overview of academic research

pressure to grow or to invest idle cash on the one hand and internal motives, on the other hand, like the presence of exceptional capabilities or personal objectives by management, many corporations seek their fortune in diversification (e.g., see Knop, 2007; Reed & Luffman, 1986; Welge & Al-Laham, 2007).

More fundamentally, there are three established theories offering a comprehensive perspective on the reasons and motives for corporate diversification: the market-power view, the agency view, and the resource-based view (Montgomery, 1994: 164–168). While the market-power view and the resource-based view generally associate positive implications of diversification on performance, the agency view leads to a negative impact of diversification on firm profitability. In addition to the arguments contained in these fundamental theories, the comprehensive review of diversification motives provided by Reed and Luffman (1986) offers additional explanations for corporate diversification including economic and technological drivers, stability of earnings and investment efficiency, as well as the adaptation to customer needs.

2.2.2.1 Market-Power View

Traditionally, the interest of economists in the diversification phenomenon stemmed from a concern for its potentially anti-competitive effects. The view argues that diversified firms will "thrive at the expense of non-diversified firms" (Hill, 1985: 828). The success of multi-business firms is, however, not linked to greater efficiency but lies in the conglomerates' access to what is termed "conglomerate power". Edwards (1955) argued that the conglomerate firm defies any analysis in terms of traditional theories, which are erected on the assumption that firms maximize profits in each of their markets but on the contrary...

> "...may possess power in a particular market not only by virtue of its place in the organization of that market but also by virtue of the scope and character of its activities elsewhere. It may be able to exploit, extent, or defend its power by tactics other than those that are traditionally associated with the idea of monopoly" (Edwards, 1955: 332)

Economists draw on three argumentations when outlining the way conglomerates can use their power in an anti-competitive way. One of the main arguments is linked to the cross-subsidization of businesses to put temporary or permanent pressure on competitors in specific industries. Multi-business firms hereby use income streams from one market to support predatory pricing activities in another. The second anti-competitive move is the so-called mutual forbearance. According to this belief, conglomerates compete less rigorously if they meet in multiple market places and realize the high level of interdependence between each other (Bernheim & Whinston, 1990). The final argument in this claim is reciprocal buying. Large, diversified firms, which are highly interrelated, use their position to keep smaller, non-diversified firms out of the individual product markets and thereby reduce or even eliminate the presence of competitive markets (Montgomery, 1994: 165).

Supporters of the market-power view therefore argue that firms will actively seek diversification in order to expand their influence base across industries and to consequently maximize the firm's profitability through the use of conglomerate, anti-competitive power.[4]

2.2.2.2 Agency View

A second important theory used to explain corporate diversification is based on the principal-agent problem. Scholars such as Mueller (1969), Jensen (1986), and Morck, Shleifer, and Vishney (1990) among others argue that in the absence of ownership of significant equity stakes, managers pursue diversification strategies to further their own interests at the expense of a firm's shareholders.

In early stages in the life cycle of a firm, management has numerous opportunities to profitably re-invest the firm's earnings. However, as businesses mature, the number of attractive investment opportunities becomes scarce, leading managers to pursue unprofitable projects instead of returning the funds to its owners. This phenomenon is generally referred to as "free cash-flow problem.[5]" In accordance with this theory, academics such as Jensen (1986) argue that managers in reality are less interested in the future growth path of the firm but pursue what he refers to as "empire-building". Diversification, in particular through the use of conglomerate mergers and acquisitions, is therefore seen as a means to increase management's influence and prestige within the firm and in the public (Mueller, 1969).

Another rationale for diversification supported by the agency view is management's desire to reduce employment risk. The business risk of a firm is closely related to the risk associated with a manager's income and career. Hence, while not of obvious benefit to investors, diversification may enable managers to reduce their personal income and employment risk (Lane, Cannella, & Lubatkin, 1998; Montgomery, 1994; Morck et al., 1990).[6]

---

[4]See Markham's (1973) seminal contribution "Conglomerate Enterprise and Public Policy" for a thorough review of the theoretical foundations and shortfalls of the market-power view and its effect on public policy.

[5]The 'free cash-flow theory' will be investigate in further detail during the outline of the rationale behind the leveraged buyout association in Section 3.2.1 'Key Characteristics of Leveraged Buyouts'.

[6]Business risk refers to the implied volatilities in earnings associated with firms invested in a single business. Originally, risk reduction has been another important justification for diversification. Investors were given the opportunity to invest in a portfolio of assets rather than buy stocks of single-business firms (Levy and Sarnat 1970). Today, however, this belief has deteriorated with the rise of highly efficient, liquid capital markets. According to capital market theory, investors can diversify away business risk themselves and can hereby achieve their desired level of risk while being better equipped to changes in the market environment. Even when market imperfections such as transaction costs are admitted, the risk-reduction benefits in diversified firms seem highly questionable given the relatively low cost of portfolio diversification in capital markets (Amihud and Lev 1981: 615). Thus, managers should not be concerned with reducing their firm-specific business risk (Amit and Wernerfelt 1990; Markides 1995).

Lastly, a manager might direct a firm's diversification in a way that increases the firm's demands for the manager's set of skills. So-called management entrenchment can arguably lead managers to invest beyond the value-maximizing level and often leads to large, mostly unrelated diversified business portfolios (Shleifer & Vishny, 1989).

2.2.2.3 Resource-Based View

The third fundamental theory supporting corporate diversification moves is the resource-based view. This theory, initially proposed by Penrose (1959), draws heavily on both transaction cost economics and evolutionary economic theory and has brought forward various notable contributions including Wernerfelt (1984, 1995), Barney (1991b) and Mahoney & Pandian (1992).

Resources are hereby best viewed as a collection of sticky and imperfectly imitable resources or capabilities that enable a firm to successfully compete against other firms (Silverman, 1999; Wernerfelt, 1984). They can range from the availability of excess production capacity, the existence of valuable by-products, the ownership of specific intellectual property or capabilities, or a market position that allows a firm to broaden its presence with new products (Ghemawat, 1986; Gort, Grabowski, & McGuckin, 1985; Reed & Luffman, 1986). Penrose (1959) suggests that these excess resources are channeled into growth in the firm's extant product markets until such growth is constrained by limits in market demand as the deployment in existing markets is less costly to the firm given its management expertise in these markets. However, when a firm generates excess resources at a faster rate than it can redeploy them in its primary markets, it will diversify (Silverman, 2002: 8–11).

Resources that are distinctive or superior to those of rivals are of particular interest to firms in their considerations to diversify as these resources can provide a sustainable competitive advantage that spans across different businesses of a diversified portfolio (Peteraf, 1993). Diversification should therefore be guided along a firm's distinctive resources to leverage them throughout the business portfolio of the multi-business firm. Managers in this context have to ask themselves "whether their strategic assets are transportable to the industry they have targeted" (Markides, 1998b: 88). Overall, the resource-based view suggests "that a firm's level of profit and breadth of diversification are a function of its resource stock" (Montgomery, 1994: 168).[7]

[7] The resource-based view will be of particular interest in the discussion of corporate involvement in the leverage of resources across different businesses and will be covered in further detail in Section 2.4.3 'Leverage of Resources and Competences across Businesses'.

2.2.2.4 Additional Motives for Diversification

In addition to the arguments contained in the above presented fundamental theories, Reed and Luffman (1986) offer some additional explanations for corporate diversification. These arguments include economic and technological drivers in a firm's market environment, stability of earnings and investment efficiency, as well as a firm's adaptation to the changing needs of its customers.

Economic and technological drivers are the underlying motive for all diversification initiatives in Ansoff's early contribution about "why companies diversify?" (Ansoff, 1958) and continue to be one of the key reasons why firms enter into new businesses (Goold & Luchs, 1993). Hereby included is the economic decline of markets, specific industry trends that require significant modifications in a company's business model or changes in the company's regulatory environment. It furthermore comprises the offsetting effect of technological obsolescence through product or process innovations (Teece, 1982). These economic and technological drivers therefore require firms to seek new sources of income and motivate CEOs to engage in diversification initiatives.

Stability of earnings and consequently efficient investment is another argument that is continuously brought forward when discussing diversification with practitioners and academics. The availability of stable earnings hereby enables diversified firms to fund profitable projects, which would not find adequate funding from external capital markets. Efficient internal capital markets allow the allocation of funds across different business units to fund attractive investment opportunities independent of the current cash flows of the respective business unit, so-called "winner-picking" (e.g., see Funk & Welge, 2008; Rajan, Servaes, & Zingales, 2000; Scharfstein & Stein, 2000; Shin & Stulz, 1998; Stein, 1997). Besides this "smarter-money" effect caused by the ability to re-allocate funds within a business portfolio, there exists moreover a phenomenon called the "more-money" effect. In this argumentation, the presence of an efficient internal capital market gives a manager access to funds a single-business firm would find difficult to obtain as external finance is often more expensive or unavailable for certain projects due to differences in information, incentives, asset specificity, control rights, or transaction costs (Alchian, 1969; Gertner, Powers, & Scharfstein, 2002; Gertner, Scharfstein, & Stein, 1994; Lamont, 1997; Myers & Majluf, 1984). Empirical evidence suggests that diversified firms generally engage in cross-divisional allocation of funds (Lamont, 1997); academic views about the efficiency of this cross-subsidization however are mixed. Some studies underpin the positive influence of stable results and the efficiency of internal capital markets. Stein (1997), building on Williamson (1975), for example makes the case that independent of agency problems any re-allocation of resources across divisions will be in the direction of increased efficiency. A study about investment efficiency after spin-offs by Gertner et al. (2002) on the other side suggests that business units improve capital allocation after spin-offs. Scharfstein and Stein (2000) furthermore argue that the rent-seeking behavior of divisional managers can distort the functioning of internal capital markets.

Finally, Reed and Luffman (1986) regard "adapting to customer needs" as another motive for diversification. Broadening of a firm's product portfolio is in their view required if firms want to meet the changing demands of clients and to satisfy the requests of diversified dealers. In particular, the ongoing consolidation within most industries and the reduction of industry entry barriers raise in Reed and Luffman's view the need for firms to broaden their business portfolios. Multi-business firms therefore gain the ability to capitalize on economies of scope based on shared customers (Nayyar, 1990: 514–516).

2.2.3 *Entry into New Businesses*

Although the question of whether a firm should diversify is critical, many academics and practitioners argue that the "how" of diversification really makes the difference about the success of diversification moves (Hill, Hitt, & Hoskisson, 1992). Following the classifications by Ramanujam and Varadarajan (1989) as well as Simmonds (1990), the entry into new businesses comprises two different dimensions: the direction of diversification and the mode of diversification.

2.2.3.1 Direction of Diversification

The direction, also called breadth of diversification, is the first decision a firm has to take when following a diversification strategy. Diversification can be viewed as way to modify a firm's business definition so as to better achieve its performance or growth objectives (Ramanujam & Varadarajan, 1989: 526). According to the business definition by Abell (1980) and consistent with the definition introduced above, a firm's diversification into new businesses can be defined by a change in customer needs it seeks to satisfy – along products, markets and resources. Typically, firms do not attempt to modify all three dimensions, and product diversification in particular has been in academics' focus.

Varadarajan (1986) and Varadarajan and Ramanujam (1987) developed a framework to cluster the diversification movements of firms and brought it into a relationship with the status of diversification the firm is currently positioned in. Varadarajan (1986) therefore uses two measures to describe the number of businesses a firm operates in as well as the number of industry groups the company is active in as highlighted in Fig. 2.4.

Hence, narrow spectrum diversification (NSD) is the diversification into a new business but within the current industry group or related diversification, broad spectrum diversification (BSD) is diversification outside the current industry focus or unrelated diversification.[8] Based on a firm's position in this matrix, it can choose

[8] Varadarajan uses a SIC-Code classification for business segments (4-digit SIC code level) and industry groups (2-digit SIC code level) based on the segmental reporting of firms in their annual reports.

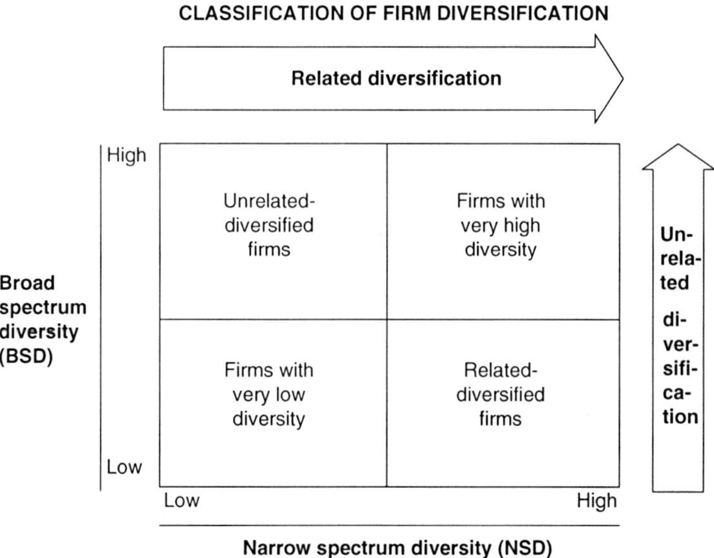

Fig. 2.4 Classification of firm diversification based on Varadarajan and Ramanujam (1987)

to either deepen its degree of diversification by moving along the broad spectrum dimension and move into other unrelated businesses or attempt to increase the degree of narrow spectrum diversification to benefit from related diversification.

In Markides and Williamson's view (1994), related diversification offers numerous advantages that go beyond mere economies of scope. While acknowledging economies of scope such as the potential to share strategic assets, e.g., common distribution systems, as important short-term benefits of related diversification (for an overview of short-term benefits e.g., see Ansoff, 1965; Nayyar, 1990, 1993; Rumelt, 1974, 1982; Teece, 1980), they argue that the real leverage comes from "exploiting relatedness to create and accumulate new strategic assets more quickly and cheaply than competitors" (Markides & Williamson, 1994: 150). The key element in their argumentation is the use and creation of core competences across different, related businesses such as the transfer of skills across different production lines or marketing divisions. "This means, that in most cases, similarities in the processes by which strategic assets are expanded and new strategic assets are created are more important than static similarities between the strategic assets that are the outcome of those processes" (Markides & Williamson, 1994: 150).

Research on the merger activity into new businesses, so-called conglomerate mergers, on the other hand provides evidence that there is a rationale for diversification into unrelated businesses (Graham, Lemmon, & Wolf, 2002; Hubbard & Palia, 1999; Lewellen, 1971; Servaes, 1996). Empirical results show that dissimilarities in mergers are in particular sources for value creation through synergies and, therefore, should encourage firms to look for acquisition opportunities outside the company's current strategic business scope while ensuring similar resource requirements (Fluck & Lynch, 1999; Harrison, Hitt, Hoskisson, & Ireland, 1991).

The two drivers influencing the direction of diversification are the resources of the firm as well as the external industry and market conditions combined with the match a firm can create between these factors (Grant, 1991; Rumelt, 1974; Stimpert & Duhaime, 1997). Porter (1987, 1996) suggests that a firm can gain competitive advantages only if it has skills or resources that can be transferred into new industries. The economics literature echoes a similar theme, suggesting a close association between the direction of diversification and the firm's transferable resources (Caves, 1982; Lecraw, 1984; Teece, 1982). An empirical study by Chatterjee and Wernerfelt (1991) shows good support for the relationship between intangible assets and more related diversification. Working at the industry level, Lemelin (1982) found that similarities in distribution and marketing channels between the origin and destination industries can serve as reliable indicators about the industry patterns a company would choose to engage in. Similarly, MacDonald (1985) as well as Montgomery and Hariharan (1991) find that firms tend to diversify into industries with similar R&D, advertising and capital expenditure intensities to those of the firms' existing businesses. Finally, studies by Silverman (1999, 2002) provide evidence that a company enters markets in which it can best exploit its existing resource base, using a firm's patent portfolio as lead indicator. Industry environment, in contrast, externally influences the direction of diversification. Christensen and Montgomery (1981) suggest that firms tend to pursue diversification more actively if their businesses are located in markets that constrain growth and profitability. Similar findings are provided by Melicher and Rush (1974) and Jacquemin (1990), who show that mergers and acquisitions are strategies commonly used when firms face increased competitive pressure and are directed towards targets with higher profitability. These findings support a hypothesis provided by Rumelt (1974), who proposed that "for a great many firms, diversification is the means employed to escape from declining prospects in their original business area. Poor absolute performance is often the result of participation in a highly competitive, non-innovative, slow growth industry" (Rumelt, 1974: 82).

2.2.3.2 Mode of Diversification

The second critical question is the mode of diversification. A firm has to choose between the two diversification options internal diversification and acquisition on external markets. Internal diversification can thereby be viewed as an organizational learning process directed at developing the knowledge necessary to enter and compete in a new industry (Kazanjian & Drazin, 1987; Normann, 1977; Pennings, Barkema, & Douma, 1994). Research regarding entry mode selection centers on the influence of financial, managerial, and legal issues on the costs and probabilities for success of diversification. It furthermore addresses the question of availability of acquisition targets and entry barriers into new industries (Lamont & Anderson, 1985; Yip, 1982). Internal diversification and acquisitions hereby differ in their financial implications, present different risks and opportunities for individual managers, and are subject to varying legal restrictions.

Theoretically, the height of barriers should have no impact on the choice of entry mode if one assumes efficiency of capital markets. This would imply that expected returns under the two modes would be equal. However, career considerations and the asymmetric impact of relatedness on barriers influence the choice of diversification mode. Hence, the cost of internal diversification varies directly with the relatedness of the existing business portfolio and the target industry. The nature and height of entry barriers, therefore, results in two influences on the mode of diversification: greater relatedness supports internal diversification while higher barriers favor an entry via acquisition (Yip, 1982: 344). Nelson and Winter's (1982) contribution portrays an incremental view of diversification; firms are inclined to stay in the vicinity of their set of competences independent of the chosen mode of diversification. Porter (1987) similarly advocates for expansion through internal development allowing firms to slowly and incrementally extent their domains. Pennings et al. (1994) hereby show that expansions are more persistent if related to a firm's core skills, fully owned, and the result of acquisition rather than of internal development. Hitt, Hoskisson, and Ireland (1990), on the other hand, provide evidence that the reduction of start-up risk is one of the key reasons why managers prefer acquisition over internal diversification and might strengthen a diminished propensity to internal development.

Various studies have then tried to provide insights into the process and the organization of entering new businesses. Kazanjian and Drazin (1987), for example, describe a detailed overview of the steps a firm has to take to implement internal diversification and elaborate on the issue of distance between proprietary and external know-how. Reed and Reed (1989), Krishnan, Miller, and Judge (1997), Morck et al. (1990) as well as Haleblian and Finkelstein (1999), furthermore, provide empirical evidence about the influence of CEO experience, management objectives and acquisition experience on the success of different ways of diversification. Using event and survey data, Capron and Shen (2007) finally illustrate that, in the case of diversification through acquisitions (external diversification), acquirers favor private targets in more familiar industries while they turn to public targets in new business domains or industries with high levels of intangible assets. Acquirers thereby attempt to eliminate information asymmetry in order to reduce transaction costs and minimize decisions errors.

2.2.4 Structure of Multi-Business Firms

Research on the organizational structure of firms has seen a shift from a focus on general design principles applicable to all kinds of organizations to a concept called "contingency theory". This research direction attempts to relate differences in organizational structure and design to the contextual conditions such as corporate strategy and market environment under which firms operate (e.g., see Ensign, 2001; Grinyer & Yasai-Ardekani, 1981; Miles & Snow, 1984; Pitts, 1980; Powell, 1992; Venkatraman & Camillus, 1984).

One important branch of this discipline has concentrated on the organizational structure of multi-business firms. The key objective of this research direction is to relate a firm's diversification strategy, i.e. unrelated vs. related diversification, to its organizational structure (e.g., see Bart, 1986; Harris & Ruefli, 2000; Miller, 1986). Chandler's (1962) seminal study of American enterprises suggested that the multi-divisional structure

(M-form) evolved as a response to the problems of managing growth and diversity within a centralized functional structure (U-form). The M-form is characterized by a separation of strategic and operations functions and offers functional autonomy of divisions with observable and measurable performance. It furthermore gives the corporate center the power to re-allocate resources generated by divisions to other divisions if attractive investment opportunities are available, allows the use of division-specific incentive schemes and offers the opportunity to employ specialized corporate staff for selected functions (Hill & Hoskisson, 1987). Mintzberg (1981) characterizes the divisionalized form of organizations as highly formalized groupings around markets with strong control systems and dominated by middle management. It typically operates in stable environments and is rather large and mature. The structure is moreover said to facilitate further growth through diversification as new businesses can merely be added next to the existing organization (Donaldson, 1982: 909). Thus, Williamson (1975) claims that multidivisional structures have information-processing advantages and therefore enable executives to effectively carry out strategic control while operating control rests with divisional management. In a diversified U-form, on the other hand, executives would be confronted with an overload of information.

Unrelated diversifiers in particular operate with divisional structures delegating day-to-day topics to the divisions and keeping strategic elements and resource allocation in the corporate center. In essence, the corporate center is reduced to the development and operation of an internal capital market where efficient resource allocation can be executed. In other words, senior management is transformed into portfolio managers who have to decide about the future shape of the overall corporate portfolio (Amburgey & Dacin, 1994; Hill & Hoskisson, 1987). Unrelated diversified firms can therefore function with small head offices and successful companies therefore operate like holding companies, giving considerable autonomy to divisions while keeping each strictly independent (Dundas & Richardson, 1982: 296–297).

Related diversified firms, on the other hand, are generally seeking to exploit economies of scope and to leverage resources and competences, which requires coordination between businesses and demands additional incentive and performance measurement systems (Hoskisson, 1987). The exploration of such synergies can be achieved through both tangible and intangible relationships (Porter, 1985). Tangible relationships are created by devices such as joint procurement of raw materials, joint development of shared technologies or production processes, joint sales forces, and joint physical distribution systems. Intangible relationships arise from the sharing of know-how and capabilities (Hill & Hoskisson, 1987; Riahi-Belkaoui, 1997). Although the M-form is commonly applied, the requirements of related diversified firms imply specific alterations in their structures (Franko, 1974: 494–497). For example, the centralization of marketing functions to achieve synergies between divisions entails that key decisions cannot be taken at the divisional level but require deep involvement in the business processes by corporate staff members. This consequently constrains the assignment of responsibility to divisional managers and brings a subjective element into performance evaluation (Hill & Hoskisson, 1987). Related diversified firms, hence, need to establish substantial corporate staff to enable coordination between businesses. Alternatively, related diversifiers of significant size can seek synergies through the implementation of intermediate structures, often called strategic business units. Firms hereby delegate the – still required – coordination task from the corporate center to this intermediate layer, which again manages different business divisions (Hoskisson, 1987; Hoskisson & Turk, 1990).

From an empirical point of view, the introduction of an M-form structure generally seems to lead to performance improvements in diversified firms. In his influential study, Rumelt (1974) found an association between a divisionalized organization and superior financial performance within diversified firms. Hoskisson's (1987) research – similar to the study provided by Armour and Teece (1978) – shows empirical support for the positive impact of an introduction of M-form structures on return on investment in the case of unrelated diversified firms while related diversified companies see a slight but not significant decrease in return.

2.2.5 *Management of Multi-Business Firms*

Structure is an important component to create an environment that enables top executives to manage a multi-business firm. The structure of a diversified company undoubtedly plays an important role for the overall performance of a firm (e.g., see Harris & Ruefli, 2000; Hoskisson, 1987), the real management task however is the day-to-day management of the diversified portfolio of the company (Mueller-Stewens, 2004: 13–14). A significant amount of academic research is therefore examining the management methods applicable in multi-business firms. Campbell, Goold, and Alexander (1995a, 1995b) and Goold, Campbell, and Alexander (1994, 1998) have, in particular, been driving the research efforts about the management of multi-business firms or, in their terms, the value a corporate parent can create for the overall business portfolio – the so-called parenting advantage. Based on their analyses and the syntheses provided by Ramanujam and Varadarajan (1989) as well as Goold and Luchs (1993), the contributions in this field of research can be categorized in four segments: (a) the governance and involvement model of top executives in individual businesses or divisions, respectively, (b) the availability of central functions and resources, (c) the realization of synergies through the horizontal leverage of resources and competences across different businesses, and (d) the portfolio management techniques of the overall business portfolio.[9]

2.2.5.1 Governance Model in Multi-Business Firms

One key dimension that has sparked the interest of academic researchers is the governance model most applicable in diversified companies; in other words, how can the corporate center best execute its shareholder function towards the individual business unit. A sizeable strategic management literature has focused on the relationship between the firm's corporate office and its strategic business units (e.g., see Allen, 1978; Baysinger & Hoskisson, 1990; Berg, 1965; Burgelman, 1983b; Hart & Banbury, 1994). All of this research is based on the premise that different businesses imply distinctive decision processes as well as varying information processing requirements, which must be accommodated by the relationship between corporate center and business units (Golden, 1992: 146–148). Research in this field, therefore, investigates different styles of corporate involvement to govern individual businesses. It furthermore studies varying approaches to strategic decision making in multi-business firms comprising the level of decision centralization and formalization as well as models describing the bilateral influence of a firm's strategy from both corporate and business unit level. This area of interest additionally covers the implications of different incentive schemes of divisional management on performance (Burgelman, 1983b; Gupta, 1987). While generally supporting the positive influence of active governance, Campbell et al. (1995b) also examine the downsides of the involvement by corporate managers and caution academics and practitioners. They claim that corporate parents regularly destroy value by "pressing for inappropriate targets, by starving businesses of resources for worthwhile projects, by encouraging wasteful investment, and by appointing the wrong managers" (Campbell et al., 1995b: 81).

2.2.5.2 Availability of Central Functions and Resources

The access to resources and services provided by the corporate center, so-called corporate resources, is a key source for creating value and achieving synergies in a diversified corporation. Corporate management hereby has to answer the question what services it should provide its businesses in order to generate additional value to the overall business portfolio; either by achieving cost synergies or by providing

[9]This section is supposed to provide a general overview of the academic literature in the field of diversification. As one of the key research objectives of this dissertation, the literature review regarding the management of multi-business firms will be further detailed in Section 2.4 'Managing Diversified Portfolios'.

an improved service level vs. a stand-alone solution within each division respectively by an outside provider (Campbell et al., 1995b: 84). Yavitz and Newman (1982) claim that multi-business firms, in order to stay competitive, have to provide their businesses with low-cost capital, outstanding executives, and specialized services such as corporate research and development or marketing. Campbell et al. (1995b), on the other hand, warn that the offering of corporate center services often holds a privileged status vs. outside suppliers and therefore protects the center from the rigors of the market. They argue that without this competitive relationship, the hoped for economies of scale in central functions can prove illusory.

2.2.5.3 Leverage of Resources and Competences across Businesses

Achieving synergies horizontally across different businesses by leveraging resources and competences is the next big area of interest in academic research. It is assumed that managers in the corporate center can identify benefits of linkages across businesses and organizational boundaries that would not be perceived by divisional management (Campbell et al., 1995b: 84). A seminal contribution in this field is Prahalad and Hamel's (1990) view on "the core competence of the corporation" and its impact on competitive advantage. They describe the core competences of a firm as the "collective learning in the organization, especially how to coordinate diverse production skills and integrate multiple streams of technologies". They, therefore, advise corporate executives to take a look beyond the boundaries installed in their companies in the form of strategic business units or divisions and to play an active role in identifying and spreading skills rather than focusing on the allocation of funds. Their views are closely oriented on the resource-based view and its role for sustainable competitive advantage (e.g., see Barney, 1991a; Ireland, Hitt, & Sirmon, 2003; Mahoney & Pandian, 1992; Newbert, 2007; Penrose, 1959; Peteraf, 1993; Sirmon, Hitt, & Ireland, 2007; Wernerfelt, 1984).

2.2.5.4 Portfolio Management in Multi-Business Firms

Portfolio management activities are the fourth element by which corporate headquarters can influence the shape and performance of a firm. Companies such as general electric, which are largely acknowledged as successful diversified firms, continuously review their portfolios in order to keep high performing divisions and divest poor performers. This portfolio analysis furthermore allows senior managers to decide about the resource allocation within the firm based on the expected future prospects of the business (Rajan et al., 2000: 77). Academic contributions therefore comprise two dimensions of portfolio management. The first part of research deals with portfolio analysis concepts. Early concepts hereby largely rely on a matrix that allows top management to evaluate a business' position according to market attractiveness and competitive position (e.g., see Bettis & Hall, 1981; Hall, 1978; Haspeslagh, 1982) while later concepts integrate value-based management approaches into the analysis (e.g., see Alberts & McTaggart, 1984; Copeland, Koller, & Murrin, 2000;

Reimann, 1988). The second part of research focuses on the implications of portfolio analysis on components such as a firm's portfolio strategy or its resource allocation (e.g., see Funk & Welge, 2008; Gertner et al., 1994, 2002; Maksimovic & Phillips, 2002), structure (e.g., see Eisenhardt & Brown, 1999), and the decision to pursue transactions such as acquisitions, divestments, alliances, business redefinitions and new ventures (e.g., see Dundas & Richardson, 1982).

2.2.6 Financial Implications of Diversification

The financial implications of diversification are probably the most acknowledged area of research with respect to multi-business firms, which has sparked controversial discussions and has been on top of the academic agenda for decades.[10] Strategic management and corporate finance have been the two disciplines that have been predominately driving the topic to shed light on the question how diversification affects a firm's financials. Generally, two branches of research can be distinguished: one regarding the effects of different levels of diversification on valuation, the other regarding the influence on a firm's financial performance.[11]

2.2.6.1 Influence of Diversification on Valuation

Research about the impact of diversification on a firm's valuation on public capital markets has been one of the focus areas of empirical investigations since the end of the 1980s (e.g., see Wernerfelt & Montgomery, 1988). The renowned finding by Lang and Stulz (1994) as well as Berger and Ofek (1995) that diversification causes a significant discount when comparing the value of the multi-business firm with the aggregate valuation of equivalent single-business firms has then brought forward a substantial amount of academic literature. The subsequent literature can be differentiated into two clusters of research. The first group of researchers is reviewing and detailing the empirical relationship tested by Lang and Stulz (1994) and Berger and Ofek (1995) by altering the measures for valuation and expanding the US-based scope of earlier studies to other international countries (e.g., see Beckmann, 2006; Denis, Denis, & Yost, 2002; Glaser & Mueller, 2006; Lamont & Polk, 2001; Lins & Servaes, 1999; Mansi & Reeb, 2002; Villalonga, 2004b). The second group of academics is investigating the grounds of this discount by testing the empirical relationship of the firm's valuation with influencing factors such as the efficiency of internal capital markets or the types of acquisitions pursued by undervalued

[10] This section is supposed to provide a general overview of the academic literature in the field of diversification. As one of the key research objectives of this dissertation, the literature review regarding the impact of diversification on the performance of multi-business firms will be further detailed in Section 2.3 'Diversification and Performance'.

[11] The measures for the level of diversification are comparable in both research direction and are illustrated in Section 2.3.1 'Measure of Diversification'.

firms (e.g., see Campa & Kedia, 2002; Denis, Denis, & Sarin, 1997; Maksimovic & Phillips, 2002; Shin & Stulz, 1998; Whited, 2001).

2.2.6.2 Influence of Diversification on Financial Performance

The second influential direction of research is largely based on the analysis of Gort (1962) and Rumelt (1974, 1982), who found a relationship between diversification and a firm's profitability. Since then, various contributions have investigated the influence of diversification on the different measures of financial performance. The first group of measures for financial performance hereby uses accounting-based indicators such as return on investment, return on assets, or return on sales to compare firms and to describe the impact of diversification on financial performance (e.g., see Bettis, 1981; Chakrabarti, Singh, & Mahmood, 2007; Chang & Howard, 1989; Grant & Jammine, 1988; Hall & St. John, 1994; Lecraw, 1984; Markides, 1995; Palepu, 1985). The second way to measure performance is based on capital-market indicators. Studies in this field use measures linked to the capital asset pricing model (CAPM) such as the Sharpe, Treynor and Jensen ratios linking stock performance with appropriate risk indicators and by those means are able to compare the return of different firms with respect to the degree of diversification (e.g., see Comment & Jarrell, 1995; De, 1992; Hoskisson, Hitt, Johnson, & Moesel, 1993; Lubatkin & Chatterjee, 1994; Miles & Huberman, 1984; Weston, Smith, & Shrieves, 1972). There is furthermore a considerable amount of studies empirically examining the influencing factors of any performance differences between different degrees of diversification such as available resources, market structure, and firm conduct (e.g., see Baysinger & Hoskisson, 1990; Chang & Howard, 1989; Christensen & Montgomery, 1981; Montgomery, 1985; Varanasi, 2005).

2.3 Diversification and Performance

As stated in the introduction of this study, the comparison of the diversification-performance relationship between publicly listed corporations and private equity firms is the first research objective of this contribution. This section will therefore detail the overview presented in Sect. 2.2.6 "Financial Implications of Diversification" and present a comprehensive outline about methods and results of prior empirical work covering the influence of diversification on a firm's financials. Several different approaches exist to define the degree of diversification. The use of these different approaches however does not correlate with the measure to quantify the impact of diversification and is therefore presented upfront independent of the spectrum of empirical studies (Sect. 2.3.1 "Measures of Diversification"). The subsequent two sections will then cover the empirical studies assessing the influence of diversification on valuation (Sect. 2.3.2) and on financial performance (Sect. 2.3.3).

2.3.1 *Measures of Diversification*

Researchers have taken considerably different approaches to evaluate a firm's degree of diversification. Although the way to assess diversification has been subject to various studies concentrating on this issue (e.g., see Chatterjee & Blocher, 1992; Hall & St. John, 1994; Hoskisson et al. 1993; Pitts & Hopkins, 1982) and has furthermore been discussed in most empirical studies investigating performance effects, there is still no single accepted indicator. Approaches range from categorical measures to continuous product count measures with one prominent hybrid model, the Entropy measure, in between (Martin & Sayrak, 2003).

2.3.1.1 Categorical Measure

Rumelt (1974), who advanced the strategic typology first developed by Wrigley (1970), offers a categorical description of diversification based on quantitative as well as qualitative data. He therefore defined ten categories of diversification as presented in Table 2.1 based on the four broad categories – single, dominant, related, and unrelated. Each of them has been clearly defined by the "specialization ratio" and the "degree of relatedness".

The specialization ratio is an entirely objective ratio determining the share of a firm's revenues in its largest single business. The degree of relatedness however is a subjective assessment of the proportion of a firm's revenues coming from its largest group of related businesses (Chatterjee & Blocher, 1992: 875). Rumelt (1974) suggests that researchers therefore look for shared facilities, similar distribution channels, common markets, and shared technologies.

Although Rumelt's categorical system provides a rich measure of diversity, it is commonly criticized for its subjectivity and complexity (Hall & St. John, 1994; Martin & Sayrak, 2003; Montgomery, 1982). Those concerns are the reason that only few researchers have attempted to replicate the classification implemented by Rumelt (e.g., see Grant & Jammine, 1988) while most studies using the categorical typology have either used Rumelt's initial sample or a subset of it (Bettis, 1981; Bettis & Hall, 1982; Bettis & Mahajan, 1985; Chang & Howard, 1989; Christensen & Montgomery, 1981; Lubatkin & Rogers, 1989).[12]

2.3.1.2 Continuous Measure

The continuous measure of diversification – also called product or business count measure – on the other hand is solely data based. Studies using this measure work with

[12]Rumelt's (1974) sample comprises 273 corporations from the US Fortune 500. It consists of a random sample selected from the top 500 firms in the US between 1949 and 1974.

Table 2.1 Overview categorical measure of diversification

General diversification	Description	Specialization ratio[a] percent	Subcategories
Single business	Firms that are basically committed to a discrete business area	95–100	• Single business • Single vertical
Dominant business	Firms that have diversified to some extent, but still obtain the preponderance of their revenues from a discrete business area	70–94	• Dominant vertical • Dominant constrained • Dominant linked • Dominant unrelated
Related business	Firms that are diversified and in which more than 70% of the diversification has been accomplished by relating new activities to the old	Less than 70%	• Related constrained • Related linked
Unrelated business	Firms that have diversified and in which less than 70% of the diversification is related to the firm's original skill or strengths		• Multibusiness • Unrelated portfolio

Source: Rumelt (1974)

[a] Percentage of firm's total assets in a discrete business area

Table 2.2 Overview continuous measure of diversification

Indicator	Description	Selected academic contributions
Numerical count	• Numerically counting number of businesses • Fails to recognize difference in size distribution of businesses	• Mansi and Reeb (2002) • Servaes (1996)
Dominant ratio	• Focus on largest business unit • Diversity as ratio of size of largest business unit relative to whole company • Fails to recognize relationship in overall portfolio	• De (1992) • Carter (1977)
Comprehensive indexes	• Weights the shares of individual businesses relative to whole company • Allows discussion about concentration level of overall portfolio • Herfindahl index typical example indicator for comprehensive indexes	• Gomes and Livdan (2004) • Lang and Stulz (1994) • Montgomery and Wernerfelt (1988)

Source: Pitts and Hopkins (1982)

reporting figures allocating a firm's businesses to the Standard Industrial Classification wsystem (SIC), which was developed by the US federal government as a way of classifying all types of business activity in the economy (Hall & St. John, 1994). Several forms of this general method can be found in academic literature ranging from simple numerical counting to complex indices as presented in Table 2.2.

Although the continuous measure is still commonly used and a close relationship between categorical and continuous measures has been observed, strategy researchers have often criticized this approach because of its failure to tap the dimension of relatedness and, therefore, allows only limited insight into the breadth of diversification (e.g., see Carter, 1977; Chatterjee & Blocher, 1992; Montgomery, 1982; Palepu, 1985).

2.3.1.3 Entropy Measure

The Entropy measure is a hybrid model of the categorical and the continuous measure and was developed by Jacquemin and Berry (Berry, 1975; Jacquemin & Berry, 1979) to overcome the previously portrayed shortcomings of the other two models while retaining some of the richness of Rumelt's categorical approach.

When combining the two techniques, a continuous measure is used to assess the level of diversification and is then transformed into strategic categories to describe the type of diversity. Hence, the Entropy measure recognizes the degree of relatedness among business segments by assuming that segments within an industry group (two-digit SIC code level) are more related to one another than segments across industry groups (Palepu, 1985).

Empirical evidence about the effectiveness of this hybrid model remains mixed. Hoskisson et al. (1993) provide confirmation for the reliability and validity of the Entropy measure as proxy for Rumelt's definition of diversification. Palepu (1985) as well as Hall and St. John (1994), on the other hand, find controversial results when applying the different methods of measuring diversification. Close variants of the Entropy measure (see in particular the refinements by Raghunathan, 1995) nonetheless have been intensively used to measure diversification in empirical studies throughout the last decade (e.g., see Amit & Livnat, 1988; Chakrabarti et al., 2007; Graham et al., 2002; Markides, 1995).

2.3.2 *Influence of Diversification on Valuation*

As indicated in Sect. 2.3.1, research on the influence of diversification on valuation is one of the two major research directions investigating the impact of diversification and has found a prominent place in academic research during the last 20 years. Contributions in this field can be distinguished in (a) studies empirically examining the relationship of diversification and a firm's value and (b) in studies looking for empirical evidence to explain any divergence in valuation between different degrees of diversification.

2.3.2.1 Relationship Diversification and Valuation

The examination of the impact of diversification on a firm's market value has gained particular interest with the two seminal studies by Lang and Stulz (1994) and Berger and Ofek (1995). With these contributions, the authors have laid out the two general methodologies for measuring value – Lang and Stulz using Tobin's q, Berger and Ofek determining excess value via asset and sales multipliers. Both approaches have in common that they compare the valuation of a multi-business firm with the imputed values for its segments as stand-alone entities. Tobin's q therefore applies a ratio between a firm's capital market valuation and the value of its assets, usually indicated by the book value (Tobin, 1969). The multiplier approach, on the other hand, uses one of three accounting items – assets, sales, or earnings – to multiply each segment's level of this item with the median ratio of single-business firms representing the firm's industry scope (Berger & Ofek, 1995). All consecutive contributions have been based on these two approaches as illustrated in Table 2.3, which provides an overview of the most acknowledged contributions in this field of research.

The majority of the studies, unfortunately most of them using different indicators for diversification, find a diversification discount; in other words the sum of a

Table 2.3 Overview selected empirical studies diversification and valuation

Empirical study	Diversification measure	Valuation measure	Sample	Uncorrected result[a] (%)	Corrected result[b] (%)
Lang and Stulz (1994)	(1) Herfindahl (2) Numerical count	Tobin's q	US	−27 to −54	–
Berger and Ofek (1995)	Binary	Asset and sales multipliers	US	−13 to −15	–
Servaes (1996)	Numerical count	Tobin's q	US	−6 to −59	–
Lins and Servaes (1999)	Binary	Asset and sales multipliers	Germany, Japan, UK	0 Germany −10 Japan −15 UK	–
Lins and Servaes (2002)	Binary	Asset and sales multipliers	Seven Asian markets	−7	–
Graham et al. (2002)	Entropy measure (modified)	Asset and sales multipliers	US	−9.6 to −13.7	−5.7 to −6.6
Campa and Kedia (2002)	Binary	Asset and sales multipliers	US	−9 to −13	0 to +30
Mansi and Reeb (2002)	(1) Binary (2) Numerical count	Asset and sales multipliers	US	−4.5	0
Villalonga (2004a, b)	Binary	Tobin's q	US	−8 to −24	+8 to +34
Villalonga (2004a, b)	Binary	Tobin's q	US	−18	+28

[a] Diversified vs. focused, results of univariate or multivariate regressions
[b] Diversified vs. focused, results of corrected analysis for sample selection biases, data or methodological issues
Source: Villalonga (2003), academic journals

firm's business segments is worth less than the aggregate value of comparable single-business firms. This relationship has originally been established with data from US firms (e.g., see Denis et al., 2002; Gomes & Livdan, 2004; Servaes, 1996) but has then been tested and confirmed in a variety of countries including Germany, France, the United Kingdom, and Japan (e.g., see Beckmann, 2006; Glaser & Mueller, 2006; Lins & Servaes, 1999). Interestingly, researchers in recent publications have started to correct their samples for selection biases, data or methodological issues[13] and have found a neutral or positive impact of diversification on value while showing negative results before these adjustments (e.g., see Campa & Kedia, 2002; Graham et al., 2002; Mansi & Reeb, 2002; Martin & Sayrak, 2003; Villalonga, 2003, 2004a, 2004b).[14]

One of the major shortcomings of the valuation research stream is the lack to integrate measures that enable the assessment of related and unrelated diversification into their studies. The results provided therefore allow only limited conclusions about how an "optimal" level of diversification could look like although many academics and practitioners claim that related diversification outperforms both focused and unrelated businesses. In addition, the setup of the valuation approach restricts the technique to non-financial firms as valuing financial players requires substantial alterations and thereby limits comparability of results. Finally, the valuation approach lacks a control mechanism for different levels of risk inherent in different business models. While valuation studies can make judgments about discounts or premiums vs. comparable peers, it does not allow a comparison across different industries or geographies.

2.3.2.2 Influencing Factors Causing Differences in Valuation

There is a broad spectrum of theoretical arguments as to why firms diversify and the positive and negative effects of such decisions. Those theoretical building blocks have been presented in Sect. 2.2.2 "Motives for diversification". Empirically, there is a growing but still limited spectrum of publications about the causes of differences in valuation.

One group of academics assesses the allocation efficiency of capital in multi-business firms. (e.g., see Ahn, Denis, & Denis, 2006; Lamont, 1997; Rajan et al., 2000; Whited, 2001). Rajan et al. (2000), for example, find that the attractiveness

[13]One of the major shortcomings of most studies is their failure to correct for the fact that many firms trading at a discount have been already trading at a discount prior to diversifying. For further detail see Lang/Stulz (1994), Campa/Kedia (2002), or Martin/Sayrak (2003).

[14]Additionally, there has been a growing number of so-called event studies, which investigate the reactions of capital markets to a firms decision to diversify or to focus such as Comment/Jarrell (1995) and Dittmar/Shivdasani (2003). They have been excluded from the overview due to the prior definition of diversification for this study along status rather than process of diversification and neither results nor methodology would contribute to the further proceeding of this study. See Montgomery (1994) for an overview of the results generated in selected event studies.

of different segments in terms of their market position and industry exposure plays only a limited role in the allocation decision. However, they show that the power structure in a firm's hierarchy and the associated power struggles among the firm's divisions have a strong effect on the decision making process and therefore causes resources to flow to inefficient investments.

A second group of contributions tries to explain the observed discount based on risk associated with multi-business firms in comparison with single-business entities. Mansi and Reeb (2002), for example, find that shareholder losses in diversification are a function of firm leverage. They furthermore observe that the common use of book values opposed to market values in the calculation associated with Tobin's q negatively influences the value of multi-business firms.

A third stream of research has targeted the behavior of investment analysts as influencing factor. Ferris and Sarin (2000) discovered that focused businesses enjoy a broader coverage by analysts than diversified firms. This consequently leads to an information and control deficit of multi-business firms and increases the variance in analyst performance estimates. Seppelfricke (2003) and Kames (2000), therefore, claim that analysts punish diversified firms with an universal discount, which is intensified by the so-called herding behavior of analysts revealed by Kim and Pantzalis (2000); in other words panel data provided by Kim and Pantzalis (2000) revealed an induced discount triggered by the prior negative assessments of other analysts.

2.3.3 *Influence of Diversification on Financial Performance*

The second branch of empirical research in this field investigates the influence of diversification on a firm's financial performance, defined from either the accounting or the capital markets perspective of performance. Based on these results, several contributions are attempting to highlight the causing factors for differences in financial performance.

2.3.3.1 Relationship Diversification and Financial Performance

Empirical studies regarding the relationship between diversification and financial performance have been in academic research since the publications of Gort (1962) and Rumelt (1974) and have been intensively researched since then in order to replicate and refine their methods and findings. Table 2.4 provides an overview of the most acknowledged studies examining the effect of diversification on financial performance.

Within this stream of research, two ways of measuring financial performance have been established. The first is measuring performance based on accounting figures such as return on assets, return on investment, return on equity or return on sales (e.g., see Bettis & Hall, 1982; Chakrabarti et al., 2007; Chang & Howard, 1989; Lecraw, 1984; Markides, 1995; Palepu, 1985; Rumelt, 1982). While these

Table 2.4 Overview selected empirical studies diversification and financial performance

Empirical study	Diversification measure	Performance measure	Sample	Key findings
Weston et al. (1972)	Numerical	CAPM	US	Positive impact of diversification in firms[a]
Bettis (1981)	Categorical	RoA	US	Related outperform unrelated diversifiers
Lecraw (1984)	Categorical	RoE	Canada	Related outperform unrelated diversifiers
Palepu (1985)	Entropy	RoS	US	Related outperform unrelated diversifiers
Bettis and Mahajan (1985)	Categorical	RoA (return and risk)	US	No significant differences between different degrees of diversification
Amit and Livnat (1988)	(1) Herfindahl (2) Entropy	CAPM, Cash flow	US	Related diversifiers with highest risk/return profile, unrelated with lowest
Lubatkin and Rogers (1989)	Categorical	CAPM	US	Related outperform unrelated diversifiers and focused businesses
De (1992)	Dominant ratio	CAPM	US	No significant differences between different degrees of diversification
Hall and St. John (1994)	(1) Categorical (2) Entropy	RoA, RoS, RoE	US	Related outperform unrelated diversifiers
Comment and Jarrell (1995)	Numerical (interest on focus moves)	CAPM	US	Focus moves lead to performance improvements for divesting firm
Markides (1995)	(1) Categorical (2) Numerical (3) Entropy	Various accounting	US	Focus moves lead to performance improvements for divesting firm
Chakrabarti et al. (2007)	(1) Herfindahl (2) Entropy	RoA	Emerging markets (six Asian)	Diversification favorable in less developed markets

Source: Academic journals
[a] Diversified firms vs. mutual funds

indicators are usually easy to retrieve, these measures make the analysis vulnerable to effects of extraordinary accounting items and differences in international accounting standards. Many studies in this direction furthermore fail to adjust for differences in risk-taking. One set of firms might therefore perform better simply because, having greater risk, they have to earn a greater expected return for their shareholders (Lang & Stulz, 1994). Market-based approaches such as risk-adjusted indicators based on a firm's stock price development (e.g., Sharpe ratio (Sharpe, 1964), Treynor ratio (Treynor, 1965), or Jensen's Alpha (Jensen, 1969)) are the second means to measure performance (e.g., see Amit & Livnat, 1988; Comment & Jarrell, 1995; De, 1992; Lubatkin & Rogers, 1989; Weston et al., 1972). They have been developed in the context of the capital asset pricing model (CAPM) and since then found broad acceptance in academic research and with participants in the world's financial markets. These measures provide the advantage of being internationally comparable and being independent of short-term accounting effects. If one accepts the assumption of efficient capital markets, using the performance of a firm on the stock markets as indicator is advantageous (Melicher & Rush, 1973; Naylor & Tapon, 1982; Reimann, 1988; Smith & Schreiner, 1969).[15]

There is an ongoing argument as to whether or not there are appropriate measures to assess relatedness in a firm's business portfolio. A recent study by Lien and Klein (2007: 5) provides evidence that there are "significant and stable efficiency effects of relatedness, and that decision makers do act in a manner consistent with the pursuit of such effects". In Lien and Klein's (2007) argumentation, the discrepancies about the performance effects in diversification studies stem from measurement problems of relatedness. The study supports earlier findings by Montgomery (1982), Pitts and Hopkins (1982) and Hoskisson et al. (1993).

Overall, the finding that related diversified firms outperform focused and unrelated diversified businesses is the key message of empirical research regarding financial performance. This conclusion has been largely consistent throughout the use of different methods of measuring performance as well as diverging ways of assessing diversification. It has, furthermore, largely been consistent across different periods of time. This stability throughout time provides evidence against Lang and Stulz's (1994) claim that one of the key weaknesses of the performance approach is the ex-post judgment of the relationship of diversification and performance; in other words a diversified firm could still be valued more than a focused business but shows weak performance in the observed period of time and therefore reduces its valuation premium. With consistent results through almost three decades of academic research, this claim appears invalid.

2.3.3.2 Influencing Factors Causing Differences in Financial Performance

Various empirical studies have consequently focused on evaluating the factors behind the above performance observations: one branch regarding firm-internal components, another examining the firm's environment (Varanasi, 2005).

The availability of internal resources is an important factor for the performance of a firm. Bettis' (1981) and Baysinger and Hoskisson's (1989) research indicates

[15] Lang and Stulz (1994) argue that the use of capital market indicators insufficiently explains the cross-section of expected returns. This however only applies to event studies that are examining the diversification process of firms. This does not apply to studies investigating the status of diversification and therefore the long-term risk-adjusted performance of a company

that advertising as well as research and development expenditures are an important determinant in the performance advantage, in particular of related diversified firms. The form of organizational structure applied in a diversified company is another component that is made responsible for differences in the diversification-performance link (e.g., see Hoskisson, 1987; Riahi-Belkaoui, 1997). There is, furthermore, considerable empirical research about the influence of internal management procedures that will be detailed in Sect. 2.4 of this document (Sect. 2.4 "Managing Diversified Portfolios").

When researchers attempt to assess the influence of firm environment on performance, they talk about the role of market characteristics such as market growth, a firm's share in the market as well as the competitive landscape. These studies indicate that the type of market in which a firm operates significantly affects the diversification-performance link (e.g., see Chang & Howard, 1989; Montgomery, 1985). Christensen and Montgomery (1981) noted that market structure variables have a moderating effect on the link between diversification and performance. Wernerfelt and Montgomery (1986) moreover found that related diversifiers, or in their words "efficient diversifiers", perform better than unrelated diversifiers ("inefficient diversifiers") when they compete in stable but highly profitable markets, while unrelated diversifiers seem to benefit more from markets that are marked by high growth.

2.4 Managing Diversified Portfolios

Developing an understanding of the management techniques applied by private equity firms to their investment portfolios is the second research objective of this study. Following the above section about the relationship of diversification and performance in corporations, this section provides a detailed overview of the theories and empirical findings investigating the management approaches of corporations with diversified business portfolios. The management concepts and relationships in corporations outlined in this section provide the basis to create an understanding of the approaches within the private equity sphere as well as to determine the similarities and differences between private equity and corporate methods. This evaluation will be the focus of the second empirical investigation of this study.

The first part of the consecutive chapter (Sect. 2.4.1) provides a general overview of the different opportunities to create value within a diversified portfolio. The further sections then focus on the key areas for value creation by a corporate parent and are structured in analogy to the brief outline within the general literature overview. They are based on the contributions by Ramanujam and Varadarajan (1989), Goold and Luchs (1993), and Goold et al. (1994) and Campbell et al. (1995a, 1995b), covering the topics "Governance Model in Multi-Business Firms" (Sect. 2.4.2), "Availability of Center Functions and Resources" (Sect. 2.4.3), "Leverage of Resources and Competences Across Businesses" (Sect. 2.4.4), and "Portfolio Management in Multi-Business Firms" (Sect. 2.4.5).

2.4.1 Value of the Parent Company

The most comprehensive view about the management of diversified portfolios is provided under the key words "value of the parent company" or "parenting advantage" and has mainly been driven by Goold et al. (1994, 1998) and Campbell et al. (1995a, 1995b). In their approach to corporate strategy, the role played by the parent is in the center of interest instead of putting a strong focus on portfolio discussions. Corporate centers genuinely incur costs; however, they can create parenting advantage if applied in the right manner (Goold et al., 1994: 6–8). Their study of various large multi-business firms such as General Electric, 3M, or Shell has brought forward insights about the different elements shaping the role of the parent. The authors, furthermore, provide an overview of areas, in which so-called parenting opportunities can be found and lay out a process to assess the need and the direction to improve fit between a firm's diversification strategy and its management approach.

In order to analyze the value corporate parenting can create, the authors distinguish four components. The authors identify the role as shareholder and the resulting governance activities as one mode to create value, so-called "stand-alone influence". Influence hereby can range from pure financial control to intense involvement on a wide range of strategic and operational issues. Another potentially beneficial influence by the parent is the availability of central functions and resources. While incurring costs, services provided by the corporate center can create value if they are "more cost-effective than what businesses could provide for themselves or purchase from outside suppliers" (Goold et al., 1994: 81). An additional parenting activity is the so-called "linkage influence". This activity refers to the active involvement by the corporate center to foster the leverage of competences and resources horizontally across individual businesses, which is generally captured in the notion of synergy. The forth component for corporate parenting is corporate development covering parent activities such as re-configuring the internal structure of the firm's portfolio, resource re-allocation between businesses as well as the acquisition and divestiture of businesses.

Campbell et al. (1995a: 126) identified ten elements as "places to look for parenting opportunities" in multi-business firms. Unfortunately, the list possesses little structure and information about the conditions under which the opportunities apply and it is difficult to derive testable hypotheses from them. Research efforts to provide empirical evidence about the different areas and their value creation potential therefore have been very scarce (Gottschalg & Meier, 2005: 7–9). In addition, the list is to a large extent generic and not specific enough to the particularities of diversified firms. Nonetheless, the following list provides a helpful and comprehensive overview about the playing field of a corporate parent.

(1) *Size and age*. Old, large, successful businesses often accumulate bureaucracies and overheads that are hard to eliminate from the inside. Small, young businesses may have insufficient functional skills, managerial succession problems, and insufficient financial resources to ride out a recession. Are those factors relevant to the business?

(2) *Management.* Does the business employ top-quality managers compared with its competitors? Are its managers focused on the right objectives? Is the business dependent on attracting and retaining people with hard-find-skills?
(3) *Business definition.* The managers in the business may have an erroneous concept of what the business should be and may consequently target a market that is too narrow or broad, or they may employ too much or too little vertical integration. The trend of outsourcing and alliances is changing the definitions of many businesses, thus creating new parenting opportunities. Is each business in the portfolio defined to maximize its competitive advantage?
(4) *Predictable errors.* Does the nature of a business and its situation lead managers to make predictable mistakes? For example, attachment to previous decisions may prevent openness to new alternatives; business maturity often leads to excessive diversification; long product cycles can encourage excessive reliance on old products; and cyclical markets can lead to overinvestment during the upswing.
(5) *Linkages.* Could the business link more effectively with other businesses to improve efficiency or market position? Are linkages among units complex or difficult to establish without parental help?
(6) *Common capabilities.* Does the business have capabilities that could be shared among businesses?
(7) *Special expertise.* Could the business benefit from specialized or rare expertise that the parent possesses?
(8) *External relations.* Does the business have external stakeholders, such as shareholders, government, unions, and suppliers, that the parent company could manager better than it does?
(9) *Major decisions.* Does the business face difficult decisions in areas in which it lacks expertise – for example, entering China, making a big acquisition, or dramatically extending capacity? Would the business experience difficulty getting funding for major investments from external capital providers?
(10) *Major changes.* Does the business need to make major changes in areas with which its management has little experience?

To assess the need of a corporate parent to get involved in individual businesses in the company's portfolio, the authors furthermore outline a process to evaluate opportunities for corporate parenting. In a first step, managers need to determine the critical success factors of each business and evaluate the opportunities of the corporate parent to add value to each business. In the second phase of the assessment, the characteristics of the parent should be revealed along such dimensions as structure, decision processes, available central functions, and skill levels. Based on this review, the parent should determine the fit between a parent's characteristics and the success and parenting requirements by different businesses in the portfolio. In a final step, the management's judgment about the value of the parent should be evaluated by assessing the impact of past parent involvement on business results.

2.4.2 *Governance Model in Multi-Business Firms*

The governance model in multi-business firms covers the so-called "standalone influence" of the corporate center towards individual business units, in other words the role as shareholder. It is closely interlinked with the principal-agent theory, which defines an agency relationship as a contract under which one or more persons (the principals) engage another person (the agent) to perform some service on their behalf (for an introduction to principal-agent-theory, e.g., see Fama, 1980; Jensen & Meckling, 1976). This involves the delegation of some decision making authority to the agent and is typically a phenomenon observed between the owner of a firm and the management in charge of running the company. In the case of a multi-business firm, corporate management is both agent (to the firm's shareholders) and principal (as owner of the individual businesses). In other words, the corporate center has to act upon its shareholder rights as owner of a portfolio of different businesses. Corporate management has to take responsibility similar to a stock-holder to actively govern the different assets in its investment basket and to secure the creation of shareholder value to the owners of the multi-business firm (e.g., see Arzac, 1986; Rappaport, 1981, 2006). Research in this field has evolved around three areas of interest: different styles of corporate involvement in general, strategic decision making in multi-business firms including decision (de-) centralization as well as formalization, and the influence of different incentive schemes of business unit managers on the unit's performance.

2.4.2.1 Styles of Corporate Involvement

Corporate headquarters need to interact on different occasions and by different means with the business units in their portfolios. Chandler Jr. (1991) distinguishes two general sorts of tasks in the responsibility of corporate management: entrepreneurial and administrative tasks. Entrepreneurial tasks comprise the corporate influence on such issues as product-market strategies, structural changes, and skill development. Administrative tasks include the agreement and monitoring of performance targets, approval of the unit's budget and investment plans, as well as the selection and replacement of business unit managers.

Based on this general classification of corporate involvement tasks, Goold et al. (1994) have outlined three generic styles of corporate management as displayed in Fig. 2.5: strategic planning, financial control and strategic control.

Corporate managers pursuing a "strategic planning" style are closely involved in the formulation of plans and decisions within individual business units, whereby corporate management has the final say on strategy. They additionally provide a clear, long-term direction for the further development of each business unit and thereby influence the unit's strategic initiatives. It is particularly used in firms with related diversified portfolios, which allows the corporate center to maintain a thorough

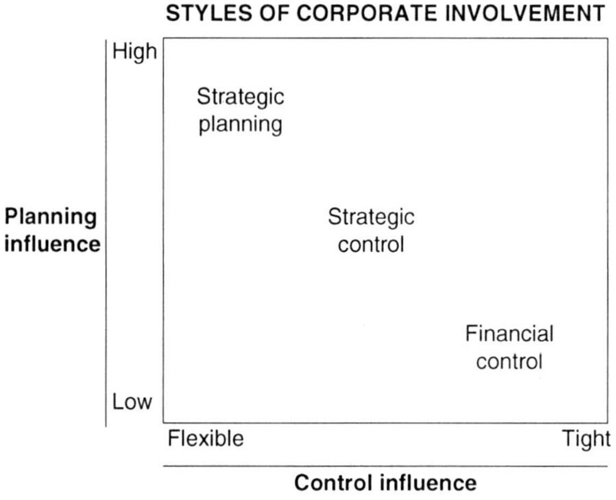

Fig. 2.5 Styles of corporate involvement based on Goold et al. (1994)

understanding of the individual businesses. According to the research of Goold and Campbell (1987: 247–251), strategic planning is a viable option if a firm is actively involved in two to three core industries before over-stretching the capabilities of the corporate center.

The management style "financial control" on the contrary is characterized by strong decentralization of planning. Business units are structured as standalone units with a high degree of autonomy and full responsibility for formulating their own strategies and plans. Corporate management focuses on the establishment of performance targets and their monitoring, often leading up to short-term objectives and project-based resource allocation. It is commonly used in firms with highly unrelated business portfolios (Goold & Campbell, 1987: 258–259).

"Strategic control" combines the two styles portrayed above. Corporate managers decentralize planning to the business unit managers but secure themselves the ability to challenge business unit strategies. Divisional managers are expected to advance strategic development in a bottom-up fashion, while corporate management consolidates and assesses the plans of the individual business units. Corporate managers may further sponsor selected strategic initiatives and by those means ensure that business unit strategies are generally in line with the overall direction intended for the corporation, however, driven by each unit's management. It is generally applicable across different diversification strategies (Goold & Campbell, 1987: 35–46).

Van Oijen and Douma (2000) developed a similar but more granular framework for the different roles of involvement for the corporate center, which distinguishes seven different, however not mutually exclusive, functions of the headquarters: (a) planning, which in analogy to Goold et al.'s (1994) "strategic planning", is mainly concerned with shaping the strategic plans for the different businesses from the corporate center; (b) evaluation, which assesses investment proposals and results by the different divisions but does not get involved in the decentralized strategic decision processes; (c) selection, which describes the job of the center of appointing key personnel for its businesses; (d) rotation, organizing exchange of staff between divisions; (e) motivation, governing its business portfolio through financial and career incentives; (f) coordination, which highlights the task of the center to provide mechanisms that encourage cooperation between business units, and (g) support, which enables corporate involvement by performing services for its businesses. The authors find, that high performing multi-business firms use the techniques "planning", "evaluation", 'selection", "motivation", and "support" to actively manage the businesses in their portfolio. These companies do not attempt to apply measures to rotate staff between divisions or to encourage cooperation between businesses.

2.4.2.2 Strategic Decision Making in Multi-Business Firms

Building on the generic styles of corporate involvement, various academic contributions have been developing models focusing on the aspect of strategic decision making in multi-business firms (for an introduction e.g., see Chakravarthy & Doz, 1992; Eisenhardt & Zbaracki, 1992; Papadakis, Lioukas, & Chambers, 1998; Paroutis & Pettigrew, 2005a; Schendel, 1992a, 1992b; Welge, Al-Laham, & Kajüter, 2000).

Burgelman (1983a, 1983b) for instance differentiates induced and autonomous strategic behavior of different business units. In the former concept, corporate managers use administrative mechanisms to shape strategy while in the latter divisional management is taking initiative to develop and implement strategy. Bourgeois and Brodwin (1984) developed five types of strategy implementation models consisting of commander, change, collaborative, cultural, and crescive model, whereby each model is associated with varying roles of corporate managers and members of the organization. The models range from strong corporate involvement as described in the commander model over corporate influence via structure, incentives or values as seen in the change and cultural model, or cooperation as illustrated in the collaborative model to the crescive model, which relies on bottom-up strategy development and limited corporate involvement. The contributions by Hart (1992) and Hart and Banbury (1994) draw another framework consisting of five styles of strategy-making in multi-business organizations, which are based on the contrasting roles of corporate center management and divisional members of the organization. Models include command, symbolic, rational, transactive, and generative. The commander model relies on strong corporate leadership while the symbolic focuses on creating a joint mission and vision. In the rational model, top management uses formal planning systems and hierarchical relationships whereas the transactive model concentrates on top managers' role as facilitator of an interactive process of strategy formation. The generative model lastly is driven by the initiative of organizational actors and corporate managers as sponsors to ensure the fit of strategy and organization.

All of the above models are based on diverse designs of the strategic decision making process. The models differentiate types of corporate involvement in strategic decision making mainly along two key dimensions – one covering the degree of centralization of decisions, the other the level of formalization of the strategy process in a multi-business firm.

Centralization refers to the degree to which the right to make strategic decisions is concentrated in the corporate center (Fredrickson, 1986: 282). In centralized settings, strategic decision making is driven by corporate management, providing only limited and targeted input opportunities for business unit managers (Calori, 1988: 86–87). It enables a high decision speed and consistency of business unit strategy with the overall strategic intend of the corporation and reduces control costs. On the other hand, it places significant cognitive demands on those managers who retain this authority and impose knowledge transfer costs from individual businesses to the corporate center (Christie, Joye, & Watts, 2003: 4–6). Given the generally accepted relationship between the strategy process model and the structural and environmental context of the firm (e.g., see Burgelman, 1983b; Noda & Bower, 1996; Paroutis & Pettigrew, 2005b), various contributions attempted to provide evidence regarding the appropriate degree of centralization in multi-business firms. Authors such as Gupta (1987) and Govindarajan (1986, 1988) therefore provide empirical evidence based on interviews and questionnaires, that business performance will be maximized through decentralization in conditions of high environmental uncertainty and non-routine production technologies while high interdependence of business units requires a centralized approach to strategic decision making. Christie et al. (2003) observed in this context that decentralization enables firms to generate specialized knowledge and is commonly found in larger and mostly unregulated multi-business firms. Hall (1987) moreover advocates for a high degree of freedom for strong business units in stable industries whereas businesses with high priority for the corporation and in industries with experienced corporate managers usually justify a larger degree of centralization. Centralized decision making is therefore commonly observed in firms with related diversification, in which the headquarters have to secure the strategic relatedness between the firms' individual businesses (Gupta, 1987: 478–482). Decentralization is conversely dominant in unrelated diversified firms, requiring little corporate involvement in strategic decision making, but attributing a key role to the corporate center as shareholder to financially control the portfolio of businesses (Lau, 1993: 59–64).

The degree of formalization describes the extent to which an organization uses rules and procedures to prescribe behavior (Hall, 1977). Formalized strategic planning is marked by an explicit process to determine a firm's long-range objectives, its strategic direction and consequently the monitoring of results. Rules and procedures, hence, contribute to the development of a firm's repertoire of behaviors and establish a formalized routine of strategic decision making (Fredrickson, 1986: 286–287). The process typically involves members of the firm's corporate management as well as members of its business divisions (Vancil & Lorange, 1975: 82–84). Informal strategy processes on the other hand are rather built on an organization-wide understanding of the company's mission and objectives. It consequently supports the implicit development of the firm's strategy and typically allows greater flexibility while at the same time being less efficient (Armstrong, 1982). Based on an empirical study, Armstrong (1982: 202–203) presents a number of conditions, under which formalized strategy processes appear favorable such as highly complex business models, high uncertainty in the market, or rapid changes in the organization or its environment. He furthermore claims that inefficient markets require stronger formalization as inefficient markets have less self-regulating power and provide little information.

2.4.2.3 Incentive Schemes in Multi-Business Firms

Incentive schemes are an important means to govern a diversified business portfolio functioning as an effective motivator of executives to achieve or even outperform their performance targets (Rappaport, 1978: 81). This research is typically linked to the principal-agent theory concentrating on the contractual relationship between shareholders as principals and managers as agents. A part of management compensation in these models is linked to up-front agreed targets, which can range from short-term oriented indicators such as earnings per share to long-term growth or profitability objectives (Hall, 1987: 88).

Incentives can take different forms, generally distinguished in pure financial contributions based on the achievement of specific targets such as bonuses and ownership rights via direct stock awards or stock option programs (e.g., see Carpenter, 2000; Goranova, Alessandri, & Dharwadkar, 2007). According to Lau (1993: 61), related diversifiers commonly base their incentive systems on the performance of the corporation whereas unrelated diversified firms use divisional achievements as the basis for their incentive calculations. In a detailed empirical study, Kerr (1985) moreover provides detailed descriptions of the formal reward systems in related and unrelated diversified firms. Related diversifiers typically use so-called hierarchy-based systems, which rely on both objective and subjective indicators, accruing to a maximum of 20–30% of salary. Incentives can comprise both bonus and stock awards. Unrelated diversifiers commonly apply so-called performance-based schemes, which are build almost exclusively on objective performance measures. They hereby address the concern that corporate managers have little insight into individual divisions and therefore cannot make subjective compensation judgments. It additionally fosters a feeling of ownership of divisional managers. They typically pay higher bonuses with 40% or above as well as stock awards.

2.4.3 Availability of Central Functions and Resources

One of the major discussion topics in the course of creating value in multi-business firms is the kind and level of resources a firm's corporate center should provide for its business units. In other words, it looks at the vertical resource relationship between the corporate center and the individual business units. According to Penrose (1959), firms will accumulate this special type of managerial resource over time and unused headquarters resources will therefore be available to the different businesses in a firm's portfolio. Based on case studies and interviews, Berg (1969), Yavitz and Newman (1982) and Hitt and Ireland (1986) identified a set of resources the corporate center should provide its business units, so-called corporate resources: the availability of low-cost capital, the access to outstanding management skills in form of corporate executives, and the supply of specialized services such as corporate research and development, or centralized marketing.

2.4.3.1 Access to Low-Cost Capital

The ability to offer low-cost capital, in particular growth capital, is one of the most widely recognized opportunities for a parent corporation to support its businesses. The access to funding at favorable cost enables business units to invest in projects it would not be able to if pursued on their own – either due to problems of access or cost of capital. Individual businesses often find it more difficult to raise money from capital markets or from banks than a larger corporation that is established in the field and that has a stable network of financial partners. A diversified firm can furthermore – without taxation – channel funds internally from divisions with strong cash flows but limited growth expectations towards the businesses with the largest growth opportunities (Berg, 1969). Regarding the costs of capital, diversified firms moreover usually experience a positive impact of diversification on the firm's rating and therefore are able to provide its businesses with funding at lower costs (Yavitz & Newman, 1982).

2.4.3.2 Availability of Management Talent

The second major area of research is the presence of management talent in the corporate center that can support individual businesses, either out of the corporate center or by transferring managerial staff to divisions to drive important initiatives. According to this view, general managerial talent is to some degree transferable across products and industries (Matsusaka, 2001). According to Katz's (1974) classification, corporate managers add human and conceptual skills to individual businesses while technical skills remain with divisional staff. Management talent from the corporate center therefore mainly contributes general business knowledge in functional or organizational areas rather than expert knowledge about specific products and markets (Andrews, 1969; Chandler Jr., 1991; Koontz, 1969). Hence, the availability of exceptional talent allows firms to react quickly to opportunities and threats by employing people familiar with the corporate culture and the firm's skills and ambitions (Yavitz & Newman, 1982: 15–16).

2.4.3.3 Supply of Specialized Services

The third and probably most controversially discussed area of parenting opportunity is the supply of distinctive competences in the form of specialized services as a headquarters resource. Research suggests that those distinctive competences are formed in functional areas such as research and development, marketing or human resources. Research by Miles, Snow, Meyer, and Coleman (1978) and Snow and Hrebiniak (1980) indicates that the availability of such specialized services is critical for the successful implementation of strategies at the business unit level. Kiechel (1982), moreover, argued that diversity can be best managed through the application of functional skills across the majority of a firm's business units. Hitt and Ireland (1986) even claim that successful formation and use of corporate level distinctive competences.[16] should increase the relatedness of a firm's business portfolio and, therefore, enable superior performance. In an exploratory research design based on a survey of 185 Fortune 1000 firms, Hitt and Ireland (1986) established a positive link between the consolidation of critical services for the firm's success in the corporate center and related diversification. Within unrelated diversifiers, on the other hand, general administration activities as well as most other corporate resources were related negatively to performance. Firms with related diversified business portfolios therefore tend to have significantly larger corporate centers than firms pursuing an unrelated diversification strategy (Collis, Young, & Goold, 2007). Campbell et al. (1995b) furthermore caution practitioners and academics, that the offering of corporate center services often holds a privileged status vs. outside suppliers and therefore protects the center from the rigors of the market. By those means, hoped-for economies of scale in central functions may remain on paper but might not find their way into reality.

2.4.4 Leverage of Resources and Competences across Businesses

The concept of cross-business synergy, in other words the positive impact of leveraging resources and competences across organizational boundaries, is central to the existence and performance of multi-business firms with diversified business portfolios (Goold & Luchs, 1993). Despite some inconsistent findings, the overall conclusion of nearly four decades of diversification research – as outlined in the earlier section "Diversification and Performance" – is that firms whose businesses are resource related achieve superior returns (Tanriverdi & Venkatraman, 2005). Unlike the previously discussed availability of central functions and resources, the leverage of resources and competences across businesses does not rely on the corporate center to provide its businesses with resources; it rather requires management to create an environment through structures, processes and incentives that fosters the sharing of resources and competences among business units.

[16] Hitt and Ireland (1986) distinguish the following competences on the corporate level: General administration, production/operations, engineering/research and development, marketing, finance, personnel/human resources, public/governmental relations.

2.4.4.1 Opportunities to Leverage Resources and Competences

The research regarding the leverage of firm's resources and competences horizontally across different businesses is largely built on the resource-based view. Followers of this approach argue that firms' resources drive value creation via the development of competitive advantage (Ireland et al., 2003). In other words, a firm's strategy needs to put strong emphasis on its resource mix rather than purely concentrating on the firm's market environment (Wernerfelt, 1984). Firm resources typically include all assets, capabilities, organizational processes, firm attributes, information, and knowledge that permit a firm to implement strategies that improve its efficiency and effectiveness (Daft, 1983; Goold & Campbell, 2002). Barney and Arikan (2001) and Priem and Butler (2001), however, highlight that the mere possession of resources does not guarantee the development of competitive advantage. This can only be achieved through the accumulation, combination, and exploitation of such resources within a firm's business portfolio. Barney (1991a), furthermore, defines four requirements a resource has to fulfill to grant its owner a sustainable competitive advantage: it must be valuable, rare, imperfectly imitable, and there must be no strategically equivalent substitute for it.

In order to create value with a resource base, firms therefore need to establish a resource management process which structures a firm's resource portfolio, bundles resources into capabilities, and leverages these capabilities while keeping environmental uncertainties in mind. Structuring activities include such elements as the acquisition, accumulation, and divestment of resources. Bundling is the sub-sequent step, which includes the stabilization and enrichment of the existing resource portfolio as well as the pioneering of new capabilities through combining different resources. The process of leveraging finally includes the mobilization, coordination and deployment of resources throughout a firm's business portfolio in order create value for customers and consequently create competitive advantage and wealth for shareholders (Sirmon et al., 2007: 275–287).

Consistent with the above findings, Prahalad and Hamel (1990) established the concept of the core competence of a firm and define a core competence as the "collective learning in the organization". Based on case studies of global companies such as General Electric, General Motors, Canon, Phillips, or Sony, the authors argue that a firm's competitive advantage depends on the development and organization-wide use of these competences. In order to be considered a core competence, it should provide a firm access to a variety of different products and markets, make a significant contribution to customer benefit, and should be difficult to imitate by competitors.

Generating superior performance, therefore, requires a firm to realize its competitive advantage and to actively seek synergies between different businesses through leveraging resources and competences (Mahoney & Pandian, 1992). Campbell and Goold (1998: 4–5) identify six sources of synergy in this context: shared know-how, shared tangible resources, pooled negotiating power towards such entities as customers, suppliers, or regulators, coordinated strategies, vertical integration of related businesses, and combined new business creation. Empirical evidence suggests that resource relatedness among business units is a critical source of cross-business synergy. Robins and Wiersema (1995), for example, developed a quantitative model to illustrate the importance of relatedness in terms of shared strategic assets such as capabilities or know-how, rather than linkages based on operations or facilities for a firm's performance. Farjoun (1998) finds in this context, that firms with high relatedness in their skill and physical base have the highest potential to generate strong performance while firms with a focus on either skill or physical base show no significant performance advantage. The contribution by Tanriverdi & Venkatraman (2005), moreover, concentrates on the knowledge relatedness of firms and finds, based on a survey throughout 303 US firms, that successful diversification requires a complementary set of product, customer, and managerial knowledge resources across businesses; this finding is supported in similar fashion by Miller (2006).

2.4.4.2 Organizational Imperatives to Leverage Resources and Competences

Implementing the principle of leveraging resources and competences implies certain organizational imperatives on multi-business firms. Typically, management is trapped in the strategic business unit mind-set, which prohibits them to recognize particular strengths and common themes across divisions. It is therefore important for top managers to take a look across a firm's organizational boundaries in order to identify important resources and core competences and to establish mechanisms that allow the leverage across different businesses (Prahalad & Hamel, 1990). In this context, Galbraith and Nathanson (1978) identify four areas of an organization that need to be addressed in order to direct a firm towards a resource-sharing organization. They distinguish mechanisms along the lines of structure, information and decision processes, people, and reward systems, whereby the latter two find particular recognition in the contributions by Gupta and Govindarajan (1986) and Kanter (1989: 90–116). Based on a survey of 58 firms, the authors provide empirical evidence that organizational familiarity of people as well as the integration of resource-sharing activity in managers' incentive plans are essential components to enable and encourage cooperation between different business units.

2.4.5 Portfolio Management in Multi-Business Firms

The previous sections have been concerned with the management of single businesses by the corporate center as well as the coordination between different existing businesses in a firm's investment portfolio. Portfolio management, in contrast, is mainly concerned with the future shape of the overall corporation. The concept of portfolio management as discipline emerged during the 1970s after the resource allocation problems of several large conglomerates due to the complexity of investment proposals coming from their divisions (Goold & Luchs, 1993: 11). Portfolio management therefore comprises the analysis of a company's portfolio, the strategy for its portfolio, and consequently the resource allocation among the different businesses.

2.4.5.1 Portfolio Analysis

Portfolio analysis is supposed to provide managers a framework, which allows the comparison of diverse existing businesses as well as new investment opportunities. The analysis is intended to support the management team of a multi-business firm to determine which businesses it should add or remove from its current scope, in other words, to determine the overall portfolio strategy. It furthermore allows management to decide how much capital to allocate to the different businesses in its portfolio.

The portfolio analysis concepts developed during the 1970s typically relied on a matrix allowing the categorization of the different businesses in a multi-business portfolio along two dimensions. One of them normally measures product/market attractiveness including elements such as profitability or market growth; the other assesses the competitive position of the different businesses in their markets including indicators such as market position or entry barriers (for a general overview see Bettis & Hall, 1981; Hall, 1978; MacMillan, Hambrick, & Diana, 1982; Welge & Al-Laham, 2007). A particular strength of such matrix concepts is that they bring "intelligent and appropriate communicational opportunities to the hard issue of portfolio management" (Hax & Majluf, 1984: 194).

Although such matrix concepts for portfolio analysis still find use, later concepts largely included value-based planning elements into the analysis of a firm's portfolio. These concepts are supposed to overcome the oversimplification of complex relationships (Clarke & Brennan, 1990; Ginsberg, 1989) and the lack of consistency with modern financial theory (Slater & Zwirlein, 1992)[17] observed in portfolio analysis based on matrices. Within value-based planning, managers are encouraged to evaluate the per-formance and outlook of each division in the same terms as the stock market and to take actions based on the value creation potential of each individual business (Alberts & McTaggart, 1984; Copeland et al., 2000; Funk & Welge, 2008; Reimann, 1988, 1989). A wide range of indicators for value measurement have become available since then and find wide use in the market. Measures commonly rely on discounted cash-flow techniques. They range from early concepts such as economic profit or economic value added, which are mainly concentrated on individual investment projects, to value measurements for the entire firm such as total return to shareholders or market value added (Arnold, 2005).

2.4.5.2 Portfolio Strategy

Building on the insights generated during a firm's portfolio analysis about the growth, profitability, and thereby value creation prospective of a firm's existing

[17]Slater/Zwirlein (1992) provide evidence, that diversification strategies built on matrix portfolio analysis are associated with value destroying investments. This observation holds true across different matrix concepts as well as risk-adjusted and market adjusted measures of return to shareholders.

businesses, multi-business firms need to set the strategy for the overall portfolio. Portfolio strategy, also referred to as portfolio planning, therefore entails the development of the future shape of the firm's business portfolio, including a decision about the future role of current businesses as well as potential investments into new areas (Alberts & McTaggart, 1984: 138; Reimann, 1989: 26). Portfolio strategy therefore is a balancing act of current businesses and investment opportunities against the supply of capital, given the predicted returns of current and potential investments (Carlesi, Verster, & Wenger, 2007; Stein, 1997). This balancing act furthermore should be consistent with the principle of modern financial theory, which demands that a firm only follows those investment opportunities that create value above its cost of capital (Slater & Zwirlein, 1992).

According to traditional theory of portfolio planning, funds in diversified firms "are not automatically returned to their sources, but instead are exposed to an internal competition" (Williamson, 1975: 147–148). Multi-business companies should con-sequently allocate their funds from less profitable businesses to more profitable businesses and seek options to advance the overall portfolio into a profitable, high-growth arena[18] (e.g., see Bettis & Hall, 1981; Hall, 1978). Recent studies (e.g., see Brandimarte, Fallon, & McNish, 2001; Carlesi et al., 2007; Dranikoff, Koller, & Schneider, 2002) however show, that only few companies actively manage their portfolios and most corporates wait too long to divest, depressing the exit price and hence creating costs for the firms.

Built on the idea of portfolio strategy and active portfolio management, Eisenhardt and Brown (1999) propose the concept of patching in order to gain flexibility in matching the portfolio strategy and the organizational setup of the firm. Patching in their definition is "the strategic process by which corporate executives routinely remap businesses to changing market opportunities. It can take the form of adding, splitting, transferring, exiting, or combining chunks of businesses" (Eisenhardt & Brown, 1999: 73–74) Patching typically comprises ongoing and mostly small changes in the organization to continuously guarantee business focus and fit between portfolio strategy, market environment and internal setup.

2.4.5.3 Internal Capital Market and Resource Allocation

The above described resource allocation in a diversified firm as consequence of its portfolio strategy creates an internal capital market within the multi-business firm. The internal capital market allows the diversified firm to fund value creating projects that external finance would not be available for. Theoretically, it can therefore fund projects a comparable single-business firm would not be able to fund and can create value for its shareholders (Gertner et al., 1994: 1211–1213).

[18]Reallocation of funds can include the transfer of cash flow from one division to the other as well as the use of one division's assets as collateral to raise financing that is then diverted to another division.

Stein (1997) highlights two pre-conditions, which are required to capture the opportunities of an internal capital market. First, there must be financing constraints from external capital markets, both for individual divisions and headquarters. Without these, every value creating project could be pursued and there would be no need for a company to deliberately restrict the number of projects they want to fund and to engage in the internal allocation of funds. Second, the headquarters must have the incentive and the authority to engage in resource allocation across businesses. This requires the corporate center to benefit from the value generated in individual projects and to be empowered to take resources away from some businesses to give it to others.

Stein (1997) then develops a theoretical model proposing that internal resource allocation is more important in markets with "underdeveloped" capital markets in the sense of information and agency problems. At the same time, he acknowledges the benefits of an internal resource allocation through the firm's headquarters – in pursuit of its own self-interest – in order to "pick winners" across the entire portfolio. Various empirical studies have addressed this topic since. They attempt to provide evidence that the failure of internal capital markets can explain the fact that diversified firms in general seem to be valued less than specialized firms. One reason for this failure could be that firms do not use their ability to allocate resources and that each division relies on its own funds. Lamont (1997) in his empirical study of firms in the oil industry, however, establishes evidence, that confirms the existence and active use of internal capital markets. Shin and Stulz (1998) find a similar relationship although less significant. They yet find no difference between the cash-flow sensitivity of segments with the best investment opportunities and segments with less attractive options and therefore conclude that firms fail to funnel funds to the prospects with the highest potential to create value. Scharfstein (1998) furthermore shows that divisions of firms with strong unrelated diversification show little relationship between investment and attractiveness indicated by Tobin's q. This link finds additional support in the contribution by Gertner et al. (2002), who find in an empirical study of 160 corporate spin-offs, that businesses after a spin-off show a stronger orientation to the value creation potential than businesses within a multi-business firm. In the same context, Klein (2005) studied the relationship of diversification and R&D investments and the role of internal capital markets. He finds a robust negative correlation between diversification and R&D intensity and provides evidence that "internal capital market inefficiencies, rather than managerial myopia, are driving the negative relationship between diversification and innovation".

In order to address the underlying cause for the internal deficiencies of diversified firms, Rajan et al. (2000) and Scharfstein and Stein (2000) show that divisional management is a key factor for the recurring failure of firms to allocate funds efficiently due to agency and information problems. They argue that divisional bargaining power and the lack of transparency of individual divisions towards corporate management prohibits the efficient functioning of internal capital markets.

Chapter 3
Introduction to the Private Equity Industry and the Role of Diversification

Once you buy a company, you are married. You are married to that company. It's a lot harder to sell a company than it is to buy a company. People always call and congratulate us when we buy a company: I say, "Look, don't congratulate us when we buy a company, congratulate us when we sell it. Because any fool can overpay and buy a company, as long as money will last to buy it." Our job really begins the day we buy the company, and we start working with the management, we start working with where this company is headed.

Henry R. Kravis, Financier and Investor, Co-Founder of KKR

Chapter 2 provided the first component of the starting position for this study by establishing an understanding about the status of academic research covering diversification in public corporations. This chapter consequently outlines the second element of the starting position required for the empirical research of this contribution by introducing the private equity industry and highlighting the role of diversification in PE settings. The chapter, therefore, gives an overview of the private equity industry comprising its definition, development, and industry structure. It furthermore presents a profile of the leveraged buyout segment within the private equity industry including elements such as the LBO market landscape, its value creation techniques, and its market trends. It then outlines the scarce academic literature regarding diversification in private equity. The chapter closes with a brief comparison between – generally public – diversified corporations and private equity firms.

3.1 Overview of the Private Equity Industry

The term private equity has recently found broad use from different directions such as academia, business practitioners, media and politicians – many of whom have used private equity as a synonym for leveraged buyout transactions and the investors behind this segment of the market. Hence, before detailing the leveraged buyout

D.O. Klier, *Managing Diversified Portfolios*,
DOI: 10.1007/978-3-7908-2173-4_3, © 2009 Physica-Verlag Heidelberg

segment of the private equity industry, this section provides a general overview of the PE industry. It therefore offers the definition of private equity as well as its historical development. It furthermore outlines the market structure of the private equity industry and in this context describes the role and distinction of the leveraged buyout segment within the overall PE industry.

3.1.1 Definition of Private Equity

Private equity is an asset class that has been an integral element of the investment universe during the past 50 years and has found particular investor as well as public interest in the 1980s and first years of the new millennium. It is part of the wider class of alternative investments, which besides PE also comprises asset classes such as hedge funds, real estate or commodities (Schmidt, 2004: 3–8). Investments in PE typically come with double-digit returns, show limited correlation with public equity markets but are associated with high risk, making the asset class attractive for institutional and private investors as yield-enhancement opportunity to their overall investment portfolio (European Private Equity & Venture Capital Association and Thomson Financial, 2005; Milner & Vos, 2003).

Private equity, according to the European Private Equity & Venture Capital Association (EVCA), can be defined as "equity capital provided to enterprises not quoted on a stock market". They furthermore define the typical application spectrum of PE as funding in order to "develop new products and technologies, to expand working capital, to make acquisitions, or to strengthen a company's balance sheet. It can also resolve ownership and management issues, a succession in family owned companies, or fund the buyout or buyin of a business by experienced managers" (European Private Equity & Venture Capital Association, 2007).

Loos (2005: 8) alternatively defines private equity as "investing in securities through a negotiated process" with the majority of investments going into an asset in which the equity is not freely tradable on a public stock market. Private equity investments are therefore less liquid than their publicly traded counterparts and are not subject to the high level of governmental regulation such as reporting and compliance requirements as firms listed on the stock market.

Complementing the definition of private equity from an activity point of view, Fenn, Liang, and Prowse (1996: 26–27) state, that PE investments typically are trans-formational, value-adding acquisitions of firms in different maturity stages. Engagements of private equity investors are largely characterized by majority ownership and typically follow an investment horizon of up to 10 years after conducting a thorough due diligence during the acquisition process. In order to create value and prepare the individual investment for its sale after the investment period, a small team of highly specialized investment managers actively monitors and advises the companies in the PE investment portfolio. During the time of investment, they retain powerful supervision and control rights over the strategic decisions of the acquired company (Bottazzi & Da Rin, 2002: 231–232).

DEVELOPMENT STAGES OF THE PRIVATE EQUITY INDUSTRY

Industry phase	Infancy (pre-1980)	Rise of venture capital (early 1980s)	Rise of buy-out funds (late 1980s-early 1990s)	Concentration and specialization (mid-1990s)	Revival and globalization (late 1990s-today)
Description	• First private fund American Research and Development (ARD) formed in 1946 • Focus on managing wealthy Americans' money and primarily funding new ventures • Annual venture capital investment less than a few hundred million dollars	• Changes to US investment and tax laws lead to increased funding • Strong contri-butions by U.S. pension funds • Major venture-backed successes (Apple, DEC, Compaq) lead to explosive growth of venture capital	• As funds increase in size, average in-vestment increases, and later-stage investments are emphasized • Ability to attack large, under-performing corporations and take them private	• Funds begin to specialize to develop industry and deal-type expertise • Increased emphasis of strategic and operational know how rather than access to capital and financial engineering • Less successful funds weeded out	• Strong growth in venture capital during end of 1990 until end of stock market boom in 2001 • Shift of growth to buyout segment • Creation of international common market place with focus on U.S. and Europe but first signs of growth in Asia and Middle East
Major players	• ARD • Thomas H Lee • Charterhouse	• Candover • Bain Capital • Clayton, Dubilier& Rice	• KKR • Carlyle	• TPG • Blackstone • 3i	• KKR Blackstone • Carlyle • Permira
Major deals	• DEC	• UPN	• RJR Nabisco • Duracell	• Continental Airlines	• TXU • LindeKion

*Grow business over 3-5 years
**Initial focus on short-term resale

Fig. 3.1 Development of the private equity industry

3.1.2 Development of the Industry

Although the private equity industry has gained particular attention during the 1980s and again since the turn of the century, the industry has developed along different phases throughout the second half of the twentieth century. Figure 3.1 provides a brief overview of the most relevant development stages of the industry including major players and deals characterizing each step in the process.

3.1.2.1 Infancy of the Industry

The start of the private equity industry dates back to the 1940s and was initiated in the United States. The first professionally managed private equity firm was established under the name of "The American Research and Development Corporation (ARD)" in 1946, a publicly traded, closed-end company. As the wealth distribution in the US was becoming concentrated in the hands of financial institutions rather than individuals, the ARD founders hoped to create a private institution that attracted institutional investors and to provide capital and managerial expertise to acquired businesses. In parallel, wealthy families started to establish similar professional organizations or funded individual businesses on a deal-by-deal basis to invest in new business ideas, so-called venture capital investments (Fenn et al., 1996; Lerner & Hardymon, 2002).

During the 1950s and 1960s, the private equity industry showed continuous growth, however annual inflows of capital never exceeded a few hundred million dollars. The industry development was still largely concentrated in the US, where the US regulatory bodies showed strong support for establishing private equity as an alternative investment vehicle. As a direct response to the short supply of private equity capital throughout the 1950s, Congress for instance passed a new legislation with the Small Business Investment Act of 1958, which paved the way for the establishment of Small Business Investment Companies (SBIC) enabling investors to provide professionally managed capital to risky companies. It furthermore allowed these new investment companies to supplement private capital with debt and were eligible for certain tax benefits (Loos, 2005: 9). However, the SBICs were also subject to certain restrictions such as their ability to take controlling stakes in firms, limitations in size, and a similar set of rules applicable to public corporations. These restrictions provided the impetus for the formation of a significant number of Venture Capital Limited Partnerships throughout the 1960s, which allowed a reduced regulatory supervision including increased flexibility to compensate investors. The establishment of limited partnerships therefore helped to attract new and more sophisticated investors compared to the publicly traded SBICs, which have been backed by mainly small private investors.

The weak state of the stock market and, therefore, the lack of ability to bring investments to the stock market in an IPO restricted the growth of private equity during the 1970s. Growth was furthermore dampened down by sharply rising capital gains tax rates, unfavorable changes in the tax treatment of employee stock options and the general shortage of qualified and entrepreneurial managers that were able to successfully restructure and run the acquired businesses. While investments into young firms in early development stages decreased significantly in the 1970s, investors developed strategies to allocate more capital to non-venture investments to avoid some of the tax and management restrictions of new venture investments. This led to the birth of the so-called leveraged buyout segment; investment volumes however remained low.

3.1.2.2 Rise of Venture Capital

The real rise of the private equity industry was spurred by another round of substantial regulatory changes in the United States. Among other alterations such as favorable modifications in the tax and securities laws, the most significant change was the US Department of Labor's decision to modify the interpretation of the "prudent man" provision governing pension fund investments in 1979 (Kaufman & Englander, 1993). Prior to this, the "Employee Retirement Income Security Act" limited pension funds from investing considerable amounts into high-risk asset classes. The new interpretation explicitly allowed pension fund managers to invest into private equity vehicles, in particular venture capital engagements fostering the growth of young businesses. This change led to an influx of capital. Whereas in 1978 only USD 424 million were invested in venture capital funds with only 15% being contributed by pensions funds, the amount invested grew to a total of USD 4 billion in 1986 with more than half coming from pension funds (Gompers & Lerner, 2000: 285).

During this time, major venture-backed successes such as DEC, Apple, or Compaq helped to increase the attractiveness of venture capital and private equity in general as an asset class. The spiral growth of venture capital was moreover supported by further regulatory changes. The "Small Business Investment Incentive Act" of 1980 redefined private equity partnerships as business development companies. This exempted venture capital investment firms from complying with the strict rules of traditional investment managers. In addition, reductions to the capital gains tax and the permission of the broader usage of stock options as compensation alternative paved the way for an eased access to investors" capital, talent, and growth of the PE industry (Tannon & Johnson, 2005: 77–78).

During this phase, European governments similarly started to change their regulatory policies in light of the success stories coming from the US to enable the growth of young businesses. The introduction of the "Unlisted Security Market" in the United Kingdom, which was a secondary market for small and medium-sized innovative and expanding firms was an important step to support the establishment of VC funds in Europe by providing them an attractive exit channel. Similar markets soon after were introduced in most other Western European countries together with improved tax and securities laws, which helped to promote an attractive environment for private equity investments in Europe.

3.1.2.3 Rise of Leveraged Buy-Out Funds

The increasing capital inflows from investors led to the creation of the first multi-billion dollar funds in the late 1980s. Encouraged by this new acquisition capacity and the rising competition for attractive new venture investments, the neglected leveraged buyout segment experienced strong rise during the late 1980s and early 1990s (Kaplan, 1991: 287–288). In 1988, there have been 125 transactions in the US market with an average acquisition price of USD 487 million in contrast to thirteen recorded transactions with USD 74 million average acquisition price in 1980. The buyout segment accounted for almost half of the increase in the value of assets traded in mergers and acquisitions between 1981 and 1989, representing 17% of all M&A activity (Lichtenberg & Siegel, 1990; Wiersema & Liebeskind, 1995). By borrowing against the firm's assets and cash flows, buyout firms were even able to attack large, underperforming firms, most prominently completed by Kohlberg Kravis Roberts & Co. with its acquisition of RJR Nabisco for USD 25 billion in 1989 (Jensen et al., 2006; Smith, 1990b). In total, 2,540 publicly quoted companies with a market value of over USD 297 billion were taken private between 1981 and 1989 (Wiersema & Liebeskind, 1995: 447).

3.1.2.4 Concentration and Specialization

Following a period of economic downturn, the private equity industry had to make some adjustments to its appearance. Whereas the number of PE funds increased by a factor of four between 1978 and 1988, the commitments from investors dropped by 68% between 1987 and 1991 and consequently forced unsuccessful PE firms out of the market. The remaining firms had to concentrate and develop a competitive edge to gain the trust of investors (Gompers & Lerner, 2000). During this time, most funds therefore have targeted a specific segment of the market (e.g. venture capital or buyout investments including sub-segments) as well as specific industries to allow the build-up of unique competences and gain reputation in the selected PE field. The pure access to capital lost in significance while the need to provide appropriate experience got to be the key to success in private equity during this stage, which has dominated most of the 1990s.

3.1.2.5 Revival and Globalization

The necessary changes within the structure of the PE industry during the mid-1990s, rising governmental support for entrepreneurial funding in industries such as life science or high tech as well as the establishment of new stock markets targeting the segment of young, high-growth firms such as the "NASDAQ" or the London-based "Alternative Investment Market" (AIM) let to another surge of the private equity segment. Driven by these changes, the venture capital segment of the market has been the front-runner and has dominated the private equity landscape, similar to the development during 1980s, until the sharp decline of the stock markets in 2001 and 2002. Since then, leveraged buyouts have been driving the private equity market with 84% of newly raised European private equity funds in 2006 being allocated to buyouts vs. 58% in 2005 and similar figures in the US market (European Private Equity & Venture Capital Association, 2008). The entire private equity market has reached new record levels – largely driven by the recent leveraged buyout boom – and is totaling in global investments of USD 734 bill ion in 2006 with strong mid-term growth expectations as illustrated in Fig. 3.2.

In parallel to the revival of private equity as a high-growth asset class, the industry began to globalize into an international market place (Cornelius, Langelaar, & van Rossum, 2007: 109–111). The majority of large US-based investment funds are by now established in the European market together with European counterparts.[1] According to the Global Private Equity report by PriceWaterhouseCoopers (2006), the industry is still heavily based in North America (35% of global PE investments in 2005) and Europe (40%); however, the market for private equity type investments is starting to develop in Asia (22%) as well as other developing regions (3%) with first deals taking place in countries such as China, Singapore, India, or Egypt.[2]

[1] For example, "Texas Pacific Group" opened its office in London in 1997, "Kohlberg, Kravis, Roberts & Co.", "E.M. Warburg Pincus & Co.", and "Clayton, Dubilier & Rice" opened offices in 1998. "The Carlyle Group" opened its London office in 1999 and by March 2000 had raised its first USD 730 million European fund.

[2] TPG for example recently completed a USD 1.5 billion transaction in Singapore together with affinity equity partners (see Guevarra, 2007), Blackstone and Apax acquired a USD 1.7 billion interest in Egyptian telecommunication company Weather (see Bryan-Low & Singer, 2007), and KKR made a USD 0.9 billion investment in Indian Flextronics Software Systems (see Range & Santini, 2007).

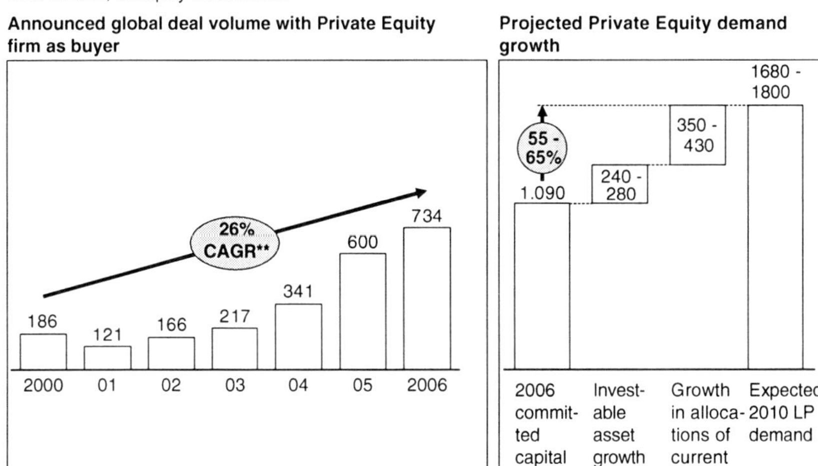

Fig. 3.2 Private equity investments 2000–2006 and projected growth

Although growth expectations for the private equity industry are high as Henry Kravis remarked at a 2007 conference – "the private equity world is its golden era right now; the stars are aligned" (Henry R. Kravis in Teitelbaum, 2007: 36) – industry experts caution investors. Rising acquisition prices paired up with rising borrowing costs pose substantial risks on debt markets and consequently revive memories of the rocky times of PE firms during the 1990s (Financial Times, 2007; Maier, 2007; Sender, Berman, & Zuckerman, 2007). "Everybody thinks private equity is the panacea – in our opinion, it's getting crazy." (Jim Leech, senior vice president of a large Canadian pension fund in Teitelbaum, 2007: 42). However – despite current, subprime-driven disruptions in the market for corporate control – the current private equity wave appears to be healthier than during the industry's boom in the 1980s with now lower levels of debt and higher earnings-to-interest ratios (Kaplan, 2007b).

3.1.3 Structure of the Industry

The private equity market consists of three major types of market participants. The first group is the issuers of private equity, in other words the firms a private equity fund invests in. The second are the private equity intermediaries, resembling the private equity firms, which manage the different investment vehicles. And third, PE investors, contributing capital to the private equity funds (Fenn et al., 1996; Ljungqvist & Richardson, 2003b).

3.1.3.1 Private Equity Issuers

Issuers of private equity represent the firms, which seek the investment by private equity funds. The nature of these firms varies widely across different sizes and stages of maturity; however, all of the firms are typically in a situation, where financing through debt or in the public equity market is difficult or not feasible. Private equity is commonly one of the most expensive options of financing for a firm as investments often involve high degrees of uncertainty with regard to the prospects of the firm's future operations (Lerner & Hardymon, 2002). After the acquisition, the firms are typically referred to as portfolio companies.

Investment targets can be distinguished based on the maturity stage the firms are in and can generally be divided into two groups, which have already been distinguished in the outline of the historical development of the PE industry: venture capital and leveraged buyout investments (e.g. see Fenn et al., 1996; Kraft, 2001). Figure 3.3 provides an overview of the two groups including the different sub-categories.

Venture capital investments are investments in firms during their early stages, for the "launch, early development, or expansion of the business" (European Private Equity & Venture Capital Association, 2007).[3] Venture capital funds typically actively support the management of the acquired company in developing and executing an adequate business plan for the venture (Gompers, 1995; Hellmann & Puri, 2002).

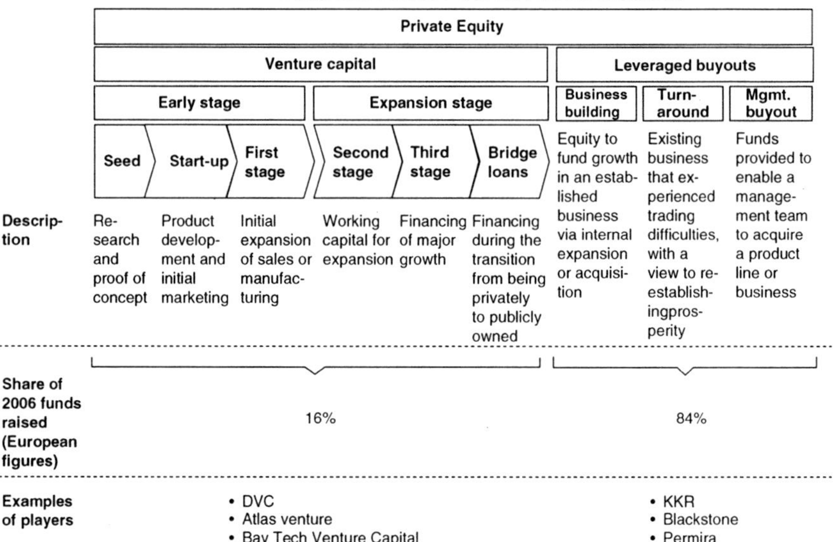

Fig. 3.3 Private equity investment stages

[3]Some, in particular European contributions use venture capital for the entire private equity market, also applying it to leveraged buyout. This study follows the predominately US definition and distinguishes private equity by maturity stages in venture capital and leveraged buyouts.

The primary exit channel for such investments is a public offering on the capital markets. Leveraged buyouts on the other hand are investments into established companies and are used to fund growth projects, to support firms in turn-around situations or to provide funding to management teams attempting to acquire a product line or business, so-called management buyouts.

3.1.3.2 Private Equity Intermediaries

The intermediaries in the private equity market are the private equity firms, which are the core element of interest in this study. They are the organizations, which manage the PE funds with the money contributed by investors and therefore are the managers of the individual assets in the firm's investment portfolio.

Private equity firms commonly manage multiple investment funds, which have been raised throughout the lifetime of the PE firms. The funds are typically established as limited partnerships, whereby the private equity firm holds the position of the general partner and the investors are the limited partners (de Malherbe, 2005: 81). Within each of the funds, investments are generally embedded in transaction-specific limited partnerships, which provide the equity for an acquisition sourced from the fund as well as the target company's management team (Baker & Smith, 1998: 170). Figure 3.4 provides an overview of a typical structure of a private equity intermediary on the example of a leverage buyout association.[4]

The general partner manages and controls the assets while the limited partners monitor the overall fund performance. Private equity funds typically raise capital for one fund at a time with an average life-span of 10 years, whereby funds are invested in the first 3–5 years after fund raising and capital is returned to investors after the liquidation of the partnership. Most PE firms raise funds by forming limited partnerships every 2–5 years and make up to two dozen investments over the life-span of the fund (Gompers & Lerner, 1999: 5–6; Povaly, 2006: 28–32).[5] Lerner and Hardymon (2002: 2) estimate that more than 80% of PE investment vehicles in the US are structured as limited partnerships with a similar share in the European market. Few firms are set up as small business investment or business development companies (both US only), publicly traded investment firms, or are the investment units of larger corporations.

In order to ensure the alignment of interest between general and limited partners, the compensation schemes of private equity investment arrangements are a critical contractual mechanism (Gompers & Lerner, 1999: 6). The terms and conditions for the private equity firm's compensation are typically fixed in the limited partnership

[4] The research of Baker and Smith (1998) is based on KKR's activities during the 1980s and early 1990s. The illustrated equity share of 5% is only used in very aggressive buyout transaction structures. It can generally be expected at levels around 20%. The general legal structure also holds for venture capital intermediaries though the capital structure for such investments is typically characterized by higher levels of equity.

[5] Gottschalg et al. (2004) show in their sample that venture capital funds even invest on average (median) in 32 (28) companies and leveraged buyout funds in 16 (12) companies.

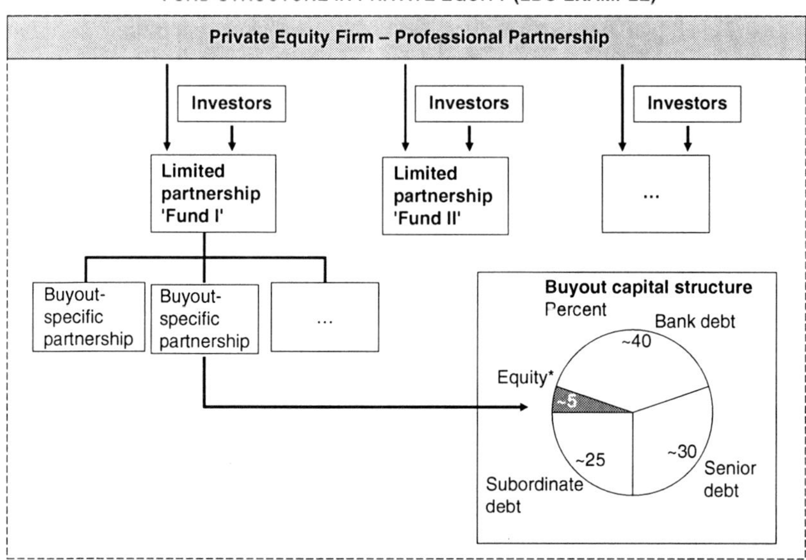

Fig. 3.4 Fund structure in private equity

agreement during fund raising and commonly provide the PE firm with three different sources of income. First, the PE manager receives an annual fixed fee for the management of the fund, which ranges between 1.5 and 3%. In addition, the fund manager receives a variable compensation of around 20% of the fund's performance. The most significant and also most effective way to guarantee the alignment of interest between investors and fund managers is the so-called "carried interest" or "carry" (Teitelbaum, 2007: 43). "Carried interest" is the term used to denote the general partners' share of the profits as remuneration for carrying the management responsibility of the investment fund and the portfolio companies contained in it. This part of the remuneration is based on the overall return of the fund after its liquidation and therefore ensures the management's focus on value creation until the fund's termination (Axelson, Stroemberg, & Weisbach, 2005: 2–5; Zong, 2005: 64). Another important means to align interests is the fact that – in contrast to corporate managers – private equity managers need to raise fresh capital for each fund and therefore rely on a solid track record and strong reputation in the market (Fenn et al., 1996).

Given the strong growth – the estimated number of private equity firms more than doubled between 2005 and 2007[6] – and the limited regulation of the market, there are no exact numbers of how many private equity firms are currently operating in the market. Based on the Private Equity Intelligence database (2007), 1,098 private

[6]The number of members in the US private equity associations (NVCA) for instance went from 454 to 866 between April 2005 and April 2007.

equity firms have been active with more than 2,700 non-liquidated funds in May 2007. Similar figures can be drawn from the two most prominent private equity associations, the European Venture Capital and Private Equity Association (EVCA) and the US National Venture Capital Association (NVCA), which claim that most active firms are members in their associations. EVCA counts 925 registered members in Europe, while NVCA states the membership of 866 firms in the United States with considerable overlaps given the global nature of the private equity market.

Drawing on the above classification along different maturity stages of a firm's investments, the landscape of private equity firms can be clustered in a similar way. There are three different groups of private equity players in the market: firstly, venture capital providers, secondly, leveraged buyout specialists, and thirdly, providers of alternative financing – primarily the hybrid form of mezzanine capital (e.g. see Das, Jagannathan, & Sarin, 2003; Kaplan & Schoar, 2004). Figure 3.5 gives an overview of the private equity landscape, providing evidence, that the leveraged buyout segment of the market is by far the dominating with more than 75% of capital. Given the general differences in their business models, the large group of providers of financing for assets such as real estate and infrastructure with more than USD 200 billion of capital as well as providers of fund-of-funds solutions with close to USD 100 billion have been excluded from this analysis.[7]

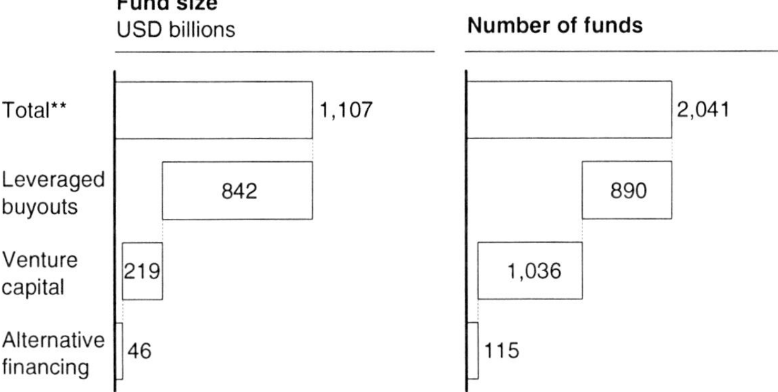

Fig. 3.5 Overview private equity investment landscape

[7]The study focuses on the comparability of private equity firms and diversified corporations. Assets other than corporate investments are therefore excluded from this analysis. Fund-of-funds are furthermore excluded to avoid double counting as their investments go into primary private equity funds.

The research objective of this study concentrates on the investigation of diversification effects and management techniques in diversified corporations and comparable private equity firms. Given the focus of leveraged buyout firms on generally larger and more mature investment targets, the empirical research of this study focuses on the leveraged buyout segment, which will be detailed further in Sect. 3.2 "Profile of the Leveraged Buyout Segment".

3.1.3.3 Private Equity Investors

The limited partners of a private equity fund are referred to as fund investors while the general partners are the fund's managers, who contribute only a small fragment of the fund's capital. Most funds have a selected group of large core investors and some smaller investors, totaling to usually not more than 15–20 investors.

Investors are typically large institutions such as pension funds, banks and insurance companies as well as some wealthy private investors. Recently, there has been an increasing contribution coming from governments via their investment offices as well as retail investors via fund-of-funds solutions. Fund-of-funds bundle the investments of numerous small private clients and invest in their name in private equity funds. Figure 3.6 provides an overview of the private equity investor landscape for the European market based on the EVCA (2008).

Private equity investments are an important means for institutional investors to enhance the overall yield of their portfolios and to diversify their risk profile. Although investments in PE typically represent only a small share of less than 10% of overall investments, the generally high returns, even after risk adjustments, enable investors to improve the return of a portfolio with the majority of investments in fixed income products (Deutsche Bank Research, 2005: 4).

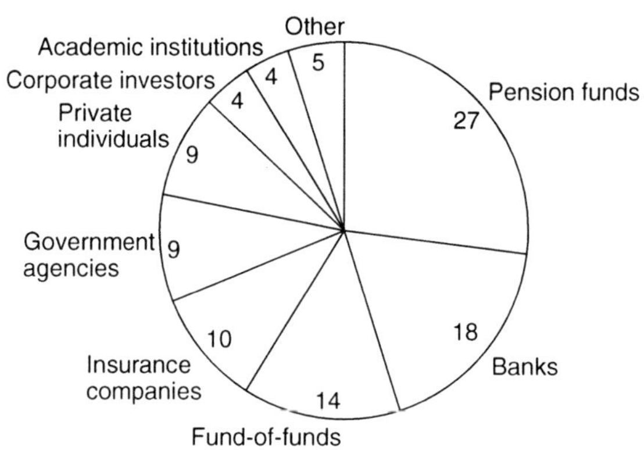

Fig. 3.6 Overview private equity investors

Investors often do not have the professional staff to make such investments themselves and hence use private equity firms to execute the investment strategy on their behalf (Lerner & Hardymon, 2002). Investment consultants often support them during the assessment and selection of investment opportunities.

3.2 Profile of the Leveraged Buyout Segment

As highlighted previously, this study focuses on the leveraged buyout segment of the private equity market. Before reviewing the academic literature regarding diversification in private equity and providing a brief comparison between the characteristics of diversified corporations and LBOs in the concluding section of this chapter, this section provides an introduction to the relevant aspects of the leveraged buyout part of the industry. It therefore presents an overview of the key characteristics of leveraged buyouts and the general LBO industry landscape. It furthermore offers insights into the performance measurement and distribution in leveraged buyouts and the status of research regarding the different value creation techniques in a leveraged buyout investment. The chapter closes with a brief outline of the most critical market trends and the industry's future outlook.

3.2.1 Key Characteristics of Leveraged Buyouts

Leveraged buyouts can be defined as transactions "in which a group of private investors, typically including management, purchases a significant and controlling equity stake in a public or non-public corporation or a corporate division, using significant debt financing, which it raises by borrowing against the assets and/or cash flows of the target firm taken private" (Loos, 2005: 11). Palepu (1990) remarks that the most obvious characteristic of LBOs is the significant increase in financial leverage; however he acknowledges several other important changes that are associated with such transactions. Buyouts are structured in order to increase management's ownership interest in the firm substantially. They furthermore lead to substantial improvements in the corporate governance by actively monitoring management's strategy and performance. A further distinction of LBOs is that investors typically lose the access to liquid public equity markets after the buyout.

The investments of leveraged buyouts are distributed broadly across different industries with strongholds in manufacturing and consumer goods as illustrated in Fig. 3.7. With regards to geography, the magnitude of buyout capital invested has historically been in the US; however, recent years have shown a strong uptake of, in particular, the European market with an annual growth of 26% between 1994 and 2004 compared to 16% in the US during the same period of time (Thompson Financial, 2007). According to the Global Private Equity Report by PriceWaterhousCoopers (2006), close to half of all new buyout investments in 2005 were going into Europe vs. 32% in the US and 25% in the Asia Pacific region. A study by Stroemberg (2008)

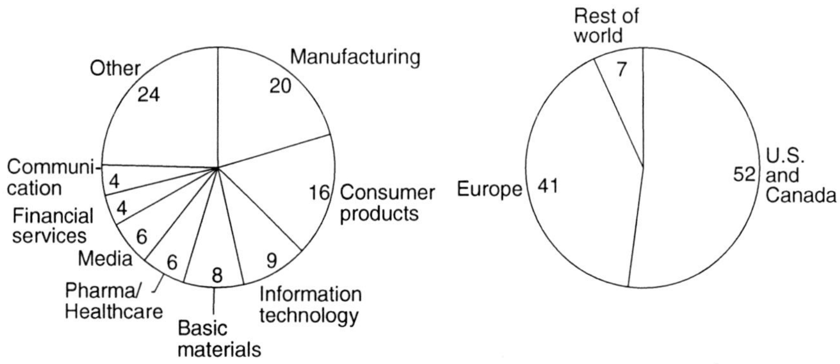

Fig. 3.7 Industry and geography distribution of leveraged buyout investments

for the World Economic Forum similarly shows that during the years 2001–2007, 46% of global buyout activity measured by deal volume occurred in continental Europe, Scandinavia and the U.K. and thereby slightly topped the deal volume in the United States and Canada with 45%.

As highlighted above, leveraged buyouts can generally be segmented in three general types of acquisitions: business building, turnaround and management buyouts. Business building and turnaround takeovers – one investing in firms with strong growth perspective, one in critical conditions – are driven by the private equity firms and often lead to the replacement of existing management (Easterwood, Seth, & Singer, 1989). In management buyouts, on the other hand, the current management of the target firm seeks support from outside investors to take control of the equity of the company or a specific product line from its previous owners. In either case, the investing firm typically targets the majority ownership of the acquired firm.

Buyout targets typically are established businesses with strong, non-cyclical cash flows in order to be able to service the financing costs imposed by the increased financial leverage. Hence, target companies moreover need to provide sufficient, unused borrowing capacity (Carow & Roden, 1997: 49–51; Kohlberg Kravis Robert & Co. and Deloitte Haskins & Sells, 1989: 66). The typical buyout targets, in particular during the 1980s, were businesses operating in medium to low technology industries with limited investment needs (e.g. see Lehn & Poulsen, 1990; Waite & Fridson, 1989). Opler and Titman (1993) furthermore found that most LBO targets had low Although the spectrum of businesses that are acquired by buyout firms is expanding into areas with stronger investment needs, the general characteristics from the buyout rise of the 1980s commonly still apply (e.g. see Kosedag & Michayluk, 2004; Peck, 2004).

3.2.1.1 Rationale for Leveraged Buyouts

Academic literature provides two different rationales why LBOs occur: on the one hand, economic approaches emphasizing ownership issues and, on the other, behavioral approaches relying on the impact of LBOs on stakeholders (Fox & Marcus, 1992: 65–73).

From an economic perspective, the leverage buyout is a means to improve the relationship between management and shareholders by improving the alignment of interest between the two parties. Whereas in traditional public markets shareholders are concerned about share price, management worries most about power and security. The strong participation of management in the performance of the investment through principal investments in unison with strong financial incentives during the investment as well as the strong involvement of PE firms in strategic decision making helps to avoid some of the obstacles observed in public corporations (e.g. see Fama, 1980; Jensen, 1986; Jensen & Meckling, 1976). This controversy, for instance, is described in the free cash-flow theory, which can be used to explain why firms become attractive buyout targets. The theory argues that when a firm's cash flows exceed its investment opportunities, these excess resources are subject to self-interested managerial discretion. Instead of distributing excess funds to shareholders, they rather "invest it at below the cost of capital" or "waste it through organizational inefficiencies" (Jensen, 1986: 323). If the board does not succeed in creating alignment of interest, the firm becomes an attractive takeover target for a leverage buyout using large free cash flows to service debt. Jensen (1989a) therefore explains the development of private equity as a "response to problems caused by the lack of effective monitoring of corporate managers" (1989a: 37). LBOs are furthermore an instrument for management to save its position in the case of a hostile takeover. Managers facing a hostile bid often initiate a buyout to secure their management seats (Fox & Marcus, 1992: 67). Lehn and Poulsen (1990), for example, found that activity in the market for corporate control either in the form of competing bids or takeover rumors was a significant predictor of the likelihood of an leveraged buyout with close to 50% of all LBOs in the late 1980s being accompanied by a competing bid or takeover speculations.

The behavioralists, on the other hand, disagree with the economists' view about the benefits of LBOs and argue that "LBOs are fraught with ethical problems and are, at best, merely redistributive" (Fox & Marcus, 1992: 70). In their view, the high premiums above the existing market price that are paid to the shareholders during the acquisition are not due to any expected uplift in the firm's value but are a result of insider information and tax advantages and occur at the expense of existing employees, tax payers and bond holders (Lowenstein, 1985; Palepu, 1990). The price premium and the return to PE investors is thereby financed by lowering the value of existing debt (e.g. see Smith, 1990b), reducing corporate taxes (e.g. see Kaplan, 1989), and shifting bargaining power from employees and unions to managers through the use of higher levels of debt and the implied threat of bankruptcy (e.g. see Shleifer & Summers, 1988).

3.2.1.2 Deal Structure

In a LBO transaction, the private equity fund buys out the equity of the current shareholders, which results in the formation of a privately held firm (Wiersema & Liebeskind, 1995: 447). The largest part of the acquisition in a buyout transaction is financed with debt with a leverage of up to 85% debt after the transaction (Kaplan, 1991) and an European average leverage of all firms involved in buyouts of 65% in 2005 even after repayments of debt (Deutsche Bank Research, 2005). The equity required for the acquisition is provided by the private equity fund and often to a smaller extent by the target firm's senior management.

The debt financing is split into different "tranches" such as senior and sub-ordinate debt and can be supplemented by alternative means of finance like mezzanine financing or securitization of carved out assets (Arzac, 1992: 17–18; Kohlberg Kravis Robert & Co. and Deloitte Haskins & Sells, 1989: 65). The non-equity components are typically borrowed against the target's future cash flows with additional securities on the target's tangible assets such as properties, plants or inventories (Arzac, 1992; Roden & Lewellen, 1995). During the first years of the investments, free cash flows are primarily used to service interest and to pay back the high level of debt before paying out dividends to investors or investing in future growth.

3.2.1.3 Buyout Process

The buyout process can be distinguished into three phases: (a) the acquisition including target selection, due diligence and the structuring of the transaction, (b) the post-acquisition management in order to create value from the buyout, and (c) the divestment (Loos, 2005; Tyebjee & Bruno, 1984).

During the acquisition phase, private equity firms first screen the market for potential investment opportunities that meet their investment criteria and offer further possibilities for value creation. As most deals are still privately negotiated, a deep knowledge of the market and contacts to decision makers are crucial qualities during this phase to establish a proprietary deal flow. Although there is an increasing trend in the market towards competitive auctions, buyout funds will continue to privately initiate transactions as returns in this type of deal are substantially more attractive. Once an appropriate target has been identified, the private equity firm needs to develop and assess a business plan for the firm and to determine an acquisition price based on the valuation of the target and the expected value creation opportunities (Tyebjee & Bruno, 1984: 1052–1053). This process, which is commonly known as due diligence, is followed by the detailed structuring of the transaction, the call for previously committed capital from investors as well as in some cases the raising of investment-specific investor funds, and the arrangement of the required debt financing.

SOURCES OF LEVERAGED BUYOUT TRANSACTIONS

Percent, all leveraged buyout transactions with and without financial sponsor, 1970-2007

Number of transactions

	1970-2000	2001-2007	All transactions
100% =	23	45	30
Public-to-private	6	7	7
Private-to-private	64	37	47
Divisional buyout	23	36	31
Financial vendor	6	17	13
Distressed	1	3	2

Transaction volume
USD billion

	1970-2000	2001-2007	All transactions
100% =	23	45	30
Public-to-private	27	29	28
Private-to-private	37	15	22
Divisional buyout	26	32	30
Financial vendor	9	23	19
Distressed	1	1	1

Source: Stroemberg (2008)

Fig. 3.8 Sources of leveraged buyout transactions

The valuation of the firm and the financial structure of the deal determine a considerable part of the overall deal performance (Axelson et al., 2005; Baker & Montgomery, 1994).

The majority of buyouts are acquisitions of companies already in private ownership, so-called private-to-private transactions, and divisional buyouts from multi-business firms as outlined in Fig. 3.8. The number of deals from each source has remained relatively stable with a slight increase in buyouts from financial vendors and a reduction in private-to-private transactions. In terms of transaction volume, public-to-private deals play a more important role given their larger size while smaller private-to-private transactions make less of a contribution to the overall deal flow.

During the investment phase, the private equity firm needs to actively work with the firm and influence the strategic decisions made by the firm's management to generate extra value in order to compensate the high return expectations of the PE investors. Traditionally, PE firms have focused on value creation through financial engineering and their involvement as active shareholders. Since the 1990s, however, leveraged buyout firms increasingly seek value creation through operational and structural changes in the asset (Kester & Luehrman, 1995). Since recently, private equity firms furthermore engage in strategically influencing the industry landscape by acquiring different, related assets and forming new entities from it.[8]

[8] The different value creation levers applied by private equity firms are detailed in Sect. 3.2.3 "Value Creation Techniques".

Individual investments are generally held less than 10 years, typically only 3–5 years. Butler (2001) shows in a sample of 200 public-to-private chemical buyouts that the average investment time is 4.4 years for investments between 1980 and 2000; however, a considerable amount of PE houses showed longer commitments to the their investments, depending on the performance of the investment and the market environment (Gompers & Lerner, 2000; Ljungqvist & Richardson, 2003b).

While contributions to shareholders are typically low during the investment, the major driver for the return of the deal is a strong exit. Divestments can take place in the form of an initial public offering, a trade sale of the portfolio company to a strategic buyer, or as a "re-leverage" and secondary buyout to another financial investor (Ainina & Mohan, 1991: 393–395; Ljungqvist & Richardson, 2003b: 18–24). The sale to a strategic buyer in a trade sale is the most common exit mode although secondary buyouts have substantially increased in popularity (Wright, Simons, Scholes, & Renneboog, 2006).[9] In unsuccessful investments, bankruptcy takes the place of the exit to end an engagement.

Figure 3.9 illustrates the results of Stroemberg's (2008) study of global LBO investments between 1970 and 2007. He finds a considerable decrease in IPOs as a way to exit buyout investments whereas the importance of financial and LBO-backed acquirers has been rising constantly since 1970.

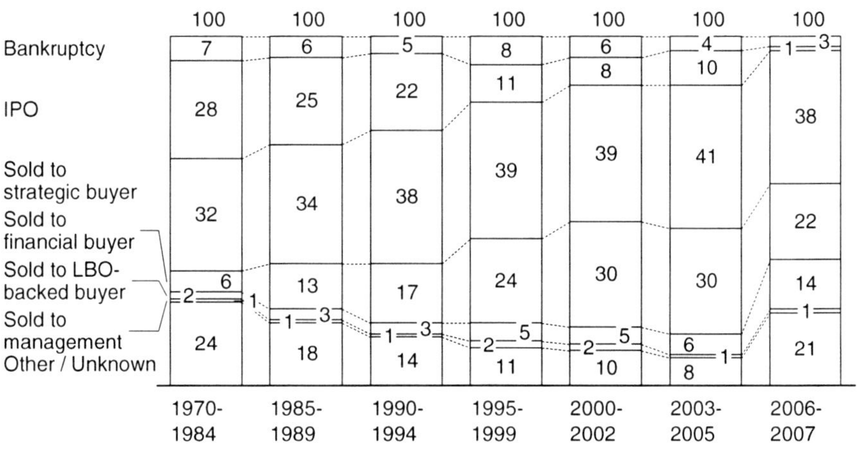

Fig. 3.9 Modes of exits for leveraged buyout investments

[9]Figures for the U.K. indicate a decrease of exits through flotation from over 30% in the late 1980s to approximately 5% in the period 2001–2005 while secondary buyouts increased from less than 10% to over 20%. Trade sales dropped from around 45% to approximately 35%. The residual is receivership.

3.2.2 *Leveraged Buyout Landscape*

The value of equity committed to leveraged buyouts as well as the number of private equity firms active in the leveraged buyout segment has been growing substantially since its inception in the 1980s. For instance, over 100 firms have been registered in 2005 with more than one billion in equity whereas the number of PE firms with comparable funding in 1989 has been only five.

According to Private Equity Intelligence (2007), there has been a total of 354 private equity firms with activities in leveraged buyouts and close to 800 active buyout funds recorded at the end of 2006. Some of these funds such as KKR, Blackstone, or TPG, the former Texas Pacific Group, have long reached the size of large blue chip firms with responsibility over various portfolio companies and many thousand employees (Schaefer, 2005).

Although the market counts a large number of players, the industry is concentrated around a limited group of large investment houses that run a number of active buyout funds. Some of them also manage investments in venture capital or alternative assets such as real estate or infrastructure; these funds are excluded from all further analysis. Most of the leading PE firms have been in the market since the uplift of buyout transactions in the 1980s and have established a track record of successful acquisitions with strong and consistent performance. The top ten private equity firms illustrated in Table 3.1 account for one third of total equity committed to buyout funds, all managing multiple funds and largely fulfilling the high return requirements of their investors. The top 50 firms are covering more than 70% of the market and the top 100 buyout firms unite 85% of the leveraged buyout segment (Private Equity Intelligence, 2007).

Table 3.1 Top ten leveraged buyout firms December 2006, buyout funds only

No.	Firm	Equity value USD billions[a]	Number of funds[b]	Geographic focus	Average fund performance Net IRR in percent[c]
1	KKR	41	7	Global	21
2	TPG (former Texas Pacific Group)	31	12	Global	30
3	Blackstone	30	6	Global	30
4	Permira	27	7	Europe	33
5	Goldman Sachs Private Equity	24	9	US	14
6	Carlyle Group	21	12	Global	28
7	Apollo Management	19	5	US	17
8	Bain Capital	18	7	US	22
9	CVC Capital Partners	18	5	Europe	29
10	Thomas H. Lee Partners	10	4	US	20

[a]Equity value of active buyout funds
[b]Number of active buyout funds
[c]Internal rate of return after fees
Source: Private Equity Intelligence

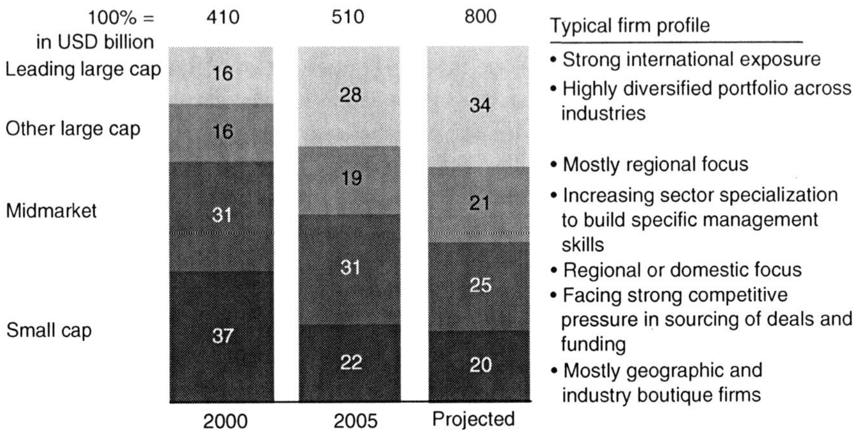

Fig. 3.10 Development of private equity firms across market caps

Growth is experienced in particular by the largest players in the market with international portfolios that are usually highly diversified across industries. These large caps are currently outgrowing the market and current fund raising indicates that this trend will continue as outlined in Fig. 3.10. Players with smaller amounts of equity, on the other hand, are facing strong competitive pressure in sourcing deals on the market and raising funds from investors. Many of these smaller funds have to start building expertise in a particular region or industry in order to competitively bid for assets and to convince investors of their ability to create value.

The majority of LBO firms has a US origin and consists of independent investment managers, although there are few large players, which are in the ownership of large financial institutions such as Goldman Sachs, Morgan Stanley, and Credit Suisse or are part of larger corporations. They typically run their investment portfolios with a small team of professional staff supported by seasoned management as advisors (Collis, Young, & Goold 2007: 383).

3.2.3 *Value Creation Techniques*

The creation of above market value during the time of investment is at the very heart of the private equity business model. The value creation methodologies on a single investment level, therefore, have found substantial coverage in public and academic literature, whereas the value creation techniques on a portfolio level have found only very limited representation in research. This section is supposed to provide an overview of the value creation techniques on the level of individual portfolio companies. The scarce literature regarding the management of the overall investment portfolio is outlined in Sect. 3.3 "Diversification in Private Equity" and is subject to further research in this study.

The management of the individual investment of a buyout firm has gone through different development stages since the ignition of leveraged buyouts some 25 years ago. During the rise of buyouts in the 1980s, the focus of LBO firms was on financial restructuring and active governance, so-called "financial and governance engineering" (Kaplan in Jensen et al., 2006: 15). While these components remain important until today, the increased competition in the search for attractive investments forced private equity firms to get involved in operational improvements and in later years strategic growth initiatives in order to achieve the returns required by investors (Anders, 1992; Loos, 2005: 21–34; Teitelbaum, 2007: 42), so-called "operational engineering" (Kaplan in Jensen et al., 2006: 16). Figure 3.11 provides an overview of the different value creation waves and the corresponding success factors and skill requirements for private equity firms, which are detailed in following.

VALUE CREATION LEVERS

		Operational engineering	
	Financial engineering and governance engineering	**Operational improvements**	**Strategic growth**
Predominant time	1980 -1990	1990 -2000	2000 -present
Key success factors	• Access to capital • Identification of financial value • Solid agency/corporate governance	• Access to deal • Knowledge of industry structure • Turnaround of operational inefficient targets	• Creation of strategic growth platforms • Active role in changing industry landscape
Required skills	• Financial restructuring • Active governance	• Operational improvements • Financial restructuring • Active governance	• Strategic industry insights • Operational improvements • Financial restructuring • Active governance
Geography	Domestic	Regional	Global

Fig. 3.11 Value creation levers in private equity

3.2.3.1 Financial Engineering

One of the key levers for value creation in a leveraged buyout is the financial restructuring and consequent de-leveraging of the target firm. As a consequence of the high debt burden taken on during the acquisition, buyout targets typically need to undertake substantial financial engineering to service the high interest rate payments. Baker and Wruck (1989) provide evidence in their case study of the O.M. Scott & Sons Company's leveraged buyout from ITT Corporation, that servicing a heavy debt load leads to improved performance. Wruck (1994) similarly shows that Sealed Air Corporation's leveraged special dividends lead to a reduction in free cash flows and consequently improved post-dividend performance. LBO firms share their deep knowledge about capital market mechanisms and financial expertise with the acquired firms to determine and implement the optimal capital structure for each investment.

Anders (1992: 85) notes, that "there is one discipline, in which the buyout firm's takeover adventures (…) are completely germane: finance." The private equity specialists actively support the chief financial officer in structuring the firm's balance sheet through the active use of capital markets. In order to de-leverage the target's balance sheet, capital market transactions can include the issuance of common or preferred stock, the use of instruments such as asset back securities based on a carved out portfolio of assets like properties or plants, as well as the liquidation of assets from the balance sheet, which are non-critical for the firm's operations (Zong, 2005: 64). LBO firms furthermore assist management in negotiating bank loans, bond underwritings, initial public offerings, and subsequent stock sales at terms an individual portfolio company would not be able to receive at a standalone basis (Cotter & Peck, 2001).

Many critics of private equity transactions on the other side argue that the high leverage drives up costs of financing and therefore hinders the execution of a firm's growth strategy. Contrary to their argumentation, empirical research (Butler, 2001; Long & Ravenscraft, 1993) showed that buyout transactions have almost no effect on the weighted cost of capital (WACC). The costs of capital in these research efforts proved to be more or less independent of leverage given the strong tax advantage of high debt levels. Another point of criticism of the high level of debt financing refers to its implication on financial distress. The large debt burden increases a firm's exposure to external shocks and can lead to financial distress or bankruptcy (Rappaport, 1990). It can furthermore make the firm short-term oriented to reduce leverage and service interest payments and thus leads to a decline in long-term competitiveness (Gifford Jr., 2001; Palepu, 1990). Conversely, Jensen (1989b) argues that the risk of default is much lower than proclaimed, since financial innovations and the interest of all parties to complete a successful workout process reduces bankruptcy risk considerably. Kaplan (1989) and Kaplan and Stein (1990)[10] furthermore provide

[10]Research by Kaplan and Stein (1990) conducted in leveraged recapitalizations of public corporations; provides only indicative evidence for the risk implications of leveraged in buyout transactions.

evidence that the systematic risk of equity in leveraged buyouts is much smaller than what would normally be predicted given the large amount of financial leverage.

3.2.3.2 Governance Engineering

Active governance is the second technique of private equity value creation and is a core element of the existence and performance of buyout investments. Beroutsos and Kehoe (2006) call the activity of private equity firms the exploitation of "governance arbitrage", in other words, realigning companies that have sub-optimal governance structures. The governance model of LBO investments comprises two key elements: the close involvement of PE managers in strategic decision making, on the one hand, and, on the other, the strong alignment between the interest of portfolio company managers and buyout investors through the PE specific incentive systems.

The corporate governance system of a firm, that underwent a buyout transaction, typically goes through a radical transformation (Kaufman & Englander, 1993; Thompson, Wright, & Robbie, 1992). The concentration of substantial parts of a firm's equity in the hands of one or few PE firms leads to the active participation by PE specialists in corporate governance (Habib, 1997: 157). As a consequence, firms in the portfolio of a PE firm experience a more active representation on typically smaller boards of directors including stronger involvement in strategic decision making as well as improved monitoring of top management's strategy and operating performance (e.g. see Adams, 2006; Cornelli & Karakas, 2008; Cotter & Peck, 2001; Jensen, 1989b; Lerner, 1995; Lowenstein, 1985; Smith, 1990a). Their involvement is particularly obvious during turnover of key members of the management team (Lerner, 1995: 316), during complex and challenging transactions (Cornelli & Karakas, 2008), as well as in setting ambitious growth and savings targets, which has become a rather routine procedure in public corporations but turns into an intense negotiation under private equity reign (Anders, 1992; Zong, 2005).

Based on the example of the US buyout specialist Clayton, Dubilier & Rice (CD&R), Kester and Luehrman (1995) developed three key principles of the governance approach of private equity firms. First, they identify more direct and informal lines of communication between the PE firm and various members of the organization, not only the chief executive officer. Second, their case study distinguishes the selective, however timely intervention of CD&R in the portfolio firm's decision making as another trait specific for PE investments. Third, their research claims trustworthiness between the partners of the PE firms and the firm's senior management as a core element of the private equity governance approach. These principles stay in clear contrast to the highly formalized communication of a public corporation with its shareholders, restraining the opportunities of involvement to few formal occasions.

Anders (1992), Kaplan and Stroemberg (2000) as well as Cotter and Peck (2001) furthermore remark that private equity firms conduct regular assessments of the portfolio company's management and are willing to quickly replace underperforming executives. Generally speaking, private equity firms as professional investors are likely to have a comparative advantage over third-party equity investors in the active governance of post-buyout organizations (Cotter & Peck 2001; DeAngelo, DeAngelo, & Rice, 1984). Henry Kravis, one of the founders of KKR, proudly remarks in this context, that no private equity backed firm has been involved in one of the major corporate scandals of the last 25 years due to the active governance executed by PE firms as owners (Henry R. Kravis in Zong, 2005: 63).

The second component that brings about significant changes in governance is the strong alignment of interest between owners and managers through changes in a firm's incentive system. The substantial ownership of equity through principal investments by the portfolio company's senior management as well as strong equity linked bonus systems create a strong motivation for managers to improve firm performance (Nikoskelainen & Wright, 2007; Palepu, 1990; Phan & Hill, 1995; Thompson et al., 1992; Weir & Wright, 2006; Weir, Laing, & Wright, 2005). Incentive systems are furthermore extended to a wide range of managers whose job performance can directly affect shareholder value. In public corporations, on the other hand, the total compensation of management, especially if part of a larger, multi-business corporation reflects a division's performance to a small extent only (Moon in Jensen et al., 2006: 22–24). Bonuses are rather paid – for a selected group of managers only – for "longevity, middle-of-the-pack performance, and for a host of other reasons that reward managers not only when companies do well" (Anders, 1992: 80). The high personal ownership in PE investments thus leads to personal costs of inefficiency (Smith, 1990b) and reduces management's incentive to shirk (DeAngelo et al., 1984; Jensen & Meckling, 1976; Smith, 1990a). Their large equity stake creates a strong positive momentum to undertake value-increasing actions and to invest only in projects above a company's cost of capital (Easterwood et al., 1989; Palepu, 1990).

With respect to efficient investment, Jensen (1989b) argues on a different note that not only the active involvement by the buyout firms as well as the strong ownership incentives reduces the above mentioned free cash-flow problem faced by many firms. The large debt burden itself limits managerial discretion and thus avoids investments below the firm's cost of capital. Grossman and Hart (1982), Jensen (1986; 1989b) as well as Baker and Wruck (1989) argue that debt can induce management to act in the interest of investors in ways that cannot be duplicated with optimally designed compensation packages. The servicing of interest reduces the available free cash flow and thereby limits the ability of management to spend extra cash inefficiently. In other words, the high debt burden forces managers to run their companies efficiently in order to avoid default (Cotter & Peck, 2001; Lowenstein, 1985).[11]

In a comparison of two case studies, one being a LBO transaction, the other a leveraged recapitalization of a public company, Denis (1994) found that the firm involved in an LBO showed a significantly higher performance uplift than the public company. He suggests that altered managerial ownership, board composition, and executive compensation induced by the buyout specialists allowed the LBO firm to outperform its public counterpart. Holthausen and Larcker (1996) moreover find

[11] Grossman and Hart (1982) furthermore outline that high debt and the implied risk of bankruptcy also put the high equity stake of managers as well as their reputation and power at risk. The high personal investment thus functions as further motivational factor.

that the superior performance of LBOs continues also after the reverse leveraged buyout, in other words the re-issuance of the firms in an IPO on public capital markets. In their empirical study, the authors find that reverse-LBO firms show a better performance than competitors in their industries for at least the four full fiscal years after the IPO and link the performance upside to the retained improvements in the firms' governance and incentive structures.[12]

3.2.3.3 Operational Engineering Phase 1: Operational Improvements

The early years of leveraged buyouts have been dominated by short-term investments and value creation largely driven through financial engineering and active governance. Given the fact that those traits of a leveraged buyout transaction have become increasingly commoditized, buyout specialists had to get involved in operational improvements to create value from the transaction and to generate the cash flows required to service the high interest rate payments (Palepu, 1990). Kaplan (in Jensen et al., 2006) summarizes this phenomenon by stating:

> *"In the late 1980s and after, more and more transactions saw buyout firms bidding against each other to do the financial and governance engineering: as a result, more of the value started to go to the sellers. Buyout firms have responded by developing industry and operating expertise that they can use to add value to their investments. This increased focus on improving operations is a big change. Given the combination of financial and governance engineering with this operational engineering,* private equity *is likely adding more overall value today (...)" (Kaplan in Jensen et al., 2006: 16).*

Jensen (1989b) suggests that the primary source of value creation from buyouts is organizational changes that lead to improvements in firms' operating performance and investment decisions. Leveraged buyouts are, therefore, likely to take place in companies that show significant potential to improve overall performance (e.g. see Baker & Wruck, 1989; Kaplan, 1989; Lichtenberg & Siegel, 1990; Smith, 1990b). While operational improvements can be triggered by management alone and be driven by the firm's high debt burden and the improved governance structure, buyout firms show an increasing support for management through strong and systematic involvement in strategic decision making. The following studies provide an overview of the operational effects of private equity, independent whether they are initiated by management or the private equity firm and are a sign of the importance of operational changes.

The investigation of the effects of buyout transactions on operational performance has brought forward a substantial amount of academic research. Kaplan (1989) provides evidence of management buyouts, showing strong improvements in operating performance even after adjusting for industry wide changes. Smith's (1990b) and Smart and Waldfogel's (1993) contributions support this argumentation confirming

[12] Holthausen and Larcker (1996) show that the superior performance is not an effect of restrictions in capital expenditure or working capital as those figures return to the industry median after the reverse leveraged buyout.

a significant relationship between buyout activities and improvements in operating cash flows. Breaking the overall firm performance down to plant-level performance, Lichtenberg and Siegel (1990) as well as Harris, Siegel, and Wright (2005) analyzed post-buyout operating enhancements in total factor productivity in plants of LBO companies. They observed significant short-term productivity improvements compared to plants in non-LBO firms. Harris et al. (2005) link productivity improvements mostly to measures undertaken by new owners to reduce the labor intensity of production via outsourcing of intermediate goods and materials.

Based on the finding that a positive relationship exists between LBO activity and operating performance, contributions by Muscarella and Vetsuypens (1990) or Wright, Hoskisson, and Busenitz (2001) provide evidence that operating performance improvements often coincide with substantial changes in the organizational structure and management processes of the firm's operations.

One particular instrument of a buyout firm to improve overall operational performance and to repay debt in the short-term is the concentration on a target firm's core businesses, in which they own a competitive edge and show high productivity (Anders, 1992: 83–84). If their distinctive competence for a business is not greater than the competition's, firms after a buyout would be forced to divest the business. They are sold to firms that have greater potential to add value to the business (Fox & Marcus, 1992). Anders (1992) in his KKR case study shows that portfolio companies stick to their core even after substantial debt reductions. Wiersema and Liebeskind (1995) and Berger and Ofek (1996) similarly show that LBO firms show substantially lower levels of diversification than comparable public benchmarks.

An additional area of cost reductions is the downsizing of firms' overheads. Singh (1990) argues that buyout targets had accumulated higher levels of organizational slack than non-buyout firms. LBOs typically "increase overhead efficiency by improving control systems, building better mechanisms for coordination and communication flow and by enhancing the speed of decision making" (Loos, 2005: 23). Hence, buyout firms are characterized by markedly less bureaucracy (Butler, 2001; Easterwood et al., 1989).

Another essential way to increase operational performance is the realization of efficiency gains in the use of corporate assets (Bull, 1989). As an immediate consequence of a buyout transaction, control on corporate spending tightens substantially and regular monitoring of budgets gains in importance (Anders, 1992; Holthausen & Larcker, 1996; Kosedag & Michayluk, 2004). The management of working capital is in the centre of such improvements including accelerated collection of receivable and the reduction of inventory. Easterwood et al. (1989) as well as Opler (1992) for instance observed sharply declining levels of inventory and receivables compared to pre-buyout levels. Liebeskind, Wiersema, and Hansen (1992) furthermore show that LBO activity results "in the creation of value through inducing managers to downsize the firm and to forego excess growth".[13] Although similar trends could

[13]Also see Kosedag and Michayluk (2004) for a summary of studies regarding the post-buyout performance of buyout targets.

be observed in many public corporations during the 1990s (Wright & Robbie, 1996), the above-depicted empirical studies provide evidence that buyout firms follow such approaches in greater consistency and effectiveness.

Studies by Kaplan (1989), Smith (1990b), Hall (1990) and Long and Ravenscraft (1993) moreover find that overall capital expenditure including areas such as research and development is considerable lower after a buyout than in non-buyout firms. Researchers therefore argue that through their restructuring activities, buyout firms sacrifice the long-term competitiveness of their portfolio companies for short- to mid-term returns (e.g. see Lei & Hitt, 1995; Long & Ravenscraft, 1993; Phan & Hill, 1995). Firms such as KKR provide evidence that this is a phenomenon only during the early years after buyout (Kohlberg Kravis Robert & Co. and Deloitte Haskins & Sells, 1989: 67). A recent academic study by Lerner, Sorensen, and Stroemberg (2008) reveals that, for 495 LBO investments during 1983 and 2005, there was no deterioration of patent quantity and in the fundamental nature of research measured by patent originality and generality.

3.2.3.4 Operational Engineering Phase 2: Strategic Growth

The increasing importance of delivering strategic growth to create value and to realize an attractive exit price in recent years underpins the argumentation of PE firms that pure cost savings will not provide the performance required by their investors (Bruining & Wright, 2002: 147; Wiersema & Liebeskind, 1995). Firms have to be in stable conditions with potential for further growth before they can be offered in the capital markets or sold to other investors via trade sale (Butler, 2001: 142–145). Wright, Hoskisson, and Busenitz (2001) argue that buyouts can no longer be viewed solely as a means to address corporate inefficiencies but as value creators through strategic growth.

While non-core businesses are typically divested (Seth & Easterwood, 1993; Wiersema & Liebeskind, 1995), the raised performance standards driven by the above described governance and incentive system require management teams to develop ambitious business plans and to generate growth. An early study by Singh (1990) already shows that buyouts coming back to the capital market had experienced substantially higher revenue growth than their industry peers. In this context, Wright et al. (2001) differentiate two different types of buyouts, one fostering efficiency, the other driving innovation and strategic change. The latter is supported by the transformation of the organization's corporate governance – in both divisional and corporate buyouts – to enable entrepreneurship containing some of the elements of a start-up firm. Herein, operating management typically enjoys high levels of freedom with, however, close monitoring of key performance indicators (Baker & Wruck, 1989). In order to drive innovation, buyouts radically deregulate operational procedures and acquire new skills whereas firms in a corporate context are under strict, short-term control mechanisms, discouraging risk-taking. In coherence with this trend towards strategic growth, buyout firms are also moving into less mature industries with stronger growth opportunities such as technology or media.

Empirical studies (e.g. see Bruining & Wright, 2002; Markides, 1998a; Zahra & Fescina, 1991) provide evidence that LBOs lead to substantial growth in new product development as well as increasing research and development staff, technological alliances and new business creation. Bruining, Boselie, Wright, and Bacon (2005) as well as Amess and Wright (2007) document an employment growth in management buyouts during the recent buyout wave. "These findings are consistent with the notion that MBOs lead to the exploitation of growth opportunities, resulting in higher employment growth. The same patterns do not emerge from MBIs, typically because the latter transactions involve enterprises that require considerable restructuring" (Cumming, Siegel, & Wright, 2007: 449).

A second means to create strategic growth and to influence the shape of the industry landscape the firms are operating in are so-called "buy-and-build" strategies (Bruining & Wright, 2002: 148). PE firms pursuing such strategies undertake add-on acquisitions of either new lines of business, expansion of the target firm's business scope in areas with distinctive competences and resources, or – most typical – in comparable firms to increase market power in a fragmented and/or subscale market and realize economies of scale (Baker & Smith, 1998; Butler, 2001; Seth & Easterwood, 1993). Pursuing such strategies can take different forms. First, PE firms can supply a portfolio company with sufficient, pre-determined funding for acquisition purposes during the initial leverage or during a re-leverage. Alternatively, the PE firm undertakes separate acquisitions and subsequently mergers the portfolio companies. By those means, private equity can help in the consolidation of industries, in particular by forming new champions out of previously neglected divisions of larger corporations (Bae & Jo, 2002). A recent study in 321 exited buyouts in the UK between 1995 and 2004 by Nikoskelainen and Wright (2007) provides evidence for the positive influence of "buy-and-build" acquisitions carried out during the holding period on the probability of a positive return.

3.2.4 *Performance of Leveraged Buyout Investments*

Private equity funds are closed-end investment vehicles, which are liquidated after the divestment of all buyout assets in the portfolio. Investors are therefore less interested in an annual return but in the overall performance of their investments after the fund's closure. This section outlines a typical distribution of returns between the PE firm and investors as well as the common performance measures used in the private equity industry. It furthermore provides an overview of the historic private equity performance benchmarked to public markets.

3.2.4.1 Performance Distribution and Measures

There is neither a global reporting standard established in the private equity industry nor do firms disclose much of their performance. However, with limited partners getting more sophisticated and the increasing popularity of fund-of-funds investments within private and retail banking clients, the transparency in the market is increasing and common performance measures are getting established (Povaly, 2006; Rettberg, 2007). Generally, there are two different views about performance in a private equity engagement.

First, the overall fund performance, which can be measured on the basis of realized investments, i.e. only divested assets are included, or on the basis of all investments the fund has conducted. If all investments are regarded, the fund regularly calculates a net asset value (NAV), which values realized investments based on the exit price and still active investments based on its cash flows. Given the fact that transaction prices can only be objectively observed during acquisitions and divestments (Kaserer & Diller, 2004), the calculation of net asset values leaves substantial room for valuation biases (Bygrave & Timmons, 1992).

The second dimension regards the fund's performance net of fees, which are computed based on the actual cash flows to investors. Figure 3.12 provides a brief overview of the typical distribution of returns in a leveraged buyout engagement. The overall performance is split into the return of principal investments to general and limited partners reduced by the fund's management fee and the return on investment. The general partners, in addition to their return on investment, receive the above mentioned "carried interest" or "carry" for bearing the entrepreneurial risk of the investment. In this illustrative example, the general partners would receive 16% of the equity value at divestment for a 1% equity stake. Performance measurement

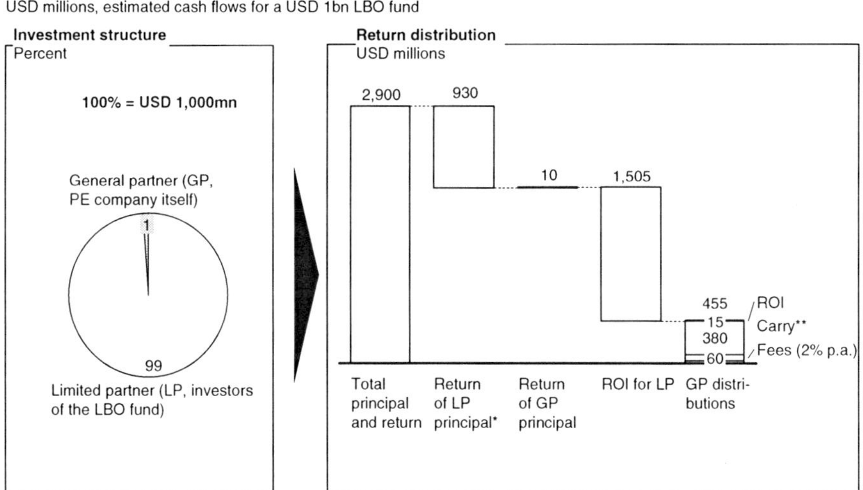

Fig. 3.12 Return distribution in leveraged buyouts

based on performance net of fees would therefore reduce the fund's return by the fees and carry charged before distributing the returns to investors (Private Equity Intelligence, 2007). This measure is commonly regarded as the most appropriate and reliable performance measurement approach (e.g. see Kaplan & Schoar, 2004; Ljungqvist & Richardson, 2003a).

A recent study by Metrick and Yasuda (2007) found a strong dependence of private equity firms on fee-based income rather than carried interest. Studying 238 private equity funds raised between 1992 and 2006, the results for the leveraged buyout segment show that – on average – less than 30% of total revenues stem from carried interest, questioning the incentive system of private equity firms.[14]

To actually measure performance, different approaches are being used. A simple metric to assess the returns of a PE investment is the use of investment multiples. Multiples describe "the ratio between the total value that the limited partner has derived from its interest in the partnership – i.e. distributed cash and securities plus the value of the limited partner's remaining interest in the partnership – and its total cash investment in the partnership, expressed as a multiple" (Private Equity Intelligence, 2007). During the active investment, this measure is also referred to as "Ratio of Distributions to Paid-in Capital". While this measure does not reflect the time value of money, it has become an accepted metric for a brief assessment of PE performance.

The more widely accepted measure of PE performance is the internal rate of return (IRR). The measure denotes the discount rate that brings the present value of all cash flows as well as unrealized gains from active investments equal to zero. During the fund's lifetime, IRR is an estimated figure given its reliance upon not only cash flows but also upon the valuation of the investors' remaining interest (Cumming & Walz, 2004; Ljungqvist & Richardson, 2003a). Although new concepts such as Kaserer and Diller's (2004) public market equivalent (PME) or the modified IRR (MIRR) attempt to avoid the deficiency of the IRR of assuming reinvestments to occur at the rate of return equivalent to the IRR, the internal rate of return remains the standard metric of measuring private equity performance (e.g. see Baker & Smith, 1998; Gompers & Lerner, 2004).[15]

3.2.4.2 Historic Performance

Based on the database provided by Private Equity Intelligence about global private equity returns in buyout transactions, data shows that buyout investments outperformed public indices over the last 15 years (Private Equity Intelligence, 2007). As illustrated in Fig. 3.13, investments in global leveraged buyout funds performed 0.9 and 1.6% better than investments in the US S&P 500 and the MSCI Europe,

---

[14]Total revenues include carried interest, management fees as well as transaction fees charged for entry and exit.

[15]Additional performance indicators can be used to assess private equity performance including means of addressing the correlation with other asset classes and the duration of private equity investments; IRR however remains the industry-standard to assess private equity performance.

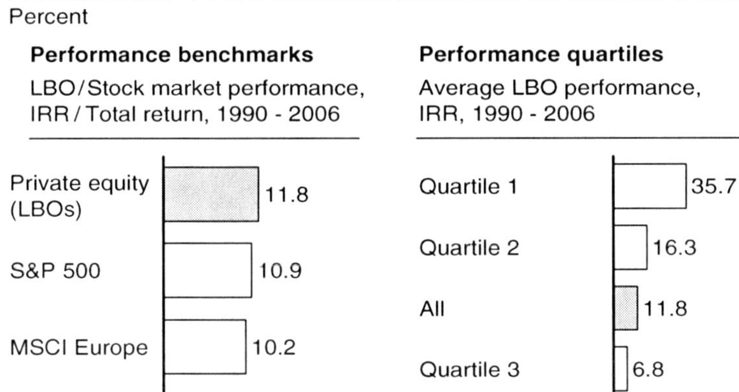

Fig. 3.13 Private equity performance benchmarks and quartiles

respectively. It furthermore shows a substantial outperformance of an investment in the global index MSCI world. However, differences between investment opportunities are large, spreading from an average performance of 35.7% in the top quartile to −11.0% in the bottom quartile.

Prior empirical studies show mixed results about the performance of buyout investments vs. public market benchmarks. Kaplan and Schoar (2004) find that the performance of US buyout funds net of fees approximately equals the performance of the S&P 500, one of the most comprehensive indices of US listed firms. They furthermore show a strong persistence of funds' performance across funds raised by individual private equity partnerships, meaning that there are firms that generally achieve a higher return than others. The authors moreover document an increase in performance with size of the fund and the years of experience of the PE firm – a result similarly supported by Nowak, Knigge, and Schmidt (2004) and Cumming and Walz (2004). Renneboog, Simons, and Wright (2007) examine the magnitude and the sources of the expected shareholder gains in 177 U.K. public-to-private buyout transactions from 1997 to 2003. The authors find that pre-transaction shareholders reaped an average 40% premium once the transaction is consummated. The study identifies pre-transaction undervaluation of target firms, increased interest tax shields, and alignment of interests as major drivers of private equity performance.

Ljungqvist and Richardson (2003a) however show – using proprietary cash-flow data – that buyout investments show a significant outperformance of public equity markets. Supporting these results, Ick (2005) provides evidence that buyout investments produce large positive excess returns. Experimenting with different ways of adjusting the returns for the implied risk, the author shows that buyout funds still match or outperform public markets, depending on the risk metric used.

Moskowitz and Vissing-Jørgensen (2002), on the other hand, show that the risk-return profile of PE investments falls short of those observed in public equity markets, however using a broader definition of private equity based on a US Survey of Consumer Finance. Constraining the analysis to the buyout segment, Gottschalg, Phalippou, and Zollo (2004) as well as Conroy and Harris (2007) similarly show that the average, risk-adjusted performance of buyout funds is considerably lower than the performance of a market portfolio, in particular given the illiquidity of such investments and the pro-cyclicability of performance. Based on new data generated by Danish pension funds, Nielsen (2006) derives a comparable conclusion stating a performance deficit of private equity investments vs. public benchmarks of 5% age points with equivalent risk. These findings are also supported for the venture capital segment as presented, among others, in the empirical study by Cochrane (2005).[16]

3.2.5 *Industry Trends and Future*

Closing the profile of the leveraged buyout segment, this section provides a brief overview of the most important trends currently influencing the shape of the industry and discusses their implications for the future development of leveraged buyouts. Key trends include the increasing occurrence of so-called club deals, the emergence of evergreen funds and listed private equity firms, the phenomenon of secondary buyouts, longer commitments as well as the changing regulatory environment for private equity firms (Anson, 2004; Stocker, 2007). Most of these trends lead to an increased similarity between LBO associations and publicly listed, diversified corporations.

3.2.5.1 Club Deals

Consortia of different LBO associations as well as cooperations between public corporations and private equity firms have conducted an increasing number of joint leveraged buyouts in recent years. In fact, research shows that, for US buyouts with a transaction value above USD 5 billion, 91% were so-called club deals (Cornelius et al., 2007: 113). These sorts of deals enable the firms to attack targets of significant market capitalization and take them private while spreading the risk of the investment. Examples of such transactions are the takeover of the Danish telecom firm TDC by Apax, KKR, Blackstone, Permira, and Providence Capital, the acquisition of the US power company TXU by KKR and TPG, or the joint bid of the Australian investment bank Macquarie and TPG for the airliner Quantas. Whereas big transactions were driven by the large conglomerates during the takeover waves of the twentieth century, a collection of LBO associations now has at least the same

[16] Also see Cumming et al. (2007) for a detailed overview of empirical studies regarding performance of private equity investments.

capability to act in the market of large-cap M&A transactions, competing with listed, mostly conglomerate-style companies for attractive assets. It furthermore leads to less focused ownership structures and therefore bears the risk of heading towards a governance model observed and criticized in publicly listed corporations (Draho, 2007: 119; Stocker, 2007).

3.2.5.2 Evergreen Funds and Listed Private Equity Firms

A second trend that currently changes the characteristics of the private equity landscape is the listing of buyout funds on public markets and thereby the creation of evergreen investment vehicles (Zimmermann, Bilo, Christophers, & Degosciu, 2005). The limited lifespan of a PE fund and therefore the definite liquidation at a pre-defined point in time was a key feature of a buyout fund and an important driver for exit-oriented wealth creation. The existence of an evergreen, publicly listed fund with potentially large numbers of small private investors takes pressure from the PE firms and could therefore lead to weaker performance (Jackson, 2006).

In addition, various private equity firms like Blackstone, Apollo, KKR, or the Carlyle Group are accessing public capital markets with the PE firm itself or are in the process of evaluating opportunities to become listed (Frankfurter Allgemeine Zeitung, 2007; Riecke, 2007a, 2007b). Such a move would consequently require the private equity players to obey with regulatory standards and will likely intensify scrutiny by investors and the public while putting the basics of their unique PE style at risk (Anders, 2007; Sender, 2007). Discounting the future proceeds of a private equity firm to the present and allowing general partners to sell their shares in the firm can lead to agency problems comparable to conventional public corporations. A lack of ownership and the torn positions of PE professionals between shareholder (of the PE firm) and investor (of the individual funds) interests can jeopardize the private equity management model.

Both, the unlimited lifetime of funds as well as the public listing of the PE firm are narrowing the gap between the LBO association and a publicly listed multi-business firm. Increasing transparency and a lack of ownership challenge the success factors of today's private equity model.

3.2.5.3 Longer Commitments

The increasing time a private equity fund remains invested in a portfolio company is another trend that brings buyout funds closer to the traditional diversified company. KKR attempted to get 20-year commitments from three of its largest investors instead of the common 10-year terms. Due to the lack of liquidity and the high acquisition prices in the market, largely driven through competition for assets and the popular auction during the sales process, longer commitments would allow buyout firms more time to find targets and to generate value through strategic growth rather than short-term operational improvements. However, longer periods of capital commitment can also lead to reduced incentives for the PE firm to deliver performance and opens the PE setting up to shortcomings observed in the public equity model (Anson, 2004: 91).

3.2.5.4 Secondary Buyouts

Anson (2004: 85–87) moreover identified the increasing use of secondary buyouts as important trend in the private equity market. Data provided by Stroemberg (2008) shows that divestments by financial vendors grew considerably from the earlier period of private equity (23% of total transactions 1970–2000) to the current private equity wave (36% of total transactions 2001–2007). Secondary buyouts occur, if PE firms are selling to one another as an exit strategy instead of pursuing traditional exit strategies such as public offerings, recapitalizations, or the sale to a strategic buyer (Lerner & Hardymon, 2002). Rather than finding new deals, private equity firms are looking at the existing private deal landscape, which Anson (2004: 86) sees as a symptom of too much capital in the industry respectively a lack of attractive investment targets.

3.2.5.5 Disclosure Requirements

The current discussion about the lack of regulation and, therefore, lack of disclosure is the final trend with important implications for the further shape of the industry and its distinctiveness towards public companies. Politicians and unionists, triggered by some large transactions and various deep and publicly discussed restructurings, have heavily criticized the value creation approaches of buyout firms. Given the size of the buyout market as well as the in-transparency associated with it, regulators are starting to evaluate means to increase the disclosure requirements for private equity firms. The British Financial Service Authority FSA for instance released a study in 2006 concluding that the "biggest buyout firms and their lenders deserve closer surveillance", however also stating that they do not see "a broad risk to the financial system" (The Economist, 2006). PE firms at the same time attempt to stall regulatory rulings by promising self-commitments to greater openness about returns, risks, and strategies of their portfolio companies (Boeschen & Gassmann, 2007).

3.3 Diversification in Private Equity

As highlighted above, academic literature regarding diversification in private equity, or more specifically in the buyout segment, is very limited. Although a sizeable group of academics is conducting research in the field of private equity, academic literature has dealt primarily with the previously outlined value creation methods on a single-asset level and the performance comparison of PE investments with public benchmarks (Lossen, 2006: 3–5). This section presents an overview of the scarce literature available regarding (a) the influence of diversification on performance and (b) the management approaches of private equity firms to diversified portfolios. When using the term private equity beyond this point, this study refers particularly to the leveraged buyout segment.

3.3.1 Diversification and Performance

Whereas the relationship of diversification and performance in publicly listed corporations is one of the areas in strategic management literature that has found intense coverage, very few contributions, all of which were published in recent years, address this issue in the context of private equity firms. Schmidt (2004) finds in a sample of 3,620 US private equity investments that a rising number of portfolio companies reduces the variation of returns of a PE portfolio due to the high risk of total loss associated with individual investments. Weidig and Mathonet (2004) make comparable observations for investments in venture capital portfolios, providing evidence that the probability of loss and total loss declines from direct investments to investments in venture capital funds, and again to funds-of-funds. Both studies however fail to address the industry diversification component of portfolio diversification.

While the above studies have focused on the effect of diversification in terms of number of investments on the associated risk of the portfolio, few contributions have included the effect of diversification across industries. Ljungqvist and Richardson (2003a) found, that the performance of investments in 73 venture capital and buyout funds since 1981 and 2001 increases significantly with the overall fund size, however, documenting a maximum at fund sizes between USD 1.1 billion and USD 1.2 billion. They furthermore show that the average fund for their sample of mainly buyout funds invests close to 40% of their capital in a single industry; however, the study provides no evidence of a significant influence of diversification across industries on the internal rate or return of the fund. Lossen (2006) observes, studying a sample of 100 PE funds containing information about 2.871 investments, that the rate of return increases with diversification across industries, in particular for the funds in the top performance quartile. He moreover shows decreasing fund performance with diversification across financing stages and no impact of diversification across countries. Finally, he finds, that the rate of return of a PE fund enhances with the number of portfolio companies. He therefore argues that private equity firms should apply an opportunistic investment approach, specializing on process know-how independent of specific industries rather than building deep industry know-how. A recent study by Cressy, Munari, & Malipiero (2007), on the contrary, supports the argumentation that there is a positive influence of industry relatedness on performance. In an analysis of 122 UK-based buyouts over the period 1995–2002, the study finds substantial improvements in operating profitability for private equity firms specialized by industry. The research reveals that the increase in profitability through industry specialization is with 8.5% almost twice as large as the difference between private equity based firms versus non-PE-backed companies with 4.5% points. In addition, Loos' (2005) study on the performance of PE deals illustrates, that the individual portfolio companies within a PE fund are largely focused firms rather than diversified companies. He however provides no evidence regarding the industry diversification on a portfolio level.

All of the above studies present valuable insights on the effects of diversification on PE performance; however, they all fail to view the investment portfolio of a private equity firm on the level of the overall firm rather than on the level of single assets or funds. As most PE firms run multiple active funds in parallel, the concentration on individual deals or funds is insufficient to draw conclusions about the effect of diversification on the performance of a PE firm and to establish a comparison to multi-business firms. Moreover, there is no consistent methodology established for the analysis of diversification – including a view on relatedness vs. unrelatedness – in private equity as presented above for the influence of diversification on performance in diversified companies.

3.3.2 *Managing Diversified Portfolios*

The relationship between academic literature regarding the management of diversified portfolios in multi-business firms and PE firms is similar to the above-illustrated gap in the academic coverage of the effect of diversification on performance. While substantial academic research has gone into the management approaches of publicly listed multi-business firms, few publications have addressed the same question in PE firms. Moreover, none of the publications has targeted the role of a private equity firm from a comprehensive, overarching perspective, that sees the PE firm in a role similar to the headquarters of a multi-business firm, the so-called "role of the parent" (e.g. see Campbell, Goold, & Alexander, 1995a, 1995b; Goold & Campbell, 1998).

The few available publications in this field of research are clustered using a consistent structure with the above literature review in diversified companies. The section therefore illustrates the existing literature regarding (a) the governance approach followed by the professional staff of a private equity house, (b) the availability of central functions and resources in PE firms, (c) the leverage of resources and competences across different investments, and (d) the portfolio management approach of PE firms.

3.3.2.1 Governance Model of Private Equity Firms

As highlighted above, active governance is one of the most important value creation levers of private equity investments. The private equity firm hereby employs elements such as active and continuous involvement in strategic decision making as well as the monitoring and immediate reaction to selected financial indicators. The buyout firm moreover makes substantial changes to the incentive schemes of the portfolio company's management (Anders, 1992; Thompson et al., 1992). While there is a substantial amount of literature about the effects of active ownership on the level of an individual portfolio company as outlined above, little research has gone into the different governance models a private equity firm as a "holding" is able to use. Elango, Fried, Hisrich, and Polonchek, (1995) distinguish three levels of involvement: "inactive", "active advice giver", and "hands-on" PE players. Involvement by the inactive group is mainly confined to attendance at board meetings. Active advice givers get involved in strategic decision making and show a faster response to changes in performance. Hands-on PE firms closely monitor individual decisions of the portfolio company and even become part of day-to-day operations. They typically hold positions in the management team and on the board (Nisar 2005). Elango et al. (1995), furthermore, found that an inactive PE specialist spent on average 6.76 h per month with an individual portfolio company, compared to 12.75 for active advice-givers, and 35.65 for the hands-on group. A similar classification was developed by Macmillan, Kulow, and Khoylian (1989) finding the clusters "laissez-faire", "moderate", and "close tracker". However, there seems to be no research attempt to determine which model is best applied in which situation, being it internal circumstances or environmental influences. Additionally, there is no empirical evidence about the link between governance model and performance or about the means of coordination within the PE house in order to guarantee a solid governance approach.

3.3.2.2 Availability of Central Functions and Resources

LBO associations typically provide only few, however important services to their portfolio companies. This becomes particularly obvious by the fact, that private equity houses are able to successfully manage large and often highly diversified portfolios and generate performance exceeding public benchmarks with only small numbers of professional staff (Baker & Smith, 1998; Collis et al., 2007). While there is no attempt made to foster synergies by consolidating support services such as personnel or accounting in the center, Berg and Gottschalg (2003) and Gottschalg and Meier (2005) recognize the availability of management talent as an important element of the parenting advantage of private equity firms. The constructive interaction between portfolio companies and buyout associations upon critical decisions as well as the management support in the form of temporary or permanent members in the management team of the acquired firms allow portfolio companies to take advantage of a PE firm as parent. Such buyout managers understand their role towards their investments as active advisors and enablers. In particular during the first 100 days or first year of an engagement, the buyout specialist actively supports the portfolio company's management in developing strategy by contributing management and industry expertise acquired in previous transactions or via experts from the market (Baker & Smith, 1998). KKR for instance runs a proprietary consulting arm that plays an active role in the development of strategic initiatives and change programs in the initial phase of an investment (Fisher, 2007; Teitelbaum, 2007). The lead representative of the buyout firm, furthermore, serves top management throughout the entire investment period as sounding board for important decisions and provides additional perspectives on elements such as strategy, markets, and external conditions (Berg & Gottschalg, 2003; Bruining & Wright, 2002; DeAngelo et al., 1984). Hite and Vetsuypens (1989) therefore argue that the "cross-utilization" of managerial talent can represent a valuable not otherwise readily available resource to the portfolio company.

Another important source of value creation from a portfolio perspective is the support by the parent in financial questions such as structuring of the balance sheet or the contacts and negotiation backing with financial institutions. As highlighted above, the PE firm's financial skill set and industry network is an important means to create value in a buyout transaction, which is provided by the LBO association and is typically utilized across the full portfolio of investments (Baker & Smith, 1998; Berg & Gottschalg, 2003; Bruining & Wright, 2002).

While there is initial literature available regarding the above illustrated types of resources provided by a PE firm, little is known so far about the impact of different levels of "corporate resources" on the performance of portfolio companies. Furthermore, there is a lack in covering the question how such resources are coordinated within the PE firm. Literature so far has concentrated on the view of an individual portfolio company instead of regarding the role of the PE firm as a "headquarters" or "parent".

3.3.2.3 Leverage of Resources and Competences

Given the nature and organizational setup of LBO associations such as the limited lifespan and the decentralized, non-integrated structure, academics argue that LBO firms are purely financial, non-strategic buyers, which typically make no attempt to leverage resources and competences horizontally among individual investments in order to realize revenue or cost synergies (Baker & Montgomery, 1994; Torabzadeh & Bertin, 1987). Loos (2005: 19–20) therefore concludes, that buyout transactions do not fall in the same domain of synergistic value creation, which is typically an important acquisition rationale for corporations, specifically for related diversifiers. However, when pursuing a "buy-and-build" strategy, LBO associations, similar to corporations, seek to acquire firms that complement an existing set of businesses and therefore follow similar motives. The recent European media deal by KKR and Permira for instance shows that the acquisition of related assets and the subsequent merger leads to value creation opportunities through both revenue and cost synergies. To the author's best knowledge, no research so far has been addressing this perspective of private equity firms.

3.3.2.4 Portfolio Management of Private Equity Firms

Private equity firms are managers of multiple investment portfolios, the private equity funds, each being liquidated after a pre-determined period of time. Consequently, PE firms have to actively manage their overall portfolios with clear entry and exit strategies. Although portfolio management is at the heart of the activities of a PE firm, the concepts applied by PE firms have very sparse representation in academic literature. This includes the formulation of PE acquisition strategies, the decision process when and how to divest as well as the question whether PE firms occasionally construct an internal capital market within a fund to funnel cash flows from one portfolio company to another. Baker and Montgomery's (1994) study is one of the few contributions addressing this element. They claim that, due to the setup as separate legal and financial entities, PE firms do not "cross-subsidize one unit's losses with the profits from another, and the failure of one unit does not threaten the health of any other companies in the LBO association's portfolio" (Baker & Montgomery, 1994: 20).

3.4 Comparison of Private Equity Firms and Diversified Corporations

The dismantling of large conglomerates was one of the major drivers for the rise of leveraged buyout firms. Conglomerates were criticized for being too diversified, too large, and essentially unmanageable. LBO associations have been active buyers of non-core businesses out of multi-business firms or been the driver behind the break-up of various large conglomerates (Bae & Jo, 2002; Berger & Ofek, 1996). Consequently, many buyout firms find themselves by now at the center of large investment empires, often with controlling interests in a widely diverse group of companies, spread across multiple industries and reaching considerable size (Baker & Montgomery, 1994: 2). The buyout firm CVC Capital Partners for instance indirectly employs 224,000 workers at the beginning of 2005 in its diverse portfolio of European investments, just slightly less than one of Europe's biggest multi-business firms Siemens with – at that point – 274,000 employees in Europe (Koltes, 2005).

The rise of LBO associations and the growing resemblance to diversified corporations caused numerous controversial debates in academic literature. Jensen (1989b: 61), for instance, argues that "the publicly held corporation (…) has outlived its usefulness in many sectors of the economy and is being eclipsed". In his view, the publicly held corporation with its fragmented ownership structure is being replaced by a new, not-listed form of organization. Rappaport (1990), on the other hand, is a representative of a group of academics arguing in favor of the public corporation. He claims that publicly held corporations "are inherently flexible and capable of renewal – properties that are crucial to stability and progress in a market-driven economy and that transitory organizations like LBOs cannot replicate" (1990: 96). From Rappaport's perception, public corporations are "vibrant, dynamic institutions" (1990: 96) rather than collections of assets. The institutional permanence towards customers, investors, employees, and other stakeholders of this organizational form is an essential condition to achieve long-term success in the market.

In order to substantiate this controversy, this section should be understood as a comparison of the key characteristics of the public corporation on the one side and the private equity firm on the other. It builds on the characteristics highlighted in Chap. 2 and the previous sections of Chap. 3. This brief comparison is supposed to facilitate the further discussion about PE success factors and their applicability in public corporations. Derived from the structure chosen by Baker and Montgomery (1994), this section compares multi-business firms and PE firms along (a) acquisition and diversification strategy, (b) portfolio and divestiture strategy, (c) the role of the parent, and (d) the role of the operating unit.

3.4.1 Acquisition and Diversification Strategy

Baker and Montgomery (1994) observe that both diversified firms and LBO associations are equally active players on the market for corporate control. However, while LBO associations are typically unrelated diversified collections of businesses, multi-business firms can own portfolios with a high level of relatedness as well as highly unrelated portfolios.

In Baker and Montgomery's (1994) view, LBO associations follow an opportunistic approach purely based on the value creation potential of the single target company. For a buyout specialist, the access to deals and the value creation opportunities based on financial engineering as well as active governance have long been the dominating decision criteria to rule for or against an acquisition. In recent years, with the increasing importance of operational improvements and strategic growth as value creation levers, the importance of industry expertise, however, appears to be increasing. This trend is supported by the above outlined move towards "buy-and-build" strategies, requiring a strong relatedness however not necessarily a complete match of assets in order to create a strong player out of a collection of subscale firms (e.g. see Butler, 2001; Seth & Easterwood, 1993).

Multi-business firms, on the other hand, typically have grown into large, diversified companies, often with different core businesses. They commonly evaluate a takeover target based on the fit in the corporate portfolio and make the purchase largely dependent upon synergy potentials between businesses. Therefore most acquisitions of a multi-business firm are in related businesses; only few firms pursue an opportunistic acquisition strategy into unrelated businesses (e.g. see Markides & Williamson, 1994; Silverman, 1999; Stimpert & Duhaime, 1997).

Funding of acquisitions by a buyout specialist is typically on a deal-by-deal basis with large amounts of newly raised debt and small amounts of called equity whereas multi-business firms finance takeovers in an intransparent mix of existing and newly raised debt and equity.

3.4.2 Portfolio and Divestiture Strategy

The research of Baker and Montgomery (1994) furthermore reveals that, while LBO associations and multi-business firms are both active acquirers, only buyout firms also actively divest companies. Their sample of 23 firms consisting of buyouts and public corporations shows that conglomerates have sold only 10% of firms bought since 1970 until the beginning of the 1990s whereas LBO associations sold more than 50%.

Due to the agreements under which private equity firms raise money in their buyout funds, they have to actively seek the exit from an investment. As illustrated above, the limited partnership agreement usually commits funds for a time span of about 10 years, after which the fund is terminated and equity as well as the fund's returns are re-distributed to investors. The primary way to pay off limited partners is by selling the assets in the fund to other financial investors, strategic buyers or in an IPO in the public market (e.g. see de Malherbe, 2005; Gompers & Lerner, 1999; Rogers, Holland, & Haas, 2002). The current induction of evergreen funds as well as longer commitment periods of funds partly reduces this automatism.

Multi-business firms on the contrary show a strong tendency to keep businesses, driven by the motives introduced in Chap. 2 including management's personal agendas as well as commitments to other stakeholders. Divested businesses are typically under-performing units while businesses that satisfy the firm's performance hurdles are unlikely to be sold (Baker & Montgomery, 1994: 9–11). Increasing pressure from capital markets to break-up highly diversified firms has led to the dismantling of some conglomerate structures (Berger & Ofek, 1996). There, however, is neither a clear incentive for management nor a requirement based on a funding agreement for systematic, pre-determined divestitures implemented in the setup of public corporations.

3.4.3 Role of the Parent

Substantial differences between a private equity firm and a public, multi-business corporation can also be observed in the role the parent company plays in a portfolio of diversified businesses. Both formats seek to be the "best parent" for their businesses by offering parenting resources to the investments in their portfolios (Gottschalg & Meier, 2005: 36). However, while corporations typically attempt to realize synergies between businesses and often have a formalized interaction process with their business units, LBO associations focus on the role of an active shareholder with continuous, informal interactions.

Buyout associations have a very flat hierarchy typical for professional service firms with a limited number of professional staff (Baker & Montgomery, 1994).[17] They are "shielded from the glare of attention" (O'Keeffe, 2005) from the larger public and can concentrate on the interaction with portfolio companies and the limited number of investors. Their management approach largely focuses their involvement

[17] Koltes (2005) outlines that the growing size of private equity firms requires an increasing professionalism in the management of the PE firm itself which might lead to the implementation of similar, value destroying structures in PE firms as criticized in the corporate centers of multi-business firms.

on selected, strategic decisions in the form of an active shareholder. Interaction is mostly informal and management of individual portfolio companies is supported by strong incentive schemes including principal investments by the target's management (Goold, Campbell, & Alexander, 1994: 43). PE firms typically provide only few services to their portfolio companies, predominantly the PE firms' management talent and financing know how (e.g. see Baker & Smith, 1998; Berg & Gottschalg, 2003; Gottschalg & Meier, 2005; Jensen, 1989b). Unfortunately, little is known about the effect of diversification on performance in PE firms as well as about the portfolio management approach of PEs and the use of different governance models or "corporate resources" in private equity settings.

A multi-business firm, on the other hand, typically holds a headquarters of substantial size with various management layers (Collis et al., 2007). The firm is under public observation and has to obey regulatory disclosure requirements. Towards its business portfolio, the multi-business firm typically plays an active role in the coordination between businesses in order to leverage resources and competences horizontally among different business units (e.g. see Mahoney & Pandian, 1992; Prahalad & Hamel, 1990; Robins & Wiersema, 1995). The headquarters furthermore provides a broad range of corporate services to the individual businesses in its portfolio including the access to low-cost capital, management talent as well as specialized services. Such services can range from administrative units such as personnel or accounting to success critical entities such as marketing or research and development (e.g. see Hitt & Ireland, 1986; Yavitz & Newman, 1982). Interaction with business units is often highly formalized with long-term planning cycles and limited flexibility for fast decisions (e.g. see Armstrong, 1982; Goold et al., 1994). Moreover, performance measurements and incentive systems are largely based on short-term accounting indicators rather than cash-flow measures (Baker & Montgomery, 1994: 19).

3.4.4 Role of the Operating Unit

The term operating unit refers to the division or strategic business unit in the setting of a multi-business firm and the portfolio company in private equity firms. The division or business unit of a public corporation is an integrated unit in a complex organizational structure whereas a portfolio company of a PE house is a largely independent legal and organizational entity.

A company in the portfolio of a private equity firm is an independent firm, which manages the company's cash flows and holds a legal status with a self-standing governance structure including executive and non-executive board members. In its original form, companies within the portfolio of a LBO association have no interactions with other operating units in the PE firm's investment portfolio (Kaufman & Englander, 1993: 69–70) and show only limited reliance on resources held in the headquarters of a private equity partnership (Jensen, 1989a: 37–39).

The division or strategic business unit of a multi-business firm on the contrary is part of a large organization. It typically has no legal status, does not manage larger amounts of cash and has no access to external capital markets. It is on the contrary highly dependent on the corporate headquarters and commonly holds close, formalized connections to the other operating units of the organization to leverage resources and competences across entities.

Nevertheless, in comparison to the strong variations between the two kinds of parenting models of "public corporations" and "private equity firms", the differences between the two forms of operating units are relatively limited. Both entities are in majority ownership and typically manage single-product businesses, that are customer-facing and are in charge of a large part of the value chain required to play in this particular market (Baker & Montgomery, 1994).

Chapter 4
General Research Design

Shades of old conglomerates in private equity

Tony Jackson, Financial Times

The leading theme of this research contribution is the parallelism between multi-business firms and private equity firms or the "shades of old conglomerates in private equity" (Jackson, 2006). This study will therefore continuously draw on the theoretical background developed and the methodological approaches applied in the research regarding the phenomenon of diversification in multi-business firms and attempt to apply the same to the private equity universe. Based on this idea, the following section will provide the general positioning in academic literature of this study (Sect. 4.1.1 "Starting Position in Academic Literature – A synthesis" and Sect. 4.1.2 "Direction of Research") as well as the guiding principles of this research effort (Sect. 4.1.3 "Two-Tier Empirical Research Design"). The detailed research methodology for each of the two empirical parts as well as the development of hypotheses and research frameworks will be outlined in the consecutive chapters "Empirical Part I – Diversification and Performance" (Chap. 5) and "Empirical Part II – Managing Diversified Portfolios" (Chap. 6).

4.1 Starting Position in Academic Literature: a Synthesis

The above review of academic literature both in multi-business firms as well as in private equity settings reveals a strong disparity in the depth of research coverage. While the phenomenon of diversification has found intensive coverage in the field of public corporations, literature regarding diversification in private equity firms is scarce. Figure 4.1 highlights this divergence, which holds true for the effect of diversification on performance as much as for the management approaches to diversified portfolios.

D.O. Klier, *Managing Diversified Portfolios*,
DOI: 10.1007/978-3-7908-2173-4_4, © 2009 Physica-Verlag Heidelberg

STARTING POSITION IN ACADEMIC LITERATURE – A SYNTHESIS

Intensive research coverage / Limited research coverage

	Multi-business firms	Private Equity firms
Performance and diversification	Intensive research existing regarding the impact of diversification on valuation and financial performance	Limited research available; in particular no coverage of Private Equity firms from a comprehensive perspective
Managing diversified portfolios	Intensive research existing providing theoretical and empirical evidence regarding the role of the parent in diversified business portfolios	Limited research available; in particular no coverage of Private Equity firms from a comprehensive perspective

Fig. 4.1 Starting position in academic literature – a synthesis

4.1.1 Diversification Research in Corporations

Diversification in multi-business firms has been approached from various academic disciplines for the last 40–50 years and has brought forward a considerable body of academic literature as outlined in Chap. 2 of this study. Research regarding performance and diversification provides a large number of methodologies to measure the effect of diversification on a firm's valuation and financial performance (e.g. see Berger & Ofek, 1995; De, 1992; Hall & St. John, 1994; Lang & Stulz, 1994; Palepu, 1985). Although results still diverge to some extent, there is little room for additional research. Diverging results largely depend on different data samples, data quality, different measures of diversification, and different time series – not on substantial methodological or theoretical arguments (e.g. see Martin & Sayrak, 2003; Villalonga, 2003).

Similarly, the management of diversified portfolios has found sizeable coverage in academic literature. The body of literature consists on the one side of comprehensive investigations of the role of the parent and the so-called parenting advantage (in particular Campbell, Goold, & Alexander, 1995a, 1995b; Goold & Campbell, 1998). On the other side, there are various studies detailing certain elements of the parenting role such as the different governance styles and interaction modes with individual businesses (e.g. see Fredrickson, 1986; Goold, Campbell, & Alexander,

1994; Hart, 1992; Hart & Banbury, 1994; van Oijen & Douma, 2000) or the corporate resources provided by the headquarters such as access to financial markets, management talent and other specialized services (e.g. see Chandler Jr., 1991; Hitt & Ireland, 1986; Yavitz & Newman, 1982). It furthermore entails contributions investigating the coordination means of corporations to horizontally leverage resources and competences across different business units (e.g. see Daft, 1983; Mahoney & Pandian, 1992; Prahalad & Hamel, 1990; Robins & Wiersema, 1995) as well as studies addressing the portfolio management mechanisms applied by the corporate center to decide about the future shape of the firm's business portfolio and about the allocation of financial resources in internal capital markets (e.g. see Alberts & McTaggart, 1984; Bettis & Hall, 1981; Hall, 1978; Lamont, 1997; Scharfstein & Stein, 2000; Stein, 1997).

4.1.2 *Diversification Research in Private Equity*

Academic research in the field of private equity on the other hand is a younger discipline, which has started to gain importance at the end of the 1980s as outlined in Chap. 3. Studies have largely been concentrated on value creation techniques on the level of individual portfolio companies as well as on performance measurements, benchmarks with public investment opportunities, and the role of PE investments as an asset class. There are very few studies addressing the diversification phenomenon in the private equity universe. To the author's best knowledge, there are particularly no publications addressing diversification on the level of a private equity firm rather than on the level of individual PE funds, which represent only part of the investment scope of a PE player. In addition, there have been no attempts to use a methodology previously applied in academic research when addressing diversification in multi-business firms. This prohibits the comparison between multi-business firms and PE houses.

Regarding the management approach to diversified portfolios, there is very limited research activity noted. A small number of publications has been addressing the interaction model of a private equity firm with its portfolio investments as well as the services provided by the PE firm for individual assets (e.g. see Anders, 1992; Berg & Gottschalg, 2003; Bruining & Wright, 2002; Gottschalg & Meier, 2005; Thompson, Wright, & Robbie, 1992). In these cases, little is known about the impact of such approaches on performance as well as about the mechanisms to coordinate center resources within the PE firm. There furthermore is very scarce literature regarding the leverage of resources and competences in PE firms and the portfolio management approach pursued. Most of all, there are no studies drawing a comprehensive picture of a private equity firm in the role of a parent to a larger number of portfolio companies, comparable to the role a corporate center of a multi-business firm plays towards its business divisions.

4.2 Direction of Research

Building on this unbalanced starting position in academic literature between multi-business firms and private equity firms, this study attempts to make a contribution to close this gap – both regarding the impact of diversification on performance as well as regarding the private equity way of managing diversified portfolios.

This section outlines the general direction of research and consequently the research questions embedded in this direction. Building on these general research questions, detailed hypotheses and research frameworks will be outlined in the empirical parts of this study in Chaps. 5 and 6 (Chap. 5 for "Diversification and Performance" and Chap. 6 for the private equity approach for "Managing Diversified Portfolios").

4.2.1 Research Direction "Diversification and Performance"

In a first step, the study aims at investigating the influence of diversification on performance in PE settings and at benchmarking the results with findings from a sample of publicly listed corporations. It is critical in this step to address the level of the entire private equity firm instead of individual funds as pursued in the past by other contributions. Only the level of the entire PE firm allows a comparison with the diversification phenomenon found within a publicly listed corporation. It hereby attempts to provide evidence along three areas of research.

4.2.1.1 Performance: Private Equity vs. Public Corporations

First of all, the study tries to construct a general comparison between the performance achieved by a sample of private equity funds and a comparable sample of publicly listed corporations, independent of the degree of diversification. It thereby seeks to find explanations about structural differences between the performance of private equity firms and the performance achieved by the management of a publicly listed corporation. The further findings then need to be adjusted for such structural differences.

4.2.1.2 Diversification and Performance in Private Equity

The study then attempts to investigate the implication of diversification on the average performance of a private equity firm, across the individual funds in its portfolio. It wants to draw conclusions about the relationship between performance and different levels or clusters of diversification, such as focused, related diversified, or unrelated diversified private equity portfolios.

4.2.1.3 Diversification and Performance: Private Equity vs. Public Corporations

Lastly, the study makes an effort to compare the relationship between diversification and performance in private equity firms with the results discovered in a comparable sample of publicly listed corporations. It thereby wants to determine whether private equity firms generally have a higher capability of achieving high performance in diversified portfolios. It furthermore tries to assess whether different degrees of diversification have a better fit in a private equity setting than in a public corporation and vice versa.

4.2.2 Research Direction "Managing Diversified Portfolios"

Based on these findings, the study then wants to explore the role of the parent in a private equity setting. It attempts to do so by addressing the different components a parent can provide its businesses, which have been introduced above. The elements of parenting activity are the governance model employed by the PE firms, the availability of central functions and resources, the leverage of competences and resources horizontally within the investment portfolio, and the portfolio management approach applied by the private equity house. The study thereby wants to investigate three dimensions within each of these components: the applicability and use of the individual components of parenting, the influencing factors of the chosen management approach with particular interest in the effect of different degrees of industry diversification on the way PE firms interact with their investment portfolios, and the mechanisms employed within the PE firm in the role of the "corporate center" to coordinate internal resources and to enable such parenting activities. The study then wants to correlate the different findings along the above outlined categories of "corporate parenting" with the achieved performance and the degree of diversification recorded in the first part of the study.

4.2.2.1 Governance Model

The governance approach of PE firms on the level of individual portfolio companies has found some representation in academic research coverage. While detailing the governance model of private equity firms, this study particularly attempts to understand the different governance styles available to PE firms and the decision processes applied by PE houses in interaction with the different investments in their portfolios. It thereby tries to understand the drivers for different governance models and the impact on performance. Additionally, the study makes an effort to shed light on the question how industry diversification affects the selection of governance models and coordination mechanisms of PE managers. Finally, it wants to understand how private equity firms are set up and coordinated in their "corporate center" to secure the appropriate amount of skills and experience required for the governance of different investments.

4.2.2.2 Availability of Central Functions and Resources

Previous academic research regarding the availability of "corporate resources" has already observed that PE firms typically provide general management skills, financial structuring know how, as well as their networks within the financial industry to their portfolio companies. Building on these findings, this study wants to establish an understanding to what magnitude such resources are available, and whether there are differences in the extent that different portfolio companies receive such resources. Particular interest will be placed on the relevance of industry-specific know-how vs. general management knowledge in order to provide such services in an effective and efficient way. The study thereby wants to investigate the influence of diversification on the applicability of specific resources of the PE firm. The paper furthermore tries to explore the coordination mechanisms of such resources within the PE firm in order to multiply existing knowledge across the different portfolio companies in the firm's investment portfolio.

4.2.2.3 Leverage of Competences and Resources

The review of contributions from academic researchers and practitioners reveals that the leverage of competences and resources across different portfolio companies plays a subordinate role in PE settings. Nevertheless, the above-described trend to drive investment performance through strategic growth and, in this context, also to employ "buy-and-built" strategies gives rise to the question how private equity firms think about the leverage of particular competences or resources available in individual firms across their portfolios. The study therefore wants to explore if such leverage mechanisms are at all in place and if so, how PE firms accomplish this task, being by transferring individual employees within the portfolio or by actively consolidating the investment portfolio and merging individual firms. It moreover wants to understand which kinds of competences and resources are in the focus of such activities and what role influencing factors such as the degree of diversification of the investment portfolio play in such efforts.

4.2.2.4 Portfolio Management

Portfolio management in a PE firm is the least covered area in previous academic research although it seems to be one of the most relevant factors for the success of the private equity investment model. This study therefore wants to make a contribution to understand the approaches and decision tools used by a private equity player to decide about the prospects of different companies in the firm's investment portfolio and the assessment of different opportunities available to the PE firms to divest their businesses. It furthermore attempts to shed light on the decision process about the direction for new acquisitions. It moreover wants to generate initial insight whether PE firms redeploy any funds contributed from portfolio companies in other investments of the same investment vehicle and thereby establish an internal capital market. If so, the study then wants to explore by what means capital is allocated. In addition, it wants to outline how the degree of diversification within the overall PE investment portfolio and within individual funds affects the portfolio management approach.

4.3 Empirical Research Design

The study is set up as an empirical investigation of the two general areas of research outlined above, (a) diversification and performance and (b) the private equity approach to managing diversified portfolios. In order to comply with the twofold direction of research and the research questions entailed, the study requires a two-tier empirical research design. The first empirical part quantitatively addresses the influence of diversification on performance; the second empirical element relies on the qualitative exploration of the management approach of private equity firms towards diversified portfolios. Both elements of the study are ordered consecutively, enabling the qualitative part of the research to draw on the sample and the findings from the assessment of diversification and performance derived in the first part of empirical research.

The following two sections describe the general empirical research design for each of the two empirical parts as guiding principles for the study. Based on these guidelines, an introduction of the detailed empirical methodology regarding such elements as data sources, sample selection and characteristics as well as the data analysis design will be provided in each of the two empirical chapters (Chap. 5 for "Diversification and Performance" and Chap. 6 for the private equity approach for "Managing Diversified Portfolios").

4.3.1 Research Design "Diversification and Performance"

This section will provide a brief introduction to the general research design and research process applied in the first part of empirical research regarding the influence of diversification on performance. It moreover presents some general remarks regarding the data collection method employed in this research contribution.

4.3.1.1 General Research Design

The part of the empirical research regarding the influence of diversification on performance is based on a quantitative research approach. Within this empirical part, the study applies a deductive, hypothesis-driven research design, which Flick (1995) considers the "classical approach" in quantitative empirical research settings and has a long tradition in academic research in the finance and strategic management discipline. Within this approach, the study develops a model before starting the data analysis based on theory and empirical evidence found previously in academic literature. Building on this model, the study then derives hypotheses, which can be tested in an empirical setting. Hypotheses in this type of research design are stated explicitly and need to be specific enough to be implemented in an empirical study design (Flick 1995). The objective in this part of empirical research is to reject or support the ex-ante defined hypotheses and, thereby, to provide confirmation of relationships derived upon theoretical considerations (Bortz & Doering, 2002).

Given the fact that there is a substantial body of literature available addressing similar methodological questions in the context of diversification research in corporations, this study intends to adapt the measures and analysis designs developed previously which have found acceptance in academic research. This includes the above-presented measures of diversification and indicators of performance as well as statistical models previously applied in academic literature. By that approach, this contribution attempts to eliminate respectively to reduce methodological shortcomings and thereby longs to increase the reliability, comparability and validity of its findings.

4.3.1.2 Research Process

Quantitative, hypothesis-driven research is structured along a standardized research process as outlined in Fig. 4.2 based on the description by Lamnek (2005) and Kromrey (2006). This process will be the basis for the first empirical part of this study presented in Chap. 5.

The first step in this research design is the review of academic literature in order to define the direction of research and consequently the research questions. The study then develops hypotheses regarding these research questions, which should be based on prior theoretical and empirical contributions. This deductive design requires the researcher to conduct a thorough investigation of the evidence presented prior to the empirical study, which in the case of this study has been outlined in Chap. 2 "Diversification in Corporations" and Chap. 3 "Introduction to the private equity Industry and the Role of Diversification". The terms used in the hypotheses then need to be clearly defined to enable empirical testing (Lamnek, 2005: 117–186).

Following the development of hypotheses, the study operationalizes the hypotheses by crafting a detailed methodology including the definition of relevant indicators and data collection approaches to test the hypotheses. The study then defines the basic population from which the research sample will be drawn as well as the selection mode to arrive at the final sample underlying the empirical analysis (Kromrey, 2006: 267–316). It then gathers the information required to conduct the empirical analysis necessary to draw statistically viable and reliable findings from the sample. The data analysis will thereby apply standardized statistical tools such as

HYPOTHESIS-DRIVEN RESEARCH DESIGN – RESEARCH PROCESS

Getting started	Developing hypotheses	Crafting detailed methodology	Selecting sample	Collecting data	Analyzing data	Reviewing hypotheses	Drawing conclusions
• Review of academic literature • Definition of problem and direction of research	• Development of hypotheses based on prior theoretical and empirical contributions • Detailed definition of terms used in hypotheses for operationalization	• Selection of indicators to test hypotheses • Determination of applicable means for data collection • Preparation of data collection	• Selection of sample for empirical study, typically random sample selection • Use of fairly homogeneous sample	• Collection of data from primary or secondary sources	• Design of statistical analysis approach • Analysis of data	• Review of hypotheses with findings from data analysis	• Summary of findings and drawing of conclusions

Source: Based on Lamnek (2005) and Kromrey (2006)

Fig. 4.2 Hypothesis-driven research design – research process

t-tests, correlations and regression analyses (e.g. see Atteslander, Cromm, & Grabow, 2006: 229–272; Watsham & Parramore, 1997: 187–226).

The study closes by supporting or rejecting the hypotheses based on the statistical results and drawing conclusions about the relationships discovered in the empirical research. It thereby intends to contribute to the generation of new theory or to modify existing theories and to provide insights for practitioners as well as academics. The study will, furthermore, provide an outlook about the need for further academic research derived from the findings.

4.3.1.3 Data Collection Method

Given the limited disclosure of private equity firms, the study uses secondary, archival data sourced from large international data vendors such as Thompson Financial, Standard & Poor's, and private equity Intelligence, which will be presented in further detail in the next chapter. These data providers gain their information from publicly available sources such as financial markets, reporting figures and press statements as well as direct data contributions from corporations, private equity firms, and private equity investors. This approach secures objectivity and reliability of the data employed in this study and furthermore allows the study to cover a larger spectrum of corporations and private equity firms than possible in a setting using primary data.

4.3.2 *Research Design "Managing Diversified Portfolios"*

In analogy with the introduction to the first empirical part of this study, the following section will provide a brief overview of the general research design and research process in the second part for empirical research regarding the PE success factors for managing a diversified business portfolio. It will moreover outline some methodological choices regarding the data collection approach employed in this research contribution.

4.3.2.1 General Research Design

The investigation of the private equity approach to diversified business portfolios is largely based on a qualitative assessment. Qualitative research can be described as "any type of research that produces findings not arrived at by statistical procedures or other means of quantification" (Strauss & Corbin, 1998: 10). Baker (1999: 8) more specifically argues that qualitative research "attempts to understand how an entire social unit such as a group, organization or community operates in its own terms". It therefore typically comes into place in broad and highly interdependent research questions as addressed in this study (Miller & Brewer, 2003: 193), where numerical approaches would fail to draw a comprehensive picture of the situation. Given the objective of this study to investigate various components of the PE management model such as coordination mechanisms and skill profiles deeply embedded in the organizational setup and culture of private equity players, only a qualitative research design appears appropriate to generate the required insights. The research design is supported by selective quantitative elements developed in the first part of empirical research.

Due to the limited theoretical and empirical coverage of the PE way of managing their portfolios, this contribution follows an exploratory research design in this part of the study. Exploratory research follows an inductive approach, which is applied in a large portion of social research (Babbie, 2002: 79). It is particularly useful in cases, in which very limited theory and evidence is available and the research aims at making a contribution to the development of a new theory. A deductive, hypothesis-driven design would require the definition of random ad hoc hypotheses without theoretical foundation (Flick, 1995: 150–151). In other words, exploratory research is associated "with theory building rather than theory testing" (Berg, 2007: 284).

In such a research design, a study typically aims at developing a set of propositions from empirical observations that establish relationships between things in a systematic manner (Henning, 2004: 14; Berg, 2007: 284–286). Propositions then can be tested further in quantitative research settings, usually focusing on one particular proposition developed in an exploratory research design. Propositions are therefore statements about concepts that may be judged true or false; they become hypotheses if formulated in a way that can be subject to quantitative empirical testing (Cooper & Schindler, 1998: 43). Exploratory research designs are, furthermore, useful to investigate the feasibility of undertaking more in-depth research on specific elements of the targeted phenomenon of the initial, exploratory approach. It moreover allows the evaluation of research methods, which can be employed further on in academic research to address questions in this particular field of research and enables the prioritization of different areas of research within the broad, exploratory design.

4.3.2.2 Research Process

Being similarly well established in academic research as the hypothesis-driven research design presented above, exploratory research also follows a standardized research process as defined for instance by Eisenhardt (1989) and comparably by Yin (2003) and Stake (2005). Figure 4.3 provides a brief outline of the research process employed in this study.

The initial step of an exploratory research design is the development of a frame of reference laying out the scope of research and the central relationships in the area of research. This exploratory framework is at the heart of any exploratory research design, which builds the framework guiding the collection and interpretation of empirical evidence (Wollnik, 1977: 44–45). The frame of reference is developed based on the initial theoretical understanding of the addressed phenomenon from existing research and is refined continuously along the process if necessary due to the evidence collected. In the end, it needs to enable the researcher to develop propositions from the data collected during the research process.

After developing the exploratory framework, the researcher needs to select the cases, which will constitute the research sample of the study and determine the data collection approach applicable in the particular research setting. The selection of

EXPLORATORY RESEARCH DESIGN –RESEARCH PROCESS

Getting started	Selecting cases	Crafting instruments and protocols	Entering the field	Analyzing data	Shaping propositions	Enforcing literature	Reaching closure
• Review of academic literature • Definition of research questions • Development of exploratory framework	• Selection of cases • Deliberate sample selection based on pre-defined criteria • Use of heterogeneous sample	• Determination of applicable means for data collection • Preparation of data collection	• Collection of data within selected cases • Continuous review of exploratory framework and adjustments to framework or data collection method if necessary	• Search for relationships within individual cases • Investigation of patterns between cases	• Development of propositions based on evidence	• Review of existing literature • Illustration of agreements/ disagreements	• Summary of findings and drawing of conclusions • Description of further need for academic research

Source: Based on Eisenhardt (1989) and Berg (2006)

Fig. 4.3 Exploratory research design – research process

the sample should be deliberate along pre-defined criteria; this step is supposed to increase the validity of the study in contrast to a quantitative approach, which typically uses a random sample selection. The sample for an exploratory research design should be rather heterogeneous in its composition with different polarizing cases in order to grasp the complexity of the research object (Lamnek, 2005: 187–192; Berg, 2006: 362). For this study, this means that firms with different degrees of diversification and management approaches are sought. For the purpose of this research, they should moreover all be part of the first empirical study in order to draw on findings regarding the diversification, performance, and other quantitatively measured characteristics of these firms. The methodologies of data collection depend to a large extent on the size of the data sample and can range from interviews and surveys over the analysis of internal documentation to direct and participant observations (Yin, 2003: 85–97). In-depth case studies concentrate on a small number of cases and typically apply various data collection methods whereas the assessment of a broader sample is often pursued by a single means of data gathering (Berg, 2007: 286–294). The data collection approach used for this study will be presented below.

Data collection and data analysis of an exploratory research design are typically not consecutive but strongly interlinked. The continuous review of the data collected influences the frame of reference and, thereby, the activity of the researcher in the field and the questions asked, which proponents of interpretative approaches see as one of the key advantages of this research design (Berg, 2006: 364–368; Miles & Huberman, 1984: 21–23). The iterative process of data analysis tries to continuously find concepts within each case study that provide evidence to the research questions; it moreover attempts to discover matching patterns across different cases in the sample in order to triangulate the findings on an individual case level and find more general themes. Data is analyzed by clustering answers along different categories of the study's exploratory framework (Lamnek, 2005: 199–241; Yin, 2003: 109–140).

The end of the exploratory research approach is marked by the development of propositions outlining the discovered concepts and relationships, which are then compared with existing academic literature in the field of research. Similarities with existing research results strengthen the support for the propositions; disagreements require a more detailed investigation of the methodology employed and the influencing factors of the model. The study then concludes with the outlook for further academic research, in particular for quantitative empirical tests, building on the propositions derived in the exploratory design.

4.3.2.3 Data Collection Method

This study includes a sample of 20 private equity players in the exploratory research design. The sample will consist of firms already studied in the first part of empirical research in order to draw on the findings regarding performance and diversification and will consist of a heterogeneous group of firms, in particular with regard to the degree of diversification of the PE firms' investment portfolios. Given the limited public disclosure of private equity firms about internal questions such as the firms' organizational setup or their internal governance structures and given the depth of qualitative information required to address the above-stated research questions, the study needs to collect primary, qualitative information from private equity practitioners.

Out of the broad range of data collection methods such as document analysis, surveys, interviews, or observations, this study chooses interviews as primary means of data collection given the advantages of this approach. First of all, interviews are a feasible way of addressing private equity firms. Most PE firms are reluctant to pass out substantial information during a survey or in the form of internal documents; experience from other researchers however shows that there is a high likelihood of getting access to high ranking practitioners for personal interviews (e.g. see Baker & Montgomery, 1994; Berg & Gottschalg, 2003; Butler, 2001). Interviews, moreover, allow the researcher to constantly adjust the frame of reference underlying the exploratory research design and thereby to refine the analysis method and questions during the data collection. They furthermore provide the opportunity to tailor questions to the different cases and to detail points of particular interest (Yin, 2003: 89–92). In the private equity setting and given the complex nature of the research questions, there seems to be no other data collection method as well equipped as the interviewing approach.

There is a number of different interview methodologies available to the researcher, who has to choose the most suitable approach for the research environment and the selected research design. The different interview options can generally be distinguished into unstructured, partly structured, and structured interviews. During an unstructured interview, the researcher works without pre-defined questions and sequence for the interview. The interview is often strongly driven by the interviewee. This form of interview can for instance be found in narrative interviews or group discussions (Atteslander et al., 2006: 123; Flick, 1995: 156–159). Structured interviews form the other end of the spectrum. They work with a clearly defined set of questions put forward in a precise sequence, which gives very limited room for variation during the empirical phase. The structured interview is often used in situations such as panel research, in particular if the researcher has to rely on third-party support for conducting the interviews (Fontana & Frey, 2005). The partly structured interview combines elements from both interview approaches. It is conducted along broad discussion themes, which are supported by detailed questions. There is no given sequence to the interview, which allows the researcher to react to interesting aspects arising during the interview and thereby to interact with the discussion partner (Lamnek, 2005: 334–342).

Given the exploratory nature of this study and the fact, that private equity discussion partners are typically highly qualified managers, partly structured interviews appear to be an appropriate research method for this study (Atteslander et al., 2006: 121–125). This interview approach allows the researcher to alter the exploratory framework during the empirical phase and to adjust the interview to the style of the discussion partner. Given the broadness of the research direction, this approach furthermore offers the opportunity to detail aspects more advanced in one private equity firm and to give other components less attention. Such interviews are often referred to as guided interviews, as they are driven by the researcher along a set of discussion topics but leave enough room for the interviewee to express personal views. To support the exploratory nature of this research, the interviews will be conducted following a non-standardized approach, which employs open questions. Non-standardized interviews with open questions, in contrast a standardized interview process with closed questions, are particularly useful for the exploratory research designs as they provide no pre-defined answers and therefore allow the interviewee to express personal views about the individual discussion topics (Atteslander et al., 2006: 121–125; Yin, 2003: 89–92).

The exploratory research design is supported with data drawn from the first part of empirical research of this study, information publicly released by the private equity firms as well as external market and company reports. This additional information is used to triangulate the insights generated during the interviews in order to gain an understanding about the influencing factors and consequences of particular private equity management models. The analyses of the cohesive set of information will provide the necessary insight to substantiate the exploratory framework and to develop propositions about the underlying causes for certain strategies and management approaches in private equity firms.

Chapter 5
Empirical Part I: Diversification and Performance

Some private equity firms may well find that they have bitten off more than they can chew. But it would be wrong to assume that the challenge private equity firms pose to the public equity model is about to ease

Andreas Beroutsos, Conor F. Kehoe, Financial Times

The first empirical part of this study concentrates on the question how diversification affects performance, in private equity firms on a standalone basis and in comparison to public corporations. Many critics of the private equity phenomenon doubt the performance advantage of PEs due to the conglomerate structure of their investment portfolios, which they have accumulated throughout the past boom years of buyouts. Others on the contrary believe in the superiority of private equity in managing diversified investment portfolios. Although this controversy has been subject to public discussion in recent years, academic research has so far failed to shed light on the performance differences of private equity firms and public corporations in the light of different degrees of diversification.

This chapter first develops the hypotheses from previous theoretical and empirical contributions, which will be subject to the subsequent empirical tests. It then portrays the detailed research methodology including the data sources, the selected sample, and the applied indicators for diversification and performance. The methodological choices are based on the general remarks provided in Chap. 4. The chapter closes with the display of the empirical findings from the statistical analysis of the data sample and their interpretation.

5.1 Hypotheses

Building on the research direction highlighted in the general research design, the study follows three lead areas in this part of empirical research: (a) the comparison of performance between private equity investments and holdings in public corporations, (b) the relationship of industry diversification and performance in private equity

D.O. Klier, *Managing Diversified Portfolios*,
DOI: 10.1007/978-3-7908-2173-4_5, © 2009 Physica-Verlag Heidelberg

firms, and (c) the comparison of the diversification-performance phenomenon between private equity and public corporations.

5.1.1 Performance: Private Equity vs. Public Corporations

In a first step, the study investigates the general differences in performance between private equity investments and holdings in public corporations. Given the theoretical arguments about the existence and value creation approach of PE firms as well as the empirical evidence on the performance difference between the two asset classes – although conversely discussed – the study expects to find a significant outperformance by PE investments compared to public corporations.

From a theoretical point of view, private equity firms appear to have clear advantages over public corporations with respect to their ability to extract value from their investment portfolios. In Jensen's (1989b: 61) point of view, this form of new organizations "resolves the central weakness of the public corporation: the struggle between owners and managers" and thereby leads to a substantial reduction of agency costs. One of the most important rationales for the success of private equity is based on the free cash-flow theory. Economists hereby argue that there is a strong incentive for the management of firms under PE ownership to conduct only efficient investments and avoid such that come in below the cost of capital (Fama, 1980; Fox & Marcus, 1992; Jensen, 1986).

Empirically, results of recent contributions such as Ljungqvist and Richardson (2003a) as well as Ick (2005) provide evidence that PE firms outperform comparable public benchmarks, in particular before adjusting for different risk profiles associated with each asset class.[1] Research furthermore shows that firms with private equity owners undergo strong operational improvements (e.g. see Kaplan, 1989; Lichtenberg & Siegel, 1990; Smart & Waldfogel, 1993; Smith, 1990b) and achieve substantial strategic growth after a buyout transaction outpacing comparable companies in public ownership (e.g. see Bruining & Wright, 2002; Markides, 1998a; Zahra & Fescina, 1991).

H1: The performance of private equity investments before risk adjustments is significantly higher than the performance of holdings in public corporations.

Leveraged buyouts are typically investments in industries with stable cash flows and are most commonly found in the US and Western Europe. Given the superiority of the private equity model derived above and the stability of market conditions in

[1]The performance premium found in this studies is not undisputed. Contributions such as Moskowitz and Vissing-Joergensen (2002), Gottschalg, Phalippou, and Zollo (2004), Nielsen (2006), or Conroy and Harris (2007) provide contradicting results. Based on the research approach, this study uses the studies by Ljungqvist and Richardson (2003a) and Ick (2005) to form the study's hypotheses.

PE target segments, the study expects PE returns to exceed the performance of investments in public corporations even after adjusting the companies' risk profiles for differences such as geography or industry structure.

H2: The performance of private equity investments is significantly higher than the performance of holdings in public corporations even after adjusting for different risk profiles due to structural differences such as industry or geography distribution of investments

5.1.2 Diversification and Performance in Private Equity

In a second step, the study investigates the relationship of diversification and performance in private equity firms. The study expects that private equity firms are to a large extent unrelated diversified firms. This expectation is based on two arguments: the opportunistic acquisition strategy pursued by buyout specialists as well as the nature and organizational setup of private equity houses.

As illustrated in existing academic literature, private equity firms typically acquire businesses based on other criteria than industry relatedness. Their assessment of potential targets is largely concentrated on the firm's cash flows and the value improvement opportunities associated with the target, which can be achieved by applying the PE firm's skills and management approach. These PE-specific skills and management techniques are usually of a functional and general management nature rather than industry-specific elements. There is little concern about the fit into an existing investment portfolio as cross-asset synergies are generally not in the objective of the private equity house (Anders, 1992; Baker & Montgomery, 1994; Butler, 2001; Cotter & Peck, 2001).

In addition to the opportunistic acquisition strategy, the nature and organizational setup of private equity players contributes to the belief that PE firms are typically unrelated diversified. PE firms generally manage funds with a limited life-span, requiring the fund to divest businesses before the fund's termination (e.g. see de Malherbe, 2005; Gompers & Lerner, 1999; Rogers, Holland, & Haas, 2002). Acquired businesses are therefore not integrated into the existing business portfolio but remain separate businesses that can be divested after the PE value creation levers have been applied and the expected value can be achieved in the market. Thus, targets of PE takeovers remain separate legal and organizational entities. These characteristics of the PE business model lead to a substantial reduction of the value of related diversification, as synergies play by definition a subordinate role (Baker & Montgomery, 1994).[2]

[2]One however has to note that recent trends in the private equity industry seem to put more weight on relatedness of the assets in a PE portfolio. In particular the increasing importance of strategic growth through "buy-and-build" strategies requires the PE firm to acquire firms that have a strong relatedness in resources as well as strong strategic fit.

H3: Unrelated diversified private equity firms account for the largest share of firms within the private equity *industry*

Building on the above arguments, the study expects that the private equity business model is most suitable for the management of unrelated diversified business portfolios. While there seems to be no performance upside through industry relatedness of the portfolio, the associated risk generally decreases with unrelated diversification (e.g. see Bettis & Hall, 1982; Chang & Howard, 1989).

H4: Unrelated diversified private equity firms achieve the highest performance within the private equity industry, before risk adjustments (H4a) and after (H4b)

5.1.3 Diversification and Performance: Private Equity vs. Public Corporations

Finally, the study attempts to compare the relationship of diversification and performance found in private equity firms with results from public corporations. It is expected that the portion of unrelated diversified firms in the private equity exceeds the share in public corporations given the above argument for unrelated diversification in private equity and the relevance of relatedness in public corporations. In particular the accelerated dismantling of conglomerates during the last decades – largely supported by private equity – supports the belief that the number of firms pursuing a strategy of related diversification is substantially larger in public corporations.

Particularly driven by the resource-based view brought forward by Penrose (1959), many academics argue that the relatedness of assets should be the key criteria in the evaluation of corporate diversification decisions. They argue that a portfolio of related diversified businesses enables a firm to realize cross-business synergies from economies of scope and at the same time create and accumulate new strategic assets in a way superior to the ones available to competitors (e.g. see Ansoff, 1965; Markides & Williamson, 1994; Nayyar, 1993; Robins & Wiersema, 1995; Rumelt, 1982; Teece, 1982).

H5: The share of unrelated diversified firms is larger in private equity settings than in public corporations

Building on the above-formulated hypothesis H4, it is expected that on the private equity side of the investigation, unrelated diversified firms show the strongest performance. On the side of public corporations, theoretical and empirical evidence throughout the last two decades indicates that related diversifiers demonstrate the highest returns. Studies provided by Amit and Livnat (1988), Lubatkin and Rogers (1989) as well Hall and St. John (1994) for instance show significant excess returns of related diversified firms, using both accounting and capital market approaches for the measurement of performance. The results also hold after correction for risk effects.

H6: Unrelated diversified firms achieve the highest performance in private equity settings only, before risk adjustments (H6a) and after (H6b). Related diversifiers show the strongest returns in public corporations in both scenarios before risk adjustments (H6c) and after (H6d)

Finally, it is expected that the differences in performance between different stages of diversification are less significant in the private equity industry than what can be found in public corporations. This belief builds on the fact that private equity firms typically apply a standardized management approach to their investment portfolios, independent of different degrees of diversification and largely concentrated around the PE value creation levers (see in particular Jensen, 1989b; Baker & Montgomery, 1994). The management style of public corporations on the contrary varies strongly along different degrees of diversification. This includes elements such as the level of involvement of the corporate center (e.g. see Fredrickson, 1986; Goold, Campbell, & Alexander, 1994; Gupta, 1987; Lau, 1993; van Oijen & Douma, 2000) as well as the degree of independence of different divisions of the firm with regard to cross-divisional resource sharing (e.g. see Collis, Young, & Goold, 2007; Hitt & Ireland, 1986). Given this spread of management approaches on the side of public corporations opposed to the uniformity in private equity, this publication expects the differences in performance to be larger within the corporate sample.

H7: The differences in performance between different stages of diversification are smaller in private equity settings than in public corporations, before risk adjustments (H7a) and after (H7b)

5.2 Methodology

Building on the guiding principles of the empirical research design outlined in Chap. 4, this section introduces the detailed methodology applied in the first part of empirical research. The methodological notes include a description of the data sample as well as the measures used to indicate the degree of diversification and the different levels of performance.

5.2.1 Data Sample

To pursue the research direction of this study, it is necessary to get access to diversification and performance data for both corporations and private equity firms. The data sample is drawn from large international data vendors, which are described in Sect. 5.2.1.1. This part of the study furthermore introduces the sample selection approach and gives a brief overview of the descriptive statistics of the drawn sample.

5.2.1.1 Data Sources

Data regarding the corporate sample is, in general, publicly available and due to legal requirements largely standardized. The data items required for this research are sourced from two of the world's largest data providers, Thompson Financial and Standard & Poor's. All data regarding the accounting numbers as well as the industry classification of the selected firms is taken from "Thompson Financial Worldscope". The database includes data regarding company profile information and fundamentals for more than 40,000 global companies with more than 20 years of history. It is considered the most comprehensive and international data set available for academic research with regard to corporate samples (Ulbricht & Weiner, 2005). All items concerning the performance of firms on the world's capital markets are drawn from Standard & Poor's "Research Insight" database, which encompasses, besides general company information, all relevant historical security and market data from financial markets to assess firm stock-market performance. The database draws to a large extent on Standard & Poor's "Compustat" database and is selected for this research due to its in-depth coverage of market indicators and its well-established track record in academic literature in this field of research. Both sources are widely accepted in academic research (for a detailed assessment see Ulbricht & Weiner, 2005) and build the basis for most of the publications introduced in the above literature review with regard to the field of research "Diversification and Performance".

The private equity sample is also based on two different data providers. The performance and firm characteristics of the relevant buyout funds are sourced from private equity intelligence (Preqin), a data provider specialized in the private equity industry. The database "Preqin Performance Analyst" is one of the most comprehensive collections of PE data available in the market with performance data for over 3,400 private equity funds and close to 1,200 private equity firms. It moreover allows the differentiation of various fund types such as buyout, mezzanine or venture capital vehicles. The data of Preqin is sourced from both general and limited partners, which increases the credibility of the stated PE performance. As there is no transparency about the detailed composition of the investment portfolios of individual private equity firms available in the market, the study draws on information about the transaction history of individual private equity firms. This data is sourced from Dealogic, one of the most established information brokers regarding the activity on the global capital markets including a database tracking all mergers and acquisitions taking place in the global market ("M&A Analytics"). This database provides information regarding elements such as targets, acquirers, prices, or the share acquired during the transaction. To validate the collected information, it is compared to the limited public disclosures available from the private equity firms themselves.

All additional information required to support the analysis, such as exchange rates or other indices from financial markets, are drawn from Thompson Financial's "Datastream". The database provides historical, in-depth information for financial indicators on a global level.

5.2.1.2 Sample Selection

As indicated above, this part of research aims at investigating the diversification-performance-relationship for a comparable sample of public corporations and private equity players – or more specifically leveraged buyout houses. The study therefore applies identical sample selection criteria for both areas of interest.

The sample size of comparable studies on the side of public corporations ranges from as little as 70 to 80 (e.g. see Bettis, 1981; Lubatkin & Rogers, 1989; Rumelt, 1974; Simmonds, 1990) up to several hundred companies (e.g. see Berger & Ofek, 1995; Campa & Kedia, 2002; De, 1992; Hall & St. John, 1994; Mansi & Reeb, 2002). Small samples are used in cases when data material is not readily available and requires substantial work by the researchers while the large-scale studies in recent years rely completely on the material sourced from databases. Sample sizes containing several hundred companies have become possible with the increasing quality and standardization of publicly available data as well as the reduction of subjective indicators such as the categorical diversification clusters used by Rumelt (1974, 1982) and others in the earlier days of diversification research.

In private equity, sample sizes in academic research still remain small. One of the few studies investigating diversification in private equity by Lossen (2006) is based on 51 buyout firms. Similar sample sizes of less than 100 private equity firms can be observed in other private equity studies regarding the performance of PE firms (e.g. see Cumming & Walz, 2004; Ick, 2005; Kaplan & Schoar, 2004; Nielsen, 2006).[3] This is mainly due to the fact that there is very limited information about private equity available in public. Most studies are therefore based on the proprietary information provided by funds-of-funds or other limited partners. This source of data on the one side grants the advantage of detailed insights on individual investments. On the other side, however, these studies fail to draw an inclusive picture of a particular private equity firm and are therefore only able to draw conclusions based on the funds offered to the limited partners, who provided the data.

The approach chosen for this study investigates public corporations and private equity firms on a firm level rather than on the level of individual business units or PE funds. Given the internationality of the private equity landscape, the study is based on a population of US and European firms, both regions together representing more than 95% of global PE investments according to the private equity Intelligence database. The study is moreover focused on conglomerates or conglomerate-like structures. It therefore concentrates on large public corporations with a market capitalization above USD 5 billion and large private equity players with the sum of its fund values exceeding USD 5 billion, respectively. The private equity fund value is determined by the value of its investments, including the value of committed equity as well as debt in order to make corporations and private equity firms comparable.

Given the experience from prior studies and the substantial amount of work required to adjust the available public data for this research, the study aims at addressing a research sample of 100 firms from each group, public corporations and leveraged buyout firms. The sample size of 100 PE partnerships and accordingly 100 public corporations is – as outlined above – larger than samples analyzed in previous private equity motivated studies and is therefore expected to deliver

[3] Some of the mentioned studies contain larger numbers of private equity funds. However, if consolidated to a private equity firm level, the sample size is reduced substantially

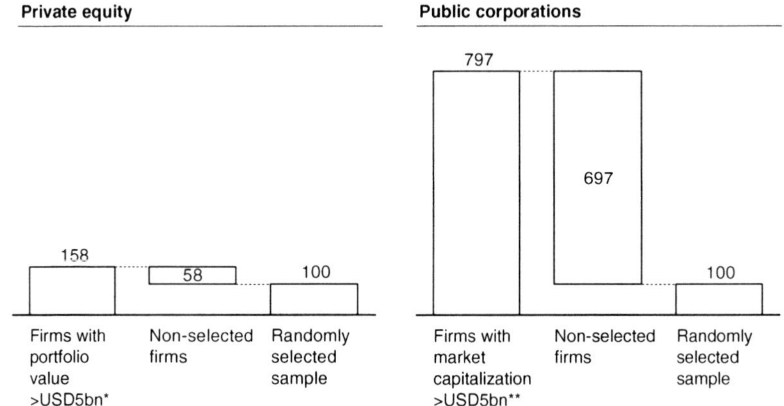

Fig. 5.1 Selection of sample

statistically viable material while ensuring the manageability of the large volumes of transaction data associated with each PE firm and its individual funds. After eliminating incomplete data sets from the data population, the sample of 100 firms is selected randomly as outlined in Fig. 5.1. The sample selection process is designed in accordance with various prior academic studies (e.g. see Bettis & Mahajan, 1985; Markides, 1995; Rumelt, 1974, 1982). Random sample selection allows an objective data selection free from selection biases in order to gain "measurable confidence in the estimates and conclusions" drawn from the sample (Maxim, 1999: 106).

5.2.1.3 Characteristics of Sample

The selected sample from both publicly listed corporations and private equity (LBO) firms consists of a selection of international players, which are among the largest players in their respective industries and geographical markets. Table 5.1 presents the selected sample. Before engaging in more detailed empirical analysis, this brief section is supposed to provide an overview of the key characteristics of the sample along such dimensions as geographical scope, portfolio structure, and fundamentals.[4]

[4] A more detailed overview of the characteristics of the selected samples of publicly listed corporations and private equity firms is provided in the appendix of this publication.

Table 5.1 Overview sample corporations and private equity firms

Corporations		Private equity firms	
Name	Country of origin	Name	Country of origin
General Electric Co	United States	Kohlberg Kravis Roberts	United States
Procter & Gamble Co	United States	Texas Pacific Group	United States
JPMorgan Chase & Co	United States	Blackstone Group	United States
Nestle CA/AG	Switzerland	Permira	United Kingdom
Wells Fargo & Co	United States	Carlyle Group	United States
DaimlerChrysler AG	Germany	Thomas H Lee Partners	United States
Hewlett-Packard Co	United States	Apollo Management	United States
Merck & Co	United States	Bain Capital	United States
ING Groep NV	Netherlands	Goldman Sachs Private Equity Group	United States
Barclays Plc	United Kingdom	CVC Capital Partners	United Kingdom
Nokia (AB) OY	Finland	BC Partners	United Kingdom
SGF SOC General De France SA	France	Credit Suisse	United States
American Express Co	United States	Madison Dearborn Partners	United States
France Telecom	France	Welsh, Carson, Anderson & Stowe	United States
Oracle Corp	United States	Forstmann Little & Co	United States
Ericsson (LM) Telefon	Sweden	Charterhouse Capital Partners	United Kingdom
Motorola Inc	United States	Candover Partners	United Kingdom
United Parcel Service Inc	United States	Clayton Dubilier & Rice	United States
LVMH MOET Hennessy L Vuitton	France	HM Capital Partners	United States
BASF AG	Germany	Cinven	United Kingdom
Carnival Corp/PLC (USA)	United States	GTCR Golder Rauner	United States
Du Pont (EJ) De Nemours	United States	Providence Equity Partners	United States
Vivendi SA	France	TA Associates	United States
Standard Chartered Bank	United Kingdom	Hellman & Friedman	United States
Prudential Financial Inc	United States	Bridgepoint	United Kingdom
Danone (Groupe)	France	Terra Firma Capital Partners	United Kingdom
Bayer AG	Germany	Vestar Capital Partners	United States
Honeywell International Inc	United States	Advent International	United States
Deutsche Post AG	Germany	Montagu Private Equity	United Kingdom
Unilever PLC	United Kingdom	Apax Partners	United Kingdom
Fedex Corp	United States	Nordic Capital	Sweden
Suntrust Banks Inc	United States	Silver Lake Partners	United States
Southern Co	United States	PAI Partners	France
H & M Hennes & Mauritz AB	Sweden	Doughty Hanson & Co	United Kingdom
Cardinal Health Inc	United States	Lindsay Goldberg & Bessemer	United States
McGraw-Hill Companies	United States	Onex Corp	United States
Northrop Grumman Corp	United States	Kelso & Company	United States
Nike Inc	United States	Industri Kapital	United Kingdom

(continued)

Table 5.1 (continued)

Corporations		Private equity firms	
Name	Country of origin	Name	Country of origin
Holcim Ltd	Switzerland	Lehman Brothers	United States
PPL Group Inc	United States	Midocean Partners	United States
CBS Corp	United States	Oak Hill Partners	United States
Novo Nordisk A/G	Denmark	Spectrum Equity Investors	United States
Kellogg Co	United States	3i	United Kingdom
Swisscom AG	Switzerland	Leonard Green & Partners	United States
Pernod Ricard SA	France	Cypress Group	United States
Norfolk Southern Corp	United States	JLL Partners	United States
Sun Microsystems Inc	United States	Berkshire Partners	United States
CRH PLC	Ireland	J.W. Childs Associates	United States
Metro AG	Germany	Summit Partners	United States
Syngenta AG	Switzerland	Willis Stein & Partners	United States
TNT UV	Netherlands	Quadrangle Group	United States
Marriott Intl Inc	United States	Code Hennessy & Simmons	United States
General Mills Inc	United States	Blum Capital Partners	United States
Omnicom Group	United States	Veronis Suhler Stevenson	United States
Clear Channel Communications	United States	Lion Capital	United Kingdom
Marsh & Mclennan COS	United States	Duke Street Capital	United Kingdom
Staples Inc	United States	Francisco Partners	United States
General Motors Corp	United States	Freeman Spogli & Co	United States
Paccar Inc	United States	Abry Partners	United States
Deutsche Boerse AG	Germany	Fenway Partners	United States
Xerox Corp	United States	New Mountain Capital	United States
Continental AG	Germany	Wellspring Capital Management	United States
Marks & Spencer Group PLC	United Kingdom	Morgan Stanley Private Equity	United States
GAP Inc	United States	Cognetas	United Kingdom
Air Products & Chemicals Inc	United States	Alchemy Partners	United Kingdom
Avon Products	United States	Castle Harlan	United States
Wolseley PLC	United Kingdom	Parthenon Capital	United States
Electronic Data Systems Corp	United States	Sun Capital Partners	United States
Beiersdorf AG	Germany	GSC Partners	United States
Boston Properties Inc	United States	Elevation Partners	United States
Starwood Hotels & Resorts	United States	Liberty Partners	United States
Ote-Hellenic Telecom Org	Greece	Diamond Castle Holdings	United States
MAN AG	Germany	Aurora Capital Group	United States
Mediaset Spa	Italy	Behrman Capital	United States
Deutsche Postbank AG	Germany	Thoma Cressey Equity Partners	United States
Grupo Ferrovial Sa	Spain	Centre Partners Management	United States
Southwest Airlines	United States	Bear Stearns Merchant Banking	United States
Sara Lee Corp	United States	Catterton Partners	United States

(continued)

Table 5.1 (continued)

Corporations		Private equity firms	
Name	Country of origin	Name	Country of origin
Freeport-McMoran Cop & Gold	United States	Barclays Private Equity	United Kingdom
Juniper Networks Inc	United States	Wind Point Partners	United States
Cie Gen Des Etablis Michelin	France	CCMP Capital Asia	United States
Wrigley (WM) Jr Co	United States	Olympus Partners	United States
Thyssenkrupp AG	Germany	Lexington Partners	United States
Sainsbury (J) Plc	United Kingdom	Odyssey Investment Partners	United States
Deutsche Lufthansa AG	Germany	Fox Paine & Company	United States
Office Depot Inc	United States	Jordan Company	United States
Saipem Spa	Italy	Reservoir Capital Group	United States
Adidas AG	Germany	Graphite Capital Management	United Kingdom
Henkel KGaA	Germany	Palamon Capital Partners	United Kingdom
Nordstrom Inc	United States	Riverside Company	United States
Parker-Hannifin Corp	United States	Charlesbank Capital Partners	United States
Smiths Group Plc	United Kingdom	Kohlberg & Company	United States
Scottish & Newcastle Plc	United Kingdom	Exxel Group	United States
Smith International Inc	United States	Harbourvest Partners	United States
Allegheny Technologies Inc	United States	KRG Capital	United States
United States Steel Corp	United States	HG Capital	United Kingdom
Smith & Nephew Plc	United Kingdom	Brockway Moran Partners	United States
Kuhne & Nagel International	Switzerland	Heartland Industrial Partners	United States
Celesio Ag	Germany	Tailwind Capital	United States
Ryanair Holdings Plc	Ireland	Towerbrook Capital Partners	United States

The sample of public corporations is balanced between US and European firms, consisting of 52% US companies and 48% representatives of the European markets. Within the European sample, firms from Germany (15%), the United Kingdom (9%), and France (7%) have the largest shares in the sample with the remaining 17% being spread across countries such as Italy, Spain, Switzerland, and the Nordic nations. The private equity sample, on the other hand, shows a stronger representation of players with US origins, consistent with the fact that the private equity phenomenon started off in the United States. The sample consists of 77% US firms and 23% European players, of which more than 90% are based in the United Kingdom. Investment activity however is increasingly moving to Europe and other international destinations.

The corporate sample has an average market capitalization of USD 35.4 billion at the end of 2006 ranging from as little as USD 7.8 billion of Ryanair to a maximum of USD 363.7 billion of General Electric. They report investments in an average of

4.3 industries classified by SIC Codes on the four-digit level.[5] The firms, on average, have 81,500 employees. In the private equity sample, the average value of the investment portfolio is USD 24.6 billion with KKR as the largest player managing investments worth more than USD 150 billion at the end of 2006. The private equity firms manage an average of five investment funds each with an average fund size of USD 1.4 billion in equity holdings, ranging from as little as USD 10–20 million to funds holding more than USD 15 billion in investors' equity.

In terms of fundamentals and vital statistics, the selected sample of public corporations has an average price/earnings (P/E) ratio of 18.6, again ranging from as little as 7.7 for United States Steel to 31.5 for Sainsbury.[6] The firms have average revenues of USD 26.6 billion and an average EBIT of USD 2.5 billion. General Motors accounts for the highest revenues with USD 190.2 billion whereas General Electric shows the highest EBIT within the selected corporate sample with USD 36.6 billion. Given the limited disclosure of private equity firms, only partial information is available about their fundamentals. The economics of the private equity firm itself are in particular not communicated to the public; however, fund performance to investors is available through selected sources, which have been outlined above. The average internal rate of return of all funds managed by the sample PE firms accrues to 16.3%, whereby the top performers such as Permira, Charterhouse Capital, or Providence Equity Partners return more than 30% average IRR to investors. Players at the bottom end of the performance scale such as Reservoir Capital, Tailwind Capital, or Heartland Industrial Partners on the other hand show overall negative returns to investors.

5.2.2 *Diversification Measures*

Selecting the approach to measure diversification is the first critical element that needs to be defined before engaging in the empirical data analysis. This section therefore lays out the general principles for the assessment of diversification as well as the application of the selected measures in the corporate and the private equity universe.

5.2.2.1 General Approach

Recent academic research efforts have been dominated by two diversification measures, which will build the basis for the empirical analysis in this study: Comprehensive indices as a form of continuous measures (e.g. see Gomes & Livdan, 2004; Lang & Stulz, 1994; Montgomery & Wernerfelt, 1988) and the Entropy measure

[5]SIC (Standard Industry Classification) Codes are a widely used approach to classified firms' business activity into generally accepted categories. The SIC Code methodology will be introduced in detail in Sect. 5.2.2 "Diversification Measures" and will be basis for all further empirical analysis. An overview of all SIC codes and industry groups is furthermore provided in the appendix of this publication.

[6]All data items have been drawn on December 31st 2006; accounting items are therefore figures for the year 2005 or 2005/2006 for companies reporting on a different business year. All market data items are for the full year 2006.

(e.g. see Berry, 1975; Chakrabarti, Singh, & Mahmood, 2007; Graham, Lemmon, & Wolf, 2002; Jacquemin & Berry, 1979; Markides, 1995; Palepu, 1985). These diversification measures replaced prior standards such as the categorical measure introduced by Rumelt (1974, 1982) and more simplistic continuous diversification measures as used by authors like Mansi and Reed (2002), Servaes (1996), or De (1992) given the improved predictive validity of these approaches (Chatterjee & Blocher, 1992).

Both indices used in this study, the Herfindahl and the Entropy measure, are based on SIC codes. The Standard Industry Classification (SIC) system was introduced by the US government as a standardized way for companies to report segmental data about their business activities and has since been adopted as a reporting requirement in most industrialized countries. Every firm hereby reports data for its different business segments on a four-digit SIC code level, which can then be aggregated to industry groups, commonly defined as the two-digit SIC code level of the SIC code system.[7] The diversification assessment for the firms in the sample is conducted with data for the year 2006 marking the end of the evaluation period.[8]

The Herfindahl index is a commonly used form of comprehensive diversification measures. It can be calculated based on various financial indicators such as sales, assets, or segment valuations. The index is the sum of the squared values of – for example – sales per segment as a fraction of total firm sales. If a firm has only one segment, its Herfindahl index is one; if a firm has on the other hand ten segments that each contribute 10% of sales, its Herfindahl index is 0.1 (Lang & Stulz, 1994: 1257). Hence the Herfindahl index falls as the degree of diversification increases, or, in other words, the concentration of the firm on a single business decreases (Comment & Jarrell, 1995: 69–70).

$$\text{Herfindahl index } H_{jt} = \sum_{i=1}^{N_{jt}} \left(X_{ijt} \Big/ \sum_{i=1}^{N_{jt}} X_{ijt} \right)^2$$

where X_{ij}, indicator attributable to a business; i, business i; j, firm j; t, fiscal year t.

The Herfindahl measure can be supplemented by two measures to triangulate the results of the more complex Herfindahl index. The first measure is based on simply counting the number of businesses of a firm; the second makes a binary classification of firms as being focused or diversified whereby a firm is categorized as diversified if it is active in two or more than two industries defined on the two-digit SIC code level and the most important accounts for less than 90% of total sales (Lins & Servaes, 1999: 2219).

The Entropy measure is an alternative index to derive additional information from the data provided in a firm's reporting and is defined as "a weighted average of a firm's diversification within sectors" (Jacquemin & Berry, 1979: 362). Whereas entirely continuous measures allow no conclusion about related or unrelated diversification, the Entropy measure has the advantage of deriving insights into the

[7]An overview of all SIC codes and industry groups is provided in the appendix of this publication.

[8]In accordance with the above argumentation, the study focuses on the status view of diversification. Changes in the degree of diversification during the 10 year analysis period are not considered relevant to the study's research objective.

different levels of diversification prevalent in a firm by assuming that segments within an industry group (two-digit SIC code level) are more related to one another than segments across industry groups (Hall & St. John, 1994; Palepu, 1985). Related diversification is hereby defined as the diversification within a two-digit SIC code, unrelated diversification as the diversification arising from operating between two-digit SIC codes (Hoskisson, Hitt, Johnson, & Moesel, 1993: 222). Thus the Entropy measure allows the decomposition of a firm's total diversity into two additive components – related and unrelated diversity – while at the same time avoiding the problems of subjectivity associated with Rumelt's (1974, 1982) categorical measures (Palepu, 1985: 244).

$$\text{Entropy index} \quad \mathrm{DT} = \mathrm{DR} + \mathrm{DU},$$

where DT, total diversity; DR, related diversity; DU, unrelated diversity.

$$\text{Total diversity} \quad \mathrm{DT} = \sum_{i=1}^{n} P_i * \ln\left(1/P_i\right),$$

where P_i, the proportion of a firm's business within the ith industry segment; n, number of industry segments which the firm participates in (four-digit SIC code).

$$\text{Related diversity} \quad \mathrm{DR} = \sum_{j=1}^{M} \mathrm{DR}_j * P_j,$$

where DR_j, diversity within industry groups;[9] M, the number of industry groups which the n industry segments aggregate into; P_j, the proportion of the firm's business within the jth industry group (two-digit SIC code).

$$\text{Unrelated diversity} \quad \mathrm{DU} = \sum_{j=1}^{M} P_j * \ln\left(1/P_j\right),$$

where M, the number of industry groups; P_j, the proportion of the firm's business within the jth industry group (two-digit SIC code).

5.2.2.2 Diversification in Corporations

The application of the selected diversification measures in the sample of corporations is fairly simple and was carried out several times before in academic studies (see in particular Berger & Ofek, 1995; Lang & Stulz, 1994; Palepu, 1985). All firms in the sample are public corporations, which are listed on large stock exchanges and therefore all publish relevant figures in their annual reports. The study's data source "Thompson Financial Worldscope" provides all relevant data items including segmental reporting

[9] Diversity within industry groups is measured by the four-digit diversification of industry group j $\mathrm{DR}_j = \sum P^j_i \ln(1/P^j_i)$ as presented in Palepu (1985: 252). P^j_i is defined as the share of the segment i of industry group j in the total sales of the respective industry group j.

figures in order to assess different degrees of diversification. Segmental reporting offers a split of a firm's revenues and assets into the different industries it operates in, containing all SIC codes associated with the firm's businesses. All residual and non-classifiable reporting figures attributed to the SIC code "9999 Non-classifiable establishments" are neglected for this study's empirical analysis in accordance with prior contributions (e.g. see Berger & Ofek, 1995; Graham et al., 2002; Lamont & Polk, 2001). Based on these elements and the adjustments described above, the Herfindahl and the Entropy measure can be calculated along firm revenues and assets and can then be used as basis for further empirical analysis.

5.2.2.3 Diversification in Private Equity

Measuring diversification in private equity firms is more complex. Given the fact that PE firms typically provide no or only fragmented information about the composition of their investment portfolios, the assessment of diversification requires a different approach. Instead of relying on partial data provided by limited or general partners and thereby only grasping part of the portfolio as seen in most prior contributions (e.g. see Lossen, 2006; Schmidt, 2004; Weidig & Mathonet, 2004), this study draws on transaction data provided by the data vendor Dealogic. By tracking all transactions, acquisitions and divestitures, the study attempts to reconstruct the actual investment portfolios of the different private equity firms in the sample. For this purpose, all transactions occurring within the 10-year horizon between January 1, 1997 and December 31, 2006 have been drawn from the database, including all types of transactions such as mergers, acquisitions, or initial public offerings. Given the limited lifespan of a PE investment fund, the transactions within a 10-year timeframe are able to closely represent a firm's investment portfolio at the end of the year 2006. The dataset provides information about the acquirer, the divestor, as well as relevant information about the target such as the transaction value, the deal type, and the industry and SIC code the target firm is operating in.

Building the diversification analysis on this set of data, all acquisitions with subsequent divestitures are removed from the sample. Furthermore all activity of specialized real estate funds such as Morgan Stanley Real Estate or Goldman Sachs Real Estate is excluded from the analysis to concentrate on the leveraged buyout segment. After triangulating the results with the publications of private equity houses and finding high correlations between the statements of PEs and the transaction analysis, the remaining list of acquisitions is then used as proxy for the current investment portfolio of the PE firms in the sample.[10] After aggregating all acquisitions,

[10] Pitts and Hopkins (1982) urge researchers to be more creative in their approach to diversification measurement in order to open up new areas of research. In the author's view, the proxy for a PE portfolio used in this study is the best outside-in assessment of the diversity of a PE portfolio available to academic research. Insider data would be more accurate but commonly does cover only individual funds rather than entire PE firms. It furthermore does not allow the coverage of a sample of 100 leading firms.

the industry structure within the PE investment portfolio can be evaluated. Consistent with the reporting standards for public corporations, only ten SIC codes per PE firm are accounted for in the empirical analysis of this study (e.g. see Amit & Livnat, 1989; Lichtenberg, 1991; Lins & Servaes, 1999).[11] The PE industry diversification is then measured by the Herfindahl and the Entropy index based on the SIC codes and the transaction values generated from the resulting set of data. The transaction value is the best quality data available for the individual investments in a PE portfolio and therefore used as lead indicator in the diversification analysis.

5.2.3 Performance Measures

The second critical component for the upcoming analysis is the definition of performance measures that will be applied in the study. Hence, this section presents the general principles for the evaluation of firm performance as well as the approach to apply the selected measures in the sample of public corporations and private equity firms.

5.2.3.1 General Approach

Given the interest of research and the nature of the hypotheses formulated above, the focus of the empirical study is on financial performance rather than valuation.[12] Within this direction of research, there are two general approaches to measure performance as presented above: an accounting-based method and an approach relying on performance to investors, also called market-based approach. This study opts for the market-based approach for three reasons. First, the quality of data available from the private equity side regarding the performance to investors is substantially better than the scarce data retrievable about the accounting-based performance measures of individual portfolio companies or the private equity investment vehicles. Second, the market-based approach integrates past and future performance elements in one measure as it is a representation of dividend yields

---

[11]Public corporations are required to publish ten SIC codes in their annual report, typically representing at least 10% of the firm's consolidated revenues or assets. While only few firms apply the latter reporting guideline, all firms limit reporting to ten SIC codes. The study therefore concentrates on the rule of a maximum of ten SIC codes. Residual or non-classifiable businesses are in accordance with public corporations grouped under SIC code "9999 non-classifiable establishments", which have been removed in comparable studies. The international work of Lins and Servaes (1999) across varying international reporting standards has particularly provided guidance for the approach chosen in this study.

[12]The focus of the study is to derive conclusions about how firms differ in managing diversified portfolios. The performance component is therefore more important than the aspect of valuation, which can be influenced by numerous factors as highlighted in Chap. 2.

and stock price movements indicating expected performance. Accounting-based indicators are purely a representation of past performance and can easily be manipulated. Third, risk adjustments based on market indicators are well established in academic research.

Financial performance is measured as the return investors gain from investing in a company's shares. The total return is therefore an aggregate value of the received dividends during the investment period as well as the gain or loss from changes in the stock price. Total shareholder return (TSR) is a measure typically employed in this context (Arnold, 2005).

$$\text{Total Return to Shareholder} \quad \text{TSR} = \left[D_1 + \left(P_1 - P_0\right)\right] / P_0,$$

where D_1, dividend per share; P_1, share price at end of period; P_0, initial share price.

Adjusting for differences in risk associated with different kinds of investments can be expressed by various measures (for an introduction see Bodie, Kane, & Marcus, 2005: 866–886). Jensen's Alpha (Jensen, 1969) represents the ability of a firm to perform better or worse than a broadly diversified market portfolio (Lubatkin & Rogers, 1989: 459). It can also be described as the risk-adjusted outperformance of an individual asset compared to the relevant market benchmark. The Sharpe measure (Sharpe, 1964) divides the excess return of an investments by the overall volatility of returns and thereby provides an alternative indicator to compare risk-adjusted returns between different investments and the market. While Sharpe's measure uses the total risk associated with the investment, the Treynor measure (Treynor, 1965) concentrates on the systematic risk of an investment and therefore corrects for potential differences in market risk associated with different investments. All three indicators appear suitable for the empirical analysis in this study (De, 1992).

$$\text{Jensen's Alpha} \quad \alpha_i = r_i - \left[r_f + \beta_i\left(r_m - r_f\right)\right] + \varepsilon_i$$

$$\text{Sharpe Measure} \quad S_i = \left(r_i - r_f\right) / \sigma_i,$$

$$\text{Treynor Measure} \quad T_i = \left(r_i - r_f\right) / \beta_i,$$

where r_i, return of investment; r_f, risk free rate of return; r_m, return of market portfolio; β_i, beta coefficient measuring the systematic risk of an individual investment; it therefore assesses the volatility of the investment above the volatility of the market portfolio; σ_i, total volatility of investment; ε_i, disruptive factor.

The risk free rate of return is approximated by the return of three months US treasury bills, adjusted for varying maturities (Bodie et al., 2005: 144). Market returns are represented by the return of the relevant stock indices of the different investments, adjusted for different time spans of the respective return measures. The systematic risk and the total volatility of the share price are represented by a single historic figure in accordance with Cunningham (1973), who observed a high consistency of risk measures for share prices over time.[13]

5.2.3.2 Performance in Corporations

Measuring performance in publicly listed corporations is a standardized approach, which is built on the market data drawn from Standard & Poor's "Research Insight" database. Performance is measured in total shareholder return (TSR) and is evaluated on a 5-year and 10-year basis ending end of December 2006. The volatilities (β_i and σ_i) required to adjust the performance data for the associated risk are directly derived from capital markets and are also taken from standard & poor's market data. All other market indicators such as the risk free rate of return (r_f) and the return of the market portfolio (r_m) are drawn from the above introduced database Thompson Financial "Datastream".

5.2.3.3 Performance in Private Equity

The evaluation of firm performance in private equity is – similar to the measurement of diversification – more complex. The performance of private equity funds itself is available; however, PE funds are not traded on public equity markets and risk indicators based on market volatilities are therefore not existing.

Performance of private equity funds is measured in "Internal Rate of Return (IRR)", which is comparable to the "total shareholder return (TSR)" (Arnold, 2005: 197). The IRR is calculated after administration and performance fees charged by the private equity firm and therefore – consistent with the TSR – entirely attributable to investors. It contains cash flows to investors as well as the current valuation of the investors' private equity investments. The performance data for individual funds of a PE firm is taken from private equity intelligence's database "Preqin Performance Analyst" and accumulated to represent the performance on the level of the PE firm.[14] Working with the vintage year of the individual funds of a firm, performance can be split into annual performance indicators. This research hereby uses 5-year and 10-year performance measures consistent with the analysis in public corporations. However, it has to be noted that some PE firms are still young enterprises and therefore not all firms in the sample contain a 10-year performance track record.

$$\text{Internal Rate of Return (IRR) solved from equation} \quad I_1 = \sum_{t=1}^{N} C_t / (1 + \text{IRR})^t,$$

where I_1, initial investment; C_t, cash flow in year t.

[13]The findings of Cunningham's (1973) study are basis for the calculation of risk figures in all relevant databases such as Datastream, Worldscope, or Research Insight/Compustat.

[14]Metrick and Yasuda's (2007) study about the economics of private equity funds for instance also uses private equity Intelligence as primary source of private equity performance data.

Due to the lack of market data, adjusting PE performance for risk requires some work-arounds. According to studies conducted by Rosenberg and Guy (1976, 1995) as well as Braun, Nelson, and Sunier (1995), it can be assumed that a firm's volatility is influenced most by the industry mix of businesses it is invested in and the degree of diversification it achieved within the firm's business portfolio.[15] This method is further supported by Jensen's (1989b) argument that the risk of default is much lower than generally expected given the interest of all parties to achieve a successful workout and the support of financial innovations – a view that finds further empirical backing by Kaplan (1989) and Kaplan and Stein (1990). Their studies show that systematic risk of equity in leveraged buyouts is considerably smaller than predicted for large levels of financial leverage. Kaplan and Schoar (2004) therefore chose a similar approach when comparing private equity returns to public equity markets. Their influential study controls for "observable differences such as industry composition and stage of investment" (Kaplan & Schoar, 2004: 9) rather than fundamental financial indicators.[16] Based on this concept, the study borrows volatility indicators for private equity firms from public corporations with a comparable business mix and degree of diversification. The study hereby uses the average volatility indicators (β_i and σ_i) of the public corporations featured in the corporate sample of the study that match the business portfolio characteristics regarding industry mix and degree of diversification.

5.3 Empirical Results

By applying the methodology outlined above, the upcoming section highlights the empirical results of testing the seven hypotheses derived in Sect. 5.1. The section follows a structure consistent with the hypotheses, first testing the general performance comparison between private equity firms and public corporations. It then highlights the empirical findings of the relationship of diversification and performance in private equity settings and closes by contrasting private equity houses and public corporations in terms of the link between diversification and performance.

---

[15]The studies by Rosenberg and Guy (1976, 1995) use technical and fundamental indicators to predict the beta of individual firms. Both studies show that the strongest predictive power of a firm's business risk is associated with the industry mix and degree of diversification of the business portfolio as opposed to other fundamental characteristics such as capital structure, market capitalization, or earnings growth.

[16]The study by Kaplan and Schoar (2004) was based on a sample of venture capital and buyout firms. Their analysis therefore distinguishes different stages of investment. This distinction is not relevant for this research, which is focused on the leveraged buyout segment. Other studies such as Ick (2005) and Conroy and Harris (2007) use historical performance of private equity investments to measure risk. These studies however face substantial problems given the lack of continuous market information about private equity investments.

5.3.1 Performance: Private Equity vs. Public Corporations

The first two hypotheses are addressing the performance relationship between private equity firms and public corporations, "Hypothesis 1" dealing with the pure performance as reported by the individual firms, "Hypothesis 2" correcting the performance for differences in the associated risk profile and market environment.

5.3.1.1 Hypothesis 1

The first hypothesis states that the financial returns of private equity investments significantly outperform the holdings in public corporations. The descriptive statistics of the analysis are illustrated in Table 5.2.

The analysis of the two samples of 100 firms each reveals that the performance of PEs is substantially higher than in public corporations. In particular the 5-year performance figures of PEs more than double those of investments in public equity while still showing considerably higher performance in the 10-year investment horizon.

Interestingly, the range of performances shows strong similarities in the 5-year investment period between private equity investments and holdings in public corporations with a total span of 78% points in public equity and 76% points in

Table 5.2 Descriptive statistics H1: "Performance in private equity firms and public corporation"

		Private equity	Public corporations	Total
5-year performance	Number of firms	96	97	193
	Mean	0.1712	0.07	0.1204
	Median	0.173	0.065	0.121
	Std deviation	0.11832	0.14343	0.14067
	Variance	0.014	0.021	0.02
	Std error of mean	0.1208	0.01456	0.01013
	Min	−0.35	−0.32	−0.35
	Max	0.42	0.47	0.47
	Range	0.76	0.78	0.81
10-year performance	Number of firms	80	82	162
	Mean	0.1611	0.1207	0.1406
	Median	0.1575	0.1218	0.1332
	Std deviation	0.12836	0.07113	0.10508
	Variance	0.016	0.005	0.011
	Std error of mean	0.01435	0.00785	0.00826
	Min	−0.53	−0.06	−0.53
	Max	0.42	0.32	0.42
	Range	0.95	0.38	0.95

private equity. However, the range diverges substantially in the 10-year horizon; the analysis in public corporations reveals a range of 38% points from −6 to 32% while PE investments span from −53 to 42%, covering a total range of 95% points. The performance data thereby displays the increased risk associated with PE investments, which is moreover highlighted by the increased spread in variance and standard deviation between the two samples when comparing the 5-year and the 10-year investment horizon.

In order to test the above described performance comparison for its significance, the study employs an independent sample *t*-test as well as the Mann–Whitney *U* test respectively the Wilcoxon signed rank test as displayed in Table 5.3.

The independent sample *t*-test assesses the null hypothesis, that the means of the two samples are equal: H_0: $\mu_1 = \mu_2$. The *t*-statistics provide evidence, that the performance of the two samples are unequal on a 5% significance level; one can therefore reject the null hypothesis that the performance means of the two samples are equal for the 5-year and the 10-year investment period. For the 5-year performance analysis, the test also holds true on a 1% significance level and a 99% confidence interval, respectively, which is not displayed in Table 5.3.

The Mann–Whitney *U* test respectively the Wilcoxon signed rank test supports the above empirical finding. The Mann–Whitney test/the Wilcoxon signed rank test assesses whether the two sampled populations are equivalent in location. The observations from both groups are combined and ranked, with the average

Table 5.3 Significance tests H1: "Performance in private equity firms and public corporations"

		Private equity		Public corporations
5-year performance	• Mean	0.1712		0.07
	• Mean difference		−0.101	
	• *T*-statistic			
	– *t*-statistics equal variances assumed		−5.344[a]	
	– *t*-statistics equal variances not assumed		−5.349[b]	
	• Mann–Whitney *U* test			
	– Mean rank	119.44		74.79
	– Sum of ranks	11,466		7,255
	– Mann–Whitney *U*		2,502	
	– Wilcoxon *W*		7,255	
	– *Z*		−5,552	
	– Asymp. sig (two-tailed)		0	
10-year performance	• Mean	0.1611		0.1207
	• Mean difference		−0.040	
	• *T*-statistic			
	– *t*-statistics equal variances assumed		−2.489[c]	
	– *t*-statistics equal variances not assumed		−2.472[d]	
	• Mann–Whitney *U* test			
	– Mean rank	92.20		71.06
	– Sum of ranks	7,376		5,827
	– Mann–Whitney *U*		2,424	
	– Wilcoxon *W*		5,827	
	– *Z*		−2868	
	– Asymp. sig (two-tailed)		0.004	

[a]95% confidence interval −0.13856 to −0.06385; significance level 0.000
[b]95% confidence interval −0.13853 to −0.06388; significance level 0.000
[c]95% confidence interval −0.07254 to −0.00835; significance level 0.014
[d]95% confidence interval −0.0783 to −0.00806; significance level 0.015

rank assigned in the case of ties. The number of ties should be small relative to the total number of observations. If the populations are identical in location, the ranks should be randomly mixed between the two samples. The values outlined in Table 5.3 provide evidence that the two populations are in fact not in the same location. The test therefore supports the original hypothesis that the performance in private equity investments is significantly higher than the return of holdings in public equity.

Based on the descriptive statistics and the two statistical tests, one can conclude that the empirical study of the two samples supports "Hypothesis 1". The performance of investments in the population of private equity firms seems to be significantly higher than the performance of holdings in the population of public corporations. One however has to note the increased risk of long-term PE investments as indicated by the difference in variance observed in the 10-year investment horizon.

5.3.1.2 Hypothesis 2

The second hypothesis of this empirical study claims that private equity firms outperform public corporations even after adjusting for differences in the risk profile of the different firms in the sample and for controlling for the market environments of the investments. The study uses the above introduced risk-adjusted performance measure "Jensen's Alpha", "Sharpe's measure", and "Treynor's measure" for the analysis. Each of these measures gives the opportunity to correct the recorded performance for the different risk profiles of each investment. The descriptive statistics of this part of the empirical study are displayed in Table 5.4.

The descriptive statistics of the sample highlight the fact that private equity firms sustain the superior performance vs. public corporations seen in the empirical results of "Hypothesis 1" even after risk adjustments. Each of the indicators reveals higher performance measures on the side of PE investments, equally true for 5-year and 10-year investments.

Jensen's Alpha offers the opportunity to assess the outperformance of different investments compared to the market, including an adjustment for different industry risk profiles. The values determined for the selected samples clearly point to a higher performance by PE firms vs. public corporations. Although the spread between the performance measures is narrowing when extending the analysis period from 5 to 10 years, the test statistics in Table 5.5 portray a sound statistical evidence for a performance premium in PE investments. The results of the t-test as well as the findings of the Mann–Whitney *U* test respectively the Wilcoxon signed rank test can be drawn on to reject the null hypothesis that the means of Jensen's Alpha between the two samples are equal (H_0: $\mu_1 = \mu_2$). There is statistical evidence that "Hypothesis 2", stating a higher performance of PE investments vs. holdings in public corporations, can be supported. The above-noted increased variance, in this case measured by standard deviation, of PE performance results and the substantial

Table 5.4 Descriptive statistics H2: "risk-adjusted performance in private equity firms and public corporations"

		Private equity	Public corporations	Total
5-year performance	Number of firms	96	97	193
	Jensen's Alpha			
	• Mean	0.0892	−0.0157	0.0365
	• Median	0.1003	−0.0081	0.0407
	• Std deviation	0.11658	0.15163	0.14488
	• Range	0.79	0.83	0.83
	Sharpe's ratio			
	• Mean	0.0058	0.0019	0.0038
	• Median	0.006	0.0014	0.004
	• Std deviation	0.00504	0.00569	0.00571
	• Range	0.03	0.03	0.03
	Treynor's ratio			
	• Mean	0.1456	0.0657	0.1054
	• Median	0.1476	0.0494	0.0977
	• Std deviation	0.13121	0.16412	0.16597
	• Range	0.78	0.93	0.98
10-year performance	Number of firms	80	82	162
	Jensen's Alpha			
	• Mean	0.0569	0.0114	0.0338
	• Median	0.0622	0.0204	0.0317
	• Std deviation	0.12389	0.07959	0.10601
	• Range	0.97	0.4	0.97
	Sharpe's ratio			
	• Mean	0.0049	0.0035	0.0042
	• Median	0.0048	0.0035	0.0041
	• Std deviation	0.00532	0.00329	0.00445
	• Range	0.04	0.02	0.04
	Treynor's ratio			
	• Mean	0.124	0.1038	0.1138
	• Median	0.1292	0.08	0.1075
	• Std deviation	0.12872	0.11274	0.12094
	• Range	0.97	0.62	0.99

decrease in the measures of public corporations find additional support in the descriptive statistics of Jensen's Alpha.

The additional risk-adjusted indicators, Sharpe's measure and Treynor's measure, provide consistent indications with Jensen's Alpha as shown in Table 5.4. Sharpe's ratio, which puts firm performance in relationship with the overall volatility of an investment, shows a statistically significant performance premium in private equity investments; the relevant statistical indicators of the *t*-statistics and the Mann–Whitney *U* test/Wilcoxon signed rank test are displayed in Table 5.6.

Similar results are achieved when using Treynor's ratio, which uses systematic risk to calibrate performance figures. The significance tests presented in Table 5.7 give further support for the hypothesis that there is a significant difference in performance between the two samples and the underlying population, respectively.

The empirical evidence presented in the descriptive statistics in connection with the above displayed statistical tests supports "Hypothesis 2" along all three risk-adjusted performance indicators. private equity investments seem to show a stronger performance than public equity holdings even after adjusting the investments for diverging industry risk profiles and market environments.

Table 5.5 Significance tests H2: "Jensen's Alpha in private equity firms and public corporations"

		Private equity		Public corporations
5-year performance	• Mean	0.0892		−0.0157
	• Mean difference		−0.105	
	• *T*-statistic			
	– *t*-statistics equal variances assumed		−5.386[a]	
	– *t*-statistics equal variances not assumed		−5.393[b]	
	• Mann–Whitney *U* test			
	– Mean rank	119.24		74.99
	– Sum of ranks	11,447		7,274
	– Mann–Whitney *U*		2,521	
	– Wilcoxon *W*		7,274	
	– *Z*		−5,503	
	– Asymp. sig (two-tailed)		0	
10-year performance	• Mean	0.0569		0.0114
	• Mean difference		−0.045	
	• *T*-statistic			
	– *t*-statistics equal variances assumed		−2.787[c]	
	– *t*-statistics equal variances not assumed		−2.772[d]	
	• Mann–Whitney *U* test			
	– Mean rank	93.68		69.62
	– Sum of ranks	7,494		5,709
	– Mann–Whitney *U*		2,306	
	– Wilcoxon *W*		5,709	
	– *Z*		−3.263	
	– Asymp. sig (two-tailed)		0.001	

[a]95% confidence interval −0.14338 to −0.06652; significance level 0.000 [b]95% confidence interval −0.14334 to −0.06655; significance level 0.000

[c]95% confidence interval −0.07771 to −0.01325; significance level 0.006 [d]95% confidence interval −0.07793 to −0.01303; significance level 0.006

Table 5.6 Significance test H2: "Sharpe measure in private equity firms and public corporations"

		Private equity		Public corporations
5-year performance	• Mean	0.0058		0.0019
	• Mean difference		−0.004	
	• *T*-statistic			
	– *t*-statistics equal variances assumed		−5.052[a]	
	– *t*-statistics equal variances not assumed		−5.056[b]	
	• Mann–Whitney *U* test			
	– Mean rank	117.73		76.48
	– Sum of ranks	11,302		7,419
	– Mann–Whitney *U*		2,666	
	– Wilcoxon *W*		7,419	
	– *Z*		−5,129	
	– Asymp. sig (two-tailed)		0	
10-year performance	• Mean	0.0049		0.0035
	• Mean difference		−0.001	
	• *T*-statistic			
	– *t*-statistics equal variances assumed		−1.995[c]	
	– *t*-statistics equal variances not assumed		−1.984[d]	
	• Mann–Whitney *U* test			
	– Mean rank	90.19		73.02
	– Sum of ranks	7,215		5,988
	– Mann–Whitney *U*		2,585	
	– Wilcoxon *W*		5,988	
	– *Z*		2,328	
	– Asymp. sig (two-tailed)		0.02	

[a]95% confidence interval −0.00543 to −0.00238; significance level 0.005 [b]95% confidence interval −0.00543 to −0.00238; significance level 0.000

[c]95% confidence interval −0.00275 to −0.00001; significance level 0.048 [d]95% confidence interval −0.00276 to 0; significance level 0.049

Table 5.7 Significance tests H2: "Treynor measure in private equity firms and public corporations"

		Private equity		Public corporations
5-year performance	• Mean	0.1456		0.0657
	• Mean difference		−0.080	
	• *T*-statistic			
	– *t*-statistics equal variances assumed		−3.733[a]	
	– *t*-statistics equal variances not assumed		−3.737[b]	
	• Mann–Whitney *U* test			
	– Mean rank	115.91		78.29
	– Sum of ranks	11,127		7,594
	– Mann–Whitney *U*		2,841	
	– Wilcoxon *W*		7,594	
	– *Z*		−4,678	
	– Asymp. sig (two-tailed)		0	
10-year performance	• Mean	0.1240		0.1038
	• Mean difference		−0.020	
	• *T*-statistic			
	– *t*-statistics equal variances assumed		−1.063[c]	
	– *t*-statistics equal variances not assumed		−1.061[d]	
	• Mann–Whitney *U* test			
	– Mean rank	87.98		75.18
	– Sum of ranks	7,038		6,165
	– Mann–Whitney *U*		2,762	
	– Wilcoxon *W*		6,165	
	– Z		−1,738	
	– Asymp. sig (two-tailed)		0.083	

[a]95% confidence interval −0.12210 to −0.03767; 0.000 significance level
[b]95% confidence interval −0.12206 to −0.03771; significance level 0.000
[c]95% confidence interval −0.05771 to 0.01733; 0.289 significance level
[d]95% confidence interval −0.05778 to 0.01739; significance level 0.290

5.3.2 *Diversification and Performance in Private Equity*

After characterizing the general performance differential between private equity and public equity investments, this section addresses the relationship between diversification and performance in the private equity industry only. "Hypothesis 3" focuses on the different modes of diversification while "Hypothesis 4" is directed towards the link between diversification and performance.

5.3.2.1 Hypothesis 3

Private equity firms are characterized by high degrees of diversification as illustrated in the descriptive statistics of the private equity sample on Table 5.8. The private equity firms in the sample are – on average – invested in close to nine different industry segments (N) and over six different industry groups (M).[17]

The Herfindahl index (H), which measures the total degree of diversification, can take values from "0" to "1", whereby "1" characterizes an entirely focused firm

[17] Industry segments are measured on the four-digit SIC code level; industry groups are assessed on the two-digit SIC code level. The characteristics of the SIC code method are highlighted in Sect. 5.2.2 "Diversification Measures".

Table 5.8 Descriptive statistics H3: "diversification in private equity"

	M	N	H	DT	DR	DU
Number of firms	100	100	100	100	100	100
Mean	6.2100	8.7300	0.2465	1.7675	0.3624	1.4051
Median	7.0000	10.0000	0.1735	1.9774	0.2878	1.5474
Standard deviation	2.0807	2.5539	0.1851	0.5452	0.2742	0.5221
Variance	4.3290	6.5220	0.0340	0.2970	0.0750	0.2730
Standard error of mean	0.2081	0.2554	0.0185	0.0545	0.0274	0.0522
Minimum	1.00	1.00	0.10	0.00	0.00	0.00
Maximum	10.00	10.00	1.00	2.29	1.09	2.12

Note: *H*: Herfindahl index; DT: total diversification; DR: related diversification; DU: unrelated diversification; *M*: number of industry groups; *N*: number of industry segments

with 100% of its business stemming from one investment. The private equity sample of this study bears a Herfindahl index of 0.2465, indicating a high degree of diversification. This finding is further supported by the total degree of diversification (DT) assessed by the Entropy measure which averages at 1.7675 and can be differentiated in related diversification (DR) and unrelated diversification (DU). The total diversification is largely driven by unrelated diversified firms, which account for 1.4051 index points, related diversification closes the gap to the total degree of diversification with only 0.3624 points.

In order to assess "Hypothesis 3", the sample of PE firms is distinguished by the mode of diversification the firms follow. As highlighted in Table 5.9, the sample can be segmented by the degree of related and unrelated diversification to form a four-field matrix as applied by Palepu (1985) in his influential study to determine the usefulness of the entropy measure. Two approaches are at hand to construct this segmentation, one splitting the portfolio in equal sizes, the other applying equal ranges to the degree of relatedness and the degree of unrelatedness (De, 1992).

Firms in the first quadrant show a relatively high degree of related diversification (0.66 in equal size portfolios/0.74 in equal range portfolios) with at the same time lower unrelated diversification (1.05/0.96). The average number of industry groups (5.00/4.74) is slightly lower than in the overall sample; the number of industry segments (8.74/8.61) remains nearly unchanged to the figure in the overall sample. The second quadrant is marked by firms that follow both high related and unrelated diversification. The total level of diversification is the highest within these firms (H 0.12/0.13; DT 2.20/2.17). Firms in the third quadrant are highly unrelated diversified (1.85/1.82); however, these PE players show only limited signs of relatedness (0.18/0.19). Firms in this part of the sample consequently have an above-average number of industry groups (7.77/7.76) in their portfolios. The fourth quadrant ultimately contains firms

Table 5.9 Diversification in private equity H3: – modes of diversification

Measured in means

Degree of relatedness (DR)		Equal size portfolios: Low DU	Equal size portfolios: High DU	Equal range portfolios: Low DU	Equal range portfolios: High DU
High	*n*	31	19	23	20
	H	0.25	0.12	0.25	0.13
	DT	1.71	2.20	1.70	2.17
	DR	0.66	0.45	0.74	0.49
	DU	1.05	1.75	0.96	1.69
	M	5.00	6.89	4.74	6.65
	N	8.74	10.00	8.61	10.00
Low	*n*	19	31	20	37
	H	0.50	0.16	0.51	0.17
	DT	1.01	2.03	1.00	2.00
	DR	0.09	0.18	0.12	0.19
	DU	0.92	1.85	0.88	1.82
	M	4.95	7.77	4.60	7.76
	N	6.05	9.58	5.95	9.62

Columns: Low / High = Degree of unrelatedness (DU)

Note: *H*: Herfindahl index; DT: total diversification; DR: related diversification; DU: unrelated diversification; *M*: number of industry groups; *N*: number of industry segments; *n*: number of firms

with low levels of unrelated and related diversification. They moreover reveal the lowest level of overall diversification (H 0.50/0.51; DT 1.01/1.00).

In addition to the above presented statistical evidence, the analysis presented in Table 5.10 provides a comparison of unrelated and related diversification in private equity firms. The index of unrelated diversification proves to be significantly larger than the measure of related diversification. With the results of the correlation analysis as well as the paired samples *t*-test, one can reject the null hypothesis stating that unrelated and related diversification play an equal role in PE settings (H_0: DU=DR).

The data regarding diversification in private equity firms provides clear evidence that PE firms have larger degrees of unrelated diversification than related diversification. The majority of PE players therefore have investments, which are not devoted to businesses related to a pre-dominant industry focus but spread across various industry groups.

5.3.2.2 Hypothesis 4

Knowing that unrelated diversification plays a dominating role in private equity investment portfolios, the interesting question is the effect of such high levels of unrelated diversification on performance.

Building on the sample segmentation into diversification portfolios of equal size and equal range introduced in "Hypothesis 3", one can calculate the performance

Table 5.10 Comparison related and unrelated diversification H3: "diversification in private equity"

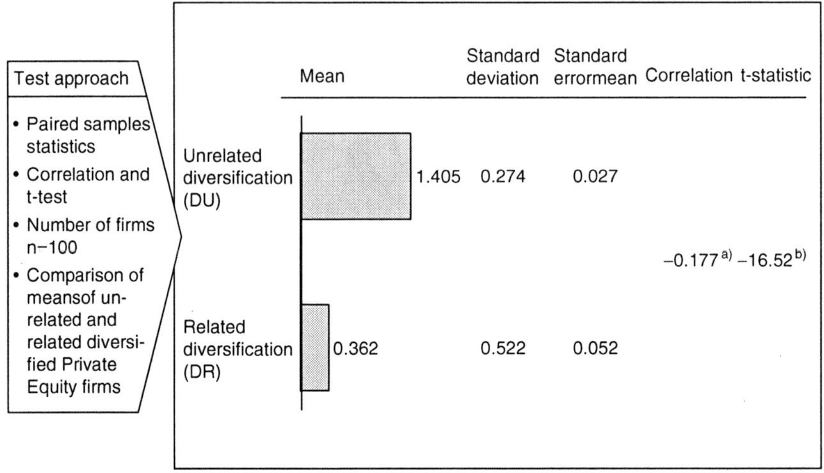

Test approach
- Paired samples statistics
- Correlation and t-test
- Number of firms n–100
- Comparison of meansof un-related and related diversi-fied Private Equity firms

	Mean	Standard deviation	Standard errormean	Correlation	t-statistic
Unrelated diversification (DU)	1.405	0.274	0.027	−0.177 [a)]	−16.52 [b)]
Related diversification (DR)	0.362	0.522	0.052		

[a]Significance: 0.079

[b]95% confidence interval: −1.1675 to −0.9174; df 99; significance level 0.000

measures for each diversification cluster. The analysis uses performance metrics consistent with the statistics presented in "Hypothesis 1" and "Hypothesis 2": Internal rate of return (IRR) for performance before risk adjustments and Jensen's Alpha (α), Sharpe's measure (S) and Treynor's measure (*T*) for risk-adjusted performance.

Table 5.11 presents the performance of PE investments on a 5-year time horizon. Independent of the way the portfolio is cut, firms with a high degree of related diversification and relatively low degrees of unrelated diversification show the highest performance of all investment portfolios. Firms with investments focused around a limited amount of industry groups outperformed those with investments spread across unrelated businesses along all performance indicators.

The 10-year view provided in Table 5.12 draws a comparable picture. Firms with low degrees of unrelated diversification show the strongest performance; however, the relationship between low and high degrees of unrelated diversification is ambiguous between the equal size and the equal range portfolio analysis. Within the equal size portfolio, firms, which are focused on limited investments and, thereby, have low degrees of related and unrelated diversification, have the strongest overall performance. In equal range portfolios, PEs with high-relatedness and low-unrelatedness in their investment portfolios outperform all other modes of diversification across the full range of performance measures.

Narrowing the statistical analysis to the two portfolios most relevant for testing the hypothesis, Tables 5.13 and 5.14 provide statistical results comparing the portfolio

Table 5.11 Diversification and performance in private equity H4: – modes of diversification (5-year)

Measured in means of 5-year performance indicators

Degree of relatedness (DR)	Equal size portfolios: Degree of unrelatedness (DU) Low	Equal size portfolios: Degree of unrelatedness (DU) High	Equal range portfolios: Degree of unrelatedness (DU) Low	Equal range portfolios: Degree of unrelatedness (DU) High
High	n : 30 IRR : 0.19 α : 0.10 S : 0.006 T : 0.16	n : 19 IRR : 0.16 α : 0.09 S : 0.005 T : 0.14	n : 22 IRR : 0.20 α : 0.12 S : 0.007 T : 0.17	n : 20 IRR : 0.17 α : 0.09 S : 0.006 T : 0.15
Low	n : 16 IRR : 0.18 α : 0.09 S : 0.006 T : 0.14	n : 31 IRR : 0.16 α : 0.08 S : 0.005 T : 0.14	n : 18 IRR : 0.15 α : 0.06 S : 0.004 T : 0.11	n : 36 IRR : 0.16 α : 0.08 S : 0.006 T : 0.15

NOTE: n: number of firms; IRR: Internal rate of return; α: Jensen's Alpha, S: Sharpe's measure; T: Treynor's measure

Table 5.12 Diversification and performance in private equity H4: – modes of diversification (10-year)

Measured in means of 10-year performance indicators

Degree of relatedness (DR)	Equal size portfolios: Degree of unrelatedness (DU) Low	Equal size portfolios: Degree of unrelatedness (DU) High	Equal range portfolios: Degree of unrelatedness (DU) Low	Equal range portfolios: Degree of unrelatedness (DU) High
High	n : 26 IRR : 0.17 α : 0.07 S : 0.005 T : 0.13	n : 16 IRR : 0.14 α : 0.04 S : 0.004 T : 0.11	n : 18 IRR : 0.19 α : 0.09 S : 0.006 T : 0.15	n : 18 IRR : 0.16 α : 0.06 S : 0.005 T : 0.13
Low	n : 13 IRR : 0.20 α : 0.08 S : 0.006 T : 0.11	n : 25 IRR : 0.14 α : 0.04 S : 0.004 T : 0.10	n : 15 IRR : 0.14 α : 0.03 S : 0.004 T : 0.09	n : 29 IRR : 0.15 α : 0.05 S : 0.005 T : 0.12

NOTE: n: number of firms; IRR: Internal rate of return; α: Jensen's Alpha, S: Sharpe's measure; T: Treynor's measure

Table 5.13 Significance tests H4: "diversification and performance in private equity" (5-years)

t-statistics with equal variances assumed; 95% confidence interval; based on 5-year performance indicators

		Equal size portfolios		Equal range portfolios	
		High DR – low DU	Low DR – high DU	High DR – low DU	Low DR – high DU
	n	30	31	22	36
Performance (IRR)	Mean	0.19	0.16	0.20	0.16
	t	1.011		1.529	
	Mean difference	0.032		0.040	
	Confidence interval	−0.029 to 0.090		−0.010 to 0.089	
Jensen's Alpha	Mean	0.10	0.08	0.12	0.08
	t	0.770		1.418	
	Mean difference	0.023		0.036	
	Confidence interval	−0.037 to 0.082		−0.014 to 0.086	
Sharpe measure	Mean	0.006	0.005	0.007	0.006
	t	0.794		1.305	
	Mean difference	0.001		0.001	
	Confidence interval	−0.002 to 0.004		−0.001 to 0.004	
Treynor measure	Mean	0.16	0.14	0.17	0.15
	t	0.394		0.901	
	Mean difference	0.012		0.027	
	Confidence interval	−0.050 to 0.075		−0.031 to 0.084	

*Significant at 0.10 level (two tailed) **Significant at 0.05 level (two tailed) ***Significant at 0.01 level (two tailed)

Table 5.14 Significance tests H4: "diversification and performance in private equity" (10-years)

t-statistics with equal variances assumed; 95% confidence interval; based on 10-year performance indicators

		Equal size portfolios		Equal range portfolios	
		High DR – low DU	Low DR – high DU	High DR – low DU	Low DR – high DU
	n	26	25	18	29
Performance (IRR)	Mean	0.17	0.14	0.20	0.15
	t	0.768		1.591*	
	Mean difference	0.030		0.049	
	Confidence interval	−0.049 to 0.110		−0.017 to 0.116	
Jensen's Alpha	Mean	0.07	0.04	0.09	0.05
	t	0.543		1.482	
	Mean difference	0.021		0.044	
	Confidence interval	−0.057 to 0.099		−0.021 to 0.109	
Sharpe measure	Mean	0.005	0.004	0.006	0.005
	t	0.645		1.368	
	Mean difference	0.001		0.002	
	Confidence interval	−0.002 to 0.004		−0.001 to 0.005	
Treynor measure	Mean	0.13	0.11	0.15	0.12
	t	0.425		1.093	
	Mean difference	0.017		0.037	
	Confidence interval	−0.061 to 0.094		−0.035 to 0.108	

*Significant at 0.10 level (two tailed) ** Significant at 0.05 level (two tailed) *** Significant at 0.01 level (two tailed)

with high relatedness and low unrelatedness (high DR – low DU) and the portfolio with low relatedness and high unrelatedness (low DR – high DU).

The results of the *t*-test for the 5-year time horizon (presented in Table 5.13) and the 10-year horizon (presented in Table 5.14) indicate that one cannot reject the null hypothesis, which is stating equality in performance between the two selected modes of diversification for each performance measure (H_0: $performance_{HighDR\text{-}LowDU} = performance_{LowDR\text{-}HighDU}$). Even though not statistically significant, the unrelated diversified PE firms have not been dominating the related diversifiers unlike initially proposed. In fact, data reveals a contrary relationship between performance and diversification. Firms with a high degree of relatedness and a low degree of unrelatedness in their investment portfolios seem to outperform unrelated diversifiers across all performance measures.

Comparing the results of the 5-year and the 10-year investment analysis, one can draw two conclusions. First, the performance in both portfolios decreased from the 5-year investment horizon to the 10-year horizon, consistent across all performance indicators before and after risk adjustments. The performance of the PE portfolios therefore seems to go in line with the general performance trend observed in "Hypothesis 1" and "Hypothesis 2" without being affected by the firms' mode of diversification. Second however, the spread between the performance of related diversifiers and unrelated diversifiers remained relatively unchanged from the 5-year to the 10-year investment horizon. The effect of diversification accordingly appears to be consistent along time although being exposed to varying economic conditions.

Investigating the sources of differences in private equity performance, Fig. 5.2 provides an overview of the portfolio companies' industry classification along the identified diversification cluster.

The analysis clusters the industry categorization of individual portfolio companies on the two-digit SIC code level into broader industry clusters. Although there are no strong industry patterns visible, diversification cluster with superior performance – before and after adjusting for different risk profiles – are characterized by a relatively higher share of investments in industries related to growth and technology such as communication, information technology, and substantial parts of the media business.[18] These businesses typically are associated with elevated growth expectations. Private equity firms with a higher ratio of unrelated investments and according to the above presented analysis weaker performance, on the other hand, appear to have a larger share of their investments in more mature markets such as consumer products or basic materials.

The analysis of variance presented in Fig. 5.3 reveals additional information about the sources of outperformance of related diversifiers. The analysis reveals that the strong performance of high DR – low DU firms is mostly driven by a large

[18]According to modern financial theory, risk adjustments should convert superior performance in selected equities back to the mean after adjusting for different risk profiles. However, data in this analysis shows that investments in high growth industries seem to outperform investments with a stronger focus on mature markets – even after adjusting for different risk profiles

H4: INDUSTRY ANALYSIS

Percent; equal size portfolios; 5-year performance measures

	High DR - Low DU	Low DR - Low DU	High DR - High DU	Low DR - High DU
	100	100	100	100
Basic Materials	5	4	8	13
Communication	11	9	5	3
Consumer Products	11	9	14	19
Financial Services	7	11	6	8
Information Technology	26	22	18	15
Manufacturing	8	12	21	15
Media	13	7	4	5
Pharma	10	4	7	6
Other*	9	22	17	16
IRR	0.19	0.18	0.16	0.16
Jensen's Alpha	0.10	0.9	0.09	0.08
Sharpe's measure	0.006	0.006	0.005	0.005
Treynor's measure	0.16	0.14	0.14	0.14

*Includes utilities, transportation, construction, and various service industries

Fig. 5.2 Industry analysis – modes of diversification

H4: ANALYSIS OF VARIANCE

Percent; equal size portfolios; performance before risk adjustmenst; 5-year IRR

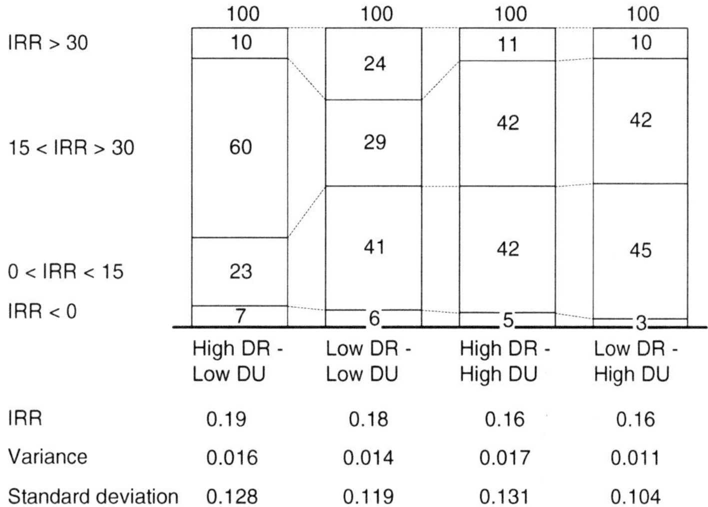

Fig. 5.3 Analysis of variance – modes of diversification

base of firms with a solid performance between 15 and 30%, not by a selected number of firms with an extraordinary performance.

The lower performance of firms in the remaining diversification clusters is mostly driven by a larger share of firms in the performance range of 0–15% with generally lower variance of performance.

Measuring diversification in terms of number of industry groups presents comparable findings. Table 5.15 puts performance in a relationship with number of industry groups.[19] The analysis shows, that firms with an average number of four to five industry groups show the highest performance levels, in particular in the 10-year investment horizon. Less diversified or more diversified players do not achieve these performance levels, even though highly diversified firms show a strong average performance in a mid-term investment horizon but appear to lose their competitive position for the 10-year investment period.

To gain a better understanding of the related diversified cluster, Tables 5.16 and 5.17 offer a deep dive into the cluster high DR – low DU. One could argue that relatedness is a function of size and that larger private equity firms naturally grow into a more related diversified portfolio while smaller firms are less related. One could moreover argue that performance is mostly driven by those large private equity players, which are able to create relatedness within large, diversified investment

Table 5.15 Performance and number of industry groups

Measured in means

		1 – 3	4 – 5	6 – 7	8+
5-year performance	IRR	0.16	0.19	0.16	0.18
	Jensen's Alpha	0.07	0.11	0.07	0.10
	Sharpe measure	0.005	0.006	0.005	0.006
	Treynor measure	0.11	0.15	0.13	0.17
	n	11	16	40	29
10-year performance	IRR	0.14	0.21	0.15	0.16
	Jensen's Alpha	0.04	0.11	0.04	0.06
	Sharpe measure	0.004	0.007	0.004	0.005
	Treynor measure	0.09	0.17	0.11	0.13
	n	9	13	37	21

[19] Industry groups are measured on the two-digit SIC code level.

Table 5.16 Deep dive related diversified private equity firms – portfolio size

Measured in means; equal range portfolios, $n = 23$

		Large players[a]	Small players[b]
5-year Performance	IRR	0.21	0.20
	Jensen's Alpha	0.14	0.11
	Sharpe measure	0.008	0.007
	Treynor measure	0.20	0.15
10-year Performance	IRR	0.20	0.20
	Jensen's Alpha	0.09	0.09
	Sharpe measure	0.006	0.007
	Treynor measure	0.16	0.15
Diversification	Herfindahl	0.19	0.30
	DT	1.94	1.52
	DR	0.82 (42% of DT)	0.68 (45% of DT)
	DU	1.12 (58% of DT)	0.84 (55% of DT)

[a]Committed equity > 5 billion [b]Committed equity < 5 billion

Table 5.17 Deep dive related diversified private equity firms – number of industry groups

Measured in means; high DR – low DU cluster based on equal range portfolios

		1 – 3	4 – 5	6 –7	8+
5-year performance	IRR	0.17	0.22	0.19	0.21
	Jensen's Alpha	0.08	0.14	0.11	0.13
	Sharpe measure	0.006	0.008	0.007	0.007
	Treynor measure	0.14	0.18	0.18	0.16
	n	3	11	7	1
10-year performance	IRR	0.10	0.28	0.14	0.20
	Jensen's Alpha	–0.01	0.18	0.04	0.10
	Sharpe measure	0.002	0.010	0.004	0.006
	Treynor measure	0.05	0.24	0.09	0.15
	n	3	8	6	1

portfolios with balanced industry risk profiles. The analysis in Table 5.16 however reveals that the difference in the 5-year and 10-year performance between larger and small players is very small.[20] The absolute diversification level of large private equity firms is higher than in small players; the relative distribution of the related and the unrelated measure is however comparable indicating a similar relevance of relatedness in both size categories.

Table 5.17 presents the relationship of number of industry groups and performance within the high DR – low DU segment. The analysis reveals that, in accordance with the full sample analysis, firms with an average of four to five industry groups show the highest performance indicators. These firms are able to achieve relatedness with a limited number of industry groups while maintaining a level of diversification to overcome high correlations of performance with individual industries.

The above-presented cluster analysis is able to provide valuable insights about phenomena observed in a number of companies with similar characteristics. Consistent with the approach of the De (1992), the cluster analysis can be supplemented by a multivariate analysis based on the individual firm level. Multivariate data analysis allows the discussion of the impact and magnitude of influence of varying factors; the analysis relies on dependent, independent, and control variables.

The multivariate analysis uses the above-introduced performance figures IRR, Jensen's Alpha, Sharpe measure and Treynor measure as dependent variable and the diversification measures Herfindahl index and Entropy measure as independent variables. In addition to these variables, the study introduces three control variables, which represent further characteristics of the private equity firm. The following control variables are included in the multivariate analysis.

(1) *Size of investment portfolio*. The size of the investment portfolio is measured by the value of the companies in the firm's investment portfolio. One has to consider a positive impact of portfolio size on the professionalism of private equity firms in managing investments and in managing diversification as indicated by prior studies (e.g. see Ljungqvist & Richardson, 2003a; Schmidt, 2004; Weidig & Mathonet, 2004).
(2) *Number of funds*. The number of funds counts the number of investment vehicles a PE firm is currently actively managing. Liquidated funds are excluded from this analysis.[21] The number of funds can impact the performance of PE investments in different ways. An increasing number of funds can potentially impose organizational and legal boundaries to the portfolio that limit parenting activities such as portfolio management and leverage of competences and resources. At the same time, a larger number of funds can increase the active parenting in

[20]Statistical comparison of the two sub-samples does not allow a rejection of the null hypothesis of equal means.

[21]Excluding liquidated funds guarantees that the variable "number of funds" is not a mediator variable for measuring the experience of private equity professionals. Experience will be assessed using the lifetime of a firm since the year of vintage of a firm's first fund.

such fields as specialized resources or active governance if funds each are specialized in particular industries.[22]

(3) *First year of vintage*. The first year of vintage is determined by the oldest fund of a private equity firm, independent of the fact whether the fund is active or liquidated. The first year of vintage is a way to measure the experience of the PE firm. One can expect a higher performance in experienced private equity firms (e.g. see Gottschalg & Meier, 2005; Loos, 2005).

The control variables "portfolio size", "number of funds", and "first year of vintage" have been selected for the fact that all three are likely to contain a strong relationship with the performance of a private equity firm while at the same time being measurable from the dataset underlying this study. Moreover, the control variables "portfolio size" and "first year of vintage" have shown a significant influence on private equity performance in prior academic contributions as outlined above and should therefore not be neglected in this study.

The multivariate analysis uses a linear regression model. The variables used in the different models of the regression analysis are contained in the correlation matrices of Table 5.18 for 5-year performance figures and Table 5.19 for 10-year performance figures.

Table 5.18 Correlation matrix "diversification and performance in private equity" (5-year)

5-year performance, Pearson correlation, two-tailed

	(1)	(2)	(3)	(4)	(5)	(6)	(7)	(8)	(9)	(10)	(11)
Herfindahl	1										
DT (2)	−0.960**	1									
DR (3)	−0.333**	0.334**	1								
DU (4)	−0.827**	0.869**	0.177	1							
Portfolio size (5)	−0.165	0.208*	0.182	0.121	1						
Number of funds (6)	−0.179	0.190	0.260**	0.062	0.461**	1					
First year of vintage (7)	0.285**	−0.313**	−0.296**	−0.171	−0.286**	−0.581**	1				
IRR (8)	−0.178	0.143	0.130	0.080	0.258*	0.213*	−0.204*	1			
Jensen's Alpha (9)	−0.195	0.160	0.135	0.095	0.245*	0.216*	−0.226*	0.989**	1		
Sharpe measure (10)	−0.189	0.149	0.124	0.089	0.233*	0.223*	−0.189	0.976**	0.979**	1	
Treynor measure (11)	−0.234*	0.207*	0.126	0.149	0.220*	0.250*	−0.233*	0.877**	0.907**	0.920**	1

* Correlation is significant at 0.05 level (two tailed) ** Correlation is significant at 0.01 level (two tailed)

[22] Given the setup of former private equity studies, information about the influence of number of funds has not been subject for research. Prior studies typically evaluated private equity questions either on a transaction or a fund level instead of addressing the private equity firm as a larger entity.

Table 5.19 Correlation matrix "diversification and performance in private equity" (10-year)

10-year performance, Pearson correlation, two-tailed

	(1)	(2)	(3)	(4)	(5)	(6)	(7)	(8)	(9)	(10)	(11)
Herfindahl	1										
DT (2)	−0.960**	1									
DR (3)	−0.333**	0.334**	1								
DU (4)	−0.827**	0.869**	0.177	1							
Portfolio size (5)	−0.165	0.208*	0.182	0.121	1						
Number of funds (6)	−0.179	0.190	0.260**	0.062	0.461**	1					
First year of vintage (7)	0.285**	−0.313**	−0.296**	−0.171	−0.286**	−0.581**	1				
IRR(8)	−0.063	0.059	0.161	−0.020	0.197	0.117	−0.262*	1			
Jensen's Alpha (9)	−0.098	0.093	0.172	0.009	0.179	0.130	−0.293**	0.988**	1		
Sharpe measure (10)	−0.081	0.072	0.168	−0.011	0.166	0.117	−0.241*	0.981**	0.988**	1	
Treynormeasure (11)	−0.112	0.115	0.170	0.033	0.122	0.124	−0.256*	0.920**	0.950**	0.946**	1

* Correlation is significant at 0.05 level (two tailed) ** Correlation is significant at 0.01 level (two tailed)

The correlation analysis for 5-year performance indices in Table 5.18 provides valuable insights about the influencing factors of private equity performance. Diversification by itself is perceived positive, indicated by a negative relationship in Herfindahl (1) and a positive association of the total diversification measure DT (2) of the Entropy index.[23] In addition, one can note that related diversification DR (3) has a stronger positive influence on performance than unrelated diversification DU (4). This relationship becomes even more obvious in Table 5.19, which displays 10-year performance numbers. In this case, there is a strong positive association of the related diversification measure but a negative or almost neutral influence of the unrelated diversification measure. These findings provide evidence supporting the positive relationship between related diversification and private equity performance established above. The results however are not statistically significant on a 1 or 5% significance level.

Beyond the performance-diversification relationship, there is a substantial amount of additional insight available in the correlation analysis. Both, 5-year and 10-year performance figures are positively affected by the portfolio size, the number of funds, and the experience of the private equity firms with varying

[23] The Herfindahl index reflects low diversification in a number close to "1" and high diversification in a number close to "0". A negative correlation of Herfindahl and performance therefore shows that increasing diversification leads to increasing performance figures.

significance levels.[24] This observation holds for the 5-year and 10-year investment horizon.

The transformation of the correlation analysis into a regression model provides the opportunity to explain the relationships and interdependences within different explanatory variables and their impact on the dependent variable (Dielman, 1991: 130). The results of the regression analysis are presented in Tables 5.20–5.23 using the different performance measures applied in the study as dependent variables.

Within each regression analysis, a different model is employed to assess the effect of the dependent variables on performance. Models (1)–(3) use the Herfindahl index (*H*) as diversification measure whereas models (4)–(6) are based on the Entropy measures for related diversification (DR) and unrelated diversification (DU). The models include varying independent variables to investigate the impact of individual components on the dependent variable.

The regression analyses substantiate some of the evidence presented above. The presence of diversification measured by the Herfindahl index has positive or neutral

Table 5.20 Regression analysis "diversification and performance in private equity" (IRR)

Performance measure internal rate of return (IRR)

	5-year performance						10-year performance					
Independent variables	(1)	(2)	(3)	(4)	(5)	(6)	(1)	(2)	(3)	(4)	(5)	(6)
H	−0.178*	−0.143	−0.118				−0.003	−0.036	−0.033			
DR				0.151*	0.105	0.070				0.162	0.130	0.060
DU				0.108	0.076	0.061				0.008	−0.190	−0.064
Portfolio size		0.237**	0.191*		0.233**	0.191*		0.192*	0.177		0.179	0.179
Number of funds			0.057			0.054			−0.084			−0.096
First year of vintage			−0.093			−0.098			−0.274**			−0.258*
n	96	96	96	96	96	96	80	80	80	80	80	80
R^2	0.032	0.087	0.102	0.028	0.080	0.095	0.004	0.040	0.095	0.026	0.057	0.102

* Significant at 0.10 level (two tailed) ** Significant at 0.05 level (two tailed) *** Significant at 0.01 level (two tailed)

[24] Portfolio size and number of funds are positively correlated with all performance indices, first year of vintage is negatively correlated with all performance measure; experience can be assessed by calculating 1-(first year of vintage), which would lead to a positive correlation of experience and performance.

Table 5.21 Regression analysis "diversification and performance in private equity" (Jensen's Alpha)

Independent variables	5-year performance (1)	(2)	(3)	(4)	(5)	(6)	10-year performance (1)	(2)	(3)	(4)	(5)	(6)
H	−0.195*	−0.163*	−0.133				−0.098	−0.074	0.003			
DR				0.158*	0.116	0.074				0.179*	0.152	0.071
DU				0.129	0.095	0.076				0.040	0.018	−0.032
Portfolio size		0.221**	0.174		0.216**	0.170		0. 168	0.144		0.153	0.144
Number of funds			0.051			0.369			−0.073			−0.084
First year of vintage			−0.121			−1.017			−0.297**			−0.282**
n	96	96	96	96	96	96	80	80	80	80	80	80
R^2	0.038	0.086	0.106	0.033	0.078	0.098	0.010	0.037	0.103	0.031	0.054	0.109

*Significant at 0.10 level (two tailed) ** Significantat 0.05 level(two tailed) *** Significant at 0.01 level (two tailed)

Table 5.22 Regression analysis "diversification and performance in private equity" (Sharpe measure)

Independent variables	5-year performance (1)	(2)	(3)	(4)	(5)	(6)	10-year performance (1)	(2)	(3)	(4)	(5)	(6)
H	−0.189*	−0.158	−0.137				−0.081	−0.059	0.003			
DR				0.146*	0.106	0.071				0.172	0.146	0.082
DU				0.116	0.088	0.077				0.019	−0.002	−0.041
Portfolio size		0.209**	0.152		0.206	0.151		0.158	0.137		0.144	0.138
Number of funds			0.101			0.099			−0.056			−0.069
First year of vintage			-0.060			-0.067			−0.239*			−0.222
n	96	96	96	96	96	96	80	80	80	80	80	80
R^2	0.036	0.079	0.095	0.029	0.069	0.086	0.007	0.031	0.074	0.029	0.048	0.083

* Significant at 0.10 level (two tailed) ** Significant at 0.05 level (two tailed) *** Significant at 0.01 level (two tailed)

Table 5.23 Regression analysis "diversification and performance in private equity" (Treynor measure)

Independent variables	5-year performance (1)	(2)	(3)	(4)	(5)	(6)	10-year performance (1)	(2)	(3)	(4)	(5)	(6)
H	−0.234**	−0.206**	−0.176				−0.112	−0.097	−0.031			
DR				0.170*	0.124	0.076				0.182*	0.165*	0.095
DU				0.179*	0.153	0.137				0.065	0.051	0.011
Portfolio size		0.190*	0.116		0.183*	0.113		0.108	0.076		0.090	0.073
Number of funds			0.119			0.122			−0,030			−0.040
First year of vintage			−0.093			−0.099			−0.244*			−0.225*
n	96	96	96	96	96	96	80	80	96	80	80	80
R^2	0.055	0.090	0.118	0.047	0.079	0.108	0.013	0.024	0.118	0.033	0.041	0.078

* Significant at 0.10 level (two tailed) ** Significant at 0.05 level (two tailed *** Significant at 0.01 level (two tailed)

impact on performance, depending on the performance measure. This means that diversification by itself has a positive impact on performance as diversification is the highest when the Herfindahl measure has the lowest values. When distinguishing diversification in related (DR) and unrelated (DU) modes of diversification, one observes a consistently positive influence of related diversification on performance while the impact of unrelated diversification varies between negative, neutral, and positive along the different measures of performance. The findings for the Herfindahl index and related diversification are weakly significant on a 10% level in most regression models when used as single independent variable, however lose significance if additional independent variables are included in the analysis.

The impact of adding the size of the portfolio to the analysis adds explanatory power to the analysis, which is furthermore improved by including number of funds and the experience of the private equity firm to the analysis. The experience of the private equity firm is particularly valuable in accounting for the varying performance levels among private equity players. Interestingly, once one adds experience to the regression model, portfolio size loses significance in most of the regression models and therefore appears to act as a proxy for experience, which is neutralized once the experience variable is included in the model.

With R^2 values ranging between 8 and 12%, this study achieves values above most comparable, cross-sectional studies in public corporations. Typical cross-sectional studies in this field such as the empirical contributions by Berger and Ofek (1995), Lins and Servaes (1999), Glaser and Mueller (2006), or Chakrabarti et al. (2007) show R^2 values considerably below 10%.[25]

Overall, the comparison of diversification and performance in private equity shows a substantial performance gap between portfolios consisting of related diversified firms vs. portfolios with mostly unrelated diversified private equity players, contradicting the initial hypothesis, which expected a beneficial association of the private equity management model and mostly unrelated diversified firms. The results of this study indicate a superior performance of firms with high relatedness in their investment portfolios. The results, however, do not prove to be statistically significant. On an individual firm level, the regression analysis shows a positive association of related diversification and performance; the results, however, are statistically not significant if additional independent variables are included in the analysis. The size of the investment portfolio and particularly the experience of the private equity firm add substantial explanatory power to the analysis of private equity performance figures.

5.3.3 Diversification and Performance: Private Equity vs. Public Corporations

Building on the insights gained from analyzing the relationship of diversification and performance in private equity firms, the following sections attempt to draw a comparison of the diversification-performance link observed in public corporations with the results of private equity firms. "Hypothesis 5" focuses on the level and mode of diversification, "Hypothesis 6" investigates the diversification-performance relationship in the corporate as well as the private equity sample, and "Hypothesis 7" assesses the variance in performance in both samples.

5.3.3.1 Hypothesis 5

Given the nature of private equity investments as largely financially driven transactions with strong levels of independence during the investment period, the study expects a higher share of unrelated investments in private equity firms than in public corporations. This assumption is supported by the observable trend in public markets to increase focus and relatedness.

---

[25]The seminal study of Berger and Ofek (1995) shows R^2 values between 2 and 8%, R^2 values in the international benchmark study by Lins and Servaes (1999) range from 3 to 14%, and the study of German corporations by Glaser and Mueller (2006) shows R^2 values between 1 and 9%.

Table 5.24 summarizes the descriptive statistics of the comparison of diversification levels between private equity firms and public corporations. The results highlight, that the overall level of diversification as well as the level of relatedness and unrelatedness are – on an absolute basis – substantially higher in private equity portfolios. From a relative perspective, relatedness plays a more important role in public corporations.

The total diversification measured by the Herfindahl and the total diversification index (DT) of the Entropy measure show a clear sign of higher diversification in private equity, indicated by a smaller Herfindahl as well as a significantly higher total diversification measure in the PE sample. This analysis holds true for the sales as well as the asset measure for diversification in public corporations, although diversification measured by asset size is stronger than by sales. The Herfindahl index of private equity investment portfolios is between 35% for assets and 50% for sales smaller than the same measure in the business portfolios of public corporations. The total diversification measure of the Entropy index on the other hand is approximately three times as high for PE firms than for public corporations.[26]

From an absolute standpoint, related and unrelated diversification is substantially higher in PE portfolios than in corporations. The measure of related diversification

Table 5.24 Descriptive statistics H5: "Diversification in private equity firms and public corporations"

		Private equity	Public corporations	
			Sales	Assets
General characteristics	Number of firms (n)	100	100	80
	Mean of industry groups (M)	6.21	1.96	1.96
	Mean of industry segments (N)	8.73	4.34	4.34
Herfindahl (H)	Mean	0.25	0.50	0.38
	Range	0.10 –1.00	0.17 –1.00	0.12 –1.00
Entropy measure: Total diversification (DT)	Mean	1.77	0.56	0.61
	Range	0.00 –2.29	0.00 –1.72	0.00 –1.74
Entropy measure: Related diversification (DR)	Mean	0.36	0.20	0.17
	Range	0.00 –1.09	0.00 –1.11	0.00 –1.26
Entropy measure: Unrelated diversification (DU)	Mean	1.41	0.36	0.33
	Range	0.00 – 2.12	0.00 – 1.51	0.00 – 1.56

[26]The sales of public corporations in the sample appear to be more concentrated than the distribution of assets across businesses. This would most likely result in substantial differences in return measures across the different businesses within a corporation. This analysis however is not part of this study.

is almost twice as high in PE while the index of unrelated diversification exceeds the same index in corporations by more than four times. This absolute relationship is statistically tested in Table 5.25, which provides statistical evidence, that all measures of diversification are higher in private equity settings than in the holdings of public corporations. The statistical analysis helps to reject the null hypothesis that the overall levels of diversification in the two samples are equal (H_0: *diversification private equity = diversification public corporations*).

From a relative point of view, the results of the analysis take a different form. In public corporations, related diversification describes between 28% of total diversification based on assets and 36% based on sales figures. In private equity, the related diversification describes only 20% of the overall diversification, the rest being contributed by unrelated diversification.

The analysis of the diversification matrix supports this observation. At this point, the study constructs portfolios with equal ranges, using the maximum observed range of the related diversification measure (DR) and the unrelated diversification measure (DU) across both samples. The study then counts the number of firms in each of the resulting clusters. The results of this analysis are presented in Table 5.26. Testing these results, the study uses a chi-square test to assess the hypothesis that the number within each diversification cluster is equal. The chi-square test provides evidence to reject the null hypothesis of equal distribution on

Table 5.25 Significance tests H5: "Diversification in private equity firms and public corporations"

Measure		Private equity	Difference	Public corporations
Herfindahl (H)	Mean	0.2469		0.5033
	Mean difference		0.256	
	T-statistics		8.213[a]	
Entropy measure: Total diversification (DT)	Mean	1.7675		0.5639
	Mean difference		−1.204	
	T-statistics		−16.206[b]	
Entropy measure: Related diversification (DR)	Mean	0.3624		0.2015
	Mean difference		−0.161	
	T-statistics		−3.802[c]	
Entropy measure: Unrelated diversification (DU)	Mean	1.4051		0.3624
	Mean difference		−1.043	
	T-statistics		−15.597[d]	

Equal variances not assumed, sales-based measures used for corporate sample

[a]95% confidence interval 0.19487 to 0.31803; significance level 0.000 [b]95% confidence interval −0.24433 to −0.07745; significance level 0.000

[c]95% confidence interval −1.34999 to −1.05709; significance level 0.000 [d]95% confidence interval −1.17488 to −0.91082; significance level 0.000

Table 5.26 Comparison "modes of diversification"

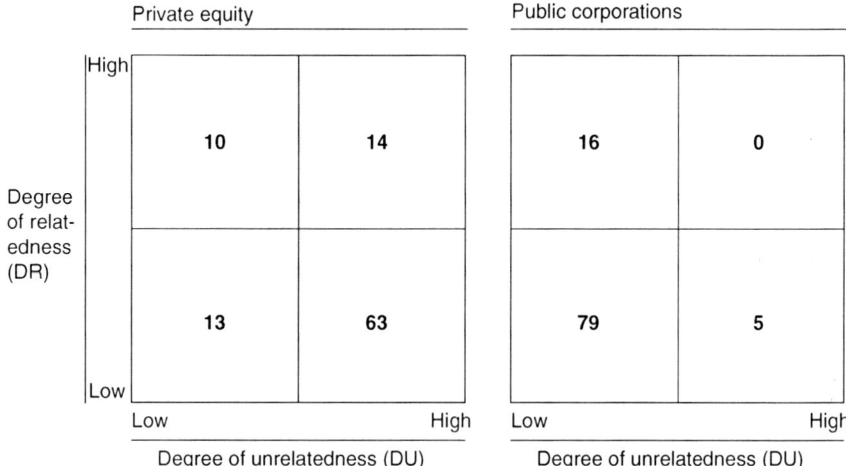

Degree of relatedness (DR)	Private equity: DU Low	Private equity: DU High	Public corporations: DU Low	Public corporations: DU High
High	10	14	16	0
Low	13	63	79	5

Equal range portfolios based on maximum ranges of both samples (DR 0.00 -1.11, DU 0.00 -2.02)[a], n=100

[a] Sales-based measures used for corporate sample

a 1% level of significance with a chi-square of 77.36 for private equity companies and a 95.66 for public corporations.

The portfolios resulting from using identical criteria for division show significant differences. The majority of private equity firms (63%) is located in the bottom-right quadrant of the matrix, which describes firms with highly unrelated portfolios and limited degrees of relatedness. The remaining firms are distributed evenly across the remaining quadrants of the matrix. In public corporations, the majority of firms (79%) is located in the bottom-left quadrant of the matrix, which characterizes firms focused on one or a very limited number of businesses. Firms in this quadrant have low degrees of both related and unrelated diversification. 16 out of the remaining 21% are then located in the top-left quadrant of the matrix, indicating a highly related portfolio of businesses with at the same time low levels of unrelatedness.[27] Only 5% of firms are in the bottom-right quadrant. These firms could be considered what is generally called conglomerates with highly unrelated businesses.

In summary, the comparison of levels and modes of diversification between private equity firms and public corporations reveals interesting findings. The overall

[27] The ranges presented in Table 5.24 further support this result. Although the mean is significantly below the value in private equity, the range of relatedness in public corporations exceeds the maximum values in private equity settings. This indicates that firms are either highly related diversified or show a low overall level of diversification.

level of diversification is substantially higher in private equity firms; however, diversification in private equity settings is mostly driven by unrelated diversification. Public corporations on the other hand – while featuring lower overall levels of diversification – show a higher share of either focused or related diversified organizations. The results provide evidence to support "Hypothesis 5", stating that unrelated diversification plays a more important role in private equity firms than in public corporations.

5.3.3.2 Hypothesis 6

The above analysis indicated that – while not statistically significant – a portfolio of private equity firms with related diversification tends to show a stronger performance than a portfolio of unrelated diversified PE partnerships. Previous studies in the field of diversification in public corporations similarly presented evidence that related diversification outperformed firms with focused or unrelated diversified business portfolios (e.g. see Amit & Livnat, 1988; Hall & St. John, 1994; Lubatkin & Rogers, 1989).

The objective of this study is to draw a comparison between the relationship of diversification and performance found in private equity firms and public corporations by using a corresponding measurement approach. The study hereby uses two models to distinguish different clusters of diversification. The first approach relies on portfolios constructed along equal ranges within each of the two independent samples. In other words, the approach for private equity firms introduced in "Hypothesis 4" is replicated within the sample of public corporations. This approach is most suited to determine the influence of relative differences of diversification on performance. The second model on the other hand uses the maximum observed range across both samples as introduced in "Hypothesis 5". This technique allows the study to draw conclusions about the influence of absolute differences of diversification between the two samples. Tables 5.27 and 5.28 outline the results based on independent samples for 5-year and 10-year performance measures. Tables 5.29 and 5.30 illustrate the empirical findings of the joint range analysis.

When using independent ranges, the results for the private equity sample represent the findings in "Hypothesis 4". Furthermore, one can observe the general findings from "Hypothesis 1" and "Hypothesis 2" about the overall performance gap between private equity firms and public corporations. Private equity firms outperform holdings in public corporations for both 5-year and 10-year investment horizons and for performance measures before and after risk adjustments.

In the mid-term investment horizon of 5 years represented in Table 5.27, private equity firms with related diversified business portfolios show the strongest performance figures, with and without risk adjustments. For public corporations, the results found in this study are on the contrary. The firms with the strongest performance are located in the low DR – low DU segment, which contains firms with a relatively focused business portfolio. For this investment period, this segment is the only one

Table 5.27 Comparison "diversification and performance" in private equity and public corporations (5-years, independent ranges)

Degree of relatedness (DR)	Private equity: Low DU	Private equity: High DU	Public corporations[a]: Low DU	Public corporations[a]: High DU
High	n : 22 IRR : 0.20 α : 0.12 S : 0.007 T : 0.17	n : 20 IRR : 0.17 α : 0.09 S : 0.006 T : 0.15	n : 19 TSR: 0.03 α : −0.06 S : 0.000 T : 0.02	n : 12 TSR: 0.06 α : −0.01 S : 0.002 T : 0.06
Low	n : 18 IRR : 0.15 α : 0.06 S : 0.004 T : 0.11	n : 36 IRR : 0.16 α : 0.08 S : 0.006 T : 0.15	n : 35 TSR: 0.11 α : 0.03 S : 0.004 T : 0.11	n : 34 TSR: 0.05 α : −0.04 S : 0.001 T : 0.05

Degree of unrelatedness (DU)

Equal range portfolios based on independent samples, 5-years performance.

[a]Based on sales measures. NOTE: n: number of firms; IRR: internal rate of return; TSR: total return to shareholder; α: Jensen's Alpha, S: Sharpe measure; T: Treynor measure

Table 5.28 Comparison "diversification and performance" in private equity and public corporations (10-years, independent ranges)

Degree of relatedness (DR)	Private equity: Low DU	Private equity: High DU	Public corporations[a]: Low DU	Public corporations[a]: High DU
High	n : 18 IRR : 0.19 α : 0.09 S : 0.006 T : 0.15	n : 18 IRR : 0.16 α : 0.06 S : 0.005 T : 0.13	n : 19 TSR: 0.12 α : 0.00 S : 0.003 T : 0.09	n : 12 TSR: 0.10 α : 0.00 S : 0.003 T : 0.09
Low	n : 15 IRR : 0.14 α : 0.03 S : 0.004 T : 0.09	n : 25 IRR : 0.15 α : 0.05 S : 0.005 T : 0.12	n : 35 TSR: 0.12 α : 0.02 S : 0.004 T : 0.11	n : 34 TSR: 0.12 α : 0.01 S : 0.004 T : 0.11

Degree of unrelatedness (DU)

Equal range portfolios based on independent samples, 10-years performance

[a]Based on sales measures. NOTE: n: number of firms; IRR: internal rate of return;TSR: total return to shareholder;α: Jensen's Alpha, S: Sharpe measure; T: Treynor measure

Table 5.29 Significance tests "diversification and performance" in private equity and public corporations

		High DR – Low DU		Low DR – High DU	
		Private equity	Public corporations*	Private equity	Public corporations*
	n	22	19	36	32
Performance (IRR/TSR)	Mean	0.20	0.03	0.16	0.05
	t	–4.664***		–3.780***	
	Mean difference	–0.171		–0.114	
	Confidence interval	–0.247 to –0.096		–0.175 to –0.054	
Jensen's Alpha	Mean	0.12	–0.06	0.08	–0.04
	t	–4.579***		–3.811***	
	Mean difference	–0.183		–0.120	
	Confidence interval	–0.265 to –0.101		–0.183 to –0.057	
Sharpe Measure	Mean	0.007	0.001	0.006	0.001
	t	–4.960***		–3.606***	
	Mean difference	–0.007		–0.005	
	Confidence interval	–0.010 to –0.004		–0.007 to –0.002	
Treynor Measure	Mean	0.17	0.02	0.15	0.05
	t	–4.162***		–2.845***	
	Mean difference	–0.157		–0.095	
	Confidence interval	–0.233 to –0.080		–0.162 to –0.028	

t-statistics with equal variances not assumed; 95% confidence interval, based on 5-year performance indicators, diversification measures based on independent ranges
* Significant at 0.10 level (2 tailed). ** Significant at 0.05 level (2 tailed). *** Significant at 0.01 level (2 tailed). NOTE: Sales based measures used for public corporations

Table 5.30 Comparison "diversification and performance" private equity and public corporations (5-years, joint ranges)

Degree of relatedness (DR)	Private equity: Low DU	Private equity: High DU	Public corporations[a]: Low DU	Public corporations[a]: High DU
High	n : 10 IRR : 0.17 α : 0.09 S : 0.006 T : 0.16	n : 14 IRR : 0.20 α : 0.12 S : 0.006 T : 0.14	n : 16 TSR : 0.05 α : –0.03 S : 0.001 T : 0.04	n : – TSR : – α : – S : – T : –
Low	n : 13 IRR : 0.13 α : 0.05 S : 0.004 T : 0.10	n : 63 IRR : 0.17 α : 0.09 S : 0.006 T : 0.15	n : 79 TSR : 0.07 α : –0.02 S : 0.002 T : 0.07	n : 5 TSR : 0.11 α : 0.03 S : 0.003 T : 0.10

Degree of unrelatedness (DU)

Equal range portfolios based on maximum range of both samples, 5-years performance

[a]Based on sales measures. NOTE: n: number of firms; IRR: Internal rate of return; TSR: Total return to shareholder; α: Jensen's Alpha, S: Sharpe measure; T: Treynor measure

with a positive Jensen's Alpha. In other words, only those relatively focused firms outperform the market. Other clusters on the diversification matrix perform considerably below market. Most remarkable, related diversified firms show the lowest performance of the overall sample.

For the 10-year investment horizon presented in Table 5.28, the results for the private equity sample remain consistent with the mid-term horizon, putting related diversifiers at the top of the sample. In public corporations, the performance differences have almost evened out, showing a strong tendency to the mean. Firms with relatively focused business portfolios show an average performance equal to that of related and unrelated diversified corporations. The mean performance is close or equal to market performance with Jensen's Alpha close to zero for all modes of diversification.

Table 5.29 outlines the results of the independent sample *t*-tests. The test results provide statistical evidence, that there is a significant difference between returns of private equity investments and holdings in public corporations for both related and unrelated diversified business portfolios. The test results remain significant for the 10-year investment horizon when accepting a 5% significance level for the probability of committing a type I error.[28]

When using joint ranges based on the maximum spread of the measures for related and unrelated diversification in both samples, performance results change. The results outlined in "Hypothesis 5" showed the relative importance of unrelated diversification in private equity firms and related diversification in public corporations. Given the relevance of those different modes of diversification in both samples, the use of a common range shifts a large number of firms in the private equity sample further onto the side of unrelated diversification while moving corporations towards the relatedness side of the diversification matrix. The influence of this change on financial performance is presented in Table 5.30 for 5-year performance measures and Table 5.31 for 10-year performance measures.

Regarding 5-year performance figures, the strongest performance in private equity firms is found in firms that have both high relatedness and unrelatedness in their portfolios. Portfolios with either high relatedness or high unrelatedness show comparable performance characteristics. Within the sample of public corporations, the highest performance is now found in the cluster of high unrelatedness. This cluster however is narrowed down to a total of five companies, which limits the reliability of this observation.

With regards to 10-year performance measures, the different modes of diversification are more balanced. In the private equity sample, the two clusters containing firms with high degrees of relatedness are illustrating a performance some seven respectively 8% points above those firms with low levels of relatedness. For public corporations, there is no such pattern perceptible.

[28] The study provides the results of the 5-year performance analysis at this point as the sample of firms that contain 5-year performance figures (overall private equity $n = 96$) is larger than that with 10-year performance figures (overall private equity $n = 80$).

Table 5.31 Comparison "diversification and performance" in private equity and public corporations (10-years, joint ranges)

Degree of relatedness (DR)	Private equity: Low DU	Private equity: High DU	Public corporations[a]: Low DU	Public corporations[a]: High DU
High	n : 6 IRR : 0.22 α : 0.12 S : 0.008 T : 0.19	n : 12 IRR : 0.22 α : 0.11 S : 0.007 T : 0.16	n : 16 TSR: 0.14 α : 0.04 S : 0.004 T : 0.14	n : – TSR: – α : – S : – T : –
Low	n : 11 IRR : 0.15 α : 0.05 S : 0.004 T : 0.10	n : 51 IRR : 0.14 α : 0.04 S : 0.004 T : 0.11	n : 79 TSR: 0.12 α : 0.01 S : 0.003 T : 0.10	n : 5 TSR: 0.14 α : 0.03 S : 0.004 T : 0.12

Degree of unrelatedness (DU)

Equal range portfolios based on maximum range of both samples, 10-years performance

[a] Based on sales measures. NOTE: n: number of firms; IRR: Internal rate of return; TSR: Total return to shareholder; α: Jensen's Alpha, S: Sharpe measure; T: Treynor measure

Overall, the results do not support the initial hypothesis, which expected unrelated diversification to be a major driver in private equity firms and related diversified public corporations to perform best. Within the study's sample, related diversification appears to positively influence performance in private equity firms whereas there is no consistent relationship between different modes of diversification and performance observable in public corporations.[29]

5.3.3.3 Hypothesis 7

The last hypothesis is centered on the performance differences between different modes of diversification. The discrepancy in performance of public corporations is expected to be significantly larger than in the study's sample of private equity firms. This relationship is anticipated given the greater common base of the management approach followed by private equity firms found in previous academic studies than the broad spectrum of management models observed in public corporations.

---

[29] Section 5.4.3 "comparison private equity vs. public equity" provides possible explanations for this empirical finding, which appears contradictory to various prior publications. However, other academic contributions such as Bettis and Mahajan (1985) or De (1992) provide consistent empirical results.

To test this hypothesis, the study first approaches the overall level of diversification found in the two samples before detailing the relationship between different modes of diversification. The detailed analysis is based on the two portfolio analysis approaches used in the previous sections of the study; one being based on independent portfolio ranges, the other on a joint maximum range over both samples. The general analysis of variance is presented in Table 5.32 while the results of the more detailed analysis are outlined in Fig. 5.4 (using independent ranges) and Fig. 5.5 (using a joint range over both samples).

Overall, the variance of all performance measures is larger in the sample of public corporations than in the private equity sample. Even though the maximum range of performance measures for public corporations exceeds the same in private equity firms only slightly, the variance measure is considerably larger in the corporate sample. Using a Levene's test for equality of variances, the results of the analysis are significant on a 5% level for Jensen's Alpha only. For Jensen's Alpha, one can therefore reject the null hypothesis stating equal variances (H_0: σ^2 *private equity* $= \sigma^2_{Public\ Corporations}$). The results do not prove to be statistically significant on a 5 or 10% level for the remaining performance measures. The analysis is presented with 5-year performance figures given the larger number of PE firms with 5-year data; results however remain valid for 10-year performance measures.

Table 5.32 Comparison "performance variance"

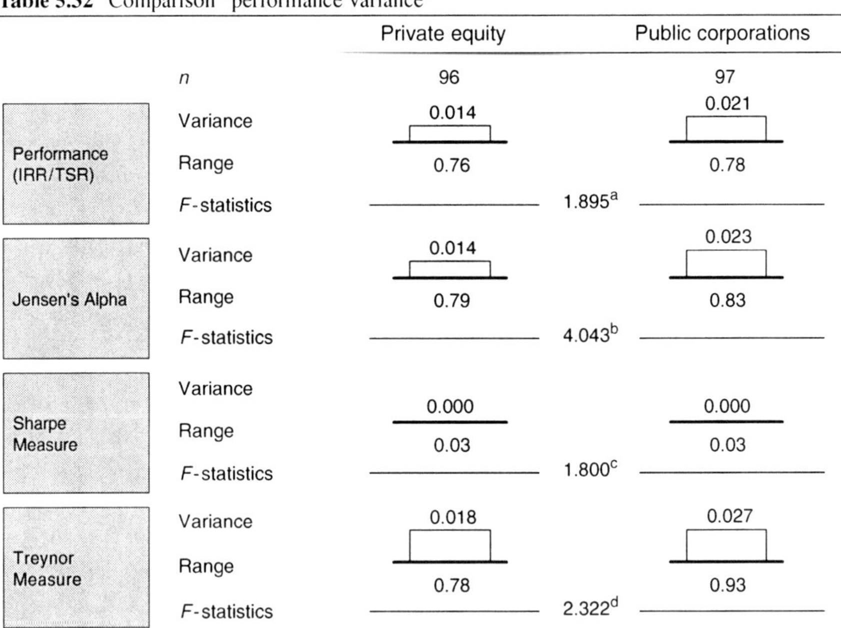

		Private equity		Public corporations
	n	96		97
Performance (IRR/TSR)	Variance	0.014		0.021
	Range	0.76		0.78
	F-statistics		1.895[a]	
Jensen's Alpha	Variance	0.014		0.023
	Range	0.79		0.83
	F-statistics		4.043[b]	
Sharpe Measure	Variance	0.000		0.000
	Range	0.03		0.03
	F-statistics		1.800[c]	
Treynor Measure	Variance	0.018		0.027
	Range	0.78		0.93
	F-statistics		2.322[d]	

5-year performance, Levene's test for equality of variances, 95% confidence interval

[a] Level of significance 0.170
[b] Level of significance 0.046
[c] Level of significance 0.181
[d] Level of significance 0.129

H7: COMPARISON 'PERFORMANCE VARIANCE ACROSS MODES OF DIVERSIFICATION'

Percent, equal range portfolios based on independent samples; 5-year performance before risk adjustments*

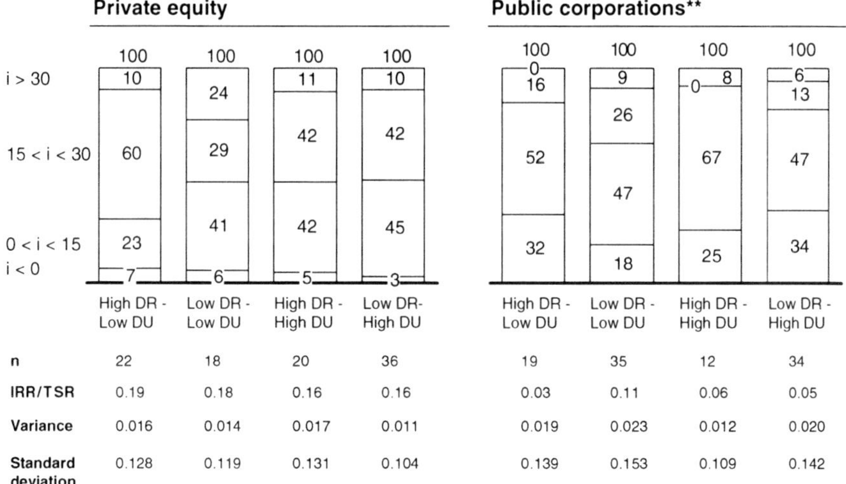

	Private equity: High DR - Low DU	Low DR - Low DU	High DR - High DU	Low DR- High DU	Public corporations: High DR - Low DU	Low DR - Low DU	High DR - High DU	Low DR - High DU
n	22	18	20	36	19	35	12	34
IRR/TSR	0.19	0.18	0.16	0.16	0.03	0.11	0.06	0.05
Variance	0.016	0.014	0.017	0.011	0.019	0.023	0.012	0.020
Standard deviation	0.128	0.119	0.131	0.104	0.139	0.153	0.109	0.142

*i measures performance; IRR for Private Equity; TSR for public corporations
**Based on sales measures

Fig. 5.4 Comparison "performance variance across modes of diversification" (independent ranges)

On the level of individual modes of diversification based on independent DR and DU ranges (Fig. 5.4), one can examine two dimensions. On the one hand, one can compare the mean performances between individual modes of diversification. On the other hand, one can determine the variance within each cluster.

Comparing the means of performance, there is a spread of 3% points in the private equity sample. The spread ranges from 16% in unrelated diversifiers and firms with both high unrelated and related portfolios to 19% for related diversifiers measured by internal rate of return. For the corporate sample, this difference is substantially larger. There is a spread of 8% points between 3% for related diversifiers and 11% for relatively focused companies in terms of total return to shareholder.

Within each mode of diversification, the variance in performance is larger in public corporations for all clusters but the one containing firms with both high relatedness and unrelatedness (high DR – high DU). For private equity companies, the strongest variance is found for firms with high relatedness or both high related and high unrelated portfolios whereas relatively focused firms show the highest variance in the sample of public corporations. In addition, the analysis reveals that the share of public corporations with negative performance over the last 5 years is considerably larger than in the private equity sample.

Using joint range portfolios for the comparison of performance variance, the difference in the performance spread evens out. The spread in the corporate sample is six% compared to 7% in the private equity sample. Within each mode of

H7: COMPARISON 'PERFORMANCE VARIANCE ACROSS MODES OF DIVERSIFICATION'

Percent, equal range portfolios based on maximum range of both samples; 5-year performance before risk adjustments*

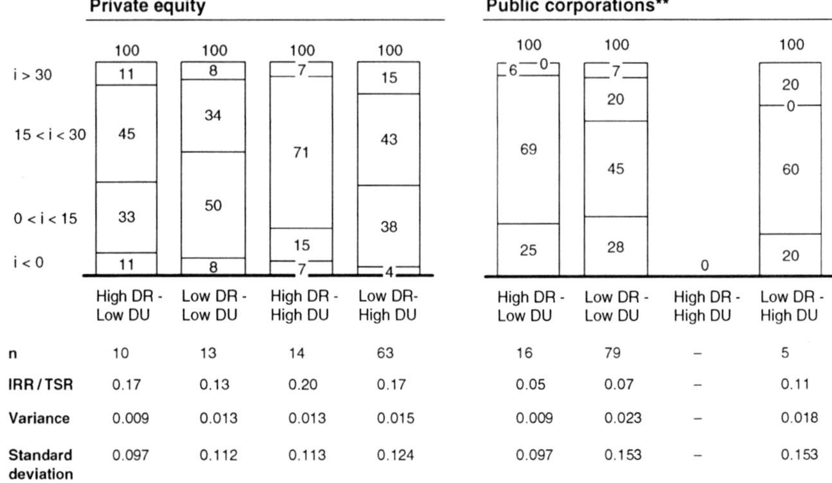

* i measures performance; IRR for Private Equity; TSR for public corporations

** Based on sales measures

Fig. 5.5 Comparison "performance variance across modes of diversification" (joint ranges)

diversification, unrelated diversifiers show the highest variance in PE settings whereas relatively focused companies reveal the highest variance in the corporate sample. Both clusters contain the highest number of firms within each sample.

Overall, the above results provide considerable evidence for the initial hypothesis. The differences in performance appear to be larger in public corporations than in private equity firms. The results are significant for Jensen's Alpha and are consistent for all other performance measures.

5.4 Discussion of Results

The results of the study's first empirical part offered a broad spectrum of findings, structured along seven hypotheses. To gain a better understanding of the overall implications of these outcomes, this section is intended to illustrate the underlying constructs within the private equity world and the implications for public corporations. The section starts with a review of the diversification strategies observed in private equity and the implications on performance, thereby addressing one of the main objectives of this study. It then highlights the different performance drivers in private equity and derives opportunities for public corporations. The section closes by outlining the study's research limitations.

5.4.1 *Diversification in Private Equity*

The above empirical findings offer insights along the two lines of academic research that have been at the core of the discussion of diversification in public corporations. On the one hand, the study provides findings regarding the status of diversification in private equity firms and references it to diversification in public corporations. On the other hand, the empirical results contain information about the relationship of diversification and performance.

5.4.1.1 Status of Diversification

The empirical results of the study outline an unambiguous picture of diversification in private equity firms. Overall, diversification is high and unrelatedness is the major driver of diversification.

The results show that the overall level of diversification in private equity firms is high with an average Herfindahl of 0.25 and an Entropy total diversification measure DT of 1.77. These measures indicate an overall level of diversification that is significantly larger in private equity firms than in public corporations. The private equity Entropy measure for instance tops the same measure in public corporations by some three times. The number of industry segments and groups further accentuates this relationship. Private equity firms are – on average – invested in close to nine industry segments and more than six industry groups while public corporations hold slightly more than four industry segments in approximately two industry groups. The largest share of private equity companies is managing a portfolio invested in six to seven industry groups.

Unrelated diversification is the major driver for diversification. The Entropy measure for unrelated diversification (DU) is with 1.41 significantly larger than the related measure (DR) with 0.36. Related diversification therefore explains only 20% of total diversification. In public corporations on the other side, relatedness is substantially more important in explaining total diversification with up to 35% and a broader spread of relatedness measures.

On average, the portfolios of private equity firms show structures that are very comparable to conglomerate structures. Conglomerate portfolio structures are found in highly unrelated diversified multi-business firms. However, one has to recognize that unrelated diversification is not the only model of diversification observed in the selected private equity sample. Whereas the majority of firms are active in a multitude of industries, there is a considerable number of PE partnerships in the sample that concentrate their activities on one or few industries groups. The number of industry groups ranges from one up to ten different industry groups and the measure of relatedness within industry portfolios goes as high as 1.09, more than three times the mean. This evidence indicates, that Jensen's (1989a: 37) argument that leveraged buyouts "are similar in many respects to diversified conglomerates" might not be entirely true. Although unrelated diversification is the major driver of diversification in private equity, numerous alternative, more related models can be observed in the industry.

The findings of this study are largely consistent with findings of comparable studies. The studies by Schmidt (2004) and Lossen (2006) provide evidence for high levels of diversification in private equity, which are even exceeded by this study given its broader definition of the private equity investment portfolio. The unit of analysis in prior studies is private equity funds while this study uses the PE partnership level as unit of analysis. Even though one has to recognize that deliberate diversification in private equity happens to a large extent on the level of individual funds, this analysis provides a unique and clear-cut picture of the general industry exposure of the firm as a management entity. Investigating diversification on a fund level can offer insights into the risk-return profile of one particular fund investment. The approach chosen in this study pioneers an understanding of private equity as an institutionalized management model that outlasts the lifetime of individual funds and that can be compared to traditional multi-business firms.

5.4.1.2 Relationship Diversification and Performance

The analysis of the relationship between diversification and performance is less clear-cut. Diversification overall tends to have a positive influence on performance. However, within diversification, only related diversification shows consistent positive associations with performance.

The empirical results of this study imply that diversification generally has a positive influence on performance. The results of the regression analysis show that a smaller Herfindahl index leads to higher performance indicators, independent whether performance is measured before or after risk adjustments. On this level, one therefore can expect higher performance by firms that are invested in a larger number of industry groups than by firms that are highly focused on a small number of dominating investments. These results are further supported by the fact that firms with investments in a small number of industry groups (one to three) show the lowest performance figures.

Although diversification in general has a positive influence on performance, only related diversification shows consistent positive implications while unrelated diversification has no unambiguous association with performance. Private equity firms with higher relatedness in their investment portfolios show a stronger performance than unrelated diversified companies, consistent across performance measures, portfolio compositions, and investment horizons. The highest performing private equity partnerships are generally those firms that are invested in a limited amount of industry groups (four to five) and build relatedness within these industry groups. Even though these results are consistent in every analysis, they show only weak or no statistical significance.

The results of this study are in line with the general findings by prior studies in the field of diversification in private equity. Schmidt (2004) and Weidig and Mathonet (2004) find a positive influence of diversification on a private equity fund's risk-return profile. Lossen (2006) and Cressy, Munari, & Malipiero (2007) similarly find a positive influence of industry diversification on private equity returns. However, none of the prior has addressed the issue of relatedness and unrelatedness within a diversified investment portfolio. Moreover, prior studies have not provided an observation whether there are a particular number of industry groups that seem to enable superior returns.

5.4.2 *Performance Drivers in Private Equity*

The above outline of the relationship between diversification and performance highlights that there are portfolio compositions more likely to deliver high investment performance than other modes of diversification. However, diversification is clearly only a piece in the performance puzzle of private equity. This section therefore attempts to outline and explain the performance drivers in private equity firms.

5.4.2.1 Diversification and Risk-Return

The empirical results of the study show that diversification is a key component of the private equity model. Higher levels of diversification improve the risk-return profiles of private equity investments by reducing performance volatility. Schmidt (2004) similarly showed that a private equity firm is able to reduce its diversifiable risk by almost 80% when the portfolio increases to 15 investments.

Private equity firms are specifically interested in a strong track record with consistent performance levels. Although inconsistent with the Modigliani and Miller (1958) theorem and West's (1967) transition of the theorem to portfolio diversification, investors in private equity are typically large institutional investors that are looking for stable returns and are not willing to bet on the success of individual industries. Given the information asymmetry and insufficient liquidity of private equity investments, risk diversification does not happen exclusively on the investor level but on the level of the private equity firm's funds.

Risk reduction through diversification is particularly important for investment models such as private equity, which are built around non-permanent capital. private equity firms are highly dependent on short-term and mid-term economic trends and on the resulting opportunities to acquire and divest companies. Firms therefore tend to decrease their overall exposure to particular industries and minimize correlations within their investment portfolios.

5.4.2.2 Related Diversification

Diversification appears to be a critical success factor for a private equity firm; however, the mode of diversification matters. Related diversification in a selected set of industries tends to promise the highest rate of return for a private equity partnership and its investors.

The selection and oversight of private companies is characterized by considerable information asymmetries and principal agent problems (Chan, 1983; Gompers, 1995; Amit, Brander, & Zott, 1998). Specialization in particular industries through related diversification appears to provide private equity firms the ability to overcome some of those obstacles. The exposure to a limited number of industries with substantial scale in those industries can offer a related diversified private equity firm a competitive advantage and the opportunity to improve the selection of acquisition targets, the management of a firm's investment portfolio, and the successful exit from an investment.[30]

During the acquisition process of a new target, information asymmetry exists between the private equity firm as acquirer, the management team, and the vendor of the target company. Private equity firms generally run an intense, multi-stage selection process to overcome such information asymmetries (Birley, Muzyka, & Hay, 1999; MacMillan, Zemann, & Subbanarasimha, 1987; Tyebjee & Bruno, 1984). However, knowledge about particular industries enables a private equity manager to further reduce the information gap and improve the selection and valuation results. One can expect that related diversified PE players are able to build greater industry expertise and consequently have a greater likelihood of making promising acquisitions than unrelated diversified firms.

After the acquisition, two elements appear to enable related diversifiers to extract greater returns from their portfolio companies: the ability to exercise stronger corporate governance and the opportunity to add value as a parent.

On the one side, agency problems exist between the buyout firm (the principal) and the management team of a portfolio company (the agent). Even though the strong incentive systems implemented in a private equity ownership model help to reduce agency problems (Palepu, 1990; Phan & Hill, 1995; Smith, 1990a, 1990b; Thompson, Wright, & Robbie, 1992), personal interests of managers might continue to differ from the interests of the PE firm and its investors. According to Gompers (1995; 1465–1466), three likely types of agency costs and asymmetric information exist in private equity investments. First, management might invest in strategies and projects that have high personal returns such as recognition or further career options but low expected monetary payoffs to shareholders. Second, given that management equity stakes are essentially call options, a strong incentive exists to pursue high-variance strategies. Third, private information might allow a manager to continue projects with negative net present values or undertake inefficient

[30] Lossen (2006) makes similar remarks in his study about diversification in private equity funds. His data shows that specialization in particular financing stages can improve the performance of private equity investments whereas no impact of country specialization and a negative impact of industry focus is found. The study however fails to distinguish between related and unrelated diversification and consequently uses a very narrow definition of industry specialization.

investments while this information is shielded from the private equity firm.[31] A stronger expertise in particular industries can allow private equity managers to overcome some of the costs associated with agency and asymmetric information. Managers with experience in a number of related investments are more likely to draw on comparable cases to assess management performance and investment decisions.

On the other side, to achieve the returns required by investors, various private equity players have shown a transition of their investment model to a more actively involved management style. Buyout specialists play a stronger role in strategic and operational changes to create value and to generate sufficient cash flows to service interest payments (Bruining & Wright, 2002; Fox & Marcus, 1992; Kaplan, 1989; Palepu, 1990; Wiersema & Liebeskind, 1995). Related diversification can enable private equity professionals to add more value to a portfolio company given their accrued industry experience in strategic and operational questions. Managers of unrelated diversified portfolios have a smaller likelihood of coming across questions and industries that they have addressed before. This argument is closely connected to the resource-based view of diversification in corporate settings. Building on this theory, private equity managers should – as much as corporate managers – attempt to use their set of skills in familiar areas as long as attractive investment opportunities are available in the field (Penrose, 1959; Silverman, 2002).

Finally, a stronger degree of relatedness in a PE firm's investment portfolio can allow for a stronger position in the exit phase. The amount of information held by the private equity firm and the knowledge of the industry landscape and potential benefits for strategic investors can help a private equity partnership to achieve higher exit prices than an unrelated diversified investor without a strong position in the industry.

5.4.2.3 Management Experience

Closely linked to relatedness is experience, which proved to be the most significant explanatory factor for performance differences in private equity firms. The time since a private equity firm issued the first fund was able to add substantially to the power of the performance analysis of the study's private equity sample. On a similar note, Kaplan and Schoar (2004) show a strong persistence in performance across different funds of the same private equity general partnership. In their view, the persistence of results is most likely driven by heterogeneity in the skill set of general partners and the limited scalability of human capital. Persistence of high returns is of particular importance in the private equity world given the non-permanent nature of capital. Private equity professionals are obligated to return capital to investors after the lifetime of each fund, typically after 10 years, and then need to raise fresh

[31] Gompers (1995) focuses his research on venture capital investments. His findings however appear applicable more generally to private equity as way of financing.

capital for new funds. The evaluation process by limited partners is largely based on the performance of prior funds. Lossen's (2006) study similarly shows a positive association of performance with firm experience; his results however are not significant and based on a fund rather than firm sample.[32]

Time since inception of the first fund embodies a number of variables including a network and brand easing access to transactions, the management expertise and network of experienced managers that can be employed in one of the firm's investments, as well as knowledge about potential buyers and standing contacts with investors. All of these can be considered elements brought about by the "experience" of a private equity firm.

For acquisitions, experience allows a firm to build up a network as well as a brand to attract and find available deals in the market. Being in the private equity sphere for a longer period of time provides private equity managers with contacts to search for deals. Furthermore, after having executed a number of successful deals in particular industries, transactions will start to find the private equity firm in those industries. Moreover, those more established firms will most likely be associated with higher credibility by financiers to raise bridge loans, find co-investors, and get access to debt required for the transaction, potentially even at lower cost. A young firm will not have the luxury of being established in the market and will have to put a higher level of activity forward to get into the deal flow.

After the initial acquisition, more experienced firms will have a higher likelihood of extracting value from an investment through active involvement in strategic decision making. Established firms will moreover have access to a network of executives and advisors, with whom they have worked before and who can be approached if the need for strategic advice arises. A younger player in the market will have to work harder to establish the same level of management expertise and network of competences. Information about the market is of further importance when it comes to exits. Established firms will most likely have more information about potential buyers and the advisors most suitable for particular transactions.

Furthermore, established players are able to present a track record to investors and have an established base of investors. Most institutional investors are investing in the same firms on a continuing basis based on trust and the firm's performance record. Positioning a new player in the market without a long standing performance record and investor network will require a stronger investment case and potentially a risk premium.

Finally, established private equity firms most likely have gained the ability to read different economic conditions and understand the implications on the private equity model. Different economic cycles can significantly influence the acquisition and divestiture opportunities and thereby affect the depth of involvement and the

---

[32] In addition to these studies, Loos (2005) finds a concave curve in his study about performance and fund manager experience. He however provides no results about the relationship between performance and private equity firm experience but focuses on the characteristics of individuals.

modes of value creation in PE investments. Experienced firms may pass on transactions during highly competitive periods and play a more active role on capital markets when they see sound market environments.

Wruck (2007) refers to this phenomenon as the "routinization" of the private equity approach to reorganization for value creation. The establishment of a relationship-oriented, organizationally-focused business over a PE firm's existence provides the ability for the firm to create a competitive advantage over less experienced market participants. Building on Jensen and Meckling's (1992) view, the contribution of private equity experience is a question of specific vs. general knowledge. Whereas general knowledge is inexpensive to transmit among agents, specific knowledge takes time to create and is costly to transfer among agents (Chapman, 2007).

Ultimately, the argumentation about the positive influence of experience on private equity performance is closely linked to theories of behavioral learning (e.g. see Bower & Hilgard, 1981; Cyert & March, 1963; Haleblian & Finkelstein, 1999; Mazur, 1994) and organizational learning (e.g. see Crossan, Lane, & White, 1999; Fiol & Lyles, 1985; Huber, 1991). These theories argue that experience allows firms to establish routines and procedures for managing their investments and thereby achieve higher investment performance. Experienced organizations moreover have a higher ability of reflecting on changes in a firm's environment. Haleblian and Finkelstein (1999) for instance establish a positive relationship of experience gained by an organization and performance in corporate mergers by analyzing acquisitions from a behavioral learning point of view. Their study documents that the more similar a firm's acquisition targets are, the better they perform.

5.4.2.4 Explaining the Unexplained

The above performance drivers help in determining what creates more or less successful private equity players. Although results are comparably strong for a cross-sectional analysis, those characteristics of a firm, that can be measured through the investment portfolio and data points such as diversification, fund size or first year of vintage explain only part of performance differences between private equity players. There is a substantial part of private equity performance that cannot be explained by the firms' investment portfolios or levels of experience.

Explaining this unexplained part of private equity performance will require a look into the specific ownership and management models pursued by individual firms as well as an investigation of the set of skills accessible for a private equity firm. As indicated by Lossen (2006: 36), those unobserved differences in management styles between private equity firms are arguable the cause for differences in performance. Consequently, this interest in explaining the unexplained part of private equity performance creates the fundamental motivation for the second, exploratory part of this study, which is presented in Chap. 6 "Empirical Part II: Managing Diversified Portfolios".

5.4.3 *Comparison Private Equity vs. Public Equity*

Beyond the findings about performance drivers in private equity firms, the study provides evidence about the relationship between different modes of diversification and performance in public corporations and draws a comparison between the two ways of ownership – private and public equity.

5.4.3.1 Diversification and Performance in Public Equity

The analysis of the diversification-performance link in public corporations reveals that in the long-run, performance across different modes of diversification converts to the mean. While an advantage of focus can be observed in the 5-year investment horizon, the performance difference levels out in a 10-year analysis to 12% in focused, related diversified and unrelated diversified public companies.[33]

The phenomenon of long-term conversion to the mean highlights the difficulty of multi-business firms to find strategies that enable them to enhance the value of a firm's business portfolio. In particular the long-praised advantage of related diversification in multi-business firms is not substantiated by the analysis. Arguing from a resource-based view standpoint, related diversification should be able to create value as resources can be leveraged across a firm's business portfolio. However, if this use generates excess administrative costs, the value creation stemming from the joint use of resources is reversed. Inefficient corporate infrastructure can turn a legitimate reason for diversification into a zero-sum or value-destroying game. Bettis and Mahajan (1985) furthermore argue, that related diversified firms are by definition in specific core businesses and cannot easily, if at all, change core industries. In their view, this suggests that "bad luck in the initial choice of an industry early in a firm's history may lock a related firm out of superior performance" (Bettis & Mahajan, 1985: 796). Ultimately, none of the three modes of diversification – focus, related diversification, and unrelated diversification – appears to provide a systematic advantage for adding value to a firm's business portfolio.

Prior literature has produced two contradicting results. A first group of researchers including Lecraw (1984), Palepu (1985), or Hall and St. John (1994) have found a positive influence of related diversification on financial performance whereas a second group including Bettis and Mahajan (1985) and De (1992) has provided evidence, that there is no significant performance differential between different modes of diversification. The results of this study support the latter group of academic publications for the corporate sphere.

[33] These results are based on the analysis using independent diversification ranges. The only mode of diversification with below-average performance of 10% is both high unrelated and high related diversification. This particular segment of multi-business companies however is eliminated if joint ranges are used for the analysis.

5.4.3.2 Impact of Ownership

While there has been substantial coverage of the prior observations in previous academic literature, the comparison of the diversification-performance relationship between private equity firms and publicly listed companies is unique to this study. The empirical evidence of this study shows that the returns achieved by private equity firms are considerably better than what you can expect from holdings in public equity – before and after risk adjustments. In the mid-term, the internal rate of return in private equity is more than twice as high as in public corporations. Although the performance gap is narrowing to approximately 4% points in the longer 10-year investment horizon, the findings for the longer term highlight the same performance superiority and are statistically significant.

The sustained performance superiority of private equity firms indicates advantages in the private equity management and ownership model over public corporations. Active ownership appears to matter providing private equity firms with the ability to add value to their investment portfolios. The systematic overview provided by Baker and Montgomery (1994) as well as contributions by Jensen (1989a, 1989b), Kaufman and Englander (1993), Gompers and Lerner (1999), or Berg and Gottschalg (2003) outline a number of factors that play a potential role in support of the above findings. Those factors, each in comparison to public corporations, include the stronger divestiture activity revealed by private equity firms, the smaller however actively involved private equity partnership in the sense of a "corporate center", as well as the higher level of independence of individual portfolio companies within the investment portfolio of a private equity firm.

A particular ability to achieve superior performance compared to their peers as well as public corporations is revealed by those firms showing higher levels of related diversification. In accordance with the above findings about the influence of related diversification on performance in private equity firms, related diversified private equity firms appear to be able to successfully apply the advantages of the resource based view while reducing agency costs and costs from asymmetric information. At the same time, those firms seem to have found a way to contain administrative costs. This observation is particularly true for private equity firms that focus their investment activities on an average of four to five industry groups and exploit the advantages of relatedness within those sectors.

The results of previous academic studies regarding the pure performance comparison between private and public companies range from a PE outperformance to a significant performance deficit of private equity companies when compared to public market benchmarks. The results of this study are in line with such contributions as Ljungqvist and Richardson (2003a) or Ick (2005). No prior publications have investigated the performance differences among different modes of diversification.

The empirical findings of part one reveal advantages in the ownership and management model of private equity firms. The investigation of the individual key success factors of the private equity management model will be subject of the second empirical part of this study. The results are presented in Chap. 6 "Empirical Part II: Managing Diversified Portfolios".

5.4.4 *Limitations of Research*

Concluding the study's first empirical part, a number of research limitations need to be addressed. Overall, the study attempts to use the performance and diversification metrics that have received the highest level of acceptance in the academic community and which have been going through academic assessments for several decades. However, research limitations arise – in particular given the pioneering work of this study in the private equity field. Limitations of the quantitative part of this contribution mainly include quality issues in the study's data as well as the validity of the applied performance and diversification measures. Finally, the treatment of consortium deals presents a problem more particular to the private equity industry.

Data for public markets shows a high level of quality. The study's sample includes some of the largest global companies with continuous market data provided through two of the world's leading vendors. On the private equity side, reliable data is less accessible. The performance data is based on contributions by general and limited partners to London-based private equity intelligence. Although the mix of general and limited partners should lead to substantial quality improvements, there is still substantial management discretion and a lack of continuous market data in private equity. In addition, both samples reveal survivorship biases given that only the success models survived and made it above the sample cutoff criteria. The bias has an effect on the analysis of performance drivers in private equity firms, in particular in terms of experience. For the comparison study of private equity firms and public companies, the survivorship bias is present in both samples and thus has – under the assumption of a comparable effect – less impact on the power of the study's findings.

The validity of the measures used in this study to assess performance is arguable very high. Total return to shareholders (in public corporations) and the internal rate of return (in private equity firms) in combination with their risk-adjusted variations provide a useful basis to measure performance while overcoming accounting or measurement problems observed in other performance indicators. One fact however is noteworthy in this context. Private equity firms that have not yet been closed base performance calculations on interim valuations, which might misstate the real value of an investment. Performance figures for not yet liquidated funds might therefore be misstated substantially.

The validity of the measures regarding diversification reveals a number of limitations. In public corporations, the attribution of revenue and assets to individual business segments lies partly in management discretion. For private equity, the lack of regulatory disclosures required the construction of a portfolio proxy through the use of transaction data to assess industry diversification. Additionally, the metrics to evaluate related and unrelated diversification based on SIC Codes have found regular criticism as such industry classifications are unable to capture a potential resource relatedness of businesses even though they are in different SIC industry groups (see Martin & Sayrak, 2003: 49–52 for an useful overview).

Finally, the occurrence of consortium deals can present a limitation to the study's findings. Generally, only the lead firm will be deeply involved in a portfolio company's strategic and operational changes whereas non-lead firms have weak incentives for time-consuming activities (Bottazzi, Da Rin, & Hellmann, 2004). The effect of industry specialization is therefore most relevant for lead firms whereas co-investors mostly contribute capital to the transaction or participate for "window dressing" reasons (Lakonishok, Shleifer, Thaler, & Vishny, 1991) to demonstrate a track record of successful investments to investors (Admati & Pfleiderer, 1994; Cressy et al., 2007; Cumming, 2005a, 2005b). The dataset is unable to distinguish between lead and non-lead investors.

Chapter 6
Empirical Part II: Managing Diversified Portfolios

The alchemy of LBOs; no it isn't black magic
Paul A. Butler, The McKinsey Quarterly

While the first empirical part of this study was able to establish relationships between diversification, relatedness, experience and performance, the majority of performance differences cannot be explained by looking at private equity portfolios. Instead, one is required to investigate the different management models and characteristics of private equity firms and how those differences lead to superior or inferior performance. The alchemy of the management models of private equity players is what ultimately explains the success factors of a good private equity player and will highlight what it will take for a public corporation to learn from private equity.

Even though a significant part of private equity performance remains unexplained by the study's first empirical part, its findings raise important questions for the second part of the study. For instance, the observed tendency of related diversified firms to show superior performance over unrelated diversifiers challenges the way different management models choose to exploit the relationship between diversification and performance. One can expect that bringing parenting advantage to private equity portfolios requires different models in related diversified firms than in unrelated diversifiers. Moreover, the relationship between experience and performance provides evidence for a routinization of the private equity management model over the lifetime of a firm. Some firms must have found management models that enable them to consistently deliver superior performance by adding value to their investment portfolios.

As highlighted in the literature review and the outline of the study's research direction, little is known about the functioning of leveraged buyout players in the role of a parent. In addition, most of what is known stems from a time when private equity players have been closer to what you would consider a corporate raider (e.g. see Anders, 1992; Baker & Montgomery, 1994; Kaufman & Englander, 1993) than to today's well established management approach. This part of the study therefore offers an empirical approach to the question how private equity firms manage diversified portfolios and how they take on the role as a parent in a portfolio of diverse investments.

Empirical part one also showed that investments in private equity firms perform substantially better than holdings in public companies and more specifically in

D.O. Klier, *Managing Diversified Portfolios*,
DOI: 10.1007/978-3-7908-2173-4_6, © 2009 Physica-Verlag Heidelberg

multi-business firms. So far, limited effort has been made to understand the differences between the management models of private equity firms and traditional multi-business firms and to outline opportunities for multi-business firms to apply some of the key success factors of the private equity management model. The few publications available moreover lack a comprehensive assessment of the private equity firm as a parent of diversified portfolio companies and only target selective opportunities to create parenting advantage (e.g. see Barber & Goold, 2007; Gottschalg & Meier, 2005; Pozen, 2007). Ultimately, this part of research wants to find potential answers to the question what traditional multi-business firms can learn from private equity.

This chapter opens with a description of the exploratory framework, which is used as guidance for the empirical analysis. It then highlights the methodology used to analyze the various dimensions of the exploratory framework. The chapter consequently closes by outlining and discussing the empirical results and findings of the second empirical part of this study.

6.1 Exploratory Framework

As outlined in the general research design presented in Chap. 3, the second empirical part of this study builds on an exploratory research design. Following such qualitative designs, an exploratory framework is required as a starting position of empirical analysis (Eisenhardt, 1989). This section presents the framework used in this research setting.

6.1.1 General Structure

The general exploratory structure of this study's research framework is closely aligned with the traditional structure–conduct–performance paradigm rooted in industrial organization research. The framework initially developed by Mason (1939) and Bain (1968) and critical for Porter's (1983, 1985, 1987, 1996) contributions considers the economists' view of strategy and is based on the belief that firm conduct and consequently performance critically depend on the industry's environment. The framework is particularly advantageous given its comprehensive nature. It allows the analysis of a broad spectrum of industry and firm characteristics and enables the recognition of relationships between individual components of the framework; it is therefore especially useful for an exploratory research design and its demand for a broad spectrum of input variables. The framework's power is moreover drawn from the fact that it incorporates performance as integral part into the analysis while many other strategic frameworks miss the consistent connection between market conditions, strategy, and effect on outcome.

Although slightly varied in the sense that structure in this paper's research entails multiple firm-specific characteristics in combination with market environment, the structure–conduct–performance framework is a useful tool to guide this study's research efforts. The general research structure therefore rests on three elements:

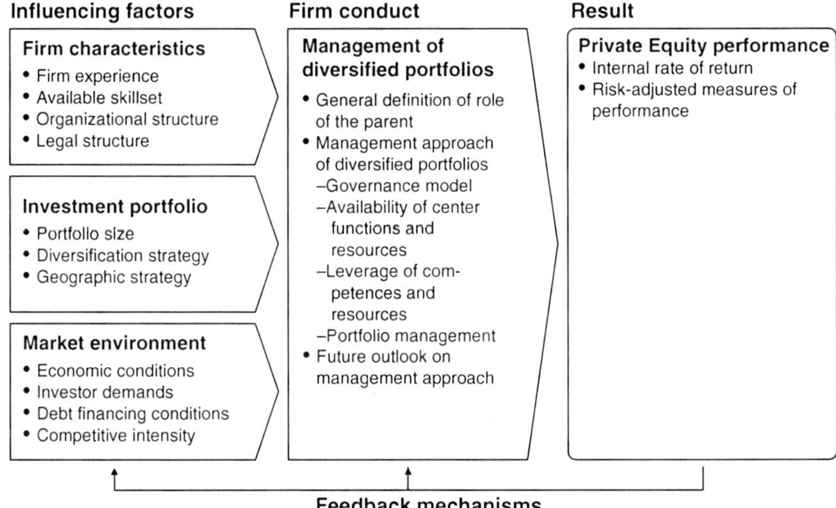

Fig. 6.1 Exploratory framework

Influencing factors, firm conduct, and resulting performance as highlighted in Fig. 6.1 and detailed in the consecutive sections. In addition, the framework entails a feedback mechanism in order to overcome the criticism of the structure–conduct–performance framework of being static and one-directional. The incorporated feedback mechanism is designed to assess the impact of "performance" as well as "firm conduct" on prior steps of the exploratory framework.

6.1.2 Influencing Factors

Influencing factors are all factors that can shape the way a private equity firm interacts with its portfolio companies. This study structures the influencing factors in three categories: (a) the PE firm's characteristics representing the factors determining the private equity firm headquarters or what is comparable to a "corporate holding", (b) the investment portfolio covering the characteristics of the portfolio companies in the PE firm's investment portfolio or what is comparable to the "business units" in a corporate setting, and (c) the market environment representing the external influences on the management style of a private equity player.

6.1.2.1 Firm Characteristics

Firm characteristics describe the elements that constitute the make-up of a PE partnership's headquarters. Most importantly, the experience of the private equity firm and the skill set comprised in the private equity firm are investigated in this part of research. It is expected, that the experience of a PE firm as well as the skills present in the firm are critical determinants of the management approach chosen by the firm. Players with long standing experience and a broad skill set ranging from financial engineering to deep operational expertise allow a PE partnership to execute a parenting role that differs substantially form the style one can expect in a young firm with mostly financial background. Experienced players would most likely tend to be heavily involved in the firm's strategic decision making and would probably hold a certain amount of center functions available for the business as found in Gottschalg and Meier (2005: 32–33) and Loos (2005: 217–278). Inexperienced PE firm on the other hand might focus on financials and oversight, much like the financial control role in traditional multi-business firms described by Goold and Campbell (1987: 111–145).

Another perspective covered in this category is the organizational and legal structure of a private equity firm as potential influencing factor on the management approach chosen towards the firm's portfolio companies. One can for instance expect that a firm structured in industry groups is a more active parent and is more active in leveraging resources across businesses than a firm organized along functions or regions. One can furthermore expect that legal structures impact the ability of a PE firm to manage its investment portfolio. A firm with few large funds might show a stronger portfolio management activity and ability to draw on the combined strengths of a portfolio than a firm with small, dedicated vehicles.

6.1.2.2 Investment Portfolio

The properties of the investment portfolio of a private equity partnership are the second important category of influencing factors. One element with potentially high impact on the parenting role is the pure size of the portfolio, which might allow a stronger exchange of resources across portfolio companies and an increased portfolio management activity as expressed in prior empirical studies (e.g. see Ljungqvist & Richardson, 2003a; Schmidt, 2004; Weidig & Mathonet, 2004). One can furthermore expect a correlation of portfolio size and the skill set available in the headquarters even though no direct relationship of portfolio size and PE performance was found in the first empirical part of this study. It is assumed that larger firms in general have a higher capability of attracting top talent given their presence in the market.

A second element of potential influence is the status of industry diversification within the investment portfolio, which is moreover at the very heart of this study. As indicated in the quantitative analysis of the firms' financials, one can expect a relationship between diversification strategy and management approach. Strong industry relatedness could allow a firm to develop a deeper understanding of operational practices and therefore provide the firm with the ability to have stronger involvement in strategic decision making. High relatedness can moreover offer the opportunity to present a substantial amount of center functions and resources to support the individual businesses. In addition, industry relatedness might foster a strong portfolio management and leverage of resources including such activities as buy-and-build strategies or the transfer of tangible and intangible resources.

As a third influencing factor, geographical scope is considered. One can expect that the more a portfolio is geographically spread, the less opportunity a firm has to actively manage the portfolio and the less center resources will be made available to the businesses in the investment portfolio.

6.1.2.3 Market Environment

The third category of influencing factors is market externalities. The components general economic conditions, investor demands, availability of debt financing and the associated conditions, as well as competitive intensity are included in the analysis to control activities by the PE for changes in the market place. One can, for instance, expect that an increasing demand for return by investors can lead the PE firm to a more active role in managing its investments. Similarly, an increasing competition for attractive targets in the market can eventually lead to higher acquisition costs and thereby trigger the need for more active involvement to make up for the higher up front investment. Economic conditions and availability of debt financing can have comparable influences. A sluggish economy or expensive respective scarce debt financing can require private equity players to bring a stronger parenting advantage to the portfolio to meet the return targets negotiated with the firms' limited partners.

6.1.3 Firm Conduct

The dimension firm conduct contains the key area of interest for this part of the study. Driven by the influencing factors, firm conduct covers the management approach chosen by a private equity house towards its portfolio companies. The research dimensions for this part of the exploratory framework are based on prior research about parenting and the management of diversified portfolios in multi-business firms and are aligned with the structure and findings outlined in Chap. 2 of this study, "Diversification in Corporations".

The section comprises three dimensions: (a) the general definition of the role as a parent, (b) the specific use of the four dimensions of corporate parenting in private equity firms, and (c) an outlook on current trends and developments in management practices of PE firms.

6.1.3.1 General Definition of Role a Parent

The general definition of how private equity is involved as a parent determines all further decisions about specific alternative management approaches. Once a firm identifies a certain parenting role, everything naturally should fall into place; it is therefore critical to understand the general tone prevalent in the different firms involved in the exploratory phase. The general parenting design can range from a pure investor role with some oversight activities to a hands-on industry specialist with deep operational expertise. The study furthermore attempts to understand the rationale behind the selected role with reference to the above-outlined influencing factors such as experience, industry diversification, or market externalities.

6.1.3.2 Specifics of Management Approach

After establishing a general understanding of the parenting role, the study then investigates the particular characteristics of the PE management approach. The individual elements of managing diversified portfolios are therefore deductively derived from the above-introduced corporate parenting theory by Campbell et al. (1994, 1998) and Campbell, Goold, and Alexander (1995a, 1995b). Each of the four major categories of corporate parenting "governance model", "availability of center functions and resources", "leverage of competences and resources", and "portfolio management", is broken down further to build a granular structure to analyze the parenting activities of a private equity firm as outlined in Fig. 6.2. This granular structure is based on academic contributions about the management models and techniques of traditional multi-business firms within each of the four

ACTIVITIES TO CREATE PARENTING ADVANTAGE

	Criteria	Description
Governance model	• Leverage as disciplinary tool	Use of high levels of leverage to reduce inefficient investments
	• Equity stakes	Requirement for management to invest own funds
	• Value-driven compensation system	Use of strong incentive system based on cash metrics
	• Willingness to replace management	Early replacement of non-performing management
	• Active board position	Execution of active shareholder role
	• Active management involvement	Active involvement in strategic decision making
Availability of center functions and resources	• Access to capital	Network of financial institutions and negotiation support
	• Access to financing talent	Professionals with financial skill set
	• Access to management talent	Professionals with general management and industry specific skill set
	• Access to other center functions (e.g., legal, purchasing)	Consolidation of selected services such as legal support or purchasing of key supplies
Leverage of resources and competences	• Informal platform for interaction	Installation of informal platform for regular exchange between executives
	• Targeted bilateral introductions	Targeted introductions of executives with potential for cooperation
	• Formalized systems (e.g. processes, targets, incentives)	Installation of formalized system to manage cooperation across portfolio
Portfolio management	• Internal capital markets	Installation of internal capital market for resource allocation
	• Regular portfolio reviews	Process for regular assessment of portfolio
	• Use of buy-and -build strategies	Active search of buy-and-build opportunities

Fig. 6.2 Activities to create parenting advantage

categories of corporate parenting, which have been introduced in Chap. 2 "Diversification in Corporations".

The study attempts to gain an understanding of the use of individual parenting activities by private equity firms. It then assesses the mechanisms and processes used within the PE partnerships and throughout their investment portfolios to apply different elements of the parenting framework.

6.1.3.3 Outlook on Future Industry Practices

Finally, the outlook on future industry practices can offer valuable insights about the future development of the industry, in particular when contrasted to the world of public equity. Looking back at the development of the private equity industry since the 1980s, substantial changes have occurred that brought the private equity management model much closer to the model seen in public corporations – but still outperforming investments in public equity. While the focus of PE in the early days was largely on financial engineering and financial oversight, today's PE firms are typically actively involved in their portfolio companies. Understanding the current trends can help to predict the future of the PE model as well as the model's long-term advantages over public equity markets.

6.1.4 Private Equity Performance

The performance of private equity investments marks the result of firm internal and external influencing factors and the way private equity partnerships deal with those factors – the firm conduct. Private equity performance is measured in accordance with the indicators used in the first empirical part of this study. On the one hand, the study uses the internal rate of return as a measure before risk adjustments. On the other hand, risk adjustments are introduced with the measures Jensen's Alpha, Sharpe's measure, and Treynor's measure.

6.1.5 Feedback Mechanisms

Industrial organization frameworks such as the structure–conduct–performance concept have often been framed for being static while it was clear that changes in strategic behavior often are dynamic processes that occur in rapidly shifting environments and therefore require a more dynamic analysis (e.g. see Bresnahan & Schmalensee, 1987; Spence, 1979). A common approach to address this criticism is the introduction of feedback loops to the original structure–conduct–performance framework, which link conduct and outcome back to the original starting position.

The use of feedback mechanisms enable the study to explore the influence of different performance levels on the shape of the private equity firm and the profile of the investment portfolio. It furthermore allows drawing conclusions about changes in firm conduct based on varying performance levels. The achieved outcome will most likely have an impact on the portfolio strategy and management model pursued by the private equity house.

The link between conduct and influencing factors completes the framework by investigating the influence of different behaviors on the characteristics of the private equity partnership and its investment portfolio. One can for instance expect that experiences with certain parenting styles influence the decision about new acquisitions. Positive impact of active parenting can for example cause a private equity firm to pursue further investments in related industry groups and therefore alter the portfolio composition of the firm.

6.2 Methodology

The general research design presented in Chap. 4 "General Research Design" already defined the most critical design choices. The study relies on exploratory research and will use guided interviews as primary means of data collection to arrive at propositions regarding the PE management approach to diversified portfolios. Having the general research design defined, this section outlines some of the specific methodological considerations in order to operationalize the exploratory research design of the second empirical part. The section presents the selected sample, the sources of information, the structure of the interviews, and the analytical design to explore the management model of private equity firms.

6.2.1 Sample for Exploratory Research

The exploratory research in this section is highly related to the analysis conducted in the quantitative research of empirical part one. The consecutive descriptions of the unit and level of analysis, the selection of the study's sample, and the characteristics of the sample will highlight the link between the two empirical studies.

6.2.1.1 Unit and Level of Analysis

One of the major shortfalls of prior empirical research about diversification in private equity is the studies' focus on individual funds or portfolio companies instead of targeting the PE firm at the partnership level. Similar to the quantitative analysis, the unit of analysis is therefore the private equity firm. The definition "firm" thereby comprises all individual funds and portfolio companies the individual firm is invested in as well as the headquarters of the private equity partnership.

The level of analysis for this study is the PE firm's headquarters. The objective of the study is to gain an understanding of the parenting role of PE players. It therefore studies the activities of the entity most comparable to a corporation's holding, which can be found in the private equity partnership. The analysis of the headquarters level includes all activities within the center as well as interactions with individual funds and portfolio companies as these interactions arguably are the major source of value created by "corporate parenting". The study furthermore takes the above-presented external influencing factors into account creating a three-tiered analysis design: market externalities, headquarters activities, as well as affected units and processes on fund and portfolio company level. According to Scott (2001), a model that can "trace the effects of salient and influential processes across two or more levels" (Scott 2001: 196) provides researchers with the most informative power.

6.2.1.2 Selection of Sample

While the quantitative analysis was based on a large sample covering 100 private equity players, qualitative research can be based on smaller sample sizes in particular for exploratory research designs. Exploratory research attempts to create an in-depth understanding of relationships and activities within the firms under review. The study therefore selects 20 private equity firms as research objects.

Exploratory research typically makes an effort to gain access to a diverse sample of research objects (Lamnek, 2005: 187–192). The selection of the research sample is based on the results of the quantitative analysis regarding performance and diversification found in empirical part one of this effort. The particular focus of this part of research lies on firms that have either a high degree of relatedness (high DR – low DU) or a high degree of unrelatedness (low DR – high DU), defined based on the equal range portfolios introduced in empirical part one. However, a limited number of firms with high degrees of relatedness and high degrees of unrelatedness (high DR – high DU) as well as both low degrees of relatedness and low degrees of unrelatedness (low DR – low DU) are included in the analysis to triangulate the findings of related and unrelated diversifiers.[1] Within each of these clusters, the selected sample is supposed to cover both low and high performers as well as both US and European PE players to correct for any inherent strategic and geographical ambiguities. In addition, the sample seeks to feature firms of varying sizes and ages to control for effects imposed by the pure portfolio dimension and the implied higher potential for industry relatedness.

6.2.1.3 Characteristics of Sample

The sample consists of a total of 20 private equity players with seven firms in the category relatedness (high DR – low DU), six firms with high degrees of unrelatedness (low DR – high DU), four private equity players with both high relatedness and

[1] Players with both high degrees of relatedness and unrelatedness have a substantial number of investments in multiple industries; players with both low degrees of relatedness and unrelatedness are dominated by individual investments in a limited number of industry groups.

high unrelatedness (high DR – high DU) and three players with both low levels of relatedness and unrelatedness (low DR – low DU). Figure 6.3 presents the featured sample including key indicators regarding performance, diversification, and size.[2]

Private equity players focused on a narrow investment portfolio as well as related diversified players show the strongest performance as measured by internal rate of return on a 10-year horizon (27.7% for low DR – low DU and 22.6% for high DR – low DU). Firms with both high related and unrelated diversified portfolios rank 2.4% below related diversifiers, slightly above the selected firms with highly unrelated diversified portfolios (18.3%). The performance characteristics also hold for the risk-adjusted performance measures used in this study.

Largely focused private equity firms in the exploratory sample have the largest amount of committed equity, some 40% above more diversified portfolio configurations. They moreover have the lowest degree of total diversification (DT 1.5) followed by related diversified firms (DT 1.8).

Twelve firms out of the sample have an US origin with the remaining eight firms being founded in the European market. However, all 20 firms in the sample have

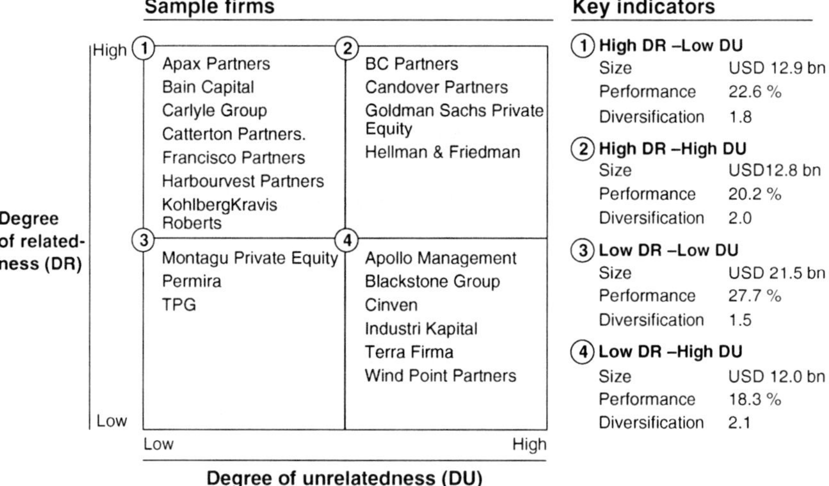

Fig. 6.3 Characteristics of sample

[2] A short profile of all firms included in the exploratory research design is attached in the appendix of this publication. The information contained in the profiles is solely based on publicly available information about the private equity players. All information gained during the exploratory research is used for aggregate research only.

global investment portfolios with strongholds in the US and Europe and selected investments in Asia and other regions. Eleven of the 20 firms were interviewed in the US whereby one European firm was interviewed in the US and two firms with US roots were part of the nine European interview participants.

6.2.2 *Sources of Information*

While the first part of research in this study was solely based on third-party data, exploratory research is generally based on multiple data sources in order to get an in-depth understanding for the relationships within the research object (Yin, 2003: 85–97). This part of the study's empirical research therefore uses multiple sources of data to derive conclusions about the management approach of private equity firms towards diversified portfolios.

The major insight is expected from the interaction with private equity practitioners during guided interviews, which have been introduced in Chap. 4 "General Research Design"; however other sources are important to gain sufficient insight on the dimensions of the exploratory framework: influencing factors, firm conduct, and performance. Figure 6.4 provides an overview of the different sources of information used for the exploratory part of this study, which will be detailed in following.

SOURCES OF INFORMATION FOR EXPLORATORY RESEARCH

	Dimension of exploratory framework	Information sources: Dataset	Interview	Company/ analyst reports	Market reports
Influencing factors	• Firm characteristics	✓	✓	✓	
	• Investment portfolio	✓	✓	✓	
	• Market environment		✓		✓
Firm conduct	• General defintion of role of parent		✓		
	• Specifics of management approach		✓		
	• Future outlook on Private Equity management approach		✓		
Per-formance	• Private Equity performance	✓			

Fig. 6.4 Sources of information for exploratory research

Interview partners are partners or seasoned investment professionals in the selected private equity firms overseeing a larger number of investments, who at the same time have an understanding of the practices of the overall firm.[3]

6.2.2.1 Influencing Factors

Information about the characteristics of the private equity firm including the firm's skills and organizational as well as legal structure will be obtained during the interviews with private equity practitioners and supplemented by information available to the public in company as well as analyst reports. The experience of the firm can be obtained through the vintage years of its funds contained in the data sample of empirical part one.

Insights regarding the PE investment portfolio is largely embedded in the quantitative information obtained in empirical part one. The analysis of the transaction history of the study's 100 PE firms provides insight about the industrial and geographical diversification of the firms' investment portfolios. The size of the portfolio is contained in the dataset acquired with the performance data.

The market environment about debt financing conditions, investor demands, and competition is assessed through industry reports and additional information gained during the interviews.

6.2.2.2 Firm Conduct

The investigation of firm conduct is at the very heart of the exploratory research design. Understanding the practices and key success factors of private equity firms in handling large, diversified portfolios is the focus of this part of analysis. All components, general definition of parenting role, the specific components of the management approach to diversified portfolios as well as the outlook on future practices are explored in interviews with practitioners from private equity firms.

6.2.2.3 Private Equity Performance

The assessment of PE performance is based on the data sample analyzed in the first empirical part of the study. The above-studied dataset provides the internal rate of return as performance measure before risk adjustments as well as the risk-adjusted measures Jensen's Alpha, Sharpe measure, and Treynor measure. This data will

[3] For the purpose of this study, all interview information is used on an aggregate level only. The information about each firm obtained during the interview is treated anonymously and all company data not already obtained in the study's first empirical part or available to the public remains confidential.

provide the information required to assess the success of particular and potentially diverging private equity management strategies.

6.2.3 Structure of Interview

The general structure of the interview follows the exploratory research framework outlined above and the information requirements, which are to be assessed during the interview with private equity practitioners. The interview is therefore structured along four elements "firm characteristics and portfolio strategy", "role of the parent", "management approach to diversified portfolios", and "outlook on future industry practices".[4]

First of all, the interview intends to deepen the understanding of the private equity firm. The interview therefore investigates the experience[5] and skill set[6] available in the PE player as well as its organizational and legal structure. The first part of the interview furthermore addresses the composition of the firm's investment portfolio including its industry diversification and geographic strategy.

Second, the interview attempts to get an in-depth understanding of the general definition of a firm's parenting role including the impact of the different influencing factors such as firm characteristics, investment portfolio, and market environment. Particular focus is placed on the impact of diversification on the parenting approach and the opportunities to create a parenting advantage in related and unrelated diversified portfolios.

Third, the interview addresses the specific management approaches contained in corporate parenting along the granular structure outlined above. Within each of the four dimensions "governance model", availability of center functions and resources', "leverage of resources and competences", and "portfolio management", the study wants to gain an understanding of the use of different management approaches, the impact of different influencing factors as well as the coordination mechanisms found within the PE partnership to coordinate scarce resources across the portfolio.

The interview then closes with questions regarding the outlook on future industry practices. In this section, the interview is expected to highlight current trends in the private equity field and to provide insights about the impact of such changes on the parenting role of private equity firms.

[4] The interview guide underlying the qualitative empirical part of this study is provided in the appendix of this publication.

[5] The experience of the private equity firm is generally measured by the time since its inception respectively the time since the vintage of the firm's first fund.

[6] The skill set of the private equity firm is assessed through the typical recruiting sources. People with financial skills generally are recruited from leading investment banks, management skills are generally found in former management consultants or seasoned managers, and deep operational knowledge typically stems from former long-term industry practitioners.

6.2.4 Design for Data Analysis

In accordance with the general design principles outlined in Chap. 4 "General Research Design", the study's exploratory research design approaches the management models of private equity firms on a case-by-case basis and then aggregates the collected data to find overarching clusters. These clusters build the foundation to derive propositions about the success factors of private equity and the learning opportunities of traditional multi-business firms.

In a first step, every firm is analyzed and rated along the exploratory framework including influencing factors, firm conduct and performance. The analysis of firm conduct hereby draws on the granular structure of corporate parenting developed for the study's exploratory framework and applied during the guided interviews. The comprehensive set of information about every firm is used to gain an in-depth case-by-case picture for each firm in the sample.

In a second step, the linkages and feedback mechanisms between the individual elements of the exploratory design are analyzed to get a collective view of every private equity firm. This part of research again takes place on a case-by-case basis and aspires to gain information about relationships between elements such as skills, diversification, or geographic origin and the management styles used to govern the portfolio as much as the link between parenting activities and performance. It finally attempts to understand the feedback mechanisms connecting performance and parenting style with a firm's influencing factors.

In a third step, the study investigates the overarching relationships between cases. It consequently seeks patterns across multiple case studies thereby attempting to find more general themes about the overall management models of private equity firms in diversified investment portfolios as well as the individual influencing factors, parenting activities, and performance levels that characterize different management models. The objective of this step in the exploratory research design is to find a small number of clusters that are able to describe the majority of cases analyzed in this part of empirical research.

These overarching clusters are then used for the further discussion of the study's empirical results and form the basis for the development of propositions about the key success factors of private equity and the learning opportunities for traditional multi-business firms.

6.3 Empirical Results

This section displays the empirical results of the qualitative research of this study. The section first outlines the general management models observed in private equity firms (Sect. 6.3.1). It then details the individual models including firm characteristics, a detailed description of the management models along the above-mentioned components governance, headquarters role, leverage of resources, and portfolio management, as well as the management models' impact on performance (Sects. 6.3.2–6.3.4). The section closes with trends in the private equity industry and the effects on the PE management model (Sect. 6.3.5).

6.3.1 Management Models in Private Equity

The exploratory research provided an insight into an industry that is more diverse than often described in academic or media contributions and perceived by business practitioners, politicians, and the public. Most prior contributions outline a management model that is unison across the entire private equity industry. This study, however, shows that one can observe different management approaches, which define the role and opportunities for value creation by the private equity firm within its investment portfolio.

To derive different management models, the study created clusters along different dimensions of the study's exploratory framework. These dimensions included quanti-tative criteria such as portfolio size, first year of vintage, or level of diversification as well as qualitative criteria such as parenting activity and skill profiles. The analytical design providing the most explanatory power includes the two dimensions parenting style and mode of diversification as key dimensions. Along those lead dimensions, 80% of the firms sampled in this study can be classified into two general management models. Only 20% have strongly diverging characteristics and are therefore categorized as hybrid management models. Other analytical designs are not able to deliver comparable results. Figure 6.5 highlights the two key dimensions and the two general management models in private equity, which will then be detailed in following.

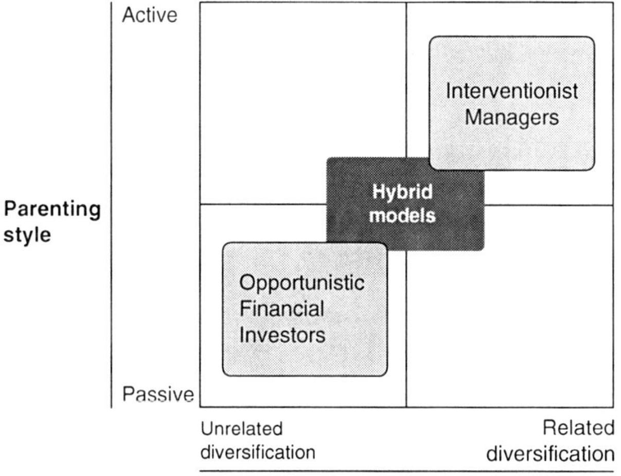

Fig. 6.5 Private equity management models

6.3.1.1 Key Dimensions

Two key dimensions characterize the private equity management model. On the one hand, the private equity parenting style; on the other hand, the mode of industry diversification of the private equity investment portfolio.

The study finds large discrepancies in the way private equity firms handle their role as parents towards a portfolio of diversified businesses. The parenting style dimension is therefore the first critical component in finding an overarching management model in private equity firms. Generally, there are firms with an active approach towards their investment portfolios while other firms act as a passive parent. Active parenting is characterized by a deep parenting footprint of a private equity firm across multiple dimensions of the parenting framework with strong involvement by the PE partnership in strategic and financial questions whereas passive parents generally focus their activities on few particular elements of the parenting spectrum. The classification as active vs. passive parent is primarily based on the study's interviews with private equity practitioners.

As improvement to the classification along parenting styles, the mode of diversification proves to be the most powerful component whereas other factors add only limited explanatory power to the analysis. The mode of diversification describes the direction of industry diversification measured for the individual private equity firm. Some firms pursue an opportunistic investment strategy in unrelated business sectors. Other firms on the contrary deliberately chose a limited number of industries and concentrate their investment activities on those industries, thereby creating a portfolio with related diversified businesses. The classification of the level of diversification and the firm's investment strategy are based both on the quantitative research results of the study's first empirical part as well as the interviews with private equity practitioners.

Within the sample of this study, other components such as portfolio size or time since inception of a private equity firm do not appear to be distinguishing factors of different management models. No pattern can be recognized between these elements and private equity conduct as a parent in a portfolio of diversified businesses.

6.3.1.2 Private Equity Management Models

Based on the two key dimensions, one can distinguish two general management models in private equity firms, "opportunistic financial investors" and "interventionist managers".

"Opportunistic financial investors" are private equity firms with investment portfolios spread across multiple industry groups, whereby no critical size is achieved in any of those industry groups (unrelated diversification). The parenting style of those firms is considered passive with limited and highly focused involvement in the activities of the firms' portfolio companies. Areas of interest for "opportunistic financial investors" center around changes in the financial and governance structure of their portfolio companies in the early stages of the investment.

The investment portfolio of "interventionist managers" on the other side consists of mostly related diversified businesses whereby most firms achieve relatedness of their investments in more than one industry group. These firms pursue an active parenting style with generally deep intervention in strategic and financial questions. The level of involvement remains high during the holding period of the investment.

In addition to those two models, one can observe a number of hybrid management models. Some hybrid management models can be found in firms on a transition path from one management model to another while others appear persistent over time.

6.3.2 *Characteristics of Opportunistic Financial Investors*

The "opportunistic financial investor" management model is long established and can be considered the classic private equity management model. It has first been created in the early 1980s and has dominated the private equity world throughout its first boom during the late 1980s. This traditional private equity model can still be observed in numerous private equity players today and stands behind the success stories of some of the world's largest private equity firms. It is also the basis for most academic publications during the late 1980s and 1990s and remains the standard definition of private equity in many of today's PE contributions.

6.3.2.1 General Profile and Investment Portfolio

"Opportunistic financial investors" generally originated in the US and have gone global from their US base. Their business grew from a domestic American business in the 1980s over Europe in the 1990s to a business with global footprint in the recent private equity wave. An increasing number of firms are getting established in Asia or are transforming their investor relations offices in those countries into investment offices. Most firms by now have a global office footprint; however, most of these "opportunistic financial investors" operate out of the large financial hubs and have limited local presence in the countries they are invested in.

The skill profile of "opportunistic financial investors" has a strong spike in topics related to financial engineering. The vast majority of the firms' investment professionals have a background in investment and debt banking, generally accounting for more than 90% of the firms' work force. The skills acquired during the staff's time in banking comprise in particular financial valuation of target companies and the ability to engineer the capital structure of an acquisition. One of the interviewed private equity managers described the investment bankers' skill set as "oriented on the balance sheet rather than on the income statement"; in other words capital structures and asset sales play a more important role in those firms than EBITDA growth through top-line growth and cost reductions. The firms' teams are typically supplemented by selected senior managers, who have previously been top-executives in a broad range of industry firms. While operational experience is an important motivation to bring these managers on board, their professional network appears to outweigh operational expertise. Networks allow access to proprietary deal flow and are an essential element for the success of a private equity firm. As one private equity manager of a leading US firm puts it: "Industry hires are door openers".

Organizationally, there is no prevalent structure found in "opportunistic financial investors". Some of the largest PE firms use geographic regions as their primary organizational distinction while others are organized by industry groups or along individual funds. Other firms finally organize their investment professionals in a general pool and employ them opportunistically on incoming transactions. One of the largest firms claims that "the teams of individual US buyout funds work 100% independent of each other" giving up any advantages of industrial or functional knowledge sharing. Responsibilities for specific investments generally remain with the deal team, which often consists of two partners and additional associates for support.

The investment portfolio of "opportunistic financial investors" is characterized by unrelated diversification. Investors with this management model generally invest opportunistically in a broad industry portfolio without respect of the existing portfolio and skills potentially available in the private equity partnership. 85% of the firms' total diversification (mean total diversification DT 1.88) is explained by unrelated diversification (mean unrelated diversification DU 1.60 vs. mean related diversification DR 0.28). The average number of industry groups is, on average, more than seven (2-digit SIC count 7.25) with individual firms ranging up to ten.[7] A senior investment professional at a mid-size private equity firm with strong financial focus highlights that – in his view – "a broad pipeline across different industries is crucial for the success of private equity firms". He argues that the flexibility to react to different industry cycles and the consequent changes in deal flow outweigh any advantages of sector focus.

From an industry preference point of view, one finds that "opportunistic financial investors" have a higher share of investments in mature industries vs. growth industries. An above average share of investments lies in companies in the basic material, consumer products, and manufacturing industry as well as in utilities. Those investments in general provide more stable cash flows and require lower amounts of investments during the holding period than acquisitions in industries with high growth opportunities and large investment requirements such as telecommunication, information technology or pharmaceuticals. A manager in one of the largest firms in the financial investor definition explains that they don't need "huge growth to get our returns" and that investments generally are "more on the side of more stable businesses".

Closely linked to the observation of industry preferences, one finds that "opportunistic financial investors" generally invest and operate with higher levels of leverage. Managers in these firms generally remark that they "feel comfortable with high levels of leverage" and stress the "disciplining function" of high levels of leverage

---

[7]Ten industry groups (defined on the two-digit SIC Code level) is by methodological definition the upper limit for the number of industry groups possible to be assigned to individual firms.

in reference to Jensen's (1986) free cash-flow theory. The high leverage of most engagements gives management limited latitude over new investments but focuses management's attention on bottom-line growth to pay down debt.

6.3.2.2 Description of Management Model

The "opportunistic financial investor" would describe itself as "the more reactive player rather than the very focused, proactive investor". This type of investor defines its role as a provider of capital combined with a strong skill set in financial issues such as deal and capital structure as well as deep process knowledge about mergers and acquisitions. More cynically, a competitor describes this PE model as "excellent financial engineers but lack of understanding of individual businesses". They don't see their role in the active intervention with management decision making and support on strategic and operational questions. A senior manager of a firm that classifies his partnership as a "financial investor" states clearly that "we only get involved in management decision making if there is a significant problem or if there is an opportunity that requires financing".

Value creation in the view of financial investors comes from "being able to buy right, with the right capital structure, the right cost of capital and the right incentives". In their belief, "capital efficiency is the most important thing in a company – by bringing in capital efficiency, you added more value than with anything else you could do". If one decomposes value creation in EBITDA growth, de-leveraging, and multiple expansion, many financial opportunists would argue that the largest part of value creation comes from de-leveraging and multiple expansion. De-leveraging basically means "reducing the cost of the operating capital while retaining an option on the upside of the equity holding – you just have to wait and the option will be worth more." Driving performance through multiple expansion is related to the speculation on particular industry cycles and differences in multiples rather than realizing opportunities for improvement and growth in individual businesses.

Figure 6.6 outlines the parenting activities of "opportunistic financial investor" along the four major elements to create parenting advantage. The numerical findings reveal a strong focus of private equity firms in this investor class on financially driven activities while avoiding active involvement in management's strategic decision making.

The governance function in "opportunistic financial investors" is dominated by two characteristics: high levels of leverage with the consequent debt burden and strong alignment of interest. In accordance with Jensen's (1986) free cash-flow theory, the agent's ability to undertake value-destroying investments is reduced by the obligation to pay down debt and service interest payments. private equity firms in general and financial investors in particular value high levels of debt as "terrific disciplinary tool". Strong alignment of interest is provided by the equity stake and incentive plan outlined for the management team of portfolio companies. If the particular portfolio company achieves high levels of performance for the PE firm's investors, they are rewarded with what one of the PE managers calls a "juicy compensation package".

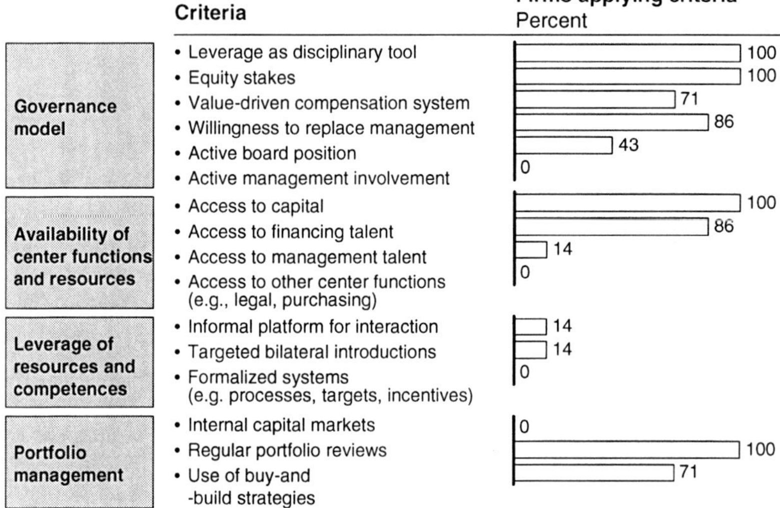

Fig. 6.6 Parenting activities "opportunistic financial investors"

Management performance is highly transparent and measured on the level of individual portfolio companies, not the performance of an overall fund or even the private equity firm. PE firms implemented a successful model that instills a clear message with top management: "If I do well, I walk off wealthy". On the flip side, financial investors are generally much faster in replacing non-performing management. While having a higher upside, executives in portfolio companies also face a higher risk of losing their jobs than typically observed in the divisions of traditional multi-business firms. The head of a leading firm in this segment states that "if things go bad, my first job is to change management". Management is often considered a "black box" that is replaced if the firm does not achieve the required performance standards.

Interaction with management occurs both formally in board meetings as well as informally if particular issues arise. However, interaction between private equity management and portfolio company management is very selective and generally focused on financial performance indicators and selected strategic measures. "Opportunistic financial investors" generally have small professional teams and seek limited intervention with strategy and operational decisions in their portfolio companies. In investment cases that require deep operational expertise, financial investors often seek the support of a consortium partner. Besides the spreading of risk and access to capital, operational expertise in specific industries is a key driver for the increasing occurrence of so-called club deals as less active financial investors seek the partnership with PE firms with stronger operational and industry expertise.

In general, financial investors provide their portfolio companies with limited resources out of the private equity partnership. The key expertise that is leveraged across the firms' investment portfolios is finance-driven and includes financial engineering skills and access to capital markets. PE firms consolidate all financing activities and are generally in charge of any change in the capital structure of individual portfolio companies. A partner in one of the industry's leading firms is convinced that financial engineering still "offers tremendous potential for superior returns" and only the largest private equity houses have "the capabilities to implement complex capital structures" with techniques such as securitization or sale-and-lease-back transactions. PE professionals are furthermore the single point of access to capital markets and hold the relationships of coverage groups in financial institutions to negotiate interest rates and financing terms. Beyond finance activities, there are limited services provided by the financial investors. Private equity in this investor group has limited operational capacity and expertise to function as sparring partner or consultant to the management team of portfolio companies and there is no attempt to consolidate any services such as purchasing or talent development in the hands of the private equity firm.

The horizontal leverage of resources between the investments within a firm's investment portfolio is also limited in the case of financial investors. They acknowledge that the expertise acquired during the buyout process adds to the knowledge base for further transactions in the same industry or geography. However, once a company is part of a firm's investment portfolio, limited activity can be observed. At most, there are occasional informal introductions of portfolio companies' top managers, who could profit from interaction with each other. However, financial investors stress the importance of respecting the arm's length principle. The principle requires a clear accountability of potential revenues or cost savings to individual companies as different firms are often part of different investment funds and therefore belong to different investor groups. In addition, the firms in a private equity portfolio are meant to remain liquid assets. PE firms in the financial investor category are therefore concerned that attempts to leverage resources horizontally across a firm's portfolio could eventually establish rigid connections between companies and thereby reduce the assets' tradability in an IPO or trade sale on the capital markets. "You always run into problems during the exit if you link your portfolio companies. You need to unbundle them and that creates a mess". Furthermore, private equity firms in general provide no internal capital market. By the fund's legal structure, all capital flows from individual portfolio companies have to be returned to investors and fresh capital has to be called respectively new capital has to be raised to finance investments in other portfolio companies.[8] A cash rich business can therefore not be used to cross-subsidize investments in other businesses as generally practiced in multi-business corporations.

"Opportunistic financial investors" actively pursue "buy-and-build" strategies with the particular focus on achieving higher multiples with larger companies.[9] This strategy is of particular interest in fragmented industries with substantial opportunities

[8] Private equity firms typically can call committed capital in the first 5 years of a fund's lifetime; after this period, funds have to negotiate new capital injections by either existing or new investors.

[9] Large companies historically trade at higher multiples on capital markets than small companies. Private equity firms take advantage of this phenomenon by combining companies to create larger assets.

to create larger assets while avoiding regulatory constraints. PE managers however remark, that – independent of potential follow-on acquisitions – the initial investment is required to "stand on its own feet" and generate the performance required by the PE firm's investors. "buy-and-build" strategies are therefore mainly used to further enhance performance.

Financial investors generally show a holding period of their individual portfolio companies of 3–5 years. Holding periods, however, can vary based on opportunities that arise during the investment. Such opportunities include an attractive exit opportunity through a trade sale, a good IPO market or the possibility to refinance and extract a special dividend during the holding period. "An asset is always for sale – and then you evaluate if that is the biggest price you can get." Refinancing is particularly interesting to private equity firms given the deep knowledge about the firm as opposed to a new investment, which generally entails substantial business risk.

6.3.2.3 Review of Performance

The "opportunistic financial investors" featured in this study's research show an average 5-year performance of 19 and 14% in the 10-year investment horizon. Performance deviates from low double-digit performance levels to performances close to 30%.[10]

Within this study, the firms with a strong financial orientation all have an US origin. The size of the overall portfolio has no impact on performance within this investor segment.

6.3.3 Characteristics of Interventionist Managers

The "interventionist manager" model is a comparably young model in private equity firms. It evolved out of the traditional financial investor model and was largely established during the current private equity wave. This model of active parenting in a portfolio of related businesses poses a number of new challenges and particular requirements on skills, setup, and management activities of private equity firms.

6.3.3.1 General Profile and Investment Portfolio

"Interventionist" private equity firms have their origins in the United States as well as in Europe. Many of the firms have evolved out of previously more opportunistically driven financial investors. Geographically, one finds two types of "interventionist"

---

[10]The influence of different management models on performance is discussed in further detail in Sect. 6.4.1 "Comparison of Management Models and Impact on Performance".

firms. One part of the firms has a global footprint with presence in the US, Europe, and since recently Asia. In particular firms with a focus on large-cap targets have realized that most of their targets are – as one PE manager explains – "large global firms, which require a global presence to properly understand the business and manage the asset". A manager in one of the industry's largest firms accordingly expressed his firm's geographic strategy as "global reach, local presence" and their ambition to "seek local sourcing and local execution". A founding partner in another firm mentioned that "we have a strong belief in local expertise with strong local presence and a relatively large team on the ground". The other part of PE firms in this investor segment has a regional approach. These firms concentrate their engagements in particular areas of the US, European or Asian market with a focus on mid-cap targets and rely on their strong local network and know-how to source, monitor and support investments.

From a skill perspective, "interventionist manager" firms offer a stronger expertise in strategic and operational topics. The majority of a firm's employees have a consulting or industry background whereas only a small fraction of firm members come with an investment or debt banking experience. A number of firms within the top 20 of the world's largest PE firms consist of up to 80% of former top management consultants and industry hires. This observation is particularly true for firms with a European background that often tap non-investment banking talent pools to recruit new investment professionals but also holds true for many US-based firms. The staffs' diverse background provides firms with skills required for an in-depth understanding of opportunities and risks of individual businesses. In the eyes of a PE firm's founder and managing director, "balance sheet skills are necessary, but ultimately business sense and strategic vision drive performance".

"Interventionist" firms generally follow a clear organizational pattern. These firms are organized in industrial groups as primary organizational premise and many of them consider themselves "industry-sector specialists" and as firms with "strong sector orientation". The number of industry groups can range from as little as two to three to as many as eight or nine in some of the largest PE firms. The professional team is allocated to these sectors and has the responsibility to develop industry networks and build up sector-specific knowledge. Sector teams share resources only in cases of a strong imbalance of deal flow between industry teams. Beyond the sector organization, some private equity houses have maintained selected special functions such as financing or legal that overarch the firms' organizational setup.

In terms of industry diversification, private equity firms with an "interventionist manager" approach have a higher share of related assets in their investment portfolios than "opportunistic financial investors" with close to 40% of diversification being explained by related diversification (mean related diversification DR 0.59 vs. mean unrelated diversification DU 1.17). Overall diversification, however, is almost as high as in the financial investor group (mean total diversification DT in "interventionists" 1.77 vs. mean total diversification DT in "opportunistic financial investors" 1.88). The average number of industry groups in "interventionists" featured in the exploratory research part of the study is 5.75 and thereby lower than in financial investors.

From an industry perspective, investments in growth industries find a higher representation in "interventionist" firms than in "opportunistic financial investors". "Interventionists" display a higher share of investments in information technology, communication businesses, media firms, and pharmaceuticals. Most of these businesses require a larger amount of follow-on investments after the acquisition and generally more free cash flow at hand after interest payments.

The average leverage in "interventionist managers" is – according to interviewed PE managers – "conservative" and in some firms results in an average of two times EBITDA. Lower levels of leverage provide portfolio companies with more potential for growth investments as well as borrowing capacity for follow-on acquisitions: "we want the cash to stay in the businesses to reinvest it and grow" (managing director of a US mid-market PE firm).

6.3.3.2 Description of Management Model

The "interventionist manager" model is characterized by a more active investment approach and a focus on "operational and strategic expertise". Interventionist investors show a strong commitment to operational involvement and describe themselves as "hands-on investors" that pursue a "consulting-like approach" with their investments. Investors in this category stress their deep understanding of focus industries and individual businesses and their willingness to "roll up our sleeves and let things get dirty" whereas financial engineering skills are described as necessary but a rather "commoditized set of skills" as pointed out by a US large cap fund manager.

While financial issues are important to the interventionists' investment case, the value is created through strategic and operational changes in the business. In the interventionists' argument, "everybody can do financial tricks, but this does not differentiate you as an investor". Value creation happens through the transformation of businesses to generate growth. If one decomposes value creation in EBITDA growth, de-leveraging and multiple expansion, "interventionist managers" state that the majority of value is created through EBITDA growth, which contains both cost reductions and revenue growth. One investor with long-standing history in the private equity field even claims that "today, we don't buy any company anymore where we don't see any revenue growth potential". A much smaller share of value is created through de-leveraging and several investors don't even accept multiple-expansion as value creation in the initial investment case for a target given the speculative element of multiple expansion.

For the parenting approach of "interventionist managers", Fig. 6.7 reveals a concentration of these private equity firms on the interaction with the management teams of their portfolio companies and the active support through center management resources and selected additional functions. "Interventionists" furthermore show a stronger level of activity to support cooperation between companies.

Governance in "interventionists" is generally understood as "sparring partner" or "day-to-day coach" relationship between the private equity management and the management teams of individual portfolio companies. Whereas leverage remains

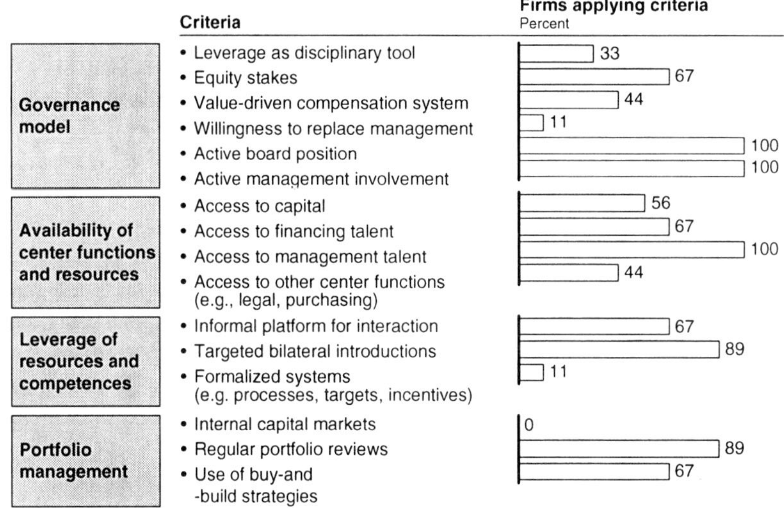

Fig. 6.7 Parenting activities "interventionist managers"

an important governance tool to avoid inefficient investments, the generally lower levels of debt provide room for new investments in growth projects. Private equity firms in this investor category are deeply involved in strategic and financial decisions and interact with management on a regular basis – formally through board meetings and informally on a "consultant-like basis". Boards are generally smaller after a leveraged buyout and therefore allow less politics but more effective interaction and decision making. A European mid-market investment professional explains that decision making "is generally decentralized in the portfolio companies; however PE professionals are actively involved in strategic decision making and retain the right to take key decisions to the PE firm's investment committee".[11]

Intervening PE investors often exchange management teams early on during the investments, ideally during the development of the investment's business plan and generally "change individual positions rather than the entire top management". During the holding period, investors typically try to work with the management team and refrain from replacing top management unless absolutely necessary.

Hands-on monitoring and involvement in strategic dimensions can be accomplished by different means. Some private equity firms have established investment teams with deep operational expertise that are in charge of acquiring and managing

[11] The private equity firm's investment committee is generally involved in decision making if major investments or strategic shifts are up for decision that have not been part of the initial investment thesis.

the firms' investment portfolios and thereby avoid the separation of performance responsibility between dealmakers and operating managers. Other players have opted for separate groups and thereby promote the institution of deeper transaction and operational expertise. One group generally focuses on the transaction process during acquisition and exit while the other group concentrates on the monitoring and interaction with management to increase performance while an asset is in the firms' investment portfolio. In the latter case, one observes two ways of allocating responsibility: In some firms, the responsibility over the individual investments remains with the investment professional in charge of buying the asset and operational expertise is "purchased" similar to an outside consulting firm or external group of advisors. In other private equity houses, the responsibility is split between investment and operating professionals or is temporarily handed over to operational partners. The split model has the advantage that each group is able to build distinctive knowledge and networks relevant to their task and to focus their time on the things they are best equipped to do. As one PE manager puts it, "deal partners should not be distracted from their origination focus while others know how to monitor and transform a company. You always have to ask yourself, is this the best use of your time?"

Given the high levels of involvement by an interventionist private equity firm, players in this investor category generally seek to invest outside of consortium deals or to be the lead firm in a group of rather passive, financially oriented investors. A managing director in a large European PE firm states clearly that "we don't do club deals and we only do deals where we gain full control". Another lead partner in a US firm explains that "consortium deals are good as long as the deal is good – they become a nightmare in bad investments as suddenly everybody wants to get involved". "Interventionist managers" therefore prefer to be the "only cook in the kitchen" and have majority control to enforce their ownership position. The recent trend to equity bridges is a mechanism to guarantee the lead position even in large deals. Banks provide the required equity bridge in a deal that is syndicated to passive investors after the transaction is completed.[12] The driving private equity firm is therefore in a clear leadership for further interaction with management.

The active involvement in strategic decision making is supported by the alignment of interest between the private equity firm and top management. The incentive schemes of top management provide them with a package that allows them to "make big figures" if performance is improved and the private equity firm reaches a successful exit.

Interventionist private equity firms provide their portfolio companies with a number of services from the private equity partnership. First of all, they make a substantial amount of management talent available to the top management team of a portfolio asset. Private equity professionals generally spend a substantial amount of time on the development of strategic initiatives during the first 100 days and offer further support on strategic issues to management in strategy workshops or

[12]Passive investors can include other private equity firms that restrict their role in the engagement to a passive co-investment as well as investors that generally act as limited partners in PE funds but are given selective opportunities to make direct co-investments.

via informal meetings functioning as sparring partner by "simply asking the right questions". "In many ways, it looks like a 100-day plan that, say, GE would implement once they buy a company." The management support function is particularly strong in firms with established industry groups and a strong sector focus given the in-depth strategic and operational expertise accrued over time. Firms with experienced industry teams claim that they are more "empathetic with management teams" and are able to "provide better guidance" than less sector-focused players in the private equity field. Since most private equity firms have developed into global players, they furthermore assist their portfolio companies in areas such as finding management talent and addressing accounting, legal, and regulatory issues in foreign geographies where local market understanding is required. One private equity firm even describes its local reach as "way to get into deals" as some companies need expertise in certain markets to drive their expansion strategies forward – in particular expansions involving M&A activities. In addition, "interventionist managers" provide access to financial markets and financial engineering know how to their portfolio companies in case changes in the firms' capital structure or refinancing is required and use their combined negotiation power with financial institutions to improve financing terms.

As a recent trend, "interventionist" firms also start consolidating purchasing activities to a center competence, which can be either internally organized or provided by an outside expert. Joint purchasing can involve non-core elements such as the joint negotiation of IT licenses, packaging, telecommunication and insurance deals, or the status at large logistics providers. It can however also stretch into core business activities if substantial gains for the performance of the business portfolio can be achieved. If for example the sugar or steel price is a critical driver of performance for the overall portfolio, some "interventionist" firms have started to consolidate activities and counterparties and use their stronger position to reduce prices on the raw material markets or with selected suppliers, respectively.

Horizontally, the leverage of resources between portfolio companies remains limited as PE firms avoid the reduction of tradability of assets and the lack of accountability for management actions. However, there are selected areas, where "interventionists" engage to enable synergies between businesses. First of all, they acquire industry expertise that can be levered in subsequent or parallel investments. This knowledge base is particularly fruitful in firms that consolidate related investments in industry groups and therefore create centers of competence in those focus sectors. Beyond this, "interventionist" firms provide an informal platform for companies to engage bilaterally. PE professionals make introductions and host conferences that bring top managers of different portfolio companies together to exchange knowledge and create potential business connections. One PE manager even states that "if things are roughly equivalent, we expect that we keep them in the family". Given the informal nature of those activities, private equity firms keep assets tradable and at the same time avoid the creation of expensive and binding interaction processes and targets that generally lead to large cost positions in multi-business firms. Interventionist investors therefore "create the forum but just the forum". Beyond this informal platform, only few private equity firms actively search for cooperation opportunities between businesses.

Only one large European firm featured in the sample stated that they would – for example – actively pursue distribution opportunities for their media holdings through retail outlets owned by other portfolio companies and build those synergies into the initial investment case. Internal capital markets are not established given the previously outlined legal structure of private equity funds.

"Interventionist managers" actively use "buy-and-build" strategies to grow the business. This strategy is of particular interest to this type of investor as "you put more money at work at a time when you already know which direction the investment is going – it's like doubling up once you have seen the cards". While buy-and-build strategies generally entail substantial integration efforts, these strategies at the same time reduce organic growth requirements to reach the PE performance hurdles.

The holding period of "interventionist" firms are with an average of 3–5 years comparable to financial investors. Investment periods however vary due to the fact that investors generally want to grasp a substantial part of the strategic shift of the company before they exit the investment. The question they are most interested in is: "Can we add more value to the company? If not, we should sell!" At the same time, private equity firms are constraint by the capital market environment and the demand of their investors. Pension funds – generally the largest PE investors – require a rather stable cash flow to fund their obligations to pensioners. The general timing for the point of exit is typically defined early on during the holding period and reviewed regularly by the PE firm's investment committee. Some private equity managers argue that the pressure to sell due to non-permanent capital and the clear timing of the exit window reduce agency costs within the PE firm. By being put on the spot by investment committees, private equity professionals are unable to carry failing businesses forward and "hope for the best" as one can observe in various public corporations.

6.3.3.3 Review of Performance

The "interventionists" featured in the exploratory part of this study achieved an average 5-year performance of 24% and an average 10-year performance of 28%. The performance spreads from high single-digit internal rates of return to performance figures in the low forties.[13]

The firms categorized as "interventionist managers" have both US and European origins. Within the sample, size again is no differentiating factor. The firm with the strongest performance is one of the study's smallest firms followed by one of the largest players in the private equity industry.

[13] The influence of different management models on performance is discussed in further detail in Sect. 6.4.1 "Comparison of Management Models and Impact on Performance".

6.3.4 Hybrid Management Models

The "opportunistic financial investor" and the "interventionist manager" are the two genuine private equity management models observed in the exploratory research part of this study. While the majority of companies studied in this effort fit in one of the two management models,[14] there are hybrid cases that present some characteristics of both management models. One can observe permanent and transitional hybrids. Permanent hybrids have developed a strategic niche that is based on key elements of both management models. Transitional hybrids are traditional financial investors but initiated more interventionist behaviors.

6.3.4.1 Permanent Hybrids

Permanent hybrids are private equity firms that pursue investment strategies that focus their involvement on very particular functional skills but lack a more general intervention approach. Some players in the private equity arena have developed particular skills on such questions as the internationalization of domestic leading companies and use their functional niches to reach their performance hurdles. While those firms generally developed deep "interventionist" approaches on those dimensions, they behave like "opportunistic financial investors" on most other dimensions of the private equity management model. Permanent hybrids, furthermore, lack the sector focus of most "interventionist" players.

6.3.4.2 Transitional Hybrids

Transitional hybrids describe private equity firms that have a joint origin with financial investors but have started to implement an operational expertise in selected areas and appear to be on a path towards the "interventionist manager" model.

On the one side, there are transitional hybrids that have started a more "interventionist" approach in selected industry groups. A number of firms generally have a financial investor perspective on their investments; they however realized that in their largest sectors, there is significant potential for value creation if they bundle knowledge and show a stronger involvement in the strategic changes of their portfolio companies. Kaplan (2007a: 11) confirms that "there's more convergence among financial engineers and operators than there was 20 years ago". Some players have therefore established industry groups for their one to two historically dominant industries and a general pool for the remaining opportunistic investments. In those

[14] The two general management models "Opportunistic Financial Investor" and "Interventionist Manager" explain 80% of the firms sampled in this study. Only the remaining 20% are represented by the hybrid models outlined in this section.

selected industries, transitional hybrids have already established mechanisms to engage in strategic decision making and to leverage key resources across the investment portfolio. In the remaining investment portfolio, the focus of investment professionals remains on financial issues. Increasing experience in a number of industries and the institutionalization of the intervention approach will potentially lead to a shift of the entire private equity firm to the "interventionist" side of the management model spectrum.

On the other side, there are private equity players that have established small operational units of former strategy consultants, operating executives and former CEOs that are specialized on intervening in "unintentional turnarounds". This is the case if portfolio companies run into difficulties that have not been foreseen in the original investment case. In most firms, these operational experts so far account for less than 10% of the firm's professional staff; however, their importance for above market returns is increasingly recognized even by more financially oriented players. One senior private equity manager in a firm that is largely characterized as an "opportunistic financial investor" admits that "we have realized that this particular source of value creation (from financial engineering) is not enough any more and therefore we decided to strengthen our operating expertise". Positive experiences with these small specialized turnaround teams will eventually lead to a stronger appreciation of the benefits of active involvement and lead to an intensifying practice of the "interventionist" management model.

6.3.4.3 Review of Performance

Private equity firms with a hybrid management model show an average 5-year performance of 20 and 22% in the 10-year investment horizon.[15] Performance ranges from low double-digit levels to internal rates of return in the high thirties.[16]

Firms with a permanent hybrid strategy and therefore a clear strategic focus tend to be smaller in portfolio size than private equity firms on a transitional path. Firms in this category have both US and European origins.

6.3.5 Trends in the Private Equity Management Model

The transition of private equity firms from the traditional model of "opportunistic financial investors" to "interventionist manager" is an overall trend that can be observed in the private equity industry since the 1980s. Changes in the market environment have caused several financial investors – however clearly not all – to

[15] To maintain interview confidentiality and anonymity, the performance review of permanent and transitional hybrids is combined given the small number of firms within this category.

[16] The influence of different management models on performance is discussed in further detail in Sect. 6.4.1 "Comparison of Management Models and Impact on Performance".

change to a more interventionist approach. This section briefly highlights the starting position of leveraged buyout firms in the 1980s. It then highlights the changes in the market place and closes with the management model that is most likely dominating the way going forward. This section draws on KKR as a case study to highlight the transformation of one of the oldest private equity firms since the 1980s.[17]

6.3.5.1 Starting Position of Private Equity Management Model

The traditional leveraged buyout model is a classic opportunistic investor with strong focus on changes in a firm's capital structure and the consecutive sale of non-core assets as well as the creation of an effective governance structure by creating strong incentives for the portfolio companies' management teams. "Value in those transactions was created mainly at the time of the deal", remarks Carl Ferenbach, Managing Director at Berkshire Partners (Ferenbach in Jensen et al., 2006: 18). Beyond this, private equity firms showed limited involvement in the portfolio companies' strategic and operating decisions and soon became known as "Barbarians" (Anders, 1992) because of the profits they realized and the publicly perceived conditions they left divested companies in.

In the early days of private equity, the industry was comparably small in size and was run by a limited number of firms. The key success factors of the original investors were the access to capital and a deep understanding of financial engineering options. Value was created by de-leveraging the firm and realizing gains from splitting up larger, poorly performing entities. In the interaction with management, "financial strategies commanded the most attention" (Baker & Smith, 1998: 105). The unrivaled financial skill set of private equity firms during this period has been supported by improvements in the governance mechanisms through increasing management ownership and thereby creating an alignment of interest between the principal (the private equity firm representing its investors) and the agent (the management team of the portfolio companies).

KKR is one of the most prominent examples for the private equity model of the 1980s, which set a milestone for the industry in 1989 with the broadly and controversially discussed acquisition of RJR Nabisco. In KKR's mission statement in 1982, one finds a clear definition of KKR's role during this period:

> "Assist each company in its acquisition program, divestiture and capital investment program, as well as advise the companies as to timing and the best alternatives for obtaining additional capital or achieving liquidity for the investors." (Baker & Smith, 1998: 100)

The firm's mission statement provides evidence that the investment focus in the 1980s was clearly evolving around changes in an asset's capital structure and through

[17] Given the anonymity promised to the study's participants, the well documented example of KKR appears valuable to further illustrate the observed trends in private equity management models. All information used to highlight the transformation of KKR is based on public information and is not drawn from any interviews conducted during the exploratory research of this study.

consecutive acquisitions and divestitures after the initial investment. This is further supported by the fact that 21 out of the first 24 investment professionals of KKR had a banking or law background (Baker & Smith, 1998: 178), both with higher relevancy for transactions and changing the firm's balance sheet than for strong involvement in strategy shifts.

Baker and Smith (1998), who intensively studied KKR's management model during this period, portrayed the firm's activities close to the description of an "opportunistic financial investor": "KKR monitored the companies it controlled, but it did not attempt to exercise managerial authority over them. (...) KKR's primary responsibilities were to watch over its companies on a close and continuous basis, to help structure executive compensation, to intervene in timely fashion when management ran into serious problems, and to engineer corporate financings and refinancings, acquisitions and divestitures" (Baker & Smith, 1998: 169).

6.3.5.2 Changing Market Environment

Since the first boom of private equity in the 1980s, three changes have transformed the market environment, in which private equity operates: improved access to capital, an increasing level of competition, and considerable improvements in the way public corporations are managed.

Whereas raising capital has been one of the key challenges for private equity in its early days – "the availability of financing was our biggest challenge" (Kravis, 2004) – capital has become nearly a commodity. Institutional investors such as large pension funds, private investors as well as an increasing number of sovereign wealth funds have been eager to provide large sums of equity to leading private equity firms to enhance their returns in a low-yield market environment. At the same time, financial institutions have been willing to provide high levels of debt financing to fund leveraged buyouts. Access to capital has therefore lost its original distinguishing character in the private equity industry, which was further supported by the low-interest environment in recent years.

The success of private equity during its first wave has caused a substantial number of new players to enter the market. "Our success in building businesses by leveraging our flourishing capital markets has led to increased competition from traditional private equity investors as well as from outside the industry" (Kravis, 2004). The pure skill of increasing leverage to drive returns has been commoditized and is no longer a distinguishing factor in the private equity universe. "Anyone could run an LBO model" says one private equity manager while another PE professional adds that "financial restructuring was clearly the first low hanging fruit to go – the commoditization of financing skills however has largely eliminated this source of value creation". A senior managing director at a leading firm furthermore points out that the increasing competition combined with a rising transparency in the market made it "extremely hard to find a hidden jewel".

Finally, public corporations have considerably improved their management model and are – on average – better managed than during the 1980s and early

1990s. In the US and most European markets, nearly all publicly listed companies have part of their equity owned by the companies' management teams to guarantee alignment of interest. Furthermore, "an emphasis on increasing shareholder value has become an important driver in powering a dynamic and prosperous (US) economy". Kravis (2004) furthermore adds that "it is no longer as easy as it once was to increase the value of our companies, in part because we, as investors and general partners in this industry, have institutionalized some enduring business values in the United States and in many other parts of the world that have made businesses more efficient and better run and, as a result, more valuable".

6.3.5.3 Private Equity Management Model Going Forward

The fundamental changes in the private equity market environment have let to two diverging private equity management models. One model, the "opportunistic financial investor", is closely related to the investors during earlier waves of private equity and is still found in some of the industry's largest players. The other model, the "interventionist manager" model, has shifted its focus from financial engineering to "acting more like industrialists" or what one private equity professional calls "company building". Many of the buyout firms responded to the changing market environment by "developing industry and operating expertise that they can use to add value to their investments" (Kaplan, 2007a: 11). So far, the question of which of the management models is more successful remains unanswered in academic research and in the opinion of practitioners. Section 6.4.1 will provide an evaluation which of these models is able to produce higher returns based on the results of this study; nevertheless both models co-exist in the market place.

The "interventionist" management model relies on a new set of skills. It involves access to proprietary deal flow in connection with deep strategic and operational expertise in selected industry sectors. The increasing competition has led to high valuations and multiple bids for individual targets. Investors with a strong reputation for deep operational expertise can expect a better standing with industry managers and owners of target companies and thereby get access to better and partly proprietary deal information. Strong strategic and operational insight is then also required to extract the value from an investment that is necessary to achieve the return expectations of investors. While the right capital structure is still an important part of the "interventionist" management model, the majority of value is created by increasing efficiency in the business and driving growth. Section 6.4.2 will outline propositions about the key success factors of private equity in the current market environment.

Going forward, most private equity managers see a stronger move towards the "interventionist manager" model and greater industry orientation with several financially oriented investors starting the assessment of portfolio groups and the intensified use of external advisors to support the improvement of business performance. One PE professional clearly states: "you need to get your hands dirty to keep future returns on the levels expected by investors". In addition, most private equity managers expect holding periods to lengthen, not only due to the downturn in the market but also given the increased management activity. However, a strong adherence to the "opportunistic financial investor" model remains or is even reaffirmed in some of the industry's largest and most established firms: "we believe that investors should stay investors and should not become managers" (managing director of US firm).

KKR's transformation from an "opportunistic financial investor" to an "interventionist manager" has begun in the late 1990s. "This was a time when my partner George Roberts and I were frankly dissatisfied with the performance of the firm. We were making too many mistakes. KKR had been a pioneer in the private equity industry, but continued industry leadership in an increasingly competitive and complex business environment, we believed, required fundamental rethinking of our methods", says Kravis (2006). The firm's founders realized that pure financial engineering did not guarantee the performance the firm was renowned for. "If we were to differentiate ourselves, we had to understand the industry and the company (…). We had to understand the economic drivers, the metrics, the risks inherent in the business, and the opportunities to create additional value" (Kravis, 2006).

The firm consequently made substantial changes to its management approach and decided to build deep expertise in specific industries. Starting in 2000, KKR organized its investment professionals into industry teams and charged those professionals with becoming experts in their fields. The firm furthermore broadened the experience background of its employees by hiring "a broad range of strategic, consulting, operating, and finance backgrounds" (Kravis, 2006) with all but one senior hire being executives with several years of industry experience. In the course of those changes, KKR's management model has shifted substantially from a financial focus to a more holistic, interventionist investor approach as illustrated in the firm's current mission statement:

> "The KKR investment team sources acquisitions, works with senior managers of our portfolio companies to design ways of growing and improving their business, determines the optimal capital structure to support a company's business strategy, provides access to global network of resources that strengthen operational execution, and realizes value for investors when exiting a company" (Kohlberg Kravis Robert & Co., 2008).

Finally, KKR has implemented an in-house consulting arm, called Capstone, that supports investment professionals and portfolio company management in developing business plans and driving change. The group has a high resemblance of external consulting firms but holds a share in KKR's carried interest in the firm's investment portfolio to align the interests between deal makers and operators.

6.4 Discussion of Results

The results of the second empirical part of this study provide insights into the different management models, which can be found in the private equity industry. Unlike most prior publications, this study illustrates that the private equity industry is not as homogeneous as it is commonly described. The study finds vast differences between different private equity management models and is able to link those differences with the characteristics of different private equity firms and firm performance.

This section discusses the empirical results by drawing a comparison between the two general private equity management models and outlines commonalities and differences. It furthermore highlights the impact on performance of each management model. Based on these findings, the section then develops propositions about the key success factors of private equity in managing diversified portfolios and the opportunities for multi-business firms to learn from private equity. The section closes by outlining the limitations of the qualitative research element of this study.

6.4.1 Comparison of Management Models and Impact on Performance

The "opportunistic financial investor" model is the industry's traditional management model. The model relies heavily on changes in the firm's financial structure and shows strong similarities with an increasingly active generation of hedge funds in today's market. "Interventionists" on the other side are relying more and more on involvement in a firm's strategic and operational decisions and show increasingly signs of resemblance with multi-business firms or – in other words – traditional conglomerates that they have started out to dismantle in the 1980s. So far, it remains unanswered which of the models is better suited to create value in a private equity engagement while avoiding the infrastructure costs generally associated with traditional multi-business firms.

6.4.1.1 Private Equity Management Models and Value Creation Levers

Private equity firms have access to different ways of value creation by acting as a parent in a diversified business portfolio. The above-outlined generic strategies of private equity parenting highlight the opportunities for PE players to differentiate themselves from other players in the industry and to define their particular approach to create parenting advantage.

To compare both management models and to explain the effects of each model on performance, one has to connect the different management models and parenting styles with the ways of value creation accessible for private equity firms. Prior studies introduced in Sect. 3.2.3 "Value Creation Techniques" have focused on the value creation on the level of individual portfolio companies; they however lack a comprehensive analysis of the relationship between the behavior of private equity firms and value creation levers.

This study consequently links the elements of the PE management model with individual ways of value creation and then investigates the impact on performance. Figure 6.8 outlines the relationship between the elements of "corporate parenting" used to explore the private equity management model (governance approach, availability of center resources, leverage of resources across businesses, and portfolio

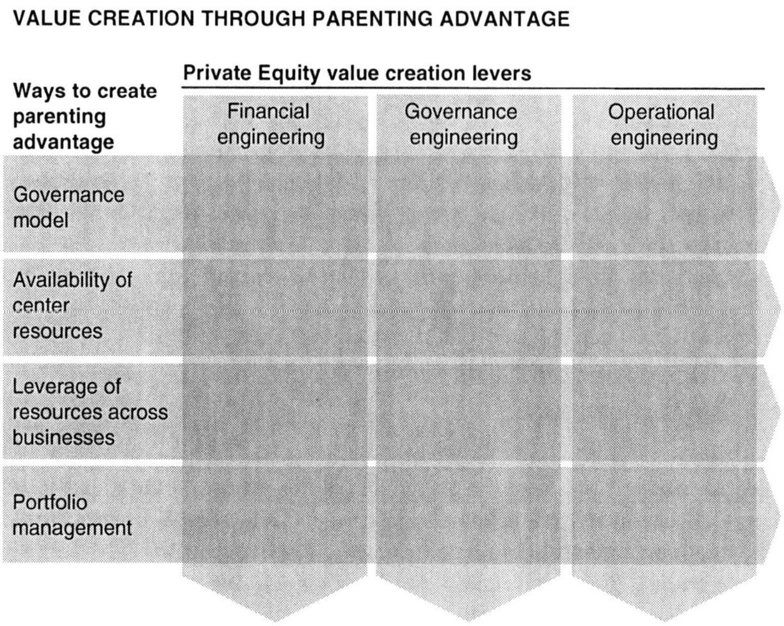

VALUE CREATION THROUGH PARENTING ADVANTAGE

	Private Equity value creation levers		
Ways to create parenting advantage	Financial engineering	Governance engineering	Operational engineering
Governance model			
Availability of center resources			
Leverage of resources across businesses			
Portfolio management			

Fig. 6.8 Value creation through parenting advantage

management) and the private equity value creation levers (financial engineering, governance engineering, and operational engineering).

Value creation through financial engineering entails the active involvement of private equity firms in the change of an asset's capital structure and the sale of non-core assets. Value creation through governance engineering requires a substantial reduction of agency costs. private equity firms approach this objective with a powerful combination of governance tools that characterize the private equity governance model. Active oversight by private equity firms gives executives in portfolio companies the distinct feeling of "having a boss", who is heavily involved in monitoring performance rather than a legal body that passes management proposals. The installation of strong incentive systems that are linked to the value created in a company is a further governance method that creates alignment of interest between principal and agent. The use of high leverage finally is another tool used by private equity firms to govern their portfolio companies and provides a solution to the free cash-flow problem of inefficient investments by implicitly imposing higher performance requirements on investment projects. Value creation through operational engineering finally involves the active support of management teams in the transformation of businesses and the realization of advantages in the overarching investment portfolio.

Comparing both management models, one finds a strong common basis between the "opportunistic financial investor" and the "interventionist manager" based on the changes in a firm's capital structure and governance approach as well as the investors' active acquisition and divestiture behavior. At the same time, the operational

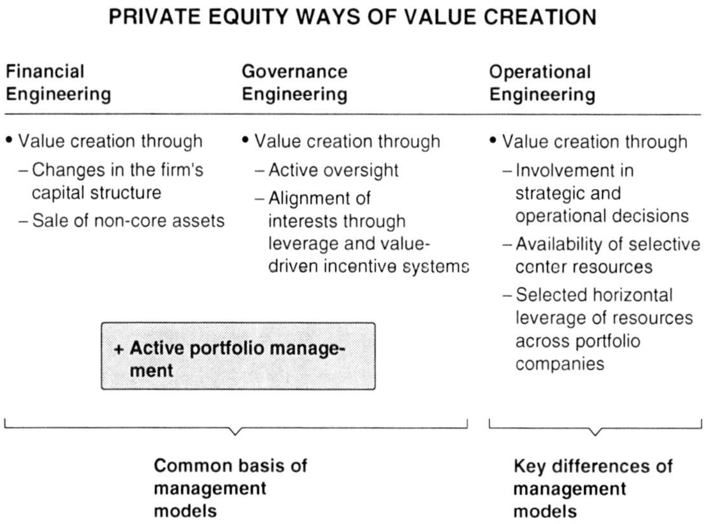

PRIVATE EQUITY WAYS OF VALUE CREATION

Financial Engineering	Governance Engineering	Operational Engineering
• Value creation through – Changes in the firm's capital structure – Sale of non-core assets	• Value creation through – Active oversight – Alignment of interests through leverage and value-driven incentive systems	• Value creation through – Involvement in strategic and operational decisions – Availability of selective center resources – Selected horizontal leverage of resources across portfolio companies

+ Active portfolio management

Common basis of management models (Financial Engineering, Governance Engineering)

Key differences of management models (Operational Engineering)

Fig. 6.9 Private equity ways of value creation

element to reduce costs and grow revenues provides a strong distinguishing factor between the two management models. The "interventionist" management model is based on the same principles as the financial investor model but developed further approaches to draw value from investments by actively intervening in strategic and operational decision making. Active parenting paired with industry expertise provides "interventionist" firms with the ability to integrate operational engineering into their management models and thereby creates a strong differentiating factor to the traditional financially oriented private equity model.

Figure 6.9 provides an overview of the private equity ways of value creation and their occurrence across management models and forms the basis for the further comparison of private equity management models in this section. Financial engineering, governance engineering as well as active portfolio management can be found in both management models while operational engineering is a unique feature in interventionist investors.

6.4.1.2 Common Basis of Management Models

The two general private equity management models share a strong common basis that is characterized by the ability of private equity houses to introduce significant changes in an asset's capital structure and governance logic, which is supplemented by an active management of the firms' investment portfolios.

Financial engineering represents the private equity firms' focus on changes in the structure of the balance sheet of their portfolio companies. The firms use substantial amounts of debt for a target's acquisition that consequently has to be paid down by the portfolio company. Through the aggressive use of leverage, private equity firms essentially create a long option on the business they acquire with only limited equity investments as potential downside. By de-leveraging the firm with the firm's cash flow, the PE firm raises its equity share and creates value for its investors – a technique that can be used repeatedly over the period of investment with reduced risk given the increasing knowledge of the business. The de-leveraging of the firm is supported by additional measures on the balance sheet side such as the sale of non-core assets and reductions in working capital. "Opportunistic financial investors" generally put a stronger focus on gains from financial engineering; both models of leveraged buyouts however are built around this way of financing acquisitions and creating value.

Governance engineering consists of three major components: active oversight, a solution to the free cash-flow problem, and value-driven incentive systems. First of all, private equity firms exercise an active oversight of their investments. Both management models play an active role on the board of a portfolio company to challenge and influence management's decisions. "Interventionist managers" in particular extend the monitoring of management beyond their formal role on the board to an informal and regular dialogue with management. These more active investors, in general, bring a stronger understanding of the respective industry and business to the task of monitoring management and can thereby add additional value to the engagement by reducing agency costs and shaping the business. The aggressive use of leverage provides a solution for the free cash-flow problem observed in traditional multi-business firms. The pressure of high leverage and the resulting obligations to make interest and principal payments implies that management has less latitude to invest the firm's funds in inefficient projects or for excess cash waiting around to be spent. Even though both private equity management models discovered in this study tend to use different levels of debt, the general mechanism of high leverage to reduce agency costs remains unchanged. Nevertheless, "interventionists" need to put a stronger focus on the selection of investment projects given the – by tendency – larger amount of free cash flow available in their portfolio companies. Finally, private equity firms transform the incentive systems in companies they acquire. Both "opportunistic financial investors" and "interventionist managers" generally require top management to invest substantial amounts of their own funds into the company and at the same time introduce a stronger link between performance and compensation. The interests of management are aligned with the interests of the private equity firm and its investors as compensation is ultimately linked to the value created between entry and exit of the PE investor as opposed to accounting-based measures found in many corporations.

By the nature of the industry, private equity investments are non-permanent and thus provide an automatism for an active management of a firm's investment portfolio. private equity firms are required to return the investor's equity within a maximum time of – in general – 10 years but typically attempt to provide stable cash flows back to investors after the initial investment period. With holding periods of individual investments generally between 3 and 5 years, private equity firms always have to be concerned with the potential exit strategy. The active portfolio management in both models of private equity investors implies a focus on immediate value creation after a target's acquisition. Regular reviews of the PE investment portfolio moreover support the realization of value in a timely manner and avoid inefficiency problems generally associated with permanent capital. private equity firms have to exit successful investments as well as failures and thereby avoid management's tendency to prolong the holding period of businesses with strong cash generation as well as of non-performing units.

The study's findings regarding financial and governance engineering confirm findings from previous research such as Palepu (1990), Anders (1992), Kaufman and Englander (1993), Long and Ravenscraft (1993), and Cotter and Peck (2001). The study adds a new perspective about the influence of the private equity partnership as a holding on individual value creation levers on portfolio company level. It therefore offers a comprehensive perspective linking private equity firm behavior with value creation on the investment level and consequently performance.

6.4.1.3 Key Differences of Management Models

While the "opportunistic financial investor" and the "interventionist manager" share a strong common basis, the use of active parenting to install operational engineering for value creation distinguishes the two management models from each other. Financial investors generally focus their activities on changes in a firm's financial and governance structure while intervening PE firms are actively involved in driving change in their portfolio companies. To install operational engineering as value creation lever in private equity investment portfolios, "interventionists" have improved the private equity partnership's parenting capabilities to exercise active ownership and have commenced to make selected center resources available to their portfolio companies as well as to support selective horizontal linkage between businesses to profit from revenue and cost synergies in the overall PE portfolio.

The leading "interventionist" players have established a limited number of industry groups and focused their investments in those sectors. These firms have then given individual professionals responsibility for the selected industries. In large players, most professionals are mainly focused on one sector while in smaller players most staff members have what one managing director calls "majors and minors like in a university" in two to three industries. Industry knowledge considerably improves the firm's ability to execute active oversight over the investment portfolio through the reduction of information asymmetries, which presents a further means to avoid agency costs. "interventionist managers" therefore are equipped with stronger capabilities to exercise the PE firms' shareholder role on the boards of their portfolio companies.

"Interventionist" players moreover get proactively involved in the development of strategies for their portfolio companies. This is achieved by a strong presence of private equity professionals during the initial phase of the investment as well as ongoing support as sparring partner and resource to support management in key decisions. "Interventionist managers" spend considerably more time with their investments and have a higher demand for operationally trained talent. "Opportunistic financial investors" generally don't provide such resources and generally lack strong industry expertise. The partnerships of mainly financial investors tend to be smaller than of interventionist players and less diverse with regards to professional backgrounds.

"Interventionist managers" furthermore started to take advantage of the scale of their portfolios to improve terms with key suppliers in both business-related and non-business-related items. As outlined above, active investors support portfolio companies in the negotiation of arrangements with key resource suppliers as well as service providers such as logistics, infrastructure, IT services, or insurance. The consolidation of market access and the support in dealing with suppliers is largely achieved without increasing the size of the PE partnership by on the one side using outside experts and on the other side focusing on a selected number of key performance drivers for the portfolio. The informality of the arrangement allows private equity firms to execute the "interventionist" approach without implementing rigid and expensive bonds between the PE partnership and individual portfolio companies. However, the consolidation of services in the private equity firm creates – to a certain extent – complexity and reduces the flexibility and accountability of individual portfolio companies. In selected cases, management teams might be required to join overall initiatives although there may be better solutions available to them. "Opportunistic financial investors" are generally not involved in attempts to create value through joint purchasing.

In addition, intervening investors selectively link companies within their portfolios to transfer knowledge but also to engage firms in bilateral business arrangements. While not supported by strict processes and targets, "interventionist" firms proactively introduce executives of individual portfolio companies with cooperation potential. "Opportunistic financial investors" are typically not involved in linking firms horizontally. Instead of drawing potential synergies from their portfolios, they stress the importance of accountability and tradability of their assets. Both criteria are reduced when introducing horizontal links in a private equity portfolio.

The study adds considerable insight about the way private equity firms influence decisions on the level of individual portfolio companies to improve operational performance. The study confirms the importance of active parenting and operational engineering as value creation levers found in previous research such as Berg and Gottschalg (2003), Gottschalg and Meier (2005), Loos (2005), and Teitelbaum (2007). It moreover highlights that operational engineering enabled through active parenting is the distinguishing factor between different private equity models, which has not been captured properly in previous research activity. The majority of prior studies uses a portfolio company or fund as unit of analysis and therefore is not able to evaluate the overarching management model pursued by the private equity firm. The study then outlines the different ways for a private equity house in the role of a holding to create value through active parenting and the organizational choices available to a private equity firm.

6.4.1.4 Impact on Performance

Both private equity management models share a strong common basis and apply financial engineering, governance engineering, and active portfolio management in principally comparable ways. However, only "interventionist managers" engage in active parenting to improve performance through operational engineering but at the same time require more talent and risk flexibility, accountability, and tradability of their investment portfolios through establishing connections throughout their assets. The analysis of the management models' impact on performance will need to show whether operational engineering can create the value required to justify the increasing number of investment professionals and the reduced flexibility in the PE investment portfolio.

On the positive side, "interventionist managers" take advantage of the effects of related diversification and experience. By focusing the overall private equity firm to a larger extend on related businesses and by implementing a stronger industry orientation in the professional team, intervening firms are able to exploit the benefits of industry relatedness. Going back to the original theories regarding diversification, the "interventionist" model has foundations in the market-power view, the agency view and the resource-based view. By addressing the supply side of the entire investment portfolio, private equity firms attempt to exercise market power similar to what multi-business firms generally do. A stronger industrial expertise furthermore enables private equity professionals to reduce agency costs by guarantying a better oversight over management and being a more active investor in shaping strategic decisions. Finally, from a resource-based perspective, PE firms employ their resources in related businesses and thereby take advantage of the skills and experiences acquired in previous and parallel transactions.

At the same time, "interventionist" firms run the risk of establishing a system that inhibits some of the major benefits of the private equity model and shows signs of multi-business firms. For one, an increasing linkage of businesses as well as the rising influence in strategic decision making limits the accountability of an asset's management team. Senior managers are potentially limited in their choices due to benefits for the overall portfolio and can therefore be held less responsible for the performance of the investment. So far, "interventionists" avoided the installation of expensive and rigid corporate-like infrastructure by maintaining all interventions informal; a risk of an ongoing institutionalizing and further loss of flexibility however exists. In addition, linking businesses and consolidating selective services can create a resistance to sell assets as fast as "opportunistic financial investors" may sell a portfolio company due to the importance for the joint purchasing power or the success of cooperations between assets. The "interventionist" model may therefore reduce tradability of a PE firm's investment portfolio. Finally, intervening investors need a larger group of investment professionals and thereby run a larger cost base in the private equity firm's "headquarters".

The results of this study indicate that operational engineering enabled through active parenting adds substantial value to the investment portfolio of a private equity firm. The comparison of performance achieved by "interventionist managers", "Hybrid" models and "opportunistic financial investors" presented in Table 6.1 reveals that "interventionist managers" outperform less active management models by a substantial premium. On a 5-year investment horizon, intervening management models generate an average outperformance of 5% age points in IRR vs. financial investors. On a 10-year timeframe, the performance gap grows considerably. "Interventionist" investors achieve an average internal rate of return of 28.1% and therefore almost twice the performance of "opportunistic financial investors" with 14.8%. The study shows comparable results for risk-adjusted measures. The size of the investment portfolio as well as the experience of the firm measured by years since the vintage of the firm's first fund have no explanatory power for the performance difference. Some of the largest and oldest private equity firms lead the performance comparison while others are at the lower end of the spectrum.

The results for the 10-year performance are particularly interesting given the changes in the market environment throughout the last decade. On the one side, liquid debt markets and covenant-light arrangements with low interest rates marked the late years in the 5-year investment horizon (specifically 2004–2006) whereas the 10-year investment period is characterized by less favorable markets

Table 6.1 Management models and private equity performance

MANAGEMENT MODELS AND PRIVATE EQUITY PERFORMANCE

Measured in means

		Interventionist Managers	Hybrids	Opportunistic Financial Investors
Management model	General definition of parenting role	Active parenting with strong industry expertise	Hybrid parenting style with permanent and transitional models	Passive parenting with focus on financial engineering
Performance measures (5 years)	IRR (in percent)	23.5	20.2	18.7
	Jensen's Alpha	0.1446	0.1069	0.1057
	Sharpe measure	0.0081	0.0078	0.0064
	Treynor measure	0.2079	0.2059	0.1648
Performance measures (10 years)	IRR (in percent)	28.1	21.5	14.3
	Jensen's Alpha	0.1657	0.1016	0.0407
	Sharpe measure	0.0099	0.0078	0.0040
	Treynor measure	0.2347	0.1909	0.0969
Diversification measures	Total diversification (DT)	1.8	1.8	2.1
	Related diversification (DR)	0.6	0.3	0.3
	Unrelated diversification (DU)	1.2	1.5	1.8

around the turn of the century.[18] Financial investors are equipped to perform particularly well in markets with easy access to relatively low-priced debt. On the other side, the strong equity markets in recent years supported private equity firms in generating high returns through multiple expansion and a friendly IPO and trade sale environment. The IPO market in Europe and the US for instance went from a EUR 20 billion transaction volume in 2003 to a record level of EUR 109 billion in 2006. Market conditions in the 5-year investment horizon have therefore been favorable for more financially oriented players that generate value primarily through changes in a firm's capital structure and multiple expansion. However, the strong difference between management models in 10-year performance illustrates the strength of the "interventionist manager" model to drive strong performance independent of debt and capital markets. Only "interventionist" firms proved to maintain high performance and were able to create value through EBITDA growth despite the challenging debt and capital markets after the burst of the stock market in 2000 and 2001.

The performance gap between "interventionist manager" models and "opportunistic financial investors" can be interpreted as the value created through active parenting. The "interventionist" management model is necessary to unlock the potential of operational engineering as value creation lever, which has been regularly discussed in business and academic literature but never properly captured. Intervening investors appear to be able to exploit the advantages of active involvement while avoiding its downsides.

To the author's best knowledge, no prior study has linked private equity management models and investment performance. This study therefore establishes a first basis to evaluate different private equity management models and to value the influence of active parenting on PE performance.

6.4.2 *Key Success Factors of Private Equity Management Model*

The comparison of management models revealed a superior performance of the "interventionist manager" model as opposed to the "opportunistic financial investor" model by adding new competences of active parenting and consequently operational engineering to the strong common basis shared by all private equity players. Developing the key success factors of the private equity management model will therefore be based on the strong common ground of private equity achievements as well as the unique parenting skills added by the "interventionist" management model.

The study develops five propositions about the key success factors of private equity as a result of the exploratory research. These propositions are shared by all "interventionist" private equity firms and are likely to build the basis for the firms' superior performance during the investment period sampled in this study. The key

[18]The 5-year period of the study's data sample includes the years 2002–2006. The 10-year period includes the years 1997–2006.

success factors are structured in accordance with the parenting framework of Campbell et al. (1994, 1995a, 1995b, 1998) to represent the general definition of a firm's role as parent, the governance model, the availability of center functions and resources, the leverage of resources and competences across a firm's portfolio, and the portfolio management approach pursued by private equity firms. All propositions are subject to further academic research with a particular focus on the quantitative test of each of these propositions.

6.4.2.1 Proposition 1: Act as Active Shareholder

Foremost, private equity firms act as active shareholders towards their portfolio companies. private equity professionals take a more active role on the boards of companies they own, whereby boards are typically smaller and consist mainly of the firms' largest investors. Board meetings are used as discussion platform and bear "tremendous amounts of conflict" rather than a formal act of passing management proposals. Active investors fulfill the belief that "everybody needs a boss", according to Cary Davis, managing director at Warburg Pincus (in Jensen et al., 2006: 24).

Partners responsible for an individual investment spend considerable time with monitoring the asset and engaging with the management team to influence strategic decisions. Many partners spend more than 50% of their time on one investment in the initial phase and one to two days a week over the investment's holding period to understand the business and develop growth opportunities – way above the mostly passive role taken by directors on public company boards or the behavior of top management in a multi-business firm vs. the management teams of its business units.

Active ownership and the active oversight of management's decisions involve the discussion of financial achievements as much as the progress of implementing the strategic initiatives developed in the business plan for each individual investment. Private equity professionals are keen to understand the status of strategic change and enforce a strong management of milestones given the limited investment period of 3–5 year.

6.4.2.2 Proposition 2: Create Alignment of Interests

The alignment of interest between investors, private equity professionals, and the top management team of portfolio companies is characteristic for the private equity industry. Particularly the relationship between private equity firms and top management is a unique factor distinguishing PE from other investment opportunities. Alignment of interest is achieved through the implementation of a strong, performance-based incentive structure with long-term focus as well as the use of high degrees of leverage.

The incentive system of private equity engagements is marked by substantial upside as well as downside potential for senior management. First of all, managers are generally required to invest some of their own funds into the transaction. Through these equity stakes, senior management can participate in value increases but at the same time suffers from reductions in the firm's valuation. On top of this, management's compensation is highly linked to the performance of the company. The measurement of performance is based on cash metrics rather than measures skewed by accounting practices or capital market trends and is determined on the portfolio company level. In most multi-business firms, a sizeable part of the incentive system is based on the success of the overall firm, which in this case would be the private equity firm or an individual fund rather than on the level of the business unit or in this case the portfolio company. At the same time, private equity investors generally react quickly to non- or under-performing management by actively supporting and ultimately replacing selective positions or entire top management teams if required. Therefore, the higher risk for management of losing their jobs partly balances the strong upside potential through PE's compensation packages.

Performance is generally measured with a mid-term to long-term focus whereas management teams of public companies are forced to meet short-term quarterly earnings targets. This 3- to 5-year orientation allows management to run businesses with a clear strategic objective and to invest substantial amounts of cash if growth opportunities are discovered. In the argumentation of private equity and public equity management, managers of public companies are essentially held back from following long-term opportunities by managing short-term earnings to meet analyst projections.

The high degree of leverage creates further alignment of interest and reduces agency costs. The high debt burden and the obligation to satisfy interest and principal payments reduce management's ability to invest excess cash in inefficient investment opportunities. Management will only use a firm's cash flow to invest in new growth projects if they bear earnings potential that will lift the value of the company; in other words investment opportunities are only pursued if the return expectations clearly exceed costs of capital.

6.4.2.3 Proposition 3: Exploit Advantages of Portfolio Relatedness

The exploitation of industry relatedness is a unique factor for the "interventionist" management model, which has been explored in this study. "Interventionist" private equity firms focus their investments in a limited number of core industry groups and create a platform to take advantage of the benefits of portfolio relatedness. Relatedness fosters the firms' ability to govern and support management as well as to realize selected synergies within the PE firms' investment portfolios.

The clustering of investments in selected industry groups and the consequent alignment of the PE firm's skills and structures enable private equity professionals to form a skill base that spans over individual investments. Leveraging the knowledge from co-existing and prior engagements allows a firm to have a stronger position on the M&A market and to exercise more effective oversight over management decisions. Deep industry knowledge reduces the problem of asymmetric information during the acquisition and exit between individual parties of a transaction. At the same time, a strong industry background can support a firm in the origination and initial negotiation of a transaction by creating stronger empathy and trust than less-informed investors as well as by building a reputation as investor in relevant industry networks. Many firms recon that an increasing share of investments comes through established networks in particular industries. To reduce agency costs, a strong industrial background enhances a firm's ability to understand and control management decisions and to interfere in critical steps along the implementation of the investment thesis. It furthermore provides the foundation to effectively influence and support management in developing a business plan and driving EBITDA growth initiatives. Leading "interventionist managers" provide substantial management talent to their portfolio companies during the initial phase of each investment and further on support the evaluation of important strategic choices. Instances range from support in transactions to the development of organic growth options or globalization programs. A stronghold in a selected number of industries furthermore allows a firm to surround itself with a group of highly skilled and experienced advisors that have a long-standing track record in particular industries. Interventionists can thereby rely on deep industry knowledge while opportunistic investors generally have to rely on ad-hoc or general management support given their lack of scale in specific industries.

"Interventionist" private equity firms not only materialize on knowledge from investments in related businesses, they have also started to implement measures to benefit from scale and realize synergies between businesses. The proceeds of scale are captured by consolidating selected services such as financial engineering, access to capital markets and – in "interventionists" – purchasing of selected core and non-core components on a level above individual portfolio companies. Intervening PE firms select key cost drivers as well as discretionary items and use the increased market power to improve overall performance. On top, leading private equity houses provide an informal platform for businesses to engage bilaterally and actively link senior executives of relevant firms to determine cooperation potential.

6.4.2.4 Proposition 4: Avoid Costs of "Corporate Infrastructure"

Private equity firms in general successfully implemented their ownership model without establishing large "corporate-center-like" vehicles to manage the firms' investment portfolios. The partnerships of private equity firms generally consist of few investment professionals and offer only a limited selection of services such as support in financing and key strategic decisions. Either of the two general PE management models therefore is able to achieve the benefits of the PE approach while avoiding the downside of building up expensive "corporate infrastructure". They avoid corporate inefficiencies by focusing their activities on key performance drivers, relying on informal governance and intervention approaches, providing businesses with a large degree of independence, and by eliminating any opportunity for cross-subsidization of individual businesses.

Private equity firms in general restrict their involvement on very selective, yet critical elements for the success of an investment. Besides an active role on the portfolio companies' boards, private equity firms engage in only few company matters.

Even "interventionist managers", which distinguish themselves through active parenting and value creation through "operational engineering", select only key strategic decisions to be involved in. Such decisions involve the development of major growth opportunities, M&A transactions, changes in the investments' capital structure, or the consolidation of market access for inputs, that bear high cost saving potentials through the scale of the overall portfolio.

All intervention by private equity firms is maintained on an informal level to avoid the inefficiencies of formalized interactions regularly observed in public multi-business firms. Monitoring, management support as well as the horizontal cooperation between individual portfolio companies is executed through mostly informal interactions between the involved parties. In this context, private equity firms also avoid the wasteful use of senior management resources of public corporations to develop and review annual budgets during an extensive budgeting process between the holding level, in this case the private equity partnership, and the divisional level, here the individual portfolio company.

The informal nature of interaction between private equity partnership and portfolio company as well as the selective informal interaction among individual portfolio companies are characteristic for the high level of independence maintained by each investment. Each business remains a separate legal entity and all funding is retained on the level of the portfolio company. Performance measurement and management compensation are based on the achievements by each business. Decisions are taken on the level of individual businesses and do not have to take potential shifts in corporate strategy into account.

Finally, private equity firms – by their legal structure – avoid the problem of cross-subsidization. Research in numerous multi-business firms documented the negative effects of internal capital markets on investment efficiency. PE firms have no choice but to return funds received from a portfolio company to their investors. Private equity thereby avoids the creation of an administration-intensive internal capital market as well as the inefficient cross-subsidization of other, less successful businesses. PE houses therefore prefer to satisfy capital requirements from within a business. If additional investments are required to support growth in individual businesses, fresh capital has to be called from existing investors or raised from new parties.

6.4.2.5 Proposition 5: Invest to Sell

The value creation levers of private equity firms are supported by the non-permanent nature of PE investments. PE players are forced to maintain an active portfolio management given the finite life of each fund and therefore face a natural limitation for the holding period of each investment. Every investment case needs to contain a clear view about exit opportunities and potential points of exit.

While many corporate acquirers are as active as private equity firms on the world's capital markets, private equity firms are considerably more active on the divestment side. Corporate owners are potentially able to implement comparable changes in a business as private equity owners and thereby create similar levels of

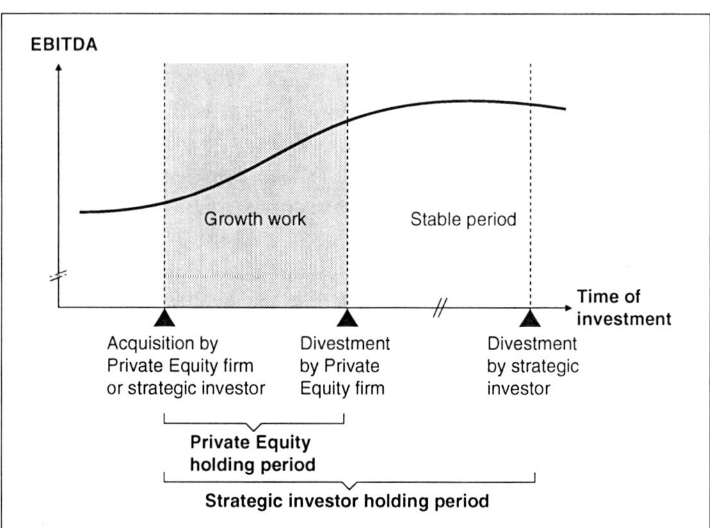

Fig. 6.10 Transformation path of portfolio company

absolute value. They however are reluctant to sell businesses as quickly as PE investors – in successful as much as unsuccessful cases – and therefore hold investments into periods of lower growth. Figure 6.10 illustrates the different holding periods of private equity investors and strategic buyers and highlights the effect of timing on overall performance. To achieve the performance required by the industry's investors, private equity firms need to implement changes quickly and then drive the divestiture of the business.

High internal rates of return are a function not only of the level of change introduced to an investment but also a function of time. Even though corporate owners – in theory – are able to achieve a comparable absolute performance as private equity houses, the concentration of private equity firms on the period of most growth work provides the strongest potential for increase in performance and valuation and supports higher relative return measures such as the industry standard measure internal rate of return.

In the business portfolio of a PE firm, all investments are constantly on the spot of attention to achieve the performance requirements within the expected holding period. The companies in the portfolio of a private equity firm receive a largely comparable amount of focus while some businesses in public equity firms often suffer a shadow existence with other businesses receiving the magnitude of management attention.

Successful exits are essential for the long-term existence of a private equity firm. The willingness of limited partners to invest new funds into PE engagements is based on the cash returns received from general partners for prior investments. Track records of positive returns are one of the major factors if not the factor for a limited partner to evaluate private equity firms. Henry Kravis' famous quote "don't congratulate us when we buy a company, congratulate us when we sell it" (Kravis in Baker & Smith, 1998: 90) is characteristic for the private equity "invest to sell" approach in order to achieve the performance requirements of the industry's limited partners.

6.4.3 Private Equity as Role Model for Multi-Business Firms

From an outside perspective, private equity firms and multi-business firms show remarkable similarities. Many of the firms are invested in large portfolios of partly related, partly unrelated businesses that are managed by an overarching entity. The holding is responsible for strategic decisions regarding the composition of the overall portfolio as well as the oversight over the individual businesses; an independent group of senior executives however is responsible for the decisions on the divisional respectively portfolio company level. Holding managers of public corporations are agents of the firm's shareholders while private equity professionals manage the funds for limited partners – in many cases the same institutional investors holding large stakes in public multi-business firms.

At the same time, there are vast differences between the two ownership and management models. Among those differences is the fact, that multi-business firms are generally led by large corporate headquarters that administer rather than manage their business portfolios. private equity companies, on the other hand, are small groups of active investors. Diversified companies generally justify their existence with synergies while private equity firms don't buy businesses for synergistic effects even though some PE players start to realize them. Multi-business firms – being mostly publicly listed companies – are moreover equipped with permanent capital with no incentive to actively trade the firms' businesses while a PE firm needs to invest with a clear view about an asset's exit opportunities.

Many executives of multi-business firms argue that being public, as most large multi-business firms are, limits their ability to adopt elements of the private equity management model and puts public companies in a disadvantage. Quarterly earnings management and costs associated with reporting and compliance are brought forward together with the fact that public companies cannot use the same level of aggressive leverage and incentive schemes observed in private equity investments given their public exposure.

Most of the differences in the two models however are not inherent and one can observe an increasing convergence in the market for corporate control. Private equity firms are getting more intervening investors and start to build more related diversified portfolios. The conglomerates of the 1960s and 1970s on the other hand have been dismantled and left behind more focused or related diversified multi-business firms with more professional management. Given the similarities in the portfolio structure of private equity firms and public multi-business firms as well as the increasing convergence between the two ownership models, one has to wonder "why public corporations cannot deliver similar levels of outperformance by using the private equity toolbox?" (Shivdasani & Zak, 2007: 32).

This section will therefore develop propositions about the transferability and applicability of the success factors of private equity into traditional – mostly public – multi-business firms. The key success factors of private equity are based on the exploratory research presented in this study while the basis for comparison in multi-business firms is drawn from previous academic literature as well as from the view of selected practitioners in private equity partnerships and public business entities.[19]

6.4.3.1 Proposition 6: Execute Active Ownership

Senior management in the holding of a public multi-business firm is often accused for being administrators rather than managers. Corporate headquarters typically consist of few experienced managers and a large group of employees with administrative duties such as controlling, accounting, compliance, etc. The senior management team itself is responsible for the overall business portfolio and has limited resources with business insight to work with divisional management and to challenge their strategic decisions.

Active ownership on the other side is key to the success of private equity investments and in particular of the "interventionist" management model. Industry experienced professionals dedicate considerable time to each investment to monitor financial results as much as influence strategic decisions. The industry knowledge paired with the high amount of attention brought to each individual portfolio company enables private equity firms to reduce agency costs and ignite strategic change at the same time.

Senior management teams of public multi-business firms need to redefine their role within the firm. Three main tasks should dominate their agenda: First of all, they have to act as active shareholders in a diversified business portfolio rather than administrative heads in a rigid business complex. Corporate headquarters need to have the resources to spend substantial time with business unit management to drive strategic changes rather than administer formalized interaction processes. Management focus needs to shift from a budget-driven control style to an active monitoring of financial results and profound involvement in strategic decisions. Interactions thereby can take place during formalized business review meetings as much as during informal, ad-hoc discussions between executives. Second, corporate management is responsible for strategic changes in the overall corporate strategy

[19] A large number of multi-business firms are publicly listed companies; however, the study's propositions are supposed to be as applicable in privately held companies that are structured along the lines of traditional multi-business firms.

such as the move into new businesses or the exit of maturing fields. Finally, senior management is responsible for the interaction with the firm's shareholders. All of the following propositions for corporate multi-business CEOs support this redefinition of their role as active investors.[20]

6.4.3.2 Proposition 7: Align Interests

The alignment of interest between limited partners, private equity professionals, and the management teams of portfolio companies is a key factor for the long-standing success of private equity firms. The alignment of interest between shareholders and company CEOs has improved substantially over the last decade with considerable growth in equity ownership by senior management as highlighted by Kravis (2004) and Jensen (in Jensen et al. 2006). A recent study by Kaplan and Minton (2006) furthermore found a rising turnover of CEOs and an increasing performance sensitivity of corporate boards. The link of compensation to performance on the divisional level, however, has made little improvements. There is a lack of clear alignment of interest between business unit performance and the compensation of business unit management. Incentive plans are often linked to the overall firm equity performance (typically in related diversified firms) or individual accounting-based measures on business unit level (typically in unrelated diversified firms) as outlined by Kerr (1985), Lau (1993), or Pozen (2007). A general lack of cash-based measures exists on the divisional level, particularly due to a lack of independence of businesses and therefore absence of clear accountability for results. Public corporations furthermore have no requirement for management to invest own funds to acquire equity stakes in the business.

Private equity firms on the contrary link performance to clearly defined cash-based performance targets on the level of individual businesses. No manager participates in the success of the fund or the overall private equity firm but incentives are exclusively linked to the business under their responsibility. Private equity firms furthermore require substantial equity investments by management teams to provide higher upside as well as downside potential for their actions. Finally, private equity firms use leverage as a way to prevent management from inefficient investments whereby the level of leverage is adjusted to the particular situation of the business.

Many of these requirements to align interest between divisional management and corporate objectives at first hand appear difficult to implement in public multi-business firms. Stewart (1990), however, developed means for public companies

[20] A number of recent contributions such as Moon (2006), Draho (2007), or Kaplan (2007a) discussed the opportunity to encourage minority engagements of private investments in public equity, so-called PIPEs, to bring the advantages of active ownership into public equity as happened in the investment of Blackstone in Deutsche Telekom or the 25% stake of Elevation Partners in Palm Computer. While this thought is valuable for the management of the overall firm, it does not address the lack of ownership within the portfolio of a multi-business firm. In the argumentation of this study, the holding of a multi-business firm itself has to become more like a private equity firm.

to benefit from the private equity incentive systems while maintaining the character of a public multi-business firm, which have been employed by numerous firms in the 1980s and 1990s but never received wider public or academic recognition. Stewart (1990) proposes the use of leveraged equity purchase plans (LEPPs) to create stronger ownership incentives and internal leveraged buyouts to bring the advantage of LEPPs to the divisional level of multi-business firms and to impose the disciplinary function of leverage to business unit management.[21]

Leveraged equity purchase plans allow substantial equity ownership by senior management even in large corporations while linking payoffs to above market returns. In a LEPP, the senior management acquires equity through stock purchases whereby most of the purchase price is funded through a loan from the company, which is secured solely by a pledge of stock and has no recourse to the personal assets of individual managers. The remaining purchase price is financed by the personal wealth of the manager and is therefore put at risk. The loan by the company then accrues interest equal to the company's cost of capital. Thus managers benefit financially only if they find investment opportunities that earn a return higher than the firm's cost of capital. LEPPs therefore provide a realistic way for management to gain significant equity ownership in a company without diluting the interest of other shareholders as seen in the use of traditional stock options or restricted stock. Moreover, LEPPs create a clear link between returns above the firm's cost of capital and personal wealth and thereby create strong alignment between the interests of shareholders and managers. There is "a direct and visible payoff for generating superior returns" (Stewart III, 1990: 128).

Internal leveraged buyouts can provide a feasible way to make leveraged equity purchase plans applicable on the business level and to make the advantages of business-specific leverage available to corporate divisions. In this model, companies use leverage at the business unit level and repatriate the funds to the parent. The debt has no recourse to the parent company and the subsidiary bears the responsibility for meeting all interest and repayment requirements. Internal LBOs enhance the financial flexibility of corporate parents and "pushes incentives of ownership down into the individual business units and hold those units accountable for performance". Stewart believes this is specifically important "in slow growth businesses where the chances for unproductive reinvestment are greatest" (Stewart III, 1990: 129). While most companies borrow at the consolidated level and then distribute cash to their business units, internal LBOs turn this relationship upside-down. Subsidiaries raise debt appropriate for the maturity state of their industry segments and are responsible for generating sufficient cash flow to ensure payment of interest and repayment of debt. The debt repayment schedule takes over for inefficient budgeting and investment approval processes. The transformation of consolidated funding activities into divisional capital structures thus provides the ability to

[21] See Stewart (1990) for a description of successful examples of leveraged equity purchase plans and internal leveraged buyouts in public multi-business firms. Examples include the internal LBO of Union Texas Petroleum or the transformation of Kaydon.

employ leveraged equity purchase plans while pushing the disciplinary function of leverage to the business unit level.[22]

6.4.3.3 Proposition 8: Redefine Corporate Center

Corporate headquarters typically host a large, labor-intensive variety of corporate services and are organized along functional lines. They generally provide a number of services to their business units regarding activities such as accounting, financing, human resources, or IT infrastructure, all of which require strong and formalized intervention with the operating procedures on the business unit level. The functional organization moreover limits the holding's opportunities to build strong centers with industry experienced managers rather than functional administrators.

Private equity firms on the contrary have small partnerships that focus on few elements for active involvement. As highlighted above, "interventionist managers" moreover established strong teams of managers with strong industry experience but – at the same time – limit their intervention on key performance drivers. Generally, they are deeply involved in financing decisions, support management in the development and selection of strategic initiatives, and selectively link companies to improve market access or establish new business opportunities within the PE investment portfolio.

Learning from the "interventionist" management model, public multi-business firms have to redefine the role, structure and breath of activities of the corporate headquarters. Besides the center's investor relations responsibility towards shareholders, managers in the corporate center have to focus their activities on managing the overall portfolio and engaging in key decision making of individual businesses. To ensure active ownership, corporate headquarters have to establish small teams that have experience in the different industries the corporation is invested in. By this means, corporate managers have the ability to engage with divisional management and to support and challenge their decision making. At the same time, corporate centers have to reduce the scope of activities offered to the overall portfolio and should focus their involvement on key performance drivers. Besides support with management talent for strategic decisions, firms have to review the importance of

[22] Several prior contributions such as Gupta and Rosenthal (1991), Denis (1994), Denis and Denis (1995), Peyer and Shivdasani (2000), or Shivdasani and Zak (2007) have investigated the use of leveraged recapitalizations to distribute cash to investors, to create acquisition currency for the company, and to bring the advantages of leverage to public companies. Leveraged recapitalizations however bring these advantages only to the holding level and have no direct consequence for individual businesses of a multi-business firm but have often been used as one-time defense mechanism against potential takeovers. Internal leveraged buyouts on the other hand affect the divisional level and can result in a new and permanent form of organizational architecture. Stewart (1990: 132) advocates for "the use of internal LBOs as a systematic and voluntary part of a company's strategy – as applicable to healthy, core businesses as to underperforming, peripheral ones".

individual services in the corporate center and increase the independence of individual businesses. Services beyond strategic decision making need to be targeted at areas critical for the company's success such as market access for key supplies, assistance in financing decisions, and the support of selective cooperation between portfolio companies. Collis, Young, and Goold (2007) find a significant relationship between the size of the corporate headquarters and the linkage among businesses as well as the headquarters involvement in functional decisions. Focusing holding activities can consequently lead to substantial headquarters reductions.

Interactions between corporate and divisional management should be informal to avoid resource-intensive processes such as the annual budgeting process commonly found in large corporations. Although often described as strategy, "this plan coordinates the deployment of resources – but it's not strategy". In Richard Rumelt's view, strategy work needs to be "a separate, non-annual, opportunity-driven process" (Rumelt in Lovallo & Mendonca, 2007: 58).

6.4.3.4 Proposition 9: Increase Independence of Businesses

The divisions of a public multi-business firm typically are part of a rigid complex of businesses held together by corporate infrastructure, which is administered by a corporate center. Interactions between divisions as well as between individual divisions and the corporate center are based on formalized processes such as the use of a joint sales force or the annual budgeting process. Resource allocations are taken on the corporate level although the senior management team of public multi-business firms spends limited time on the discussion of strategic opportunities of individual business units. Divisional management ultimately has limited freedom to act and is highly interlinked with the headquarters and other business units.

In the private equity field, portfolio companies retain a high degree of independence. The involvement by the PE partnership is focused on key strategic decisions and is based on informal interactions. Businesses are funded on the level of the individual portfolio company and no financial resources are transferred in between portfolio companies. Even though private equity firms are highly engaged in developing the capital structure for each portfolio company, each company preserves full responsibility over its cash flows and the use of them. By maintaining high levels of independence for each business, the management teams of portfolio companies can be held accountable for their results and businesses remain tradable to secure the flexibility to divest assets when appropriate.

To increase the independence of individual business units of a public multi-business firm, divisional management teams need to be taken more accountable for the developments of their divisions and businesses need to remain tradable assets. To achieve higher independence, expensive corporate infrastructure and formalized interactions within the portfolio need to be reduced, funding needs to be taken to the divisional level and performance must be evaluated on the business unit level.

While the corporate center takes the above-outlined role of an active owner, business units will be more self sustained in the "interventionist-like" model for multi-business firms and will therefore be in charge of most of the services required to run the business. Expensive corporate infrastructure with formalized interaction processes is reduced and businesses will regain responsibility over operational decisions which eventually can "reinforce the entrepreneurial energies" (Stewart III, 1990: 133) of the business.

The above-introduced means of internal leveraged buyouts provides an opportunity to exercise funding decisions and resource allocations on the business level. "Decentralization of debt transforms the nature of the relationships between business units and the parent. It limits cross-business exposure to risk, holds down the cost of equity, and enhances financial flexibility for the parent" (Stewart III, 1990: 129). The multi-business firm thereby avoids inefficiencies found in internal capital markets and furthermore gains the ability to divest shares of individual business units to existing or new shareholders. Independent businesses have a higher tradability than businesses locked into complex corporate structures and should therefore be more valuable to the company.

The business unit is given full responsibility for making investments that yield returns above the unit's cost of capital. Higher financial and operational independence provides the opportunity to assess management effectiveness on the divisional level, which links back to an improved alignment of interests between the corporate center and the business unit.

6.4.3.5 Proposition 10: Ensure Active Portfolio Management

Public corporations are generally active acquirers of businesses but rarely active sellers of businesses. Many divestitures take place when companies get into financial distress while only few companies actively manage their business portfolios. Corporate management is generally reluctant to divest strong divisions as they need to find new investment opportunities to fill their spots. On the other end of the performance spectrum, corporate management is similarly hesitant to divest underperforming businesses and substantial resources are invested before acknowledging the failure of an investment.

Private equity firms on the contrary are required by the non-permanent nature of PE capital to actively manage their investment portfolios and to be active buyers as well as active sellers of businesses. They have established regular portfolio reviews to assess the opportunities to divest businesses given the state of transformation, the future growth expectations for the business, the return requirements of investors, and the conditions on the IPO and M&A markets.

Public multi-business firms need to enforce a model of flexible ownership. The public equity model is by definition different from the model of private equity funds. Multi-business firms have the opportunity to hold onto businesses if the holding is expected to add further value to the business or if the business is of strategic importance to the overall portfolio. Based on the contribution by Barber and Goold (2007), Fig. 6.11 outlines the general portfolio management opportunities for public multi-business firms to expand their current approach of "invest to keep"

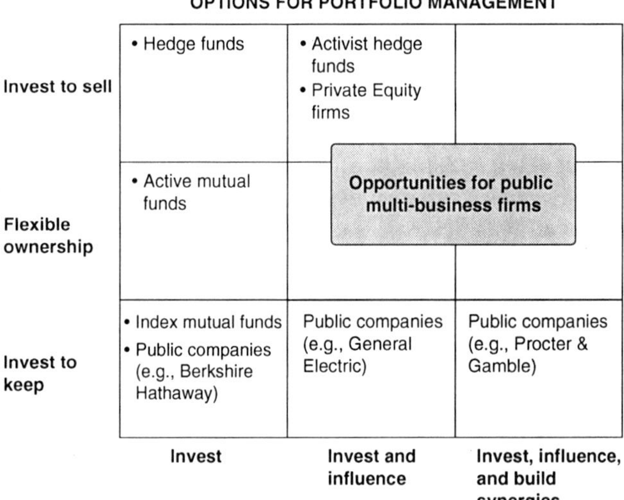

Fig. 6.11 Options for portfolio management

into a more flexible ownership approach and selectively to a PE like "invest to sell" mentality.

To enforce an active portfolio management approach, multi-business firms need to implement regular portfolio reviews that challenge the existence of every business in the portfolio of the firm. Senior management has to evaluate whether the corporation is able to add further value to the individual business or if another owner is able to extract more value from the business. The enhanced independence of each division outlined above increases the flexibility of management to divest businesses without reducing the value of the remaining portfolio by taking potentially important parts out of the overall business platform.

6.4.4 Limitations of Research

To assess the quality of research and to outline the limitations of research of this study's exploratory part, one must analyze the validity and reliability of the research approach chosen for this study. The validity of the research essentially describes how well the study's propositions represent reality and thereby assesses the quality of research. One distinguishes construct validity, internal validity, and external validity. The reliability of the propositions developed in this study describes the consistency or repeatability of the study's results and thereby assesses the quality of measurement.

Construct validity refers to the conceptualization and measures of the constructs under investigation. In this contribution, construct validity is addressed by the use of proven theoretical concepts, the triangulation of findings across different data sources, as well as the application of exploratory research. The study's qualitative research is based on the concept of corporate parenting, which has found wide recognition in the academic community as an appropriate measure for the value creation through parenting advantage. The use of interview data, company publications, as well as data collected in the first empirical part of the study allows the triangulation of findings across different sources and to detect any irregularities in the study's findings. Exploratory research finally enables the researcher to adjust perspectives and constructs during the study and thereby provides the flexibility required to address new theoretical questions.

Internal validity refers to the unambiguousness of interpretations of the study's results. It is addressed via the use of a single researcher and the application of a clear exploratory framework. A single researcher eliminates the risk of diverging perspectives and interpretations by different coders of data. The study's exploratory framework presents an explicit structure for the collection and analysis of the study's empirical data; however, the research results can be affected by the researcher's experiences and pre-assumptions.

External validity addresses the question how well the study's findings generalize back into the overall population. The study's exploratory research investigated the management models of 20 private equity firms and thereby collected insights across a broad range of business models. The study included a diverse research sample in terms of portfolio size, geographic origin, and portfolio relatedness. Its heterogeneity supports the external validity of this study. However, the interview approach with individual private equity professionals reduces the quality of research. The illustration of a PE firm's management model is influenced by the personal background and perspective of each interviewee on a firm's strategy and business model and therefore contains a subjective component. The sample size of 20 firms furthermore limits the statistical significance of the link between firm characteristics, management model, and performance found in this study. Additional quantitative research will be necessary to validate the propositions developed in this study.

Qualitative studies by their very nature will not provide the repeatability of quantitative research designs. To improve reliability, the study is based on an explicit research framework and is supplemented by quantitative data developed in the first empirical part of this study. Further academic research on the level of the overall private equity firms will be required to address any consistency concerns and to provide further insights about the private equity management model. The study is moreover focused on large, conglomerate-like private equity structures; the empirical results can therefore not provide a reliable basis for discussion of smaller private equity firms that might operate with strongly diverging portfolio strategies and management models.

Finally, the transition of private equity findings into the world of traditional multi-business firms is largely based on the depiction of public corporations in prior academic research. Potential changes in the management approach of these firms in the meantime find no representation in this study. Additional academic research will be necessary to build an empirical basis for the applicability of private equity success factors in multi-business firms.

Chapter 7
Conclusion and Outlook

> *"After looking at the successes of firms like KKR and Clayton, Dubilier & Rice, it started to become clear to me that leveraged buyouts, and what later became known as "private equity", were fundamentally a new way to think about corporate governance, a new model of management, if you will: But what surprises me is that so few public companies are actually taking advantage of this new management model. I think it's possible for public corporations to take almost all of the major competitive advantages of the private equity sector and implement them in one way or another without actually going private."*
>
> *Michael Jensen, Jesse Isador Strauss, Professor of Business Administration, Emeritus at Harvard Business School*

This contribution investigates the influence of diversification on performance in private equity firms and outlines the conduct of private equity players in the role of a parent to a portfolio of diversified businesses. The study is unique in the way that it pioneers the comprehensive analysis of the overall private equity management model and its success factors rather than the behavior of private equity professionals in individual transactions or the performance of specific investment vehicles, which have been under investigation in prior academic research. The study, furthermore, draws a comparison to the management model of multi-business firms and provides a first assessment of the applicability of private equity key success factors in traditional diversified companies.

The empirical research in this study addresses questions of high strategic relevance for private equity professionals, investors in private equity firms as much as for executives of – mostly public – multi-business firms. The implications of this study for each of these constituencies are detailed in the following sections of this chapter. It closes with an outlook for academic research in the field of private equity and defines further need for empirical studies about the opportunities for multi-business firms to learn from private equity.

D.O. Klier, *Managing Diversified Portfolios*,
DOI: 10.1007/978-3-7908-2173-4_7,

7.1 Implications for Private Equity Managers

Rising competition and less favorable debt markets strain the traditional private equity model and put increasing pressure on private equity professionals to rethink their investment approach. This study provides evidence about the influence of different portfolio strategies and management models on private equity performance and thereby offers insights for private equity managers as to what changes are required to compete in an increasing demanding market environment.

7.1.1 Portfolio Strategy

The results of the quantitative and qualitative empirical analyses provided consistent evidence that the concentration on a limited number of industrial sectors – though not on a single sector – and the creation of related diversification leads to superior performance. Even though statistically not significant on a five percent level, the consistent results of the quantitative research are underlined by the findings of the exploratory part of this study about management models and key success factors in private equity firms. The successful "interventionist" management model is generally found in firms with strongholds in particular industries to enable the establishment of transaction experience and management expertise in those selected industries.

These findings indicate that general partners face an increasing requirement to develop their firms from opportunistic investors to players with a clear industry strategy. The focus on an average of four to five industries promises a sufficient level of diversification to remain active buyers and sellers even in cyclical industries while opening up the opportunity to build industry-specific knowledge and networks and thereby improve the performance of the overall investment portfolio. Industry expertise enables a firm to have a stronger presence on the industry's transaction markets, reduces agency costs through improved supervision of management teams, and allows private equity players to better support the management teams of their portfolio companies in strategic decision making in line with the argumentation of the resource-based view.

7.1.2 Management Model

Building on the advantages of related diversified investment portfolios, the exploratory research design provides evidence for the financial superiority of "interventionist" private equity firms over the traditional type of "opportunistic financial investors". Investors with an active management approach offer considerably higher net returns to limited partners than more passive financial investors. While traditional financial investors focus their activities on the changes of an asset's capital and governance structure, so-called financial and governance engineering, "interventionist managers" have established an active parenting model to enable value creation through so-called operational engineering. This kind of PE firm acts as active investor with strong involvement in decision making regarding a firm's strategy and operations while maintaining the advantages of the traditional private equity management model. Beyond active ownership, parenting advantage is brought about by providing center resources in selected areas if critical to the success of the overall portfolio, consolidating market access in areas with significant economies of scale, and actively linking portfolio companies with potential for cooperation. All of these activities remain on an informal level to avoid the costs typically associated with extensive and inefficient "corporate-like" infrastructure.

The value of financial engineering skills deteriorated towards being almost a commodity whereas intervention in key performance drivers through active parenting and operational engineering distinguishes high performing PE firms from their peers. Private equity professionals therefore need to review their management models for opportunities to actively support the value creation in their portfolio companies. The "interventionist" management model, however, is not a completely new form of private equity ownership but appears to be the next step in the development of private equity. All activities of "interventionist" private equity firms build on the traditional performance drivers of financial investors that have to be maintained as foundations of the PE management model. The use of leverage, the alignment of interest, as well as the active role on the board of a portfolio company remain important to reduce agency costs and drive investment performance. All of the value creation levers are moreover supported by the private equity "invest to sell" approach. The implementation of the "interventionist manager" model, however, requires substantial adjustments in the portfolio strategy and skill set of a private equity firm and a change in mentality towards more active ownership.

The above-outlined shift towards related diversification in selected industries combined with a stronger team background in particular target industries are essential enablers for active ownership and the "interventionist" management model. Based on an investment portfolio with related diversification, general partners have to carefully select areas for involvement to exploit the advantages of portfolio relatedness while avoiding the costs of corporate-like infrastructure. Involvement of active investors generally includes the development of a detailed business plan during the first 100 days of an investment but also the ongoing support during the evaluation of strategic questions during the holding period with skilled management talent. Firms going towards an "interventionist manager" approach furthermore need to assess the potential benefits of joint market access for key business and non-business items such as commodities, logistics, or IT infrastructure. Finally, PE professionals should provide a platform for related businesses to interact and engage with each other. Informality of all interactions thereby ensures the independence of each business to shun the setup of firm linkages that reduce tradability and accountability of individual investments.

In terms of organizational setup, so far the jury is still out to decide which model works best. The best performing firms have installed a strong sector orientation within the private equity partnership. Regarding responsibilities along the lifetime of an asset, one, however, can observe a single-team approach with a mix of strong financial and strong operational skills as well as a split team approach with two teams, one focusing on the origination and execution of transactions, the other on monitoring and transforming portfolio companies. Recently, the majority of firms in the "interventionist manager" field or thriving to get there have implemented separate portfolio teams. While thereby enhancing focus and expertise, one at the same time risks a loss of accountability for performance within the private equity partnership.

7.2 Implications for Investors

Private equity is still a young asset class but has developed into an important part of the investment universe for both institutional as well as private investors. It allows investors to diversify and to enhance the performance of an investment portfolio. At the same time, limited transparency is available about the returns achieved by different players in the market and about the performance drivers behind the private equity management model. The study provides clear evidence that private equity as an asset class outperforms holdings in public corporations. Independent of the holding period, investments in private equity funds have generated significantly higher performance than assets in comparable companies listed on the public markets. The spread of performance in the private equity world, however, is wide and the lack of transparency in the industry poses further difficulties on the selection of private equity investment opportunities. The quantitative as well as the qualitative part of this study provide insights into the determinants of private equity performance that can assist private equity investors in the evaluation of individual private equity players.

To initiate the evaluation of private equity firms, the assessment of few key characteristics of private equity firms can reduce the number of potential investments considerably without developing a deeper understanding for particular management models of different PE houses. The results of this study highlight that the level of experience is the most important criteria for selecting a firm. Players with longstanding expertise in private equity seem to possess the potential to provide higher returns than less experienced firms. Diversification is also important for performance, however related diversification in selected industries rather than unrelated diversification of the overall investment portfolio of a firm across a broad range of industries should be considered in the evaluation of different private equity firms. The size of a private equity portfolio is not important in this assessment. Small firms with a particular niche can be as successful as the largest players in the industry.

Based on this selection, investors need to obtain a better understanding of the management models pursued by different private equity firms. The results of the exploratory part of this study indicate that general partners with an active management approach considerably outperform traditional, more financially oriented investors. Players with active involvement during the holding period of an investment generate higher returns than investors with a focus on value creation during the time of the deal by relying on the proceeds of financial engineering and alignment of interest. These operationally active firms therefore seem better equipped to face stronger competition for attractive assets and difficult market environments.

7.3 Implications for Corporate Managers

Since decades, executives of diversified companies have been under pressure by their shareholders to split up the firms' business portfolios into separate, more focused entities. Under the accusation of value destroying diversification, several corporations with conglomerate-like structures were dismantled. Only few multi-business firms successfully avoided such pressures by consistently delivering high performance such as general electric. The US conglomerate demonstrated that corporate management can add value to a diversified set of businesses. GE's corporate center focuses the involvement of its headquarters on selective success factors such as the function as financial umbrella or the development of general management talent with a strong orientation on costs as well as quality and thereby generated superior returns versus its peers.

At the same time, private equity firms have experienced strong growth rates, delivered consistently above market performance and strongly supported the split-up of public multi-business firms. Many top executives argue that the aggressive use of leverage, the PE incentive structures, and the freedom of quarterly reporting and compliance duties make the private equity model not applicable to traditional – mostly public – multi-business firms.

The results of this study on the contrary indicate that the most successful private equity firms have established models that create above market value through active ownership and strategic intervention – elements much closer to the traditional corporate manager. The empirical research of the study thereby raises questions about the portfolio strategy and management model pursued by traditional multi-business firms and the opportunities to learn from private equity players.

7.3.1 Portfolio Strategy

As highlighted above, the most successful private equity firms have established an investment portfolio with related diversification in a selected number of industries. On average, the best performing companies have four to five industry sectors and attempt to make most of their investments in these sectors. The industry concentration gives them the opportunity to build the skills and networks required to acquire, transform, manage, and divest companies in these industries.

For multi-business firms, this in consequence means that the increasing trend towards companies with a single industry focus as much as the broad diversification of the old conglomerates is not the optimal level of diversification to succeed in the market for corporate control. Focus on one sector exposes firms to cyclicality of industries and capital markets and thereby limits their investment and divestment opportunities. Multi-sector focus provides companies with sufficient flexibility to act while retaining the advantages of portfolio relatedness. If one believes that the private equity model and traditional multi-business firms are comparable in the principle of investing in and managing diversified portfolios, multi-business firms should follow the example of the most successful PE players and build a selected number of strong industry cores while ensuring a high level of independence for each business.

Few companies so far have realized a comparable portfolio strategy. Berkshire Hathaway is a highly successful example of a conglomerate company that has exploited many of the benefits found in private equity portfolio strategy while being a publicly listed multi-business firm. Warren Buffett's investments are largely concentrated on insurance companies, building technology businesses and firms in the consumer products field. By this approach, the US firm ensures an in-depth understanding of industries and businesses within the holding company and maintains the ability for targeted intervention in strategic questions while preserving a high level of independence for each investment.

7.3.2 Management Model

As indicated above, the success of the private equity management model does not depend entirely on advantages innate to private ownership such as the ability to use more aggressive leverage and incentive schemes nor in the avoidance of reporting and compliance costs associated with public markets. The study shows that the best performing private equity firms draw their returns from the transformation of their investments through active parenting. The "interventionist" management model relies on the ability of private equity professionals to lay the right foundations for the management teams of portfolio companies but at the same time to support and steer decision making in order to exploit growth opportunities and increase efficiency.

The management teams of traditional multi-business firms can draw on the success factors of private equity to reform their management model. Based on the altered portfolio strategy with strong core industries, headquarters need to redefine their role as active owners with focused intervention in critical decision making processes rather than mere administrators. Active ownership generally involves the proactive monitoring of financial results, the active support in business development, and the targeted involvement in key decisions greatly affecting performance such as financing, selecting key suppliers, or filling important executive positions. The informality of interaction and the high degree of independence of individual businesses avoid the costs generally found in conventional multi-business firms. Internal leveraged buyouts and the use of leveraged equity purchase programs can be used to create stronger alignment of interest between shareholders, holding management and the management teams of individual businesses while at the same time introducing the disciplinary effects of business-specific leverage. A flexible ownership approach with a stronger representation of the private equity "invest to sell" mentality encourages a focus on value creation and avoids deficits generally found in the portfolio management approach of large corporations. The transformation of a traditional multi-business firm to a private-equity-like owner of portfolio companies is an intense but according to this study's data fruitful process.

The recent reorganization at Siemens can be seen as an example for such an approach: by consolidating the firm's business portfolio into the three major industry groups industry, energy, and healthcare with a dedicated sector CEO for each group, the German conglomerate is creating a strong management focus on those core industries. Underneath each industry group, individual businesses are intended to operate independently. Siemens in that way installs industry experience in its headquarters and focuses the activities of a considerably smaller corporate center on targeted intervention with strategic decision making rather than centralizing a broad range of corporate functions. By those means, the company aims at improving the performance of its businesses across the overall portfolio while enabling the benefits of accountability and tradability of individual entities.

7.4 Outlook for Academic Research

The recent success stories of private equity firms and hedge funds have let to a revival of academic research in the field of alternative investments and private equity in particular. Studies however have mostly been driven out of an entirely financial perspective comparing the returns of PE funds with public market indices. Few studies have moreover investigated the influence of private equity in individual transactions.

This study pioneered the comprehensive view of a private equity firm in the role of a parent and as a new form of multi-business firms. It calculated diversification and performance indices on the level of the consolidated private equity firm and evaluated the relationship between diversification and performance. It moreover explored the different forms of management models available in the PE industry and developed key success factors of private equity firms to create value in their investment portfolios through parenting advantage. The study finally made a first assessment of the opportunities for traditional multi-business firms to learn from the private equity management model.

The methodology used in this contribution as well as the empirical results trigger a number of questions that need to be addressed in further academic research in the private equity discipline as well as in research regarding the management of corporations.

7.4.1 Research in Private Equity

This study presents two very different research methodologies and research objectives to provide a first overarching perspective of private equity general partners in their function as parent in a diversified business portfolio.

The quantitative part of the study used a sample of 100 private equity firms and 100 public corporations to analyze and compare the influence of industry diversification on returns to investors. It selected an established research approach from strategic management and finance research and applied it to a new dataset. Although it is the author's belief that the chosen approach is most appropriate for the study's research question, previous contributions in corporate management have experimented with different diversification and performance measures to triangulate the findings of individual studies and to address different angles of the diversification phenomenon. Additional empirical work would therefore be required to test the diversification–performance relationship with different measures. Categorical measures as well as a large variety of continuous diversification approaches are available to test the study's assessment of portfolio diversification while accounting or valuation based metrics could support the analysis of PE performance. Given the current availability of data on private equity, this study was build on portfolio proxies based on market transactions and third-party performance reporting. Current movements of the industry to stronger transparency will eventually provide the premises for larger sample studies on a firm-wide level with potentially higher quality data. Better insights regarding the influence of industry diversification on PE performance will also be necessary to advance academic research of portfolio strategy in private equity firms. This study provides a first basis to reveal those levels of diversification that seem to enable superior performance. Further academic research will be required to develop portfolio models for private equity firms that will help PE professionals to produce superior risk-return profiles.

The qualitative part of the study explored the management models of 20 private equity firms and linked the results with empirical data about portfolio diversification and performance obtained in the quantitative part of the study. It discovered two general private equity management models and outlined the specific components of "corporate parenting" of each model. Based on these profiles and each model's impact on performance, the study developed five propositions about the key success factors of the management model with the highest performance in the study's sample – the model of "interventionist managers". Further empirical studies will be necessary to test the classification of private equity firms into two general management models and to examine the relationship between management models and performance in larger samples. It will be of further interest to test the study's findings for time dependence; changing economic conditions might reverse trends observed in this study or make certain elements of the PE management model obsolete. In addition, empirical work is required to test the individual propositions about key success factors of private equity in a hypothesis-driven research setting.

7.4.2 Research in Corporate Management

The study provides insights for research regarding public equity and the management of traditional multi-business firms along two dimensions: the comparison of the diversification–performance relationship between private equity firms and public corporations as well as the propositions concerning learning opportunities for multi-business firms from private equity.

The study found a positive influence of diversification on performance in private equity firms while no relationship was discovered in public corporations. The majority of recent publications about the impact of diversification on financial performance and valuation have focused on a binary diversification measure – diversified or focused. Based on this study's findings about the positive attributes of related diversification on the private equity side, academic research should reconsider the appropriateness of different diversification measures. If this study's research results about a lack of diversification influence on performance find further support in empirical studies, one moreover has to find explanations for this phenomenon based on the theoretical foundations of diversification research – market-power view, agency view, and resource-based view.

The exploratory part outlined propositions about the key success factors of private equity based on the study's empirical results. The author then made an attempt to explain the usefulness and applicability of private equity components in multi-business firms to adopt some of the advantages and performance drivers of the private equity management model. The propositions are developed based on the comparison of existing research concerning the management approach of multi-business firms and the private equity management models found in this study. The applicability of each of these propositions needs to be evaluated in further empirical research. It will require an in-depth analysis of the pre-conditions that need to be present in traditional multi-business firms for the implementation of a PE-like management model. Further research will then be necessary to address the change process in firms adjusting to private equity success factors closing with an assessment of success rates and influence on performance.

Appendices

List of SIC Codes

The study uses the Standard Industry Classification (SIC) code system to classify investments into industry groups (two-digit SIC code level) and industry segments (four-digit SIC code level). The SIC codes below are reported per economic division on an industry group level. SIC codes have been introduced by the U.S. government to standardize industry classifications and have been internationally recognized in accounting practices and academic research.

DIVISION	A.	**AGRICULTURE, FORESTRY, AND FISHING**
	01	AGRICULTURAL PRODUCTION-CROPS
	02	AGRICULTURAL PRODUCTION-LIVESTOCK AND ANIMAL SPECIALTIES
	07	AGRICULTURAL SERVICES
	08	FORESTRY
	09	FISHING, HUNTING, AND TRAPPING
DIVISION	B.	**MINING**
	10	METAL MINING
	11	ANTHRACITE MINING
	12	COAL MINING
	13	OIL AND GAS EXTRACTION
		MINING AND QUARRYING OF NONMETALLIC
	14	MINERALS, EXCEPT FUELS
DIVISION	C.	**CONSTRUCTION**
	15	BUILDING CONSTRUCTION-GENERAL CONTRACTORS AND OPERATIVE BUILDERS
	16	HEAVY CONSTRUCTION OTHER THAN BUILDING CONSTRUCTION-CONTRACTORS
	17	CONSTRUCTION-SPECIAL TRADE CONTRACTORS

DIVISION D. MANUFACTURING

20 FOOD AND KINDRED PRODUCTS
21 TOBACCO PRODUCTS
22 TEXTILE MILL PRODUCTS
23 APPAREL AND OTHER FINISHED PRODUCTS MADE FROM FABRICS AND SIMILAR MATERIAL
24 LUMBER AND WOOD PRODUCTS, EXCEPT FURNITURE
25 FURNITURE AND FIXTURES
26 PAPER AND ALLIED PRODUCTS
27 PRINTING, PUBLISHING, AND ALLIED INDUSTRIES
28 CHEMICALS AND ALLIED PRODUCTS
29 PETROLEUM REFINING AND RELATED INDUSTRIES
30 RUBBER AND MISCELLANEOUS PLASTICS PRODUCTS
31 LEATHER AND LEATHER PRODUCTS
32 STONE, CLAY, GLASS, AND CONCRETE PRODUCTS
33 PRIMARY METAL INDUSTRIES
34 FABRICATED METAL PRODUCTS, EXCEPT MACHINERY AND TRANSPORTATION EQUIPMENT
35 INDUSTRIAL AND COMMERCIAL MACHINERY AND COMPUTER EQUIPMENT
36 ELECTRONIC AND OTHER ELECTRICAL EQUIPMENT AND COMPONENTS, EXCEPT COMPUTER
37 TRANSPORTATION EQUIPMENT
38 MEASURING, ANALYZING AND CONTROLLING INSTRUMENTS; PHOTOGRAPHIC, MEDICAL AND OPTICAL GOODS, WATCHES AND CLOCKS
39 MISCELLANEOUS MANUFACTURING INDUSTRIES

DIVISION E. TRANSPORTATION, COMMUNICATIONS, ELECTRIC, GAS, AND SANITARY SERVICE

40 RAILROAD TRANSPORTATION
41 LOCAL AND SUBURBAN TRANSIT AND INTERURBAN HIGHWAY PASSENGER TRANSPORTATION
42 MOTOR FREIGHT TRANSPORTATION AND WAREHOUSING
43 UNITED STATES POSTAL SERVICE
44 WATER TRANSPORTATION
45 TRANSPORTATION BY AIR
46 PIPELINES, EXCEPT NATURAL GAS
47 TRANSPORTATION SERVICES
48 COMMUNICATIONS
49 ELECTRIC, GAS, AND SANITARY SERVICES

DIVISION F. WHOLESALE TRADE

50 WHOLESALE TRADE; DURABLE GOODS
51 WHOLESALE TRADE; NONDURABLE GOODS

DIVISION G. RETAIL TRADE

52 BUILDING MATERIALS, HARDWARE, GARDEN SUPPLY, AND MOBILE HOME DEALERS
53 GENERAL MERCHANDISE STORES
54 FOOD STORES
55 AUTOMOTIVE DEALERS AND GASOLINE SERVICE STATIONS
56 APPAREL AND ACCESSORY STORES
57 HOME FURNITURE, FURNISHINGS, AND EQUIPMENT STORES
58 EATING AND DRINKING PLACES
59 MISCELLANEOUS RETAIL

DIVISION H. FINANCE, INSURANCE, AND REAL ESTATE

60 DEPOSITORY INSTITUTIONS
61 NONDEPOSITORY CREDIT INSTITUTIONS
62 SECURITY AND COMMODITY BROKERS, DEALERS, EXCHANGES, AND SERVICES
63 INSURANCE CARRIERS
64 INSURANCE AGENTS, BROKERS, AND SERVICE
65 REAL ESTATE
67 HOLDING AND OTHER INVESTMENT OFFICES

DIVISION I. SERVICES

70 HOTELS, ROOMING HOUSES, CAMPS, AND OTHER LODGING PLACES
72 PERSONAL SERVICES
73 BUSINESS SERVICES
75 AUTOMOTIVE REPAIR, SERVICES, AND PARKING
76 MISCELLANEOUS REPAIR SERVICES
78 MOTION PICTURES
79 AMUSEMENT AND RECREATION SERVICES
80 HEALTH SERVICES
81 LEGAL SERVICES
82 EDUCATIONAL SERVICES
83 SOCIAL SERVICES
84 MUSEUMS, ART GALLERIES, AND BOTANICAL AND ZOOLOGICAL GARDENS
86 MEMBERSHIP ORGANIZATIONS
87 ENGINEERING, ACCOUNTING, RESEARCH, MANAGEMENT, AND RELATED SERVICES
88 PRIVATE HOUSEHOLDS
89 SERVICES, NOT ELSEWHERE CLASSIFIED

DIVISION J. PUBLIC ADMINISTRATION

91 EXECUTIVE, LEGISLATIVE, AND GENERAL GOVERNMENT, EXCEPT FINANCE

92 JUSTICE, PUBLIC ORDER, AND SAFETY

93 PUBLIC FINANCE, TAXATION, AND MONETARY POLICY

94 ADMINISTRATION OF HUMAN RESOURCE PROGRAMS

95 ADMINISTRATION OF ENVIRONMENTAL QUALITY AND HOUSING PROGRAMS

96 ADMINISTRATION OF ECONOMIC PROGRAMS

97 NATIONAL SECURITY AND INTERNATIONAL AFFAIRS

DIVISION K. NONCLASSIFIABLE ESTABLISHMENTS

99 NONCLASSIFIABLE ESTABLISHMENTS

Sample Characteristics Corporations

Company Name	Country of origin	Market Capitalization	Herfindahl index Sales	Herfindahl index Assets	DR Sales	DU Sales	DT Sales	DR Assets	DU Assets	DT Assets	TRS 5Y	TRS 10Y	Jensen's Alpha 5Y	Jensen's Alpha 10Y	Sharpe' measure 5Y	Sharpe' measure 10Y	Treynor measure 5Y	Treynor measure 10Y
GENERAL ELECTRIC CO	US	363670	0,19	0,23	0,00	1,51	1,51	0,00	1,10	1,10	−0,04	0,13	−0,10	0,05	−0,0040	0,0050	−0,10	0,13
PROCTER & GAMBLE CO	US	198966	0,21	0,29	0,69	1,03	1,72	0,42	1,32	1,74	0,10	0,13	0,06	0,06	0,0048	0,0058	0,22	0,26
JPMORGAN CHASE & CO	US	160543	0,23	0,32	0,00	0,00	0,00	0,00	0,00	0,00	0,01	0,11	−0,09	−0,02	−0,0009	0,0027	−0,01	0,04
NESTLE SA/AG	CH	134809	0,20	0,19	1,09	0,60	1,69	1,15	0,56	1,70	0,03	0,14	−0,04	0,05	−0,0003	0,0061	−0,01	0,18
WELLS FARGO & CO	US	118969	0,48	0,00	0,00	0,00	0,00	0,00	0,00		0,05	0,17	0,01	0,11	0,0012	0,0085	0,06	0,41
DAIMLER-CHRYSLER AG	GE	111758	0,25	0,00	0,48	0,33	0,81	0,00	0,00		0,05	0,09	−0,05	−0,03	0,0006	0,0018	0,01	0,04
HEWLETT-PACKARD CO	US	107963	0,25	0,20	0,97	0,51	1,48	1,00	0,67	1,67	0,00	0,09	−0,11	−0,05	−0,0013	0,0014	−0,02	0,03
MERCK & CO	US	96631	0,85	0,00	0,27	0,00	0,27	0,00	0,00		−0,16	0,03	−0,22	−0,05	−0,0084	−0,0007	−0,28	−0,02
ING GROEP NV	NED	88720	0,26	0,24	0,00	0,51	0,51	0,00	0,50	0,50	−0,03	0,16	−0,16	−0,01	−0,0024	0,0044	−0,04	0,07
BARCLAYS PLC	UK	81326	0,22	0,47	0,00	0,04	0,04	0,00	0,05	0,05	0,10	0,18	−0,01	0,05	0,0023	0,0050	0,06	0,12
NOKIA (AB) OY	FIN	77742	0,43	0,30	0,09	0,67	0,76	0,18	0,69	0,87	−0,18	0,26	−0,31	0,11	−0,0064	0,0065	−0,15	0,15
SGF-SOC GENERL DE FRANCE SA	FR	72896	0,41	0,45	0,68	0,05	0,73	0,62	0,09	0,71	0,15	0,21	0,04	0,08	0,0050	0,0073	0,10	0,15
AMERICAN EXPRESS CO	US	70744	0,40	0,60	0,00	0,36	0,36	0,00	0,14	0,14	0,04	0,18	−0,04	0,07	0,0005	0,0067	0,01	0,12
FRANCE TELECOM	FR	63772	0,40	0,52	0,69	0,00	0,69	0,65	0,00	0,65	−0,21		−0,35		−0,0081		−0,14	
ORACLE CORP	US	62930	0,35	0,00	0,46	0,11	0,57	0,00	0,00		−0,16	0,15	−0,24	0,04	−0,0085	0,0045	−0,18	0,09
ERICSSON (LM) TELEFON	SWE	57779	0,89	0,45	0,22	0,00	0,22	0,24	0,29	0,52	−0,19	0,09	−0,37	−0,13	−0,0055	0,0012	−0,10	0,02
MOTOROLA INC	US	53595	0,51	0,35	0,00	0,00	0,00	0,00	0,00	0,00	0,06	0,04	−0,04	−0,09	0,0008	−0,0002	0,02	0,00
UNITED PARCEL SERVICE INC	US	51879	0,72	0,60	0,00	0,45	0,45	0,00	0,53	0,53	0,06		0,01		0,0023		0,06	

(continued)

Sample Characteristics Corporations (continued)

Company Name	Country of origin	Market Capitali-zation	Herfindahl index Sales	Herfindahl index Assets	DR Sales	DU Sales	DT Sales	DR Assets	DU Assets	DT Assets	TRS 5Y	TRS 10Y	Jensen's Alpha 5Y	Jensen's Alpha 10Y	Sharpe' measure 5Y	Sharpe' measure 10Y	Treynor measure 5Y	Treynor measure 10Y
LVMH MOET HENNESSY L VUITTON	FR	47950	0,24	0,24	0,52	0,95	1,47	0,45	0,98	1,43	0,03	0,13	−0,10	−0,04	0,0001	0,0034	0,00	0,05
BASF AG	GE	43859	0,19	0,20	1,11	0,52	1,63	1,26	0,41	1,67	0,12	0,20	0,03	0,09	0,0047	0,0085	0,10	0,18
CARNIVAL CORP/ PLC (USA)	US	43257	0,93	0,96	0,00	0,18	0,18	0,00	0,09	0,09	0,13	0,17	0,05	0,06	0,0044	0,0057	0,08	0,11
DU PONT (E I) DE NEMOURS	US	43166	0,21	0,22	0,47	0,54	1,01	0,53	0,51	1,04	0,01	0,05	−0,06	−0,04	−0,0016	0,0002	−0,04	0,01
VIVENDI SA	FR	41937	0,29	0,22	0,00	1,00	1,00	0,00	1.07	1,07	−0,15	0,03	−0,29	−0,13	−0,0075	−0,0004	−0,12	−0,01
STANDARD CHARTERED BANK	UK	39701	0,50	0,56	0,00	0,00	0,00	0,00	0.00	0,00	0,10	0,12	−0,03	−0,03	0,0029	0,0036	0,05	0,06
PRUDENTIAL FINANCIAL INC	US	38866	0,37	0,35	0,00	0,55	0,55	0,00	0.67	0,67								
DANONE (GROUPE)	FR	38266	0,42	0,38	0,97	0,00	0,97	1,04	0,00	1,04	0,04	0,13	−0,02	0,06	0,0005	0,0054	0,02	0,22
BAYER AG	GE	37193	0,33	0,39	0,51	0,00	0,51	0,49	0,00	0,49	−0,04	0,10	−0,16	−0,04	−0,0030	0,0024	−0,06	0,05
HONEYWELL INTERNATIONAL INC	US	35094	0,29	0,25	0,00	0,81	0,81	0,00	0,79	0,79	−0,02	0,07	−0,11	−0,05	−0,0027	0,0010	−0,05	0,02
DEUTSCHE POST AG	GE	33541	0,28	0,73	0,00	0,42	0,42	0,00	0,41	0,41	0,00		−0,11		−0,0016		−0,03	
UNILEVER PLC	UK	33128	0,27	0,45	0,66	0,69	1,35	0,52	0,53	1,05	0,03	0,09	−0,04	0,00	0,0001	0,0027	0,00	0,08
FEDEX CORP	US	31418	0,48	0,47	0,19	0,63	0,82	0,16	0,63	0,80	0,21	0,19	0,16	0,12	0,0072	0,0059	0,33	0,27
SUNTRUST BANKS INC	US	28916	0,26	0,18	0,00	0,64	0,64	0,00	0,61	0,61	0,06	0,10	0,01	0,04	0,0017	0,0042	0,06	0,15
SOUTHERN CO	US	26924	0,96	0,94	0,00	0,00	0,00	0,00	0,00	0,00	0,15	0,13	0,07	0,03	0,0084	0,0064	0,12	0,09
H & M HENNES & MAURITZ AB	SWE	26455	1,00	1,00	0,00	0,00	0,00	0,00	0,00	0,00	0,16	0,32	0,08	0,23	0,0056	0,0130	0,18	0,42
CARDINAL HEALTH INC	US	26223	0,70	0,29	0,00	0,42	0,42	0,00	0,64	0,64	0,01	0,16	−0,06	0,07	−0,0011	0,0051	−0,03	0,15

MCGRAW-HILL COMPANIES	US	23607	0,38	0,32	0,00	1,02	1,02	0,00	0,99	0,99	0,14	0,19	0,08	0,11	0,0059	0,0083	0,18	0,25
NORTHROP GRUMMAN CORP	US	23118	0,18	0,17	0,00	1,42	1,42	0,00	1,21	1,21	0,09	0,08	0,05	0,02	0,0028	0,0019	0,20	0,13
NIKE INC	US	22505	0,38	0,00	0,00	0,79	0,79	0,00	0,00		0,10	0,11	0,04	0,02	0,0033	0,0029	0,09	0,08
HOLCIM LTD	CH	21621	0,46	0,48	0,00	0,00	0,00	0,00	0,00	0,00	0,08	0,13	−0,04	−0,01	0,0020	0,0041	0,03	0,07
FPL GROUP INC	US	21573	0,63	0,51	0,54	0,00	0,54	0,63	0,00	0,63	0,07	0,10	0,01	0,03	0,0020	0,0032	0,07	0,12
CBS CORP	US	21400	0,48	0,37	0,59	0,40	0,99	0,00	0,56		−0,07	0,03	−0,14	−0,06	−0,0014	−0,0001	−0,11	−0,01
NOVO NORDISK A/S	DAN	20621	0,60	0,50	0,00	0,00	0,00	0,00	0,48	0,17	0,06	0,19	−0,04	0,07	0,0011	0,0066	0,03	0,15
KELLOGG CO	US	19829	1,00	1,00	0,00	0,00	0,00	0,00	0,00	0,00	0,14	0,04	0,09	−0,02	0,0075	−0,0004	0,46	−0,02
SWISSCOM AG	CH	19802	0,34	0,34	0,61	0,37	0,98	0,66	0,15	0,81	0,04		−0,01		0,0002		0,02	
PERNOD RICARD SA	FR	19658	1,00	1,00	0,00	0,00	0,00	0,00	0,00	0,00	0,23	0,19	0,18	0,13	0,0127	0,0096	0,66	0,49
NORFOLK SOUTHERN CORP	US	19547	1,00	1,00	0,00	0,00	0,00	0,00	0,00	0,00	0,29	0,08	0,22	−0,01	0,0089	0,0012	0,34	0,05
SUN MICROSYSTEMS INC	US	19517	0,54	0,61	0,00	0,65	0,65	0,00	0,35	0,35	−0,32	0,04	−0,45	−0,14	−0,0092	−0,0001	−0,14	0,00
CRH PLC	IRL	19224	0,35	0,41	1,07	0,00	1,07	0,97	0,00	0,97	0,08	0,18	−0,03	0,04	0,0009	0,0024	0,04	0,11
METRO AG	GE	19061	0,35	0,30	0,00	1,01	1,01	0,00	1,01	1,01	−0,01		−0,11		−0,0016		−0,03	
SYNGENTA AG	CH	18712	0,66	0,55	0,00	0,52	0,52	0,00	0,55	0,55	0,15		0,05		0,0053		0,12	
TNT NV	NED	18249	0,52	0,48	0,00	0,67	0,67	0,00	0,64	0,64	0,03		−0,06		−0,0003		−0,01	
MARRIOTT INTL INC	US	17852	0,26	0,21	0,00	0,07	0,07	0,00	0,08	0,08	0,10		0,01		0,0026		0,05	
GENERAL MILLS INC	US	17558	0,52	0,00	0,00	0,00	0,00	0,00	0,00		0,04	0,08	0,00	0,03	0,0009	0,0031	0,05	0,19
OMNICOM GROUP	US	17459	1,00	1,00	0,00	0,00	0,00	0,00	0,00	0,00	0,02	0,18	−0,05	0,08	−0,0008	0,0059	−0,02	0,15
CLEAR CHANNEL COMMUNI-CATIONS	US	17362	0,37	0,46	0,00	0,99	0,99	0,00	0,89	0,82	−0,07	0,12	−0,17	−0,01	−0,0040	0,0030	−0,07	0,05
MARSH & MCLENNAN COS	US	17316	0,35	0,35	0,00	0,95	0,95	0,00	0,90	0,90	−0,09	0,11	−0,17	0,00	−0,0058	0,0028	−0,12	0,06

(continued)

Sample Characteristics Corporations (continued)

Company Name	Country of origin	Market Capitalization	Herfindahl index Sales	Herfindahl index Assets	DR Sales	DU Sales	DT Sales	DR Assets	DU Assets	DT Assets	TRS 5Y	TRS 10Y	Jensen's Alpha 5Y	Jensen's Alpha 10Y	Sharpe' measure 5Y	Sharpe' measure 10Y	Treynor measure 5Y	Treynor measure 10Y
STAPLES INC	US	16606	0,42	0,35	0,39	0,00	0,39	0,62	0,00	0,62	0,24	0,17	0,16	0,06	0,0081	0,0049	0,18	0,11
GENERAL MOTORS CORP	US	16533	0,72	0,79	0,00	0,45	0,45	0,00	0,37	0,37	−0,13	−0,02	−0,21	−0,12	−0,0128	−0,0050	−0,15	−0,06
PACCAR INC	US	16215	0,92	0,60	0,00	0,26	0,26	0,00	0,64	0,64	0,30	0,27	0,21	0,16	0,0112	0,0095	0,22	0,18
DEUTSCHE BOERSE AG	GE	16115	0,25	0,77	0,00	0,52	0,52	0,00	0,01									
XEROX CORP	US	15927	0,34	0,00	0,00	0,00	0,00	0,00	0,00		0,26	−0,02	0,15	−0,17	0,0109	−0,0032	0,12	−0,04
CONTINENTAL AG	GE	15636	0,31	0,33	0,00	0,00	0,00	0,00	0,00	0,00	0,37	0,24	0,27	0,13	0,0127	0,0077	0,36	0,21
MARKS & SPENCER GROUP PLC	UK	15589	0,50	0,00	0,00	0,00	0,00	0,00	0,00		0,21	0,03	0,14	−0,06	0,0077	−0,0077	0,31	−0,03
GAP INC	US	15387	0,38	0,00	0,00	0,00	0,00	0,00	0,00		−0,07	0,12	−0,16	0,00	−0,0034	0,0025	−0,07	0,05
AIR PRODUCTS & CHEMICALS INC	US	15303	0,22	0,25	0,29	0,81	1,09	0,20	0,81	1,01	0,10	0,10	0,03	0,02	0,0038	0,0036	0,09	0,08
AVON PRODUCTS	US	14510	0,53	0,00	0,00	0,82	0,82	0,00	0,00		0,05	0,14	0,00	0,06	0,0009	0,0041	0,04	0,18
WOLSELEY PLC	UK	14364	1,00	1,00	0,00	0,00	0,00	0,00	0,00	0,00	0,26	0,14	0,14	−0,01	0,0091	0,0039	0,17	0,07
ELECTRONIC DATA SYSTEMS CORP	US	14037	0,96	0,56	0,00	0,00	0,00	0,00	0,00	0,00	−0,15	−0,06	−0,23	−0,17	−0,0064	−0,0037	−0,15	−0,09
BEIERSDORF AG	GE	14036	0,74	0,00	0,00	0,43	0,43	0,00	0,00		0,00	0,17	−0,06	0,09	−0,0015	0,0064	−0,07	0,31
BOSTON PROPERTIES INC	US	13674	0,78	0,00	0,00	0,00	0,00	0,00	0,00		0,18		0,11		0,0076		0,20	
STARWOOD HOTELS & RESORTS WRLD	US	13604	0,70	0,68	0,00	0,00	0,00	0,00	0,00	0,00	0,15	0,16	0,06	0,04	0,0044	0,0042	0,09	0,08
OTE - HELLENIC TELECOM ORG	GRE	13442	0,34	0,00	0,69	0,00	0,69	0,00	0,00		0,06		−0,03		0,0014		0,03	
MAN AG	GE	13231	0,48	0,45	0,19	0,81	1,00	0,19	1,01	1,19	0,15	0,13	0,03	−0,02	0,0042	0,0030	0,09	0,06
MEDIASET SPA	IT	13214	0,83	0,54	0,16	0,00	0,16	0,05	0,00	0,05	−0,04		−0,14		−0,0032		−0,07	
DEUTSCHE POSTBANK AG	GE	12988	0,72	0,32	0,00	0,00	0,00	0,00	0,00	0,00								

GRUPO FERROVIAL SA	MAD	12798	0,35	0,66	0,43	0,65	1,08	0,29	0,44	0,73	0,36		0,29		0,0155		0,53	
SOUTHWEST AIRLINES	US	12440	0,93	0,00	0,00	0,00	0,00	0,00	0,00		−0,06	0,14	−0,13	0,04	−0,0042	0,0043	−0,10	0,10
SARA LEE CORP	US	12382	0,17	0,16	0,63	0,91	1,54	0,57	0,96	1,53	−0,02	0,04	−0,08	−0,03	−0,0018	0,0000	−0,10	0,00
FREEPORT-MCMORAN COP&GOLD	US	12382	0,75	0,62	0,00	0,00	0,00	0,00	0,00	0,00	0,47	0,09	0,37	−0,04	0,0103	0,0010	0,31	0,03
JUNIPER NETWORKS INC	US	12045	0,45	0,00	0,00	0,00	0,00	0,00	0,00		−0,29		−0,41		−0,0073		−0,17	
CIE GEN DES ETABLIS MICHELIN	FR	11758	0,43	0,42	0,37	0,00	0,37	0,39	0,00	0,39	0,08	0,08	−0,01	−0,04	0,0016	0,0012	0,05	0,04
WRIGLEY (WM) JR CO	US	11430	1,00	1,00	0,00	0,00	0,00	0,00	0,00	0,00	0,08	0,11	0,04	0,05	0,0037	0,0053	0,17	0,24
THYSSENKRUPP AG	GE	11277	0,19	0,17	0,00	1,51	1,51	0,00	1,50	1,50	0,06	0,07	−0,05	−0,07	0,0011	0,0011	0,02	0,02
SAINSBURY (J) PLC	UK	10988	0,96	0,59	0,00	0,10	0,10	0,00	0,60	0,60	−0,02	0,01	−0,12	−0,11	−0,0027	−0,0017	−0,06	−0,04
DEUTSCHE LUFTHANSA AG	GE	10761	0,46	0,33	0,49	0,07	0,56	0,54	0,09	0,64	−0,12	0,05	−0,23	−0,09	−0,0049	0,0003	−0,12	0,01
OFFICE DEPOT INC	US	10541	0,36	0,30	0,00	0,61	0,61	0,00	0,56	0,56	0,35	0,09	0,24	−0,04	0,0099	0,0015	0,20	0,03
SAIPEM SPA	IT	10504	0,43	0,46	0,69	0,29	0,98	0,66	0,28	0,93	0,21	0,24	0,12	0,13	0,0071	0,0078	0,22	0,24
ADIDAS AG	GE	10291	0,40	0,00	0,00	0,98	0,98	0,00	0,00		0,21	0,16	0,15	0,09	0,0081	0,0055	0,41	0,28
HENKEL KGAA	GE	10270	0,26	0,26	1,06	0,00	1,06	1,08	0,00	1,08	0,08		0,02		0,0028		0,10	
NORDSTROM INC	US	10086	0,86	0,36	0,00	0,24	0,24	0,00	0,14	0,14	0,35	0,15	0,24	0,02	0,0108	0,0038	0,19	0,07
PARKER-HANNIFIN CORP	US	9844	0,58	0,59	0,18	0,58	0,76	0,14	0,50	0,64	0,10	0,13	0,02	0,02	0,0027	0,0036	0,06	0,07
SMITHS GROUP PLC	UK	9499	0,29	0,27	0,00	1,31	1,31	0,00	1,34	1,34	0,09	0,09	0,00	−0,03	0,0034	0,0025	0,07	0,05
SCOTTISH & NEWCASTLE PLC	UK	9333	0,51	0,54	0,00	0,00	0,00	0,00	0,00	0,00	0,01	0,00	−0,04	−0,06	−0,0012	−0,0021	−0,07	−0,13
SMITH INTERNATIONAL INC	US	9068	0,61	0,72	0,00	0,00	0,00	0,00	0,02	0,02	0,15	0,20	0,07	0,10	0,0042	0,0058	0,12	0,17

(continued)

Sample Characteristics Corporations (continued)

Company Name	Country of origin	Market Capitali-zation	Herfindahl index Sales	Herfindahl index Assets	DR Sales	DU Sales	DT Sales	DR Assets	DU Assets	DT Assets	TRS 5Y	TRS 10Y	Jensen's Alpha 5Y	Jensen's Alpha 10Y	Sharpe' measure 5Y	Sharpe' measure 10Y	Treynor measure 5Y	Treynor measure 10Y
ALLEGHENY TECHNOLOGIES INC	US	9030	0,44	0,31	0,30	0,00	0,30	0,30	0,00	0,30	0,22	0,08	0,09	–0,08	0,0043	0,0009	0,09	0,02
UNITED STATES STEEL CORP	US	8861	0,45	0,00	0,00	0,66	0,66	0,00	0,00		0,23	0,07	0,12	–0,08	0,0145	0,0021	0,10	0,01
SMITH & NEPHEW PLC	UK	8329	0,26	0,26	1,03	0,00	1,03	1,04	0,00	1,04	0,13	0,13	0,07	0,05	0,0056	0,0050	0,23	0,21
KUHNE & NAGEL INTERNATIONAL	CH	8274	0,31	0,19	0,00	1,31	1,31	0,00	1,56	1,56	0,33	0,30	0,23	0,18	0,0125	0,0110	0,31	0,27
CELESIO AG	GE	8220	0,68	0,47	0,00	0,43	0,43	0,00	0,66	0,66	0,16	0,10	0,11	0,03	0,0058	0,0023	0,42	0,17
RYANAIR HOLDINGS PLC	IRL	7882	0,73	0,00	0,38	0,08	0,46	0,00	0,00		0,08		–0,01		0,0009		0,06	

Source: Thompson Financial, Standard & Poors Research Insight (December 31, 2006)

Sample Characteristics Private Equity

Firm	Fund size (invested equity)*	Vintage first fund	Country of origin	Number of funds	Herfindahl index	DR	DU	DT	IRR 5Y	IRR 10Y	Jensen's Alpha 5Y	Jensen's Alpha 10Y	Sharpe' measure 5Y	Sharpe' measure 10Y	Treynor measure 5Y	Treynor measure 10Y
Kohlberg Kravis Roberts	40859	1980	US	10	0,13	0,85	1,29	2,14	0,26	0,24	0,18	0,13	0,0085	0,0075	0,20	0,18
Texas Pacific Group	30537	1994	US	11	0,31	0,34	1,35	1,68	0,30	0,25	0,20	0,12	0,0122	0,0094	0,18	0,14
Blackstone Group	29920	1987	US	13	0,24	0,27	1,54	1,81	0,24	0,20	0,14	0,06	0,0069	0,0052	0,13	0,10
Permira	26870	1988	UK	10	0,43	0,07	1,31	1,38	0,32	0,34	0,18	0,17	0,0074	0,0076	0,18	0,18
Carlyle Group	19941	1996	US	22	0,28	0,40	1,37	1,78	0,31	0,17	0,22	0,08	0,0126	0,0057	0,29	0,13
Thomas H Lee Partners	19497	1989	US	4	0,16	0,69	1,36	2,05	0,28	0,29	0,20	0,19	0,0096	0,0095	0,23	0,23
Apollo Management	19000	1995	US	4	0,12	0,21	1,99	2,20	0,17	0,10	0,11	0,03	0,0068	0,0029	0,27	0,12
Bain Capital	18382	2000	US	7	0,18	0,90	1,01	1,91	0,22		0,16		0,0093		0,37	
Goldman Sachs Private Equity Group	18275	1995	US	19	0,14	0,40	1,72	2,12	0,10	0,12	0,02	0,02	0,0027	0,0029	0,06	0,07
CVC Capital Partners	17813	1996	UK	5	0,13	0,14	2,06	2,20	0,29	0,22	0,19	0,09	0,0099	0,0067	0,24	0,16
BC Partners	15133	1997	UK	3	0,17	0,56	1,45	2,01	0,16	0,21	0,06	0,08	0,0050	0,0062	0,12	0,15
Credit Suisse Customized Fund Investment Group	14430	1992	US	21	0,13	0,27	1,92	2,19	0,16	0,12	0,10	0,05	0,0063	0,0038	0,25	0,15
Madison Dearborn Partners	14278	1993	US	5	0,16	0,71	1,33	2,04	0,21	0,20	0,13	0,10	0,0066	0,0061	0,16	0,15
Welsh, Carson, Anderson & Stowe	12392	1980	US	13	0,17	1,09	0,92	2,01	0,15	0,15	0,09	0,07	0,0055	0,0051	0,18	0,17
Forstmann Little & Co	11975	1986	US	6	0,17	0,91	1,00	1,91	−0,01	0,03	−0,08	−0,07	−0,0020	−0,0007	−0,05	−0,02
Charterhouse Capital Partners	10765	1994	UK	5	0,16	0,28	1,73	2,01	0,36	0,35	0,26	0,22	0,0145	0,0136	0,31	0,29
Candover Partners	10221	1989	UK	6	0,21	0,37	1,52	1,90	0,24	0,25	0,13	0,12	0,0099	0,0102	0,18	0,19
Clayton Dubilier & Rice	10148	1989	US	4	0,11	0,43	1,84	2,28	0,08	0,08	0,02	0,00	0,0022	0,0016	0,08	0,06
HM Capital Partners	10025	1994	US	6	0,16	0,13	1,88	2,01	0,01	0,01	−0,04	−0,07	−0,0010	−0,0019	−0,04	−0,08
Cinven	9226	1996	UK	3	0,14	0,25	1,88	2,13	0,21	0,12	0,14	0,03	0,0088	0,0036	0,35	0,14

(continued)

Sample Characteristics Private Equity (continued)

Firm	Fund size (invested equity)*	Vintage first fund	Country of origin	Number of funds	Herfindahl index	DR	DU	DT	IRR 5Y	IRR 10Y	Jensen's Alpha 5Y	Jensen's Alpha 10Y	Sharpe' measure 5Y	Sharpe' measure 10Y	Treynor measure 5Y	Treynor measure 10Y
GTCR Golder Rauner	9119	1980	US	10	0,10	0,44	1,85	2,28	0,26	0,19	0,18	0,09	0,0103	0,0066	0,24	0,15
Providence Equity Partners	8560	1991	US	6	0,23	0,23	1,47	1,70	0,33	0,34	0,25	0,24	0,0135	0,0134	0,31	0,31
TA Associates	8201	1969	US	19	0,11	0,57	1,70	2,27	0,26	0,28	0,18	0,17	0,0087	0,0090	0,21	0,22
Hellman & Friedman	8026	1984	US	4	0,13	1,01	1,11	2,12	0,26	0,23	0,18	0,13	0,0086	0,0072	0,21	0,17
Bridgepoint	7707	1998	UK	3	0,15	0,11	1,97	2,08	0,23	0,17	0,12	0,04	0,0086	0,0056	0,18	0,12
Terra Firma Capital Partners	7617	2003	UK	1	0,22	0,05	1,77	1,82	0,21		0,09		0,0072		0,13	
Vestar Capital Partners	7243	1993	US	4	0,13	0,19	1,99	2,17	0,24	0,24	0,16	0,13	0,0078	0,0074	0,19	0,18
Advent International	7156	1980	US	9	0,11	0,49	1,78	2,27	0,19	0,10	0,12	0,03	0,0077	0,0028	0,30	0,11
Montagu Private Equity	6946	1994	UK	3	0,34	0,04	1,31	1,35	0,23	0,24	0,15	0,15	0,0091	0,0094	0,30	0,32
Apax Partners	5913	1984	UK	19	0,10	0,97	1,31	2,28	0,22	0,21	0,14	0,11	0,0087	0,0077	0,29	0,26
Nordic Capital	5802	1998	SWE	4	0,15	0,61	1,47	2,08	0,29	0,30	0,19	0,18	0,0115	0,0115	0,24	0,24
Silver Lake Partners	5800	1999	US	2	0,37	0,67	0,49	1,16	0,24	0,24	0,14	0,11	0,0093	0,0089	0,14	0,13
PAI Partners	5788	2001	FR	2	0,19	0,16	1,84	2,00	0,08		–0,02		0,0019		0,05	
Doughty Hanson & Co	5239	1990	UK	6	0,11	0,44	1,83	2,26	0,28	0,28	0,21	0,19	0,0107	0,0103	0,46	0,44
Lindsay Goldberg & Bessemer	5100	2001	US	2	0,32	0,16	1,08	1,24	0,40		0,32		0,0147		0,33	
Onex Corp	5100	2003	US	2	0,11	0,34	1,90	2,24	0,21		0,10		0,0055		0,10	
Kelso & Company	4935	1986	US	5	0,11	0,25	2,00	2,25	0,17	0,17	0,11	0,10	0,0069	0,0063	0,27	0,25
Industri Kapital	4713	1989	UK	5	0,11	0,16	2,12	2,28	0,30	0,38	0,20	0,25	0,0121	0,0149	0,26	0,32
Lehman Brothers	4464	1983	US	10	0,10	0,25	2,03	2,28	0,14	0,13	0,08	0,06	0,0045	0,0040	0,19	0,17
MidOcean Partners	4282	1999	US	3	0,24	0,21	1,64	1,84	0,04	0,04	–0,04	–0,07	0,0002	–0,0002	0,00	0,00
Oak Hill Partners	4100	1999	US	2	0,90	0,02	0,26	0,28	0,07	0,07	–0,02	–0,05	0,0013	0,0009	0,03	0,02
Spectrum Equity Investors	3867	1994	US	4	0,53	0,00	0,66	0,66	0,13	0,14	0,05	0,04	0,0043	0,0044	0,10	0,10
3i	3833	1993	UK	7	0,11	0,46	1,79	2,26	0,11	0,11	0,04	0,02	0,0037	0,0032	0,15	0,13
Leonard Green & Partners	3671	1990	US	5	0,12	0,12	2,08	2,21	0,12	0,11	0,04	0,00	0,0033	0,0024	0,08	0,06

Cypress Group	3525	1996	US	2	0,14	0,24	1,85	2,10	0,04	0,04	−0,02	−0,04	0,0001	−0,0004	0,01	−0,01
JLL Partners	3268	1989	US	5	0,17	0,00	1,96	1,96	0,22	0,19	0,14	0,09	0,0088	0,0068	0,19	0,15
Berkshire Partners	3240	1984	US	5	0,11	0,40	1,86	2,26	0,31	0,32	0,23	0,22	0,0108	0,0106	0,26	0,26
J.W. Childs Associates	3085	1995	US	3	0,11	0,43	1,80	2,24	0,08	0,07	0,00	−0,03	0,0019	0,0010	0,05	0,02
Summit Partners	3000	1984	US	12	0,17	0,68	1,31	1,99	0,35	0,37	0,24	0,23	0,0098	0,0103	0,19	0,20
Willis Stein & Partners	2983	1990	US	4	0,20	0,31	1,59	1,90	0,12	0,14	0,03	0,03	0,0037	0,0041	0,07	0,08
Quadrangle Group	2880	2000	US	2	0,53	0,70	0,29	0,99	0,12		0,05		0,0040		0,09	
Code Hennessy & Simmons	2805	1988	US	5	0,13	0,52	1,65	2,17	0,18	0,18	0,10	0,07	0,0055	0,0051	0,13	0,12
BLUM Capital Partners	2789	1998	US	4	0,39	0,16	1,09	1,25	0,21	0,15	0,15	0,06	0,0095	0,0056	0,23	0,14
Veronis Suhler Stevenson	2602	1987	US	5	0,17	0,59	1,37	1,96	0,22	0,20	0,14	0,10	0,0071	0,0061	0,17	0,15
Lion Capital	2575	1999	UK	2	0,42	0,36	1,00	1,36	0,21	0,21	0,12	0,10	0,0049	0,0046	0,21	0,20
Duke Street Capital	2534	1997	UK	4	0,17	0,22	1,30	2,03	0,14	0,15	0,04	0,02	0,0042	0,0041	0,10	0,10
Francisco Partners	2500	2000	US	2	0,19	0,91	1,01	1,92	0,08		−0,02		0,0015		0,03	
Freeman Spogli & Co	2475	1988	US	3	0,32	0,35	0,93	1,28	0,17	0,15	0,08	0,04	0,0053	0,0041	0,12	0,09
ABRY Partners	2450	1989	US	7	0,20	0,98	0,92	1,91	0,30	0,38	0,23	0,29	0,0123	0,0156	0,28	0,36
Fenway Partners	2427	1996	US	2	0,18	0,25	1,64	1,89	0,08	0,08	0,00	−0,02	0,0019	0,0015	0,05	0,04
New Mountain Capital	2270	2001	US	2	0,11	0,91	1,35	2,26	0,20		0,10		0,0052		0,10	
Wellspring Capital Management	2244	1996	US	4	0,21	0,19	1,60	1,79	0,12	0,10	0,04	−0,01	0,0043	0,0026	0,08	0,05
Morgan Stanley Private Equity	2200	1987	US	1	0,15	0,21	1,86	2,08	0,04	0,04	−0,01	−0,03	0,0006	0,0000	0,02	0,00
Cognetas	2178	1990	UK	6	0,17	0,52	1,50	2,01	0,10	0,10	0,03	0,01	0,0033	0,0027	0,13	0,11
Alchemy Partners	2106	1998	UK	5	0,12	0,29	1,88	2,17	0,15	0,08	0,08	0,00	0,0059	0,0020	0,23	0,08
Castle Harlan	2054	1992	US	4	0,16	0,23	1,86	2,10	0,22	0,18	0,14	0,07	0,0072	0,0051	0,17	0,12
Parthenon Capital	2000	1998	US	3	0,85	0,04	0,28	0,33	0,09	0,07	0,00	−0,05	0,0024	0,0009	0,05	0,02
Sun Capital Partners	2000	1996	US	3	0,21	0,12	1,72	1,84	0,17	0,09	0,08	−0,03	0,0054	0,0020	0,10	0,04
GSC Partners	1932	1994	US	7	0,20	0,00	1,61	1,61	0,10	0,01	0,02	−0,09	0,0034	−0,0015	0,06	−0,03
Elevation Partners	1900	2005	US	1	0,50	0,00	0,69	0,69								
Liberty Partners	1884	1993	US	6	0,46	0,00	0,84	0,84	0,03	0,03	−0,04	−0,06	0,0000	−0,0004	0,00	−0,02
Diamond Castle Holdings	1850	2005	US	1	0,46	0,66	0,21	0,88								

(continued)

Sample Characteristics Private Equity (continued)

Firm	Fund size (invested equity)*	Vintage first fund	Country of origin	Number of funds	Herfindahl index	DR	DU	DT	IRR 5Y	IRR 10Y	Jensen's Alpha 5Y	Jensen's Alpha 10Y	Sharpe' measure 5Y	Sharpe' measure 10Y	Treynor measure 5Y	Treynor measure 10Y
Aurora Capital Group	1798	1994	US	3	0,37	0,37	0,67	1,04	0,26	0,09	0,19	0,01	0,0099	0,0022	0,28	0,06
Behrman Capital	1774	1993	US	4	0,14	0,61	1,55	2,16	0,09	0,09	0,02	−0,02	0,0027	0,0020	0,06	0,04
Thoma Cressey Equity Partners	1770	1998	US	3	0,14	0,49	1,61	2,11	0,14	−0,05	0,06	−0,16	0,0039	−0,0037	0,09	−0,09
Centre Partners Management	1722	1986	US	4	0,59	0,17	0,72	0,88	0,32	0,32	0,25	0,22	0,0128	0,0123	0,30	0,29
Bear Steams Merchant Banking	1700	1998	US	3	0,12	0,51	1,71	2,22	0,23	0,27	0,12	0,13	0,0060	0,0069	0,11	0,13
Catterton Partners	1650	1999	US	3	0,35	0,64	0,62	1,26	0,25	0,42	0,19	0,33	0,0098	0,0167	0,28	0,48
Barclays Private Equity	1603	2002	UK	1	0,14	0,24	1,89	2,13	0,36		0,26		0,0126		0,30	
Wind Point Partners	1581	1987	US	5	0,14	0,20	1,97	2,17	0,12	0,12	0,04	0,02	0,0032	0,0031	0,08	0,07
CCMP Capital Asia	1575	2005	US	1	0,33	0,00	1,42	1,42								
Olympus Partners	1548	1990	US	4	0,36	0,13	1,02	1,15	0,22	0,22	0,13	0,10	0,0046	0,0042	0,15	0,14
Lexington Partners	1515	1996	US	10	0,55	0,64	0,00	0,64	0,19	0,09	0,09	−0,03	0,0069	0,0022	0,11	0,03
Odyssey Investment Partners	1510	1997	US	2	0,10	0,45	1,83	2,29	0,02	0,10	−0,06	−0,01	−0,0005	0,0020	−0,01	0,05
Fox Paine & Company	1500	1998	US	3	0,19	0,65	1,28	1,92	0,17	0,02	0,10	−0,08	0,0062	−0,0012	0,14	−0,03
Jordan Company	1500	2002	US	1	0,18	0,00	1,76	1,76	0,02		−0,03		−0,0004		−0,02	
Reservoir Capital Group	1500	2006	US	1	0,33	0,00	1,28	1,28								
Graphite Capital Management	1438	1990	UK	3	0,28	0,27	1,32	1,59	0,07	0,22	−0,05	0,07	0,0015	0,0069	0,03	0,13
Palamon Capital Partners	1424	1999	UK	2	0,22	0,59	1,29	1,88	0,15	0,15	0,04	0,02	0,0049	0,0045	0,10	0,09
Riverside Company	1414	1995	US	7	0,23	0,28	1,57	1,85	0,28	0,27	0,19	0,18	0,0114	0,0103	0,26	0,23
Charlesbank Capital Partners	1411	2001	US	2	0,23	0,12	1,66	1,78	0,24		0,16		0,0101		0,19	
Kohlberg & Company	1376	2000	US	2	0,17	0,15	1,85	2,01	0,09		0,03		0,0028		0,11	
Exxel Group	1374	1998	US	2	0,39	0,33	1,17	1,50	−0,35	−0,53	−0,45	−0,63	−0,0154	−0,0234	−0,32	−0,49
HarbourVest Partners	1369	1983	US	19	0,34	0,51	0,58	1,09	0,07	0,10	−0,04	−0,02	0,0019	0,0025	0,03	0,04

KRG Capital	1367	2000	US	3	0,38	0,06	1,19	1,25	0,20		0,12		0,0067		0,15	
HgCapital	1356	1995	UK	6	0,13	0,29	1,88	2,17	0,16	0,16	0,10	0,08	0,0066	0,0060	0,26	0,24
Brockway Moran & Partners	1310	1998	US	3	1,00	0,00	0,00	0,00	0,11	0,22	0,04	0,11	0,0030	0,0065	0,08	0,17
Heartland Industrial Partners	1300	2000	US	1	0,11	0,63	1,61	2,24	−0,12		−0,18		−0,0078		−0,31	
Tailwind Capital	1300	2000	US	1	1,00	0,00	0,00	0,00	−0,10		−0,17		−0,0061		−0,17	
TowerBrook Capital Partners	1300	2001	US	2	0,15	0,40	1,64	2,05	0,42		0,34		0,0172		0,36	

*excludes debt component; equity + debt investments = total investment portfolio

Source: Private Equity Intelligence, Dealogic, Private Equity company publications (December 31, 2006)

Profiles of Private Equity Firms Included in Exploratory Research

All information included in the subsequent private equity profiles is based on publicly available sources such as company websites, news articles and press releases, as well as third-party databases employed for this study. Any insight generated during the interviews has been used for aggregated analysis in the second empirical part of this study only; firm-specific information is treated anonymously and is held confidential.

(1) APAX Partners

- Industry focus
  Investments in Tech & Telecom, Retail & Consumer, Media, Healthcare, Financial & Business Services
- Geographic scope (Office locations)
  Hong Kong, London, Madrid, Milan, Mumbai, Munich, New York, Paris, Stockholm, Tel Aviv
- Selected portfolio companies
  Kabel Deutschland (German cable TV network), TDC (Pan-European telecoms business), Tommy Hilfiger (Apparel retail and wholesale), CME (Central European TV network), Travelex (Foreign exchange provider), SULO (German recycling business)

(2) Apollo Management

- Industry focus
  Investments in Consumer Products, Industrials, Information Technology, Leisure, Media, Transportation, Other
- Geographic scope (Office locations)
  London, Los Angeles, New York
- Selected portfolio companies
  Aerospace specification metrics (U.S. manufacturer of aerospace supplies), AMC Entertainment (U.S. motion picture business), Berlitz International (Global operator of language schools), General Nutrition (U.S. food distributor), Ish (German cable operator), Meadowbrook Golf Group (U.S. operator of public golf courses), Rare Medium Group (U.S. IT service provider)

(3) Bain Capital

- Industry focus
  Investments in Communication, Financial Services, Healthcare, Industrial & Manufacturing, Information Technology, Retail & Consumer Goods, Other
- Geographic scope (Office locations)
  Boston, Hong Kong, London, Munich, New York, Shanghai, Tokyo
- Selected portfolio companies
  Applied Systems (U.S. software provider), Brenntag (German chemicals business), Burlington Coat Factory (U.S. retail apparel company), HCA (U.S. hospital operator), Inrix (U.S. information provider), Mattress Discount (U.S. retailer chain), Philips Semiconductors (Semiconductor division of Dutch Philips), Sun Telephone (Japanese trader and wholesaler of telecommunication equipment)

(4) BC Partners

- Industry focus
  Investments in Chemicals, Consumer Products, Healthcare, Information Services, Leisure, Other
- Geographic scope (Office locations)
  Geneva, Hamburg, London, Milan, New York, Paris
- Selected portfolio companies
  Brenntag (Global leader in chemical distribution), Bureau van Dijk (Financial information provider), FitnessFirst (Global fitness company), Foxtons (UK real estate agent), Picard (French distribution of frozen food)

(5) The Blackstone Group

- Industry focus
  Investments in Automotive, Chemicals, Consumer Products, Financial Services, Health Care, Industrial, Telecommunication, Transportation, Other
- Geographic scope (Office locations)
  Atlanta, Boston, Hong Kong, Los Angeles, London, Mumbai, New York, Paris, Tokyo
- Selected portfolio companies
  Celanese (Global manufacturer of commodity and specialty chemicals), CenterParcs (Operator of short-break holiday resorts), Nielsen (Global information and media company), Primacom (European cable operator), RGIS (Global inventory and retail services business), Republic Technology International (U.S. producer of special bar quality steel products), Sungard (Global provider of integrated software and processing solutions)

(6) Candover Partners

- Industry focus
  Investments in Financial Services, Healthcare, Industrials, Leisure, Media, Support Services, Technology, Other
- Geographic scope (Office locations)
  London, Madrid, Milan, Paris
- Selected portfolio companies
  ALcontrol (European operator of environmental and food testing laboratories), Capital Safety Group (Global specialist designer and manufacturer of height safety and fall protection equipment), DX Group (UK private mail operator), Ferretti (Italian manufacturer of yachts), UPC Norge (Norwegian telecommication and cable-TV provider)

(7) The Carlyle Group

- Industry focus
  Investments in Aerospace & Defense, Automotive & Transportation, Consumer & Retail, Energy, Healthcare, Industrial, Media, Technology, Telecommunication, Other
- Geographic scope (Office locations)
  Barcelona, Beijing, Beirut, Charlotte, Denver, Dubai, Frankfurt, Hong Kong, Istanbul, London, Los Angeles, Luxembourg, Mexico City, Milan, Mumbai, Munich, New York, Newport Beach (California), Paris, San Francisco, Seoul, Shanghai, Singapore, Stockholm, Sydney, Tokyo, Washington D.C.
- Selected portfolio companies
  Avio SpA (Italian manufacturer of aeroengines and space propulsion systems), Hertz Corporation (Global car and equipment rental business), Insight Communications (U.S. cable T.V. provider), LifeCare Holdings (Operator of long-term acute care hospitals), PQ Corporation (U.S. provider of silicate-based inorganic chemicals), Stahl Holdings (Dutch surface effects specialist)

(8) Catterton Partners

- Industry focus
  Investments in Consumer products (Retail & Restaurants, Consumer Brands, Food & Beverage, Consumer & Marketing Services)
- Geographic scope (Office locations)
  Greenwich (Connecticut)
- Selected portfolio companies

Farley's & Sathers Candy Company (Non-chocolate confectionary brands business), QuinStreet (Online market services provider), Tabi (Canadian women's specialty apparel retailer), The Lang Company (branded consumer products company), Outback steakhouse (U.S. restaurant chain)

(9) Cinven

- Industry focus
  Investments in Business and financial services, Healthcare, Industrials, Retail, Leisure and consumer, Telecom, Media, and Technology
- Geographic scope (Office locations)
  Frankfurt, London, Milan, Paris
- Selected portfolio companies
  Amadeus (Global travel distribution service provider), Avio (Leading producer of jet engines), Camaieu (French fashion retailer), Coor Service Management (Scandinavian integrated facilities management business), Dutch cable (Dutch cable operator), Gondola (U.K.-based operator of restaurants), Spire healthcare (U.K. private healthcare business)

(10) Francisco Partners

- Industry focus
  Investments in technology and technology-related companies in the sectors Hardware Systems, Semiconductors, and Software & Services
- Geographic scope (Office locations)
  London, San Francisco
- Selected portfolio companies
  AMI Semiconductor (designer and manufacturer of application-specific integrated circuits), FX Solutions (Internet-based foreign exchange trading platform), Mitel (Communication solutions provider), Smart Modular Technologies (designer and manufacturer of memory modules, memory cards and communications products), WatchGuard (Network security provider), Xcellenet (provider of software-based systems for managing remote and mobile networks and systems)

(11) Goldman Sachs Capital Partners

- Industry focus
  Investments in Consumer and Retail, Financial Services, Healthcare, Industrial, Media, Technology, Telecommunication, Other

- Geographic scope (Office locations)
  Hong Kong, London, New York, among others
- Selected portfolio companies
  Advanced Microfabrication Equipment (Chinese developer of semiconductor processing equipment), Aramarck (U.S.-based food and facilities management company), Burger King (U.S. provider of fast food), Grupo Clarin (Argentinean media business), Kion Group (European manufacturer of forklift trucks and related services), Limelight networks (U.S. online content delivery network), Pages Jaunes (French information provider), TEIN (Japanese automobile suspension manufacturer)

(12) HarbourVest Partners

- Industry focus
  Investments in Internet & Communications Infrastructure, Communication Services, Enterprise Software, Industrial, Other
- Geographic scope (Office locations)
  Boston, Hong Kong, London
- Selected portfolio companies
  Centra Software (U.S. provider of distance learning and collaboration software), Esprit Telecom Group (Pan-European digital telecommunications network), Geberit (Swiss manufacturer of plumbing products), Kamps (German industrial and retail bakery chain), Onetta (U.S. optical sub-systems developer), Trintech (Irish provider of electronic payment solutions), Velio Communications (U.S. provider of high-speed optical services)

(13) Hellman & Friedman

- Industry focus
  Investments in Financial services, Healthcare, Industrial and energy, Insurance, Media and Marketing, Professional services, Software and information services
- Geographic scope (Office locations)
  London, New York, San Francisco
- Selected portfolio companies
  Alix Partners (Global performance improvement, corporate turnaround and financial advisory services firm), Intergraph corporation (Leading provider of spatial information management software and services), Mondrian Investment Partners (U.K.-based asset manager), TexasGenco (U.S. wholesale power generation company), The Nielsen Company (Global market research business)

(14) Industri Kapital

- Industry focus
  Investments in Building Materials, Food Processing, Healthcare, Manufacturing, Media, Retailing/Wholesale/Distribution, Service, Specialized Process
- Geographic scope (Office locations)
  Hamburg, London, Oslo, Paris, Stockholm
- Selected portfolio companies
  Alfa Laval (Swedish provider of engineering solutions for heat transfer, separation, and fluid handling), Nobia (Swedish manufacturer of kitchens, doors, windows, and building products), Paroc Group (Finnish manufacturer of building insulation, technical insulation, and wall panels), Pieters (Belgium-based fish processor and distributor)

(15) KohlbergKravisRoberts & Co

- Industry focus
  Investments in Chemicals, Consumer Products, Education, Financial Services, Health Care, Hotels/Leisure, Industrial, Media/Communication, Retail, Technology
- Geographic scope (Office locations)
  Hong Kong, Menlo Park (California), London, New York, Paris
- Selected portfolio companies
  First data (Provider of electronic commerce and payment solutions), Jazz Pharmaceuticals (Pharmaceutical company focused on neurology and psychiatry), Kion Group (European manufacturer of forklift trucks and related services), ProsiebenSat1Media (Pan-European broadcasting group), ToysRUs (Specialty toy and children's products retailer), TXU (U.S. utilities company)

(16) Montagu Private Equity

- Industry focus
  Investments in Aerospace & Defense, Chemicals, Consumer Goods, Electronics and Electrical Equipment, Financial Services, Food & Beverage Products, Healthcare, Industrials, Media, Pharmaceuticals, Retail, Technology, Transportation, Other
- Geographic scope (Office locations)
  Duesseldorf, London, Manchester, Paris, Stockholm
- Selected portfolio companies
  Clinphone (U.K. clinical technologies provider), Kalle (German food & beverages producer), Maplin Electronics (U.K. electronics retail business), TMD Friction (German manufacturer of automotive supplies), Unifeeder (Danish provider of logistics and transportation services)

(17) Permira

- Industry focus
  Investments in Chemicals, Consumer Products, Industrial Products and Services, Technology, Media and Communication
- Geographic scope (Office locations)
- *Frankfurt, London, Luxembourg, Madrid, Milan, New York, Paris, Stockholm, Tokyo*
- Selected portfolio companies
  Cognis (Natural sourced chemical products), Cortefiel (Spanish clothing retailer), Holmes Place (European fitness company), Jet Aviation (Swiss executive jet aviation business), Leica Microsystems (German producer of microscopes for medical and semiconductor industries), Premiere (German Pay-TV provider), Rodenstock (German ophthalmic lenses and frames manufacturer), Takko ModeMarkt (German discount clothing retailer), TFL (German leather chemicals business)

(18) Terra Firma Capital Partners

- Industry focus
  Investments in asset-rich sectors such as Leasing, Leisure (Cinemas, Restaurants, Hotels), Real Estate, Utilities
- Geographic scope (Office locations)
  Frankfurt, London
- Selected portfolio companies
  Angel Trains (UK rolling stock leasing company), AT&T Capital (Consumer leasing business), BGCL (UK utilities company), EMI (Global music company), Infinis (UK renewable energy business), Le Meridien (Global hotel business), Odeon/UCI (European cinema chain), Tank & Rast (German motorway services business)

(19) Texas Pacific Group

- Industry focus
  Investments in Consumer Products, Energy, Pharmaceuticals, Retail, Other
- Geographic scope (Office locations)
  Fort Worth, Hong Kong, London, Luxembourg, Melbourne, Menlo Park, Moscow, Mumbai, New York, San Francisco, Shanghai, Singapore, Tokyo, Washington
- Selected portfolio companies
  Aleris International (U.S. aluminum and zinc recycler), Bally (Swiss manufacturer of footwear), Del Monte (U.S.-based producer of canned foods), Gate Gourmet (Swiss airline caterer), Intergraph (U.S. provider of information management software), Optium (U.S. specialist of optical subsystems for telecommunication devices), Smurfit Stone Container Corporation (U.S. consumer packaging business)

(20) WindPoint Partners

- Industry focus
  Investments in Business Services, Consumer Products, Healthcare, Industrial Products
- Geographic scope (Office locations)
  Chicago, Southfield
- Selected portfolio companies
  America's Powersports (U.S. network of sports dealerships), Marshfield (U.S. manufacturer of commercial architectural wood doors), Omniflight (U.S. air medical services), Summit Business Media (U.S. provider of financial information), Taylor-Wharton International (U.S. manufacturer of gas appliances), York Label (U.S. printing business)

Interview Guide 'Diversification in Private Equity'

Managing Diversified Portfolios in Private Equity Firms
Fall 2007

The idea of the study was born out of the questions why Private Equity firms show a superior performance to diversified public corporations even though their portfolio shows a comparable composition in terms of size and industry diversification. There has been an increasing coverage of this phenomenon in media under titles such as "shades of old conglomerates in Private Equity" or "the rise of the new conglomerates", however not yet substantiated with academic research. This research therefore aims at two objectives:

(i) The first empirical part of the study investigates the relationship between diversification and performance in Private Equity firms and establishes a comparison to publicly listed corporations. First results indicate two things: On the one side, Private Equity firms indeed show a stronger performance than public corporations independent of the degree of diversification in the sample firms' portfolios. On the other side, however, Private Equity firms with a high degree of related diversification outperform firms with a higher degree of unrelated diversification.

(ii) The seond empirical part of the study is concerned with the management approach Private Equity firms apply. It looks at the general role of the parent a PE firm plays towards its individual portfolio companies. It furthermore aims at detailing four components of a firm's parenting role: 'availability of corporate resources', 'leverage of competences and resources', 'governance model', and 'portfolio management'.

This interview will be aimed at investigating the second empirical part regarding the approach of Private Equity firms to the management of diversified portfolios.

Firm Characteristics and Portfolio Strategy

Investigates firm characteristics and portfolio strategy of the Private Equity firm including its industry diversification strategy

Firm Characteristics

When was your firm established? How large is the firm by now (number of employees)?

How are you internally organized?

- By transaction vs. portfolio management
- By industry groups
- By investment fund

What is the typical profile of your firm's employees?

- Investment banking background
- Consulting background
- Industry background

How is the legal setup within the LBO association? Are there any legal limitations regarding your level of involvement as active parent?

Investment Portfolio

How large is your current investment portfolio?

Do you have an industry focus in your investment portfolio? Do different individual funds have different industry specializations?

How do you decide to enter new industries? If so, do you attempt to make small deals first (for learning purposes) or start with a big investment (to gain sufficient scale in the new industry right away)?

Is the industry mix per fund strictly defined at issuance or does the industry mix follow an evolutionary strategy based on market environments and investment opportunities?

Do you have a geographic focus in your investment portfolio?

Is there another strategic premise that distinguishes your firm from other PE players in the market?

Role of the Parent

Investigates the general definition of the Private Equity firm as parent company towards its portfolio companies

How do you see the general role of your PE firm towards its individual portfolio companies?

- Financial investor: Seeks to generate majority of value at time of deal through financial and governance engineering. Gives the firm a high level of independence
- Hands-on specialist: Seeks to generate value at time of deal and during holding period through financial, governance and operational engineering. Gets highly involved in day-to-day business of PE firms and has deep operational expertise in the business

How would you split your investment performance into EBITDA growth, de-leveraging, and multiple expansion? Can you observe a trend over time?

How do you balance the need for additional investments and leverage? How do you determine your target level of leverage?

Do you see different definitions of the parent role in the Private Equity industry? Is there one more suitable than the other?

Do you see differences in a PE firm's parent role across different portfolio composition, e.g., firms with higher degree of industry relatedness in their investment portfolio vs. firms with a high degree of unrelated diversification?

What alternative influences determine the role of the PE firm as a parent? e.g.,

- Does competition intensity or pressure by investors influence to parenting role?
- Does portfolio size, experience and skill set influence the parenting approach?
- Do external market factors determine the chosen role?

What is your position towards club deals? What role do you prefer to take (lead partner, financial partner)? How does it affect your influence/ownership model?

How would you compare/distinguish the role of the holding in a conglomerate from the role of a Private Equity firm?

Do you generally believe that conglomerates could learn from Private Equity players in managing multi-business portfolios? Are there limitations to the applicability of the PE model in public corporations?

Management Approach to Diversified Portfolios

Investigates the detailed practices applied by the Private Equity firm along the dimensions 'Availability of Center Functions and Resources', 'Leverage of Competences and Resources', 'Governance Model', and 'Portfolio Management'.

Availability of Center Functions and Resources

Are there any corporate resources (e.g., access to low-cost capital, general management support, financial advice, marketing, human resources) provided by the PE firm in the role of a parent towards its portfolio companies, if so, which are these?

- Access to low-cost capital
- Access to management talent
- Supply of specialized services, e.g., financial engineering, marketing

What is the rationale behind the PE firm's offer of 'corporate resources' and what factors influence the extent to which resources are offered?

Is there any benefit achieved if 'corporate services' are provided to portfolio companies, which are related in their industry profile?

How are 'corporate resources' organized and coordinated within the PE firm and how do PE firms and portfolio companies interact?

Are there particular circumstances in Private Equity that prohibit further consolidation of services?

Leverage of Competences and Resources

Does your firm attempt to leverage competences and resources horizontally between portfolio companies?

Are there particular competences, skills, resources that you are using throughout a portfolio?

- Intellectual property, e.g. licences
- Networks, e.g., sales contacts
- Staff, e.g. management, engineers, scientists

Do you see a larger potential to leverage resources in a portfolio, which is related by industry (related diversification)? Are there other factors influencing the potential to leverage resources?

Does the opportunity to leverage resources throughout the portfolio play a role in an acquisition? Is the value creation potential of buy-and-build strategies mostly centered around the opportunity to leverage competences and resources?

What mechanisms are in place to facilitate the sharing of resources between entities?

- Targets
- Processes/committees
- Incentives

Are there any limitations in Private Equity that prohibit further leverage of competences and resources?

Governance Model

How deeply do you get involved in a portfolio company's strategic decision making?

- Financial control: Focus on review of financial indicators

- Strategic control: Regular reviews of strategic objectives after independent strategy determination by portfolio company
- Strategic planning: Strong involvement in firm's strategic planning process and decision making

How strong is the level of centralization in strategic decision making?

How strong is the level of formalization in strategic decision making? What support systems are in place to ensure an effective governance model in terms of processes, targets, incentive schemes?

What are the most critical skills to actively govern a PE portfolio?

- General management skills
- Industry knowledge
- Valuation and financial engineering skills

How does industry relatedness and unrelatedness in a PE firms investment portfolio affect the governance approach? Does industry relatedness increase the effectiveness of the PE firm and thereby its performance?

Do market conditions such as competition and availability of debt-financing influence the governance intensity and model?

How do you ensure that the most suitable PE professionals are engaged in the governance of a particular portfolio company?

Portfolio Management

How long is your average holding period for investments? What factors influence the holding period (IPO market, economic conditions, etc.)?

How do you determine which targets are acquired, which portfolio companies are divested and which firms remain in the PE firm's investment portfolio? Which tools are employed for this exercise?

What role does industry relatedness with the PE firm's current investment portfolio play in the determination whether or not to invest in a particular target?

Does the portfolio strategy also include a re-allocation of cash flows within an investment fund from firms with higher investment needs than others? Alternatively, are all cash flows directly funneled to investors rather than being reinvested in the portfolio? How do legal constraints limit opportunities to re-allocate funds?

Outlook on Future Industry Practices

Investigates the view of Private Equity professionals about the future industry approach to portfolio diversification and management of diversified portfolios

Do you see a trend in Private Equity to a stronger strategic and operational involvement in portfolio companies? Does this require different skill sets than in earlier days of PE?

Do you see a trend in Private Equity that individual firms choose a stronger focus on particular industries and consequently develop a stronger expertise in the management of firms in those industries?

Do you observe a convergence between the management approaches of Private Equity firms and multi-business firms? Will PE firms rather act like conglomerates or will conglomerates rather behave like PE houses?

How do you drive change internally (strategic direction, e.g. new industry sectors, as well as organizational setup)

Bibliography

Abell, D. F. (1980). *Defining the business: The starting point of strategic planning*. Prentice-Hall: Englewood Cliffs, NJ.

Adams, D. D. (2006). Improving board performance at private equity-backed firms. FEI Financial Executives International July–August 2006: 15.

Admati, A. & Pfleiderer, P. (1994). Robust financial contracting and the role of venture capitalists. *Journal of Finance*, *49*(2), 371–402.

Agrawal, A., Jaffe, J. F., & Mandelker, G. N. (1992). The post-merger performance of acquiring firms: A re-examiniation of an anomaly. *The Journal of Finance*, *47*(4), 1605–1621.

Agrawal, A. & Knoeber, C. R. (1996). Firm performance and mechanisms to control agency problems between managers and shareholders. *Journal of Financial and Quantitative Analysis*, *31*(3), 377–397.

Ahn, S., Denis, D. J., & Denis, D. K. (2006). Leverage and investment in diversified firms. *Journal of Financial Economics*, *79*, 317–337.

Ainina, M. F. & Mohan, N. K. (1991). When LBOs go IPO. *Journal of Business Finance & Accounting*, *18*(3), 393–403.

Alberts, W. W. & McTaggart, J. M. (1984). Value based strategic investment planning. *Interfaces*, *14*(1), 138–151.

Alchian, A. (1969). Corporate management and property rights. *Economic policy and the regulation of corporate securities*. H. G. Mainne. Washington, DC: American Enterprise Institute.

Allen, S. A. (1978). Organizational choices and general management influence networks in divisionalized companies. *The Academy of Management Journal*, *21*(3), 341–365.

Allen, S. A. (1979). Understanding reorganizations of divisionalized companies. *The Academy of Management Journal*, *22*(4), 641–671.

Ambrose, B. W. & Winters, D. B. (1992). Does an industry effect exist for leveraged buyouts? *Financial Management Spring*, *1992*, 89–101.

Amburgey, T. L. & Dacin, T. (1994). As the left foot follows the right? The dynamics of strategic and structural change. *Academy of Management Journal*, *37*(6), 1427–1452.

Amess, K. & Wright, M. (2007). The wage and employment effect of leveraged buyouts in the U.K. *International Journal of the Economics and Business*, 14(2), 179–195.

Amihud, Y. & Lev, B. (1981). Risk reduction as a managerial motive for conglomerate mergers. *The Bell Journal of Economics*, *12*(2), 605–617.

Amit, R., Brander, J., Zott, C. (1998). Why do venture capital firms exist? Theory and Canadian evidence. *Journal of Business Venturing*, *13*(November), 443–466.

Amit, R. & Livnat, J. (1988). Diversification and the risk-return trade-off. *The Academy of Management Journal*, *31*(1), 154–166.

Amit, R. & Livnat, J. (1989). Efficient corporate diversification: Methods and implications. *Management Science*, *35*(7), 879–897.

Amit, R. & Wernerfelt, B. (1990). Why do firms reduce business risk? *The Academy of Management Journal*, *33*(3), 520–533.

Anders, G. (1992). The barbarians in the boardroom. *Harvard Business Review, July–August 1992*, 79–87.

Anders, G. (2007). KKR, Blackstone IPOs put their style at risk. *The Wall Street Journal, July 18*: A2.

Andrade, G. & Kaplan, S. N. (1998). How costly is financial (non economic) distress? Evidence from highly leveraged transactions that became distressed. *The Journal of Finance, 53*(5), 1443–1493.

Andrews, K. R. (1969). Towards professionalism in business management. *Harvard Business Review, March–April 1969*, 49–60.

Ansoff, H. I. (1958). A model for diversification. *Management Science, 4*(4), 392–414.

Ansoff, H. I. (1965). *Corporate strategy*. New York: McGraw-Hill.

Anson, M. (2004). Trends in private equity. *The Journal of Wealth Management, Winter 2004*, 84–91.

Armour, H. O. & Teece, D. J. (1978). Organizational structure and economic performance: A test of the multidivisional hypothesis. *The Bell Journal of Economics, 9*(1), 106–122.

Armstrong, J. S. (1982). The value of formal planning for strategic decisions: Review of empirical research. *Strategic Management Journal, 3*(3), 197–211.

Arnold, G. (2005). *Handbook of corporate finance*. Prentice Hall: Harlow, UK.

Arzac, E. R. (1986). Do your business units create shareholder value? *Harvard Business Review, January–February 1986*, 121–126.

Arzac, E. R. (1992). On the capital structure of leveraged buyouts. *Financial Management, 21*(1, Leveraged Buyouts Special Issue), 16–26.

Atteslander, P., Cromm, J., & Grabow, B. (2006). *Methoden der empirischen Sozialforschung* (11th ed.). Berlin: Erich Schmidt Verlag.

Axelson, U., Stroemberg, P., & Weisbach, M. (2005). *The financial structure of private equity funds*. NBER working paper, September 2005.

Babbie, E. R. (2002). *The basics of social research*. Wadsworth: Stamford.

Bae, S. C. & Jo, H. (2002). Consolidating corporate control: Divisional versus whole-company leveraged buyouts. *The Journal of Financial Research, 25*(2), 247–262.

Bagozzi, R. P., Yi, Y., & Phillips, L. W. (1991). Assessing construct validity in organizational research. *Administrative Science Quarterly, 36*, 421–458.

Bain, J. S. (1968). *Industrial organization* (2nd ed.). New York: Wiley.

Baker, G. P. (1992). Beatrice: A study in the creation and destruction of value. *The Journal of Finance, 47*(3), 1081–1119.

Baker, G. P. & Montgomery, C. A. (1994). *Conglomerates and LBO associations: A comparison of organizational forms*. Harvard Business School, working paper. Boston, MA.

Baker, G. P. & Smith, G. D. (1998). *The new financial capitalists: Kohlberg Kravis Roberts and the creation of corporate value*. Cambridge, MA: Cambridge University Press.

Baker, G. P. & Wruck, K. H. (1989). Organizational changes and value creation in leveraged buyouts: The case of the O.M. Scott & Sons Company. *Journal of Financial Economics, 25*, 163–190.

Baker, T. L. (1999). *Doing social research*. Boston: McGraw-Hill.

Baldi, F. (2005). Valuing a leveraged buyout: Expansion of the adjusted present value by means of real options analysis. *The Journal of Private Equity, Fall 2005*, 64–81.

Barber, F. & Goold, M. (2007). The strategic secret of private equity. *Harvard Business Review September, 2007*.

Barney, J. (1991a). Firm resources and sustained competitive advantage. *Journal of Management, 17*(1), 99–120.

Barney, J. (1991b). Special theory forum: The resource-based model fo the firm: Origins, implications, and prospects. *Journal of Management, 17*(1), 97–98.

Barney, J. & Arikan, A. M. (2001). The resource-based view: Origins and implications. In M. A. Hitt, R. E. Freeman, & J. S. Harrison (Eds.), *Handbook for strategic management* (pp. 124–188). Blackwell: Oxford.

Bart, C. K. (1986). Product strategy and formal structure. *Strategic Management Journal, 7*(4), 293–312.

Barton, S. L. (1988). Diversification strategy and systematic risk: Another look. *Academy of Management Journal, 31*(1), 166–175.

Basu, S. (1977). Investment performance of common stocks in relation to their price-earnings ratios: A test of the efficient market hypothesis. *The Journal of Finance, 32*(3), 663–682.

Baysinger, B. & R. E. Hoskisson (1989). Diversification strategy and R&D intensity in multiproduct firms. *Academy of Management Journal, 32*(2), 310–332.

Baysinger, B. & R. E. Hoskisson (1990). The composition of board of directors and strategic control: Effects on corporate strategy. *Academy of Management Review, 15*(1), 72–87.

Beaver, G. (2001). Editorial: Management buy-outs: who dares wins? *Strategic Change September–October 2001*, 307–309.

Beckmann, P. (2006). Der Diversification Discount am deutschen Kapitalmarkt. Wiesbaden, Gabler.

Berg, A. & O. Gottschalg (2003). *Understanding value generation in buyouts*. INSEAD, working paper. Fontainebleau.

Berg, B. L. (2007). *Qualitative research methods for the social sciences* (6th ed.) Boston: Pearson Education.

Berg, N. (2006). Fallstudien als Methode betriebswirtschaftlicher Forschung. *WiSt – Wirtschaftswissenschaftliches Studium, 35*(7), 362–367.

Berg, N. A. (1965). *Strategic planning in conglomerate companies. Harvard Business Review, May–June 1965*, 79–92.

Berg, N. A. (1969). What's different about conglomerate management? *Harvard Business Review, November–December 1969*, 112–120.

Berger, P. G. & Ofek, E. (1995). Diversification's effect on firm value. *Journal of Financial Economics, 37*, 39–65.

Berger, P. G. & Ofek, E. (1996). Bustup takeovers of value-destroying diversified firms. *The Journal of Finance, 51*(4), 1175–1200.

Bernardo, A. E. & Chowdhry, B. (2002). Resources, real options, and corporate strategy. *Journal of Financial Economics, 63*, 211–234.

Bernheim, B. D. & Whinston, M. D. (1990). Multimarket contact and collusive behavior. *RAND Journal of Economics, 21*(Spring), 1–26.

Beroutsos, A. & Kehoe, C. (2006). A lesson in governance from the private equity firms. *Financial Times*. http://www.ft.com (access December 12, 2007).

Berry, C. H. (1975). *Corporate growth and diversification*. Princeton, NJ: Princeton University Press.

Bettis, R. A. (1981). Performance differences in related and unrelated diversified firms. *Strategic Management Journal*, 2(4), 379–393.

Bettis, R. A. & Hall, W. K. (1981). Strategic portfolio management in the multibusiness firm. *California Management Review, 24*(1), 23–38.

Bettis, R. A. & Hall, W. K. (1982). Diversification strategy, accounting determined risk, and accounting determined return. *The Academy of Management Journal, 25*(2), 254–264.

Bettis, R. A. & Mahajan, V. (1985). Risk/return performance of diversified firms. *Management Science, 31*(7), 785–799.

Bettis, R. A. & Prahalad, C. K. (1995). The dominant logic: Retrospective and extension. *Strategic Management Journal, 16*(1): 5–14.

Bina, C. & Teixeira, J. A. (1989). Leveraged buyouts: Robber barons of the eighties. *Challenge, September–October 1989*, 53–57.

Birley, S., Muzyka, D., & Hay, M. (1999). Management buyout: Perception of opportunity – A research note. *Journal of Management Studies, 36*(January): 109–122.

Blankenship, L. V. & Miles, R. E. (1968). Organizational structure and managerial decision behavior. *Administrative Science Quarterly, 13*(1): 106–120.

Boardman, A. E. & Carruthers, N. E. (1985). A note on the use of the CAPM as a strategic planning tool. *Management Science, 31*(12): 1589–1592.

Bodie, Z. Kane, A. & Marcus, A.J. (2005). *Investments* (6th ed.). Boston, Irwin: McGraw-Hill.

Boehmer, R. & Ruess, A. (2006). Deutschland ist gut aufgestellt. *WirtschaftsWoche, 2006-52*, 88–94.

Boeschen, M. & Gassmann, M. (2007). Private equity verspricht Offenheit. *Financial Times Deutschland, February 25*, 1.

Bolton, P. & Scharfstein, D. S. (1998). Corporate finance, the theory of the firm, and organizations. *The Journal of Economic Perspectives*, *12*(4), 95–114.

Bortz, J. & Doering, N. (2002). *Forschungsmethoden und Evaluation fuer Human- und Sozialwissenschaftler* (3rd ed.) Berlin: Springer.

Bottazzi, L. & Da Rin, M. (2002). Venture capital in Europe and the financing of innovative companies. *Economic Policy, April*, 231–269.

Bottazzi, L., Da Rin, M., & Hellmann, T. F. (2004). *Active financial intermediation: Evidence of the role of organizational specialization and human capital*. ECGI Finance working paper *49*.

Bourgeois, L. J. & Brodwin, D. R. (1984). Strategic implementation: Five approaches to an elusive phenomenon. *Strategic Management Journal*, *5*(3), 241–264.

Bowen, H. P. & Wiersema, M. F. (2005). Foreign-based competition and corporate diversification strategy. *Strategic Management Journal*, *26*(12), 1153–1171.

Bower, G. H. & Hilgard, E. R. (1981). *Theories of learning*. Englewood Cliffs, NJ: Prentice-Hall.

Brandimarte, J. P., Fallon, W. C. & McNish, R. S. (2001). Trading the corporate portfolio. *McKinsey on Finance, Autumn 2001*, 1–5.

Braun, P. A., Nelson, D. B., & Sunier, A. M. (1995). Good news, bad news, volatility, and betas. *The Journal of Finance*, *50*(5), 1575–1603.

Bresnahan, T. F. & Schmalensee, R. (1987). The empirical renaissance in industrial economics: An overview. *The Journal of Industrial Economics*, *35*(4), 371–378.

Briglauer, W. (2000). *Motives for firm diversification: A survey on theory and empirical evidence*. Wifo working papers *2000*(Nr. 126).

Bruining, H., Boselie, P., Wright, D.M., & Bacon, N. (2005). The impact on business ownership change on employee relations: Buyouts in the U.K. and the Netherlands. *International Journal of Human Resource Management*, *16*, 345–365.

Bruining, H. & Wright, M. (2002). Entrepreneurial orientation in management buy-outs and the contribution of venture capital. *Venture Capital*, *4*(2), 147–168.

Bruner, R. F. & Eades, K. M. (1992). The crash of the Revco leveraged buyout: The hypothesis of inadequate capital. *Financial Management, Spring 1992*, 35–49.

Bryan-Low, C. & Singer, J. (2007). For buyout firms, west meets mideast. *The Wall Street Journal, October 3*, C1.

Bull, I. (1989). Financial performance of leveraged buyouts: An empirical analysis. *Journal of Business Venturing*, *4*(4): 263.

Burgelman, R. A. (1983a). Corporate entrepreneurship and strategic management: Insights from a process study. *Management Science*, *29*(12), 1349–1364.

Burgelman, R. A. (1983b). A model of the interaction of strategic behavior, corporate context, and the concept of strategy. *The Academy of Management Review*, *8*(1), 61–70.

Butler, P. A. (2001). The alchemy of LBOs. *The McKinsey Quarterly*, *2001*(2), 140–151.

Bygrave, W. D. & Timmons, J. A. (1992). *Venture capital at the crossroads*. Cambridge, MA: Harvard Business School Press.

Calori, R. C. (1988). How successful companies manage diverse businesses. *Long Range Planning*, *21*(3), 80–89.

Campa, J. M. & Kedia, S. (2002). Explaining the diversification discount. *The Journal of Finance*, *57*(4), 1731–1762.

Campbell, A. (1999). Letters to the editor – Patching: Restitching business portfolios in dynamic markets. *Harvard Business Review, September–October 1999*, 172.

Campbell, A. & Goold, M. (1998). *Synergy: Why links between business units often fail and how to make them work*. Oxford: Capstone Publishing.

Campbell, A., Goold, M., & Alexander, M. (1995a). Corporate strategy: The quest for parenting advantage. *Harvard Business Review, March–April 1995*, 120–132.

Campbell, A., Goold, M., & Alexander, M. (1995b). The value of the parent company. *California Management Review*, *38*(1), 79–97.

Capital (2007). Die Herren der Heuschrecken. *Capital ,2007-5*, 124–126.

Capron, L. & Shen, J.-C. (2007). Acquisitions of private vs public firms: Private information, target selection, and acquirer returns. *Strategic Management Journal*, *28*(9), 891–911.

Carlesi, L., Verster, B., & Wenger, F. (2007). The new dynamics of managing the corporate portfolio. *McKinsey on Finance, Spring 2007*, 1–8.

Carow, K. A. & Roden, D. M. (1997). Determinants of the stock price reaction to leveraged buyouts. *Journal of Economics and Finance*, *21*(3), 49–59.

Carpenter, J. N. (2000). Does option compensation increase managerial risk appetite? *The Journal of Finance*, *55*(5), 2311–2331.

Carter, J. R. (1977). In search of synergy: A structure-performance test. *The Review of Economics and Statistics*, *59*(3), 279–289.

Casu, B. & Girardone, C. (2004). Financial conglomeration: Efficiency, productivity and strategic drive. *Applied Financial Economics*, *14*(10), 687–696.

Caves, R. E. (1982). *Multinational enterprise and economic analysis*. Cambridge, MA: Harvard University Press.

Chakrabarti, A., Singh, K., & Mahmood, I. (2007). Diversification and performance: Evidence from East Asian firms. *Strategic Management Journal*, *28*(2), 101–120.

Chakravarthy, B. & Doz, Y. (1992). Strategy process research: Focusing on corporate self-renewal. *Strategic Management Journal*, *13*(Special Issue: Strategic Process: Managing Corporate Self-Renewal), 5–14.

Chan, Y.-S. (1983). On the positive role of financial intermediation in allocation of venture capital in a market with imperfect information. *The Journal of Finance*, *38*(5), 1543–1568.

Chandler, A. D. (1962). *Strategy and structure: Chapters in the history of the American industrial enterprise*. Cambridge, MA: MIT Press.

Chandler Jr., A. D. (1991). The functions of the HY unit in the multibusiness firm. *Strategic Management Journal*, *12*(Special issue: Fundamental research issues in strategy and economics), 31–50.

Chang, Y. & Howard, T. (1989). The impact of diversification strategy on risk-return performance. *Strategic Management Journal*, *10*(3), 271–284.

Chapman, J. L. (2007). Private equity's history and impact on corporate governance – comment. *The history, impact, and future of private equity*. Washington, D.C: American Enterprise Institute for Public Policy Research.

Chatterjee, S. (1992). Sources of value in takeovers: Synergy or restructuring-implications for target and bidder firms. *Strategic Management Journal*, *13*(4), 267–286.

Chatterjee, S. & Blocher, J. D. (1992). Measurement of firm diversification: Is it robust? *The Academy of Management Journal*, *35*(4), 874–888.

Chatterjee, S., Lubatkin, M., Schweiger, O., & Weber, Y. (1992). Cultural differences and shareholder value in related mergers: Linking equity and human capital. *Strategic Management Journal*, *13*(5), 319–334.

Chatterjee, S. & Wernerfelt, B. (1991). The link between resources and type of diversification: Theory and evidence. *Strategic Management Journal*, *12*(1), 33–48.

Child, J. (1972). Organizational structure, environment, and performance. *Sociology 6*, 2–22.

Chou, D.-W., Gombola, M., & Liu, F.-Y. (2006). Earnings management and stock performance of reverse leveraged buyouts. *Journal of Financial and Quantitative Analysis*, *41*(2), 407–438.

Christensen, H. K. & Montgomery, C. A. (1981). Corporate economic performance: Diversification strategy versus market structure. *Strategic Management Journal*, *2*(4), 327–343.

Christie, A. A. Joye, M. P. & Watts, R.L. (2003). Decentralization of the firm: Theory and evidence. *Journal of Corporate Finance*, *9*(1), 3–36.

Clarke, C. J. & Brennan, K. (1990). Building synergy in the diversified busienss. *Long Range Planning*, *23*(2), 9–16.

Cochrane, J. H. (2005). The risk and return of venture capital. *Journal of Financial Economics*, *75*, 3–52.

Collis, D. J. & Montgomery, C. A. (1998). *Corporate strategy – a resource-based approach*. Boston: Irwin McGraw-Hill.

Collis, D. J., Young, D., & Goold, M. (2007). The size, structure, and performance of corporate headquarters. *Strategic Management Journal*, *28*(4), 383–405.

Comment, R. & Jarrell, G. A. (1995). Corporate focus and stock returns. *Journal of Financial Economics, 37*, 67–87.

Conroy, R. M. & Harris, R. S. (2007). How good are private equity returns? *Journal of Applied Corporate Finance, 19*(3), 96–108.

Cooper, D. R. & Schindler, P. S. (1998). *Business research methods* (6th ed.). Boston, MA: Irwin/McGraw Hill.

Copeland, T., Koller, T., & Murrin, J. (2000). *Valuation: Measuring and managing the value of companies* (3rd ed.). New York: Wiley.

Cornelius, P., Langelaar, B., & van Rossum, M. (2007). Big is better: Growth and market structure in global buyouts. *Journal of Applied Corporate Finance, 19*(3), 109–116.

Cornelli, F. & Karakas, O. (2008). Private equity and corporate governance: Do LBOs have more effective boards? In A. Gurung & J. Lerner (Eds.), *Globalization of Alternative Investments: The Global Economic Impact of Private Equity Report 2008* (working papers, Vol. 1, pp. 65–84). Geneva: World Economic Forum.

Cotter, J. F. & Peck, S. W. (2001). The structure of debt and active equity investors: The case of the buyout specialist. *Journal of Financial Economics, 59*, 101–147.

Cressy, R., Munari, F., & Malipiero, A. (2007). Playing to their strengths? Evidence that specialization in the private equity industry confers competitive advantage. *Journal of Corporate Finance, 13*(4), 647–669.

Crossan, M. M., Lane, H. W., & White, R. E. (1999). An organizational learning framework: From intuition to institution. *The Academy of Management Review, 24*(3), 522–537.

Cumming, D. (2005a). Agency costs, institutions, learning and taxation in venture capital contracting. *Journal of Business Venturing, 20*(5), 573–622.

Cumming, D. (2005b). Capital structure in venture finance. *Journal of Corporate Finance, 11*(3), 550–585.

Cumming, D., Siegel, D., & Wright, M. (2007). Private equity, leveraged buyouts and governance. *Journal of Corporate Finance, 13*(4), 439–460.

Cumming, D. & Walz, U. (2004). Private equity returns and disclusure around the world. LSE RICAFE working paper, *April 2004*(009).

Cunningham, S. W. (1973). The predictability of British stock market prices. *Applied Statistics, 22*(3), 315–331.

Cyert, R. M. & March, J. G. (1963). A behavioral theory of the firm. Englewood Cliffs, NJ: Prentice-Hall.

Daft, R. (1983). *Organization theory and design*. New York: West.

Das, S., Jagannathan, R., & Sarin, A. (2003). Private equity returns: An empirical examiniation of the exit of venture-backed companies. *Journal of Investment Management, 1*(1), 1–26.

Davis, S. J., Haltiwanger, J., Jarmin, R., Lerner, J., & Miranda, J. (2008). Private Equity and employment. In A. Gurung and J. Lerner (Eds.), *Globalization of Alternative Investments: The Global Economic Impact of Private Equity Report 2008* (working papers, Vol. 1, pp. 43–64). Geneva: World Economic Forum.

de Malherbe, E. (2005). A model for the dynamics of private equity funds. *The Journal of Alternative Investments, Winter 2005*, 81–89.

De, S. (1992). Diversification patterns and long-term corporate performance. *Managerial and Decision Economics, 13*(1), 1–13.

DeAngelo, H., DeAngelo, L., & Rice, E. M. (1984). Going private: Minority freezeouts and stockholder wealth. *Journal of Law and Economics, 27*(2), 367.

Demsetz, H. (1983). The structure of ownership and the theory of the firm. *Journal of Law and Economics, 26*(2), 375–390.

Denis, D. J. (1994). Organizational form and the consequences of highly leveraged transactions: Kroger's recapitalization and Safeway's LBO. *Journal of Financial Economics, 36*, 193–224.

Denis, D. J. & Denis, D. K. (1994). Majority owner-managers and organizational efficiency. *Journal of Corporate Finance, 1*(1), 91–118.

Denis, D. J. & Denis, D. K. (1995). Causes of financial distress following leveraged recapitalizations. *Journal of Financial Economics, 37*, 129–157.

Denis, D. J., Denis, D. K., & Sarin, A. (1997). Agency problems, equity ownership, and corporate diversification. *The Journal of Finance, 52*(1), 135–160.

Denis, D. J., Denis, D. K., & Yost, K. (2002). Global diversification, industrial diversification, and firm value. *The Journal of Finance, 57*(5), 1951–1979.

Desbrières, P. & Schatt, A. (2002). The impacts of LBOs on the performance of acquired firms: The French case. *Journal of Business Finance & Accounting, 29*(5&6), 695–729.

Deutsche Bank Research (2005). *Private Equity in Europa: Buy-outs stuetzen Wachstum, Gruendungsfinanzierung abgestuerzt. Research, Deutsche Bank, January 2005.*

Dielman, T. E. (1991). *Applied regression analysis for business and economics*. Boston, MA: PWS-Kent Publishing Company.

Dittmar, A. & Shivdasani, A. (2003). Divestitures and divisional investment policies. *The Journal of Finance, 58*(6), 2711–2743.

Dobbs, R. (2006). Creating value: The debate over public vs. private ownership. *McKinsey on Finance, Autumn 2006*, 1–7.

Dobbs, R. & Koller, T. M. (2005a). Measuring long-term performance. *McKinsey on Finance, 2005 Special Edition: Value and Performance*, 17–27.

Dobbs, R. & Koller, T. M. (2005b). Measuring stock market performance. *McKinsey on Finance, Autumn 2005*, 1–4.

Donaldson, L. (1982). Divisionalization and diversification: A longitudinal study. *The Academy of Management Journal, 25*(4), 909–914.

Draho, J. (2007). The convergence of public and private equity markets: Cyclical or structural. *Journal of Applied Corporate Finance, 19*(3), 117–124.

Dranikoff, L., Koller, T. M., & Schneider, A. (2002). Divesting proactively. *McKinsey on Finance, Summer 2002*, 1–6.

Dundas, K. N. M. & Richardson, P. R. (1982). Implementing the unrelated product strategy. *Strategic Management Journal, 3*(4), 287–301.

Easterwood, J. C., Seth, A., & Singer, R. F. (1989). The impact of leveraged buyouts on strategic direction. *California Management Review, Fall 1989*, 30–43.

Edwards, C. (1955). *Conglomerate bigness as a source of power*. Princeton: Princeton University Press.

Eisenhardt, K. M. (1989). Building theories from case study research. *Academy of Management Review, 14*(4), 532–550.

Eisenhardt, K. M. & Brown, S. L. (1999). Patching: restitching business portfolios in dynamic markets. *Harvard Business Review, May–June 1999*, 72–82.

Eisenhardt, K. M. & Zbaracki, M. J. (1992). Strategic decision making. *Strategic Management Journal 13*(Special Issue: Fundamental Themes in Strategy Process Research), 17–37.

Elango, B., Fried, V. H., Hisrich, R. D., & Polonchek, A. (1995). How venture capital firms differ. *Journal of Business Venturing, 10*, 157–179.

Ensign, P. C. (2001). The concept of fit in organizational research. *International Journal of Organizational Theroy & Behaviour, 4*(3&4), 287–306.

European Private Equity & Venture Capital Association (2007). *PE industry glossary, European Private Equity & Venture Capital Association.*

European Private Equity & Venture Capital Association (2008). *Private equity facts and figures.* http://www.evca.com (access January 23, 2008).

European Private Equity & Venture Capital Association and Thomson Financial (2005). *Pan-European survey of performance*. Research notes, 27.10.2005.

Evans, J. L. & Archer, S. H. (1968). Diversification and the reduction of dispersion: An empirical analysis. *The Journal of Finance, 23*(5), 761–767.

Fama, E. F. (1970). Efficient capital markets: A review of theory and empirical work. *The Journal of Finance, 25*(2, papers and proceedings of the twenty-eighth annual meeting of the Amercian Finance Association New York 1969), 383–417.

Fama, E. F. (1980). Agency problems and the theory of the firm. *Journal of Political Economy, 88*(2), 288–307.

Fama, E. F. & French, K. R. (1992). The cross-section of expected stock returns. *The Journal of Finance, 47*(2), 427–465.

Farjoun, M. (1998). The independent and joint effects of the skill and physical bases of relatedness in diversification. *Strategic Management Journal, 19*(7), 611–630.

Fenn, G. W., Liang, N., & Prowse, S. (1996). The economics of the private equity market. *Federal Reserve Bulletin, 82*, 26–27.

Ferris, S. P. & Sarin, A. (2000). Security analysis and corporate diversification. *Advances in Financial Economics, 5*, 105–137.

Financial Times (2007). *Debt risk time-bomb stalking the Private Equity industry*. Financial Times, FT Markets. London. *February, 27*, 40.

Financial Times Deutschland (2007). Bertelsmann to set up investment fund. *Financial Times Deutschland*: 1.

Fiol, M. C. & Lyles, M. A. (1985). Organizational learning. *The Academy of Management Review, 10*(4), 803–813.

Fisher, T. (2007). Nur 100 Tage Zeit. Wirtschaftswoche. *April 16*, 18.

Flick, U. (1995). Stationen des qualitiative Forschungsprozesses. In U. Flick, E. von Kardorff, H. Keurpp, L. von Rosentiel, & S. Wolff(Eds.), *Handbuch qualitative Sozialforschung* (2nd ed.). Weinheim: Beltz Verlag.

Fluck, Z. & Lynch, A. W. (1999). Why do firms merge and then divest? A theory of financial synergy. *Journal of Business, 72*(3), 319–346.

Fontana, A. & Frey, J. H. (2005). The interview – From neutral stance to political involvement. In N. K. Denzin & Y. S. Lincoln, *The sage handbook of qualitative research* (3rd ed.). Thousand Oaks: Sage Publications.

Fox, I. & Marcus, A. (1992). The causes and consequences of leveraged management buyouts. *Academy of Management Review, 17*(1), 62–85.

Frank, R. E., Massy, W. F., & Morrison, D. G. (1965). Bias in multiple discriminant analysis. *Journal of Marketing Research, 2*(3), 250–258.

Frankfurter Allgemeine Zeitung (2007). Blackstone will offenbar an die Boerse. *Frankfurter Allgemeine Zeitung, Finanzmarkt, March 18*, 21.

Franko, L. G. (1974). The move toward a multidivisional structure in European organizations. *Administrative Science Quarterly, 19*(4), 493–506.

Fredrickson, J. W. (1986). The strategic decision process and organizational structure. *Academy of Management Review, 11*(2), 280–297.

Froendhoff, B. (2006). Wachstumsstrategie: Zwischen Diversifikation und Fokussierung – Immer nah am Kern. Handelsblatt, Unternehmenspraxis. *February 14*, 22.

Funk, C. & Welge, M. K. (2008). *Gestaltung eines effektiven Winner-Pickings in Konglomeraten*. Universitaet Dortmund, working paper. Dortmund.

Galbraith, J. R. & Nathanson, D. A. (1978). *Strategy implementation: The role of structure and process*. St. Paul, MI: West Publishing Co.

Gertner, R., Powers, E., & Scharfstein, D. S. (2002). Learning about internal capital markets from corporate spin-offs. *The Journal of Finance, 57*(6), 2479–2506.

Gertner, R. H., Scharfstein, D. S., & Stein, J. (1994). Internal versus external capital markets. *The Quarterly Journal of Economics, November 1994*, 1211–1230.

Ghemawat, P. (1986). Sustainable advantage. *Harvard Business Review September–October 1986*, 53–58.

Gifford Jr., D. (2001). Why debt can hurt corporate growth. *MIT Sloan Management Review, Spring 2001*, 18.

Ginsberg, A. (1989). Construing the business portfolio: A cognitive model of diversification. *Journal of Management Studies, 26*(4), 417–438.

Glaser, M. & Mueller, S. (2006). *Der Diversification Discount in Deutschland: Existiert ein Bewertungsabschlag fuer diversifizierte Unternehmen?* Universitaet Mannheim, working paper 2006.

Golden, B. R. (1992). SBU strategy and performance: The moderating effects of the corporate-SBU relationship. *Strategic Management Journal, 13*(2), 145–158.

Gomes, J. & Livdan, D. (2004). Optimal diversification: Reconciling theory and evidence. *The Journal of Finance, 59*(2), 507–535.

Gompers, P. A. (1995). Optimal investment, monitoring, and the staging of venture capital. *The Journal of Finance*, *50*(5), 1461–1489.

Gompers, P. A. & Lerner, J. (1999). An analysis of compensation in the U.S. venture capital partnership. *Journal of Financial Economics*, *51*, 3–44.

Gompers, P. A. & Lerner, J. (2000). Money chasing deals? The impact of fund inflows on private equity valuations. *Journal of Financial Economics*, *55*, 281–325.

Gompers, P. A. & Lerner, J. (2004). *The venture capital cycle*. Cambridge, MA: MIT Press.

Goold, M. & Campbell, A. (1987). *Strategies and styles: The role of the centre in managing diversified corporations*. Oxford: Basil Blackwell.

Goold, M. & Campbell, A. (1998). Desperately seeking synergy. *Harvard Business Review, September October 1998*, 131–143.

Goold, M. & Campbell, A. (2002). Do you have a well-designed organization? *Harvard Business Review March 2002*, 117–124.

Goold, M., Campbell, A., & Alexander, M. (1994). *Corporate level strategy: Creating value in the multibusiness company*. New York: Wiley.

Goold, M., Campbell, A., & Alexander, M. (1998). Corporate strategy and parenting theory. *Long Range Planning*, *31*(2), 308–314.

Goold, M. & Luchs, K. (1993). Why diversify? Four decades of management thinking. *Academy of Management Executive*, *7*(3), 7–25.

Goranova, M., Alessandri, T. M., & Dharwadkar, R. (2007). Managerial ownership and corporate diversification: A longitudinal view. *Strategic Management Journal*, *28*(3), 211–225.

Gort, M. (1962). *Diversification and integration in American industry*. Princeton, NJ: Princeton University Press.

Gort, M., Grabowski, H., & McGuckin, R. (1985). Organizational capital and the choice between specialization and diversification. *Managerial and Decision Economics*, *6*(1), 2–10.

Gottschalg, O. & Meier, D. (2005). *What does it take to be good parent? Opening the black-box of value creation in the unrelated multibusiness firm*. HEC School of Management, working paper 2005.

Gottschalg, O., Phalippou, L., & Zollo, M. (2004). *Performance of private equity funds: Another puzzle*. INSEAD-Wharton Alliance Center for Global Research and Development, working paper 2004/82.

Govindarajan, V. (1986). Decentralization, strategy, and effectiveness of strategic business units in multibusiness organizations. *The Academy of Management Review*, *11*(4), 844–856.

Govindarajan, V. (1988). A contingency approach to strategy implementation at the business-unit level: Integrating administrative mechanisms with strategy. *The Academy of Management Journal*, *31*(4), 828–853.

Graham, J. R., Lemmon, M. L., & Wolf, J. G. (2002). Does corporate diversification destroy value? *The Journal of Finance*, *57*(2), 695–720.

Grant, R. M. (1991). The resource-based theory of competitive advantage: Implications for strategy formulation. *California Management Review*, *33*(3), 114–134.

Grant, R. M. & Jammine, A. P. (1988). Performance differences between the Wrigley/Rumelt strategic categories. *Strategic Management Journal*, *9*(4), 333–346.

Grinyer, P. H. & Yasai-Ardekani, M. (1981). Strategy, structure, size and bureaucracy. *The Academy of Management Journal*, *24*(3), 471–486.

Grossman, S. J. & Hart, O. (1982). Corporate financial structure and managerial incentives. In J. McCall (Ed.), *The economics of information and uncertainty* (pp. 107–140). Chicago: University of Chicago Press.

Guerrera, F. & Politi, J. (2007). Private equity comes to aid of conglomerates. *Financial Times, Companies and Markets*, 13.

Guevarra, V. (2007). TPG capital, affinity wrap up their bid for UTAC. *The Wall Street Journal October 8*, C2.

Gupta, A. & Rosenthal, L. (1991). Ownership structure, leverage, and firm value: The case of leveraged recapitalizations. *Financial Management*, *20*(3), 69–83.

Gupta, A. K. (1987). SBU strategies, corporate-SBU relations, and SBU effectiveness in strategy implementation. *The Academy of Management Journal*, *30*(3), 477–500.

Gupta, A. K. & Govindarajan, V. (1986). Resource sharing among SBUs: Strategic antecedents and administrative implications. *The Academy of Management Journal, 29*(4), 695–714.

Habib, M. A. (1997). Monitoring, implicit contracting, and the lack of permanence of leveraged buyouts. *European Finance Review, 1*, 139–163.

Haimann, R. & Osadnik, S. (2006). Renditetrimmer. *Financial Times Deutschland, Dossier Mischkonzerne June 21*, 5.

Haleblian, J. & Finkelstein, S. (1999). The influence of organizational acquisition experience on acquisition performance: A behavioral learning perspective. *Administrative Science Quarterly, 44*(1), 29–56.

Hall, B. (1990). The impact of corporate restructuring on industrial research and development. *Brookings Papers on Economic Activitiy: Microeconomics, 1990*, 85–124.

Hall, E. H. & St. John, C. H. (1994). A methodological note on diversity management. *Strategic Management Journal, 15*(2), 153–168.

Hall, G. E. (1987). Reflections on running a diversified company. *Harvard Business Review, January–February 1987*, 84–92.

Hall, R. H. (1977). *Organizations: Structure and process*. Englewood Cliffs, NJ: Prentice-Hall.

Hall, W. K. (1978). SBUs: Hot, new topic in the management of diversification. *Business Horizons, February 1978*, 17–25.

Hambrick, D. C. (1981). Strategic awareness within top management teams. *Strategic Management Journal, 2*(3), 263–279.

Hamel, G. & Prahalad, C. K. (1989). Strategic intent. *Harvard Business Review, May–June 1989*, 63–76.

Harper, N. W. C. & Schneider, A. (2004). Private equity's new challenge. *McKinsey on Finance, Summer 2004*, 1–5.

Harper, N. W. C & Viguerie, S. P. (2002a). Beyond focus: Diversifying for value. *McKinsey on Finance, Winter 2002*, 1–5.

Harper, N. W. C. & Viguerie, S. P. (2002b). Are you too focused? *The McKinsey Quarterly, 2002 Special Edition: Risk and Resilience*, 29–37.

Harrigan, K. R. (1980). The effect of exit barriers upon strategic flexibility. *Strategic Management Journal, 1*, 165–176.

Harrigan, K. R. (1981). Deterrents to divestiture. *Academy of Management Journal, 24*(2), 306–323.

Harris, I. C. & Ruefli, T. W. (2000). The strategy/structure debate: An examination of the performance implications. *Journal of Management Studies, 37*(4), 587–603.

Harris, R., Siegel, D., & Wright, M. (2005). Assessing the impact of management buyouts on economic efficiency: Plant-level evidence from the United Kingdom. *Review of Economics and Statistics, 2005*(February), 148–158.

Harrison, J. S., Hitt, M. A., Hoskisson, R. E., & Ireland, R. D. (1991). Synergies and post-acquisition performance: Differences versus similarities in resource allocations. *Journal of Management, 17*(1), 173–190.

Hart, S. L. (1992). An integrative framework for strategy-making processes. *Academy of Management Review, 17*(2), 327–351.

Hart, S. L. & Banbury, C. (1994). How strategy-making processes can make a difference. *Strategic Management Journal, 15*(4), 251–269.

Haspeslagh, P. (1982). Portfolio planning: Uses and limits. *Harvard Business Review, January–February 1982*, 58–73.

Hax, A. & Majluf, N. (1984). *Strategic management: An integrative perspective*. Englewood Cliffs, NJ: Prentice-Hall.

Healy, P. M., Palepu, K. G., & Ruback, R. S. (1992). Does corporate performance improve after mergers? *Journal of Financial Economics, 31*, 135–175.

Hellmann, T. & Puri, M. (2002). Venture capital and the professionalization of start-up firms: Empirical evidence. *The Journal of Finance, 57*(1), 169–197.

Henning, C. (2004). *Theorie und empirische Anwendungen: Festschrift fuer Franz Urban Pappi*. Frankfurt am Main: Campus Verlag.

Hill, C. W. L. (1985). Diversified growth and competition: The experience of twelve large UK firms. *Applied Economics*, *17*(October), 827–847.

Hill, C. W. L., Hitt, M. A., & Hoskisson , R. E. (1992). Cooperative versus competitve structures in related and unrelated diversified firms. *Organization Science*, *3*(4), 501–521.

Hill, C. W. L. & Hoskisson, R. E. (1987). Strategy and structure in the multiproduct firm. *Academy of Management Review*, *12*(2), 331–341.

Hite, G. L. & Vetsuypens, M. R. (1989). Management buy-outs of divisions and shareholder wealth. *Journal of Finance*, *44*(4), 953–970.

Hitt, M. A., Hoskisson, R. E. & Ireland, R. D. (1990). Merger and acquisitions and managerial commitment to innovation in M-form firms. *Strategic Management Journal*, *11*(10), 29–47.

Hitt, M. A. & Ireland, R. D. (1986). Relationship among corporate level distinctive competencies, diversification strategy, corporate structure and performance. *Journal of Management Studies*, *23*(4), 401–416.

Holderness, C. G. & Sheehan, D. P. (1985). Raiders or saviors? The evidence on six controversial investors. *Journal of Financial Economics*, *14*, 555–579.

Holderness, C. G. & Sheehan, D. P. (1988). The role of majority shareholders in publicly held corporations. *Journal of Financial Economics*, *20*, 317–346.

Holl, P. (1975). Effect of control type on the performance of the firm in the U.K. *The Journal of Industrial Economics*, *23*(4), 257–271.

Holl, P. (1977). Control type and the market for corporate control in large U.S. corporations. *The Journal of Industrial Economics*, *25*(4), 259–273.

Holthausen, R. W. & Larcker, D. F. (1996). The financial performance of reverse leveraged buyouts. *Journal of Financial Economics*, *42*, 293–332.

Hoskisson, R. E. (1987). Multidivisional structure and performance: The contingency of diversification strategy. *The Academy of Management Journal*, *30*(4), 625–644.

Hoskisson, R. E., Hitt, M. A., Johnson, R., & Moesel, D. (1993). Construct validity of an objective (entropy) categorial measure of diversification strategy. *Strategic Management Journal*, *14*(3), 215–235.

Hoskisson, R. E. & T. A. Turk (1990). Corporate restructuring: Governance and control limits of the internal capital market. *Academy of Management Review*, *5*(3), 459–477.

Hubbard, R. G. & D. Palia (1999). A reexamination of the conglomerate merger wave in the 1960s: An internal capital markets view. *The Journal of Finance*, *54*(3), 1131–1152.

Huber, G. P. (1991). Organization learning: The contributing processes and the literatures. *Organization Science*, *2*, 88–115.

Ick, M. M. (2005). *Performance measurement and appraisal of private equity investments relative to public equity markets*. CEPRES Center of Private Equity Research, working paper May 2005.

Ireland, R. D., Hitt, M. A., & Sirmon, D.G. (2003). Strategic entrepreneurship: The construct and its dimensions. *Journal of Management*, *29*, 963–989.

Jackson, T. (2006). Shades of old conglomerates in private equity trend. *Financial Times, Stock Markets & Currencies, October 31*, 44.

Jacquemin, A. P. (1990). Mergers and European policy. In A. P. Jacquemin (Ed.), *Merger and competition policy in the European community* (pp. 1–38). Oxford: Basil Blackwell.

Jacquemin, A. P. & Berry, C. H. (1979). Entropy measure of diversification and corporate growth. *The Journal of Industrial Economics*, *27*(4), 359–369.

Jensen, M. C. (1969). Risk, the pricing of capital assets, and the evaluation of investment portfolios. *Journal of Business*, *42*(2), 167–247.

Jensen, M. C. (1986). Agency costs of free cash flow, corporate finance, and takeovers. *American Economic Review*, *76*(2), 323–329.

Jensen, M. C. (1988). Takeovers: Their causes and consequences. *The Journal of Economic Perspectives*, *2*(1), 21–48.

Jensen, M. C. (1989a). Active investors, LBOs, and the privatization of bankruptcy. *Journal of Applied Corporate Finance*, *2*(1 Selection from the Senate and House Hearings on LBOs and corporate debt), 35–44.

Jensen, M. C. (1989b). Eclipse of the public corporation. *Harvard Business Review, September–October 1989*, 61–74.

Jensen, M. C., Kaplan, S. N., Ferenbach, C., Feldberg, M., Moon, J., & Davis, C. (2006). Morgan Stanley roundtable on private equity and its import for public corporations. *Journal of Applied Corporate Finance*, *18*(3), 8–37.

Jensen, M. C. & Meckling, W. H. (1976). Theory of the firm: Managerial behaviour, agency costs and ownership structure. *Journal of Financial Economics*, *3*, 305–360.

Jensen, M. C. & Meckling, W. H. (1992). Specific and general knowledge, and organizational structure. In L. Werin & H. Wijkander (Eds.), *Contract Economics*. Oxford, UK: Blackwell.

Jensen, M. C. & Ruback, R. S. (1983). The market for corporate control: The scientific evidence. *Journal of Financial Economics*, *11*, 5–50.

John, K. & Ofek, E. (1995). Asset sales and increase in focus. *Journal of Financial Economics*, *37*, 105–126.

Kames, C. (2000). *Unternehmensbewertung durch Finanzanalysten als Ausgangspunkt eines value based measurement*. Frankfurt am Main: Peter Lang.

Kanter, R. M. (1989). *When giants learn to dance: Mastering the challenge of strategy, management, and careers in the 1990s*. New York: Simon and Schuster, Inc.

Kaplan, S. N. (1989). The effects of management buyouts on operating performance and value. *Journal of Financial Economics*, *24*, 217–254.

Kaplan, S. N. (1991). The staying power of leveraged buyouts. *Journal of Financial Economics*, *29*, 287–313.

Kaplan, S. N. (2007a). Private equity: Past, present, and future. *Journal of Applied Corporate Finance*, *19*(3), 8–16.

Kaplan, S. N. (2007b). *Private equity's history and impact on corporate governance. The history, impact, and future of private equity*. Washington, DC: American Enterprise Institute for Public Policy Research.

Kaplan, S. N. & Minton, B. A. (2006). How has CEO turnover changed? *Increasingly performance sensitive boards and increasingly uneasy CEOs*. Chicago: University of Chicago, Graduate School of Business, working paper.

Kaplan, S. N. & Schoar, A. (2004). *Private equity performance: Returns, persistence and capital flows*. University of Chicago, working paper 2002.

Kaplan, S. N. & Stein, J. C. (1990). How risky is the debt in highly leveraged transactions? *Journal of Financial Economics*, *27*, 215–245.

Kaplan, S. N. & Stroemberg, P. (2000). *Financial contracting theory meets the real world: An empirical analysis of venture vapital contracts*. Chicago: Universtiy of Chicago, Center of Research in Security Price, working paper.

Kaserer, C. & Diller, C. (2004). *European private equity funds – A cash flow based performance analysis*. Technische Universitaet Muenchen, working paper. Munich.

Katz, R. L. (1974). Skills of an effective administrator. *Harvard Business Review, September–October 1974*, 90–102.

Kaufman, A. & Englander, E. J. (1993). Kohlberg Kravis Roberts & Co. and the restructuring of American capitalism. *The Business History Review*, *67*(1, Spring), 52–97.

Kazanjian, R. K. & Drazin, R. (1987). Implementing internal diversification: Contingency factors for organization design choices. *The Academy of Management Review*, *12*(2), 342–354.

Kerr, J. L. (1985). Diversification strategies and managerial rewards: An empirical study. *The Academy of Management Journal*, *28*(1), 155–179.

Kester, W. C. & Luehrman, T. A. (1995). Rehabilitating the leveraged buyout. *Harvard Business Review, May–June 1995*, 119–130.

Kiechel, W. (1982). Corporate strategies under fire. *Fortune, December 27*, 34–39.

Kim, C. & Pantzalis, C. (2000). *Analyst herding bebavior and firm diversification: Evidence from panel data*. City University of New York, working paper, New York.

Klein, P. G. (2005). *Are internal capital markets good for innovation?* University of Missouri, Contracting and Organizations Research Institute, working paper September 2005.

Knop, C. (2007). Die Zukunft der Konglomerate. *Frankfurter Allgemeine Zeitung, Wirtschaft. February, 19*, 9.

Kochhar, R. & Hitt, M. A. (1998). Linking corporate strategy to capital structure: Diversification strategy, type and source of financing. *Strategic Management Journal, 19*(6), 601–610.

Koehler, P. & Koenen, J. (2007). *Blackstone sucht den Super-Deal.* Handelsblatt, Finanzzeitung: 25.

Kohlberg Kravis Robert & Co. (2008). *KKR mission statement.* Kohlberg Kravis Robert & Co., http://www.kkr.com (access April 14, 2008).

Kohlberg Kravis Robert & Co. and Deloitte Haskins & Sells (1989). Leveraged buy-outs. *Journal of Applied Corporate Finance, 2*(1), 64–70.

Koltes, S. (2005). Sind Beteiligungsunternehmen die neuen Konglomerate? *Frankfurter Allgemeine Zeitung, Finanzmaerkte und Geldanlage, April 21*, 29.

Koontz, H. (1969). A model for analyzing the universality and transferability of management. *The Academy of Management Journal, 12*(4), 415–429.

Kosedag, A. & Michayluk, D. (2004). Repeated LBOs: The case of multiple LBO transactions. *Quarterly Journal of Business & Economics, 43*(1&2), 111–122.

Kraft, V. (2001). *Private Equity fuer Turnaround-Investitionen: Erfolgsfaktoren in der Managementpraxis.* Frankfurt am Main, Campus.

Kravis, H. R. (2004). *Keynote Speech.* Private Equity Analyst Conference 2004, New York, http://www.kkr.com (access April 14, 2008).

Kravis, H. R. (2006). Value creation in the large buyout space. SuperReturn 2006, European Private Equity & Venture Capital Summit, http://www.kkr.com (access April 14, 2008).

Krishnan, H. A., Miller, A., & Judge, W. (1997). Diversification and top management team complementarity: Is performance improved by merging similar or dissimilar teams? *Strategic Management Journal, 18*(5), 361–374.

Kromrey, H. (2006). *Empirische Sozialforschung* (11th ed.) Stuttgart: Lucius and Lucius.

Lakonishok, J., Shleifer, A., Thaler, R. H., & Vishny, R. W. (1991). Window dressing by pension fund managers. *American Economic Review, 81*, 227–231.

Lamnek, S. (2005). *Qualitative Sozialforschung* (4th ed.) Weinheim: Beltz Verlag.

Lamont, B. T. & Anderson, C. R. (1985). Mode of corporate diversification and economic performance. *The Academy of Management Journal, 28*(4), 926–934.

Lamont, O. (1997). Cash flow and investment: Evidence from internal capital markets. *The Journal of Finance, 52*(1), 83–109.

Lamont, O. A. & Polk, C. (2000). *Does diversification destroy value? Evidence from industry shocks.* University of Chicago, working paper 2000.

Lamont, O. A. & Polk, C. (2001). The diversification discount: Cash flows versus returns. *The Journal of Finance, 56*(5), 1693–1721.

Lane, P. J., Cannella, A. A., & Lubatkin, M. H. (1998). Agency problems as antecedents to unrelated mergers and diversification: Amihud and Lev reconsidered. *Strategic Management Journal, 19*(6), 555–578.

Lane, P. J., Cannella, A. A., & Lubatkin, M. H. (1999). Ownership structure and corporate strategy: One question viewed from two different worlds. *Strategic Management Journal, 20*(11), 1077–1086.

Lang, L., Ofek, E., & Stulz, R. M. (1996). Leverage, investment, and firm growth. *Journal of Financial Economics, 40*, 3–29.

Lang, L., Poulsen, A., & Stulz, R. M. (1995). Asset sales, firm performance, and the agency costs of managerial discretion. *Journal of Financial Economics, 37*, 3–37.

Lang, L. & Stulz, R. M. (1994). Tobin's q, corporate diversification, and firm performance. *Journal of Political Economy, 102*(6), 1248–1280.

Lau, C. -M. (1993). Diversify with care: Diversification strategies and organization development. *The International Journal of Organizational Analysis, 1*(1), 55–72.

Lecraw, D. J. (1984). Diversification strategy and performance. *The Journal of Industrial Economics, 33*(2), 179–198.

Lehn, K. & Poulsen, A. (1990). The economics of event risk: The case of bondholders in leveraged buyouts. *Journal of Corporation Law, 15*(2), 199.

Lei, D. & Hitt, M. A. (1995). Strategic restructuring and outsourcing: The effect of mergers and acquisitions and LBOs on building firm skills and capabilities. *Journal of Management, 21*(5), 835–859.

Lemelin, A. (1982). Relatedness in the patterns of interindustry diversification. *Review of Economics and Statistics, 64*(November), 646–657.

Lerner, J. (1995). Venture capitalists and the oversight of private equity. *The Journal of Finance, 50*(1), 301–318.

Lerner, J. & Hardymon, F. (2002). *Venture capital and private equity – A casebook*. New York: Wiley.

Lerner, J., Sorensen, M., & Strömberg, P. J. (2008). Private equity and long-run investment: The case of innovation. In A. Gurung and J. Lerner (Eds.), *Globalization of Alternative Investmens: The Global Economic Impact of Private Equity Report 2008* (working papers, Vol. 1, pp. 27–42). Geneva: World Economic Forum.

Levy, H. & Sarnat, M. (1970). Diversification, portfolio analysis and the uneasy case for conglomerate mergers. *The Journal of Finance, 25*(4), 795–802.

Lewellen, W. G. (1971). A pure financial rationale for the conglomerate merger – Papers and proceedings of the twenty-ninth annual meeting of the American Finance Association. *The Journal of Finance, 26*(2), 521–537.

Lichtenberg, F. R. (1991). The managerial response to regulation of financial reporting for segments of a business enterprise. *Journal of Regulatory Economics, 3*(3), 241–249.

Lichtenberg, F. R. & Siegel, D. (1990). The effects of leveraged buyouts on productivity and related aspects of firm behavior. *Journal of Financial Economics, 27*, 165–194.

Liebeskind, J. P., Wiersema, M. F., & Hansen, G. (1992). LBOs, corporate restructuring, and the incentive-intensity hypothesis. *Financial Management, Spring 1992*, 73–88.

Lien, L. B. & Klein, P. G. (2007). What's the matter with relatedness? *Norwegian School of Economics and Business Administration*, working paper 2007.

Lins, K. & Servaes, H. (1999). International evidence on the value of corporate diversification. *The Journal of Finance, 54*(6), 2215–2239.

Little, W. B. & Klinsky, S. B. (1989). How leveraged buyout can really work: A look at three cases. *Journal of Applied Corporate Finance, 2*(1), 71–75.

Ljungqvist, A. & Richardson, M. (2003a). *The cash flow, return and risk characteristics of private equity*. Stern School of Business, working paper January 2003.

Ljungqvist, A. & Richardson, M. (2003b). *The investment behavior of private equity fund managers*. Stern School of Business, working paper October 2003.

Long, W. F. & Ravenscraft, D. J. (1993). LBOs, debt and R&D intensity. *Strategic Management Journal, 14*(Special issue: Corporate restructuring), 119–135.

Loos, N. (2005). Value creation in leveraged buyouts. Graduate School of Business Administration, Economics, Law and Social Sciences, University of St. Gallen (HSG): *Disseration No. 3052*.

Lossen, U. (2006). *The performance of Private Equity funds: Does diversification matter?* Munich Business School, Muenchner Betriebswirtschaftliche Beitraege, working paper 2006(14).

Lovallo, D. P. & Mendonca, L. T. (2007). Strategy's strategist: An interview with Richard Rumelt. *McKinsey Quarterly, 2007*(4), 57–67.

Lowenstein, L. (1985). Management buyouts. *Columbia Law Review, 85*(4), 730–784.

Lubatkin, M. & Chatterjee, S. (1994). Extending modern portfolio theory into the domain of corporate diversification: Does it apply? *Academy of Management Journal, 37*(1), 109–136.

Lubatkin, M. & Rogers, R. C. (1989). Diversification, systematic risk, and shareholder return: A capital market extension of Rumelt's 1974 study. *The Academy of Management Journal, 32*(2), 454–465.

MacDonald, J. M. (1985). R&D and the directions of diversification. *Review of Economics and Statistics, 67*(November), 583–590.

MacMillan, I. C., Hambrick, D. C., & Diana, D. L. (1982). The product portfolio and profitability – A PIMS-based analysis of industrial-product busiensses. *The Academy of Management Journal, 25*(4), 733–755.

MacMillan, I. C., Kulow, D. M., & Khoylian, R. (1989). Venture capitalists' involvement in their investments: Extent and performance. *Journal of Business Venturing*, *4*, 27–47.

MacMillan, I. C., Zemann, L., & Subbanarasimha, P. N. (1987). Criteria distinguising successful from unsuccessful ventures in the venture screening process. *Journal of Business Venturing*, *2*, 123–137.

Mahoney, J. T. & Pandian, J. R. (1992). The resource-based view within the conversation of strategic management. *Strategic Management Journal*, *13*(5), 363–380.

Maier, A. (2007). Hoehenflug auf Pump. Financial Times Deutschland, Dossier *Restrukturierung und Finanzierung*, *April 26*, 2–4.

Maksimovic, V. & Phillips, G. (2001). The market for corporate assets: Who engages in mergers and asset sales and are there efficiency gains? *The Journal of Finance*, *56*(6), 2019–2065.

Maksimovic, V. & Phillips, G. (2002). Do conglomerate firms allocate resources inefficiently across industries? Theory and evidence. *The Journal of Finance*, *57*(2), 721–767.

Mansi, S. A. & Reeb, D. M. (2002). Corporate diversification: What gets discounted?. *The Journal of Finance*, *57*(5), 2167–2183.

Markham, J. W. (1973). *Conglomerate enterprise and public policy*. Boston: Graduate School of Business Administration, Harvard University.

Markides, C. C. (1995). Diversification, restructuring and economic performance. *Strategic Management Journal*, *16*(2), 101–118.

Markides, C. C. (1998a). Strategic innovation in established companies. *Sloan Management Review*, *39*(3), 31.

Markides, C. C. (1998b). To diversify or not to diversify. in: Strategies for growth. *Harvard Business Review*, 79–97. Boston: Harvard Business School Press.

Markides, C. C. & Williamson, P. J. (1994). Related diversification, core competencies and corporate performance. *Strategic Management Journal*, *15*(Special issue: Strategy: Search for new paradigms), 149–165.

Martin, J. D. & Sayrak, A. (2003). Corporate diversification and shareholder value: A survey of recent literature. *Journal of Corporate Finance*, *9*(1), 37–57.

Mason, C. H. & Perreault Jr., W. D. (1991). Collinearity, power, and interpretation of multiple regression analysis. *Journal of Marketing Research* *28*(August 1991), 268–280.

Mason, E. S. (1939). Price and production policies of large scale enterprises. *American Economic Review*, *9*(March), 61–74.

Mason, R. H. & Goudzwaard, M. B. (1976). Performance of conglomerate firms: A portfolio approach. *The Journal of Finance*, *31*(1), 39–48.

Matsusaka, J. G. (2001). Corporate diversification, value maximization, and organizational capabilities. *Journal of Business*, *74*(3), 409–431.

Maxim, P. S. (1999). *Quantitative research methods in the social sciences*. Oxford: Oxford University Press.

Mazur, J. (1994). *Learning and behavior*. Englewood Cliffs, NJ: Prentice-Hall.

Melicher, R. W. & Rush, D. F. (1973). The performance of conglomerate firms: Recent risk and return experience. *The Journal of Finance*, *28*(2), 381–388.

Melicher, R. W. & Rush, D. F. (1974). Evidence on the acquisition-related performance of conglomerate firms. *The Journal of Finance*, *29*(1), 141–149.

Metrick, A. & Yasuda, A. (2007). *The economics of private equity funds*. University of Pennsylvania, The Wharton School, Department of Finance, working paper September 2007.

Miles, M. B. & Huberman, A. M. (1984). *Qualitative data analysis: A sourcebook of new methods*. Beverly Hills: Sage Publications.

Miles, R. E. & Snow, C. C. (1984). Fit, failure and the hall of fame. *California Management Review*, *26*(3), 10–28.

Miles, R. E., Snow, C. C., Meyer, A. D., & Coleman, H. J. Jr. (1978). Organizational strategy, structure, and process. *Academy of Management Review*, *July 1978*, 546–562.

Miller, D. (1986). Configurations of strategy and structure: Towards a synthesis. *Strategic Management Journal*, *7*(3), 233–249.

Miller, D. J. (2006). Technological diversity, related diversification, and firm performance. *Strategic Management Journal, 27*(7), 601–619.

Miller, R. & Brewer, J. (2003). The A–Z of social research. London: Sage Publications.

Milner, F. & Vos, E. (2003). Private equity: A portfolio approach. *The Journal of Alternative Investments, Spring 2003*, 51–65.

Mintzberg, H. (1981). Organization design: Fashion or fit? *Harvard Business Review, January–February 1981*, 103–116.

Modigliani, F. & Miller, M. H. (1958). The cost of capital, corporation finance and the theory of investment. *The American Economic Review, 48*(3), 261–297.

Montgomery, C. A. (1982). The measurement of firm diversification: Some new empirical evidence. *The Academy of Management Journal, 25*(2), 299–307.

Montgomery, C. A. (1985). Product-market diversification and market power. *The Academy of Management Journal, 28*(4), 789–798.

Montgomery, C. A. (1994). Corporate diversification. *The Journal of Economic Perspectives, 8*(3), 163–178.

Montgomery, C. A. & Hariharan, S. (1991). Diversified expansion by large established firms. *Journal of Economics, Behavior, and Organization, 15*(1), 71–89.

Montgomery, C. A. & Wernerfelt, B. (1988). Diversification, Ricardian rents, and Tobin's q. *RAND Journal of Economics, 19*(4), 623–632.

Moon, J. J. (2006). Public vs. private equity. *Journal of Applied Corporate Finance, 18*(3), 76–82.

Morck, R., Shleifer, A., & Vishny, R. W. (1990). Do managerial objectives drive bad acquisitions? *The Journal of Finance, 45*(1), 31–48.

Moskowitz, T. J. & Vissing-Jorgensen, A. (2002). *The returns to entrepreneurial investment: A private equity premium puzzle?* University of Chicago, working paper 2002.

Mueller-Stewens, G. (2004). *Corporate Strategy: Erzeugung von Mehrwert auf Ebene des Gesamtunternehmens*. Universitaet St.Gallen, working paper 2004.

Mueller, D. C. (1969). A theory of conglomerate mergers. *Quarterly Journal of Economics, 83*(November), 642–659.

Murali, R. & Welch, J. B. (1989). Agents, owners, control and performance. *Journal of Business Finance & Accounting, 16*(3), 385–398.

Muscarella, C. J. & Vetsuypens, M. R. (1990). Efficiency and organizational structure: A study of reverse LBOs. *Journal of Finance, 45*(5), 1389.

Myers, S. C. & Majluf, N. (1984). Corporate financing and investment decisions when firms have information that investors do not have. *Journal of Financial Economics, 13*(2), 187–221.

Naylor, T. H. & Tapon, F. (1982). The capital asset pricing model: An evaluation of its potential as a strategic planning tool. *Management Science, 28*(10), 1166–1173.

Nayyar, P. R. (1990). Information asymmetries: A source of competitive advantage for diversified service firms. *Strategic Management Journal, 11*(7), 513–519.

Nayyar, P. R. (1993). Stock market reactions to related diversification moves by service firms seeking benefits from information asymmetry and economies of scope. *Strategic Management Journal, 14*(8), 569–591.

Nelson, R. R. & Winter, S. G. (1982). *An evolutionary theory of economic change*. Cambridge, MA: Bellknap/Harvard.

Newbert, S. L. (2007). Empirical research on the resource-based view of the firm: An assessment and suggestions for future research. *Strategic Management Journal, 28*(2), 121–146.

Nicolai, A. T. & Thomas, T. W. (2006). De-diversification activities of German corporations from 1988 to 2002: Perspectives from agency and management fashion theory. *Schmalenbach Business Review, 58*(January), 56–80.

Nielsen, K. M. (2006). *The return to pension funds' private equity investments: New evidence on the private equity premium puzzle*. Copenhagen Business School, working paper October 2006.

Nikoskelainen, E. & Wright, M. (2007). The impact of corporate governance mechanisms on value increase in leveraged buyouts. *Journal of Corporate Finance, 13*(4), 511–537.

Nisar, T. M. (2005). Investor influence on portfolio company growth and development strategy. *Journal of Private Equity, Winter 2005*, 22–35.

Noda, T. & Bower, J. L. (1996). Strategy making as iterated processes of resource allocation. *Strategic Management Journal, 17*(7), 159–192.

Normann, R. (1977). *Management for growth*. New York: Wiley.

Nowak, E., Knigge, A., & Schmidt, D. (2004). *On the performance of private equity investments: Does market timing matter?* CEPRES Center of Private Equity Research, working paper March 2004.

O'Keeffe, P. (2005). The rise of the new conglomerate. BBC News. http://news.bbc.co.uk (access November 11, 2007).

Opler, T. C. (1992). Operating performance in leveraged buyouts: Evidence from 1985–1989. *Financial Management, 21*(1, Leverage Buyouts Special Issue), 27–34.

Opler, T. C. & Titman, S. (1993). The determinants of leveraged buyout activity: Free cash flow vs. financial distress costs. *The Journal of Finance, 48*(5), 1985–1999.

Palepu, K. G. (1985). Diversification strategy, profit performance and the entropy measure. *Strategic Management Journal, 6*(3), 239–255.

Palepu, K. G. (1990). Consequences of leveraged buyouts. *Journal of Financial Economics, 27*, 247–262.

Papadakis, V. M., Lioukas, S., & Chambers, D. (1998). Strategic decision-making processes: the role of management and context. *Strategic Management Journal, 19*(2), 115–147.

Paroutis, S. & Pettigrew, A. (2005a). Strategizing in multibusiness firms: Making and executing strategy acress multiple levels and over time. *EGOS Colloquium: Unlocking Strategizing – A Practice Perspective*, Berlin, 2005.

Paroutis, S. & Pettigrew, A. (2005b). *Studying strategizing and organizing within the multibusiness firm: Capabilities, evidence and learning*. Organization Studies Summer Workshop, conference paper 2005.

Peck, S. W. (2004). The carrot vs. the stick: The rolse of incentive compensation and debt obligations in the success of LBOs. *American Business Review, 6*(June), 1–12.

Pennings, J. M., Barkema, H., & Douma, S. (1994). Organizational learning and diversification. *Academy of Management Journal, 37*(3), 608–640.

Penrose, E. T. (1959). *The theory of growth of the firm*. London: Basil Blackwell.

Perry, L. T., Hansen, M. H., Shane Reese, C., & Pesci, G. (2005). Diversifaction and focus: A bayesian application of the resource-based view. *Schmalenbach Business Review, 57*(October), 304–319.

Peteraf, M. A. (1993). The cornerstones of competitive advantage: A resource-based view. *Strategic Management Journal, 14*(3), 179–191.

Peyer, U. C. & Shivdasani, A. (2000). Leverage and internal capital markets: Evidence from leveraged recapitalizations. *Journal of Financial Economics, 59*, 477–515.

Phan, P. H. & Hill, C. W. L. (1995). Organizational restructuring and economic performance in leveraged buyouts: An ex post study. *Academy of Management Journal, 38*(3), 704–739.

Pitts, R. A. (1977). Strategies and structures for diversification. *Academy of Management Journal, 20*(2), 197–208.

Pitts, R. A. (1980). Toward a contingency theory of multibusiness organization design. *The Academy of Management Review, 5*(2), 203–210.

Pitts, R. A. & Hopkins, H. D. (1982). Firm diversity: Conceptualization and measurement. *The Academy of Management Review, 7*(4), 620–629.

Porter, M. E. (1983). Industrial organization and the evolution of concepts for strategic planning: The new learning. *Managerial and Decision Economics, 4*(3), 172–180.

Porter, M. E. (1985). *Competitive advantage: Creating and sustaining superior performance*. New York: Free Press.

Porter, M. E. (1987). From competitive advantage to corporate strategy. *Harvard Business Review, 5*(3), 43–59.

Porter, M. E. (1996). What is strategy? *Harvard Business Review, November–December 1996*, 61–78.

Povaly, S. (2006). Private equity exits: An analysis of divestment process management in relation to leveraged buyouts. Graduate School of Business Administration, Economics, Law and Social Sciences, University of St. Gallen (HSG): *Dissertation No. 3238.*

Powell, T. C. (1992). Organizational alignment as competitive advantage. *Strategic Management Journal, 13*(2), 119–134.

Pozen, R. C. (2007). If private equity sized up your business. *Harvard Business Review, November 2007.*

Prahalad, C. K. & Bettis, R. A. (1986). The dominant logic: A new linkage between diversity and performance. *Strategic Management Journal, 7*(6), 485–501.

Prahalad, C. K. & Hamel, G. (1990). The core competence of the corporation. *Harvard Business Review, May–June 1990*, 79–91.

PriceWaterhouseCoopers (2006). *Global Private Equity Report 2006*, http://www.pwc.com (access June 6, 2007).

Priem, R. J. & Butler, J. E. (2001). Is the resource-based view a useful perspective for strategic management research?. *Academy of Management Review, 26*(1), 22–40.

Private Equity Intelligence (2007). *Private Equity Intelligence – Performance analyst, Private Equity Intelligence (Preqin).*

Raghunathan, S. P. (1995). A refinement of the entropy measure of firm diversification: Toward definitional and computational accuracy. *Journal of Management, 21*(5), 989–1002.

Rajan, R., Servaes, H., & Zingales, L. (2000) The cost of diversity: The diversification discount and inefficient investment. *The Journal of Finance, 55*(1), 35–80.

Ramanujam, V. & Varadarajan, P. (1989). Research on corporate diversification: A synthesis. *Strategic Management Journal, 10*(6), 523–551.

Range, J. & Santini, L. (2007). Buyout firms have to settle for smaller stakes in India. *The Wall Street Journal, June 7*, C1.

Rappaport, A. (1978). Executive incentives vs. corporate growth. *Harvard Business Review, July–August 1978*, 81–88.

Rappaport, A. (1981). Selecting strategies that create shareholder value. *Harvard Business Review, May–June 1981*, 139–149.

Rappaport, A. (1990). The staying power of the public corporation. *Harvard Business Review, January–February 1990*, 96–104.

Rappaport, A. (2006). 10 ways to create shareholder value. *Harvard Business Review, September 2006*, 66–77.

Reed, R. & Luffman, G. A. (1986). Diversification: The growing confusion. *Strategic Management Journal, 7*(1), 29–35.

Reed, R. & Reed, M. (1989). CEO experience and diversification strategy fit. *Journal of Management Studies, 26*(3), 251–270.

Reimann, B. C. (1988). Managing for the shareholders: An overview of value-based planning. *Planning Review, 16*(1), 10–22.

Reimann, B. C. (1989). Creating value to keep the raiders at bay. *Long Range Planning, 22*(3), 18–27.

Renneboog, L. D. R., Simons, T., & Wright, M. (2007). Why do public firms go private in the U.K.? The impact of private equity investors, incentive alignment and undervaluation. *Journal of Corporate Finance, 13*(4), 591–628.

Rettberg, U. (2007). *Bruecke fuer private equity*. Handelsblatt, Finanztrends. *March 30*, 30.

Riahi-Belkaoui, A. (1997). Multidivisional structure and productivity: The contingency of diversification strategy. *Journal of Business Finance & Accounting, 24*(5), 615–627.

Riecke, T. (2007a). *KKR lotet Boersengang aus*. Handelsblatt, Finanzzeitung. *June 25*, 26.

Riecke, T. (2007b). Spiessrutenlauf an die Boerse. Handelsblatt. *June 22*, 2.

Robins, J. & Wiersema, M. F. (1995). A resource-based approach to the multibusiness firm: Empirical analysis of portfolio interrelationships and corporate financial performance. *Strategic Management Journal, 16*(4), 277–299.

Roden, D. M. & Lewellen, W. G. (1995). Corporate capital structure decisions: Evidence form leveraged buyouts. *Financial Management, 24*(2), 76–87.

Rogers, P., Holland, T., Haas, D. (2002). Private equity disciplines for the corporation. *The Journal of Private Equity, Winter 2002*, 6–8.
Rosenberg, B. & Guy, J. (1976). Prediction of beta from investment fundamentals. *Financial Analysts Journal, July–August 1976*, 62–70.
Rosenberg, B. & Guy, J. (1995). Prediction of beta from investment fundamentals. *Financial Analysts Journal, January–February 1995*, 101–112.
Rumelt, R. P. (1974). *Strategy, structure and economic performance*. Boston, MA: Division of Research, Harvard Business School.
Rumelt, R. P. (1982). Diversification strategy and profitability. *Strategic Management Journal*, *3*(4), 359–369.
Schaefer, D. (2005). *Die neue Wirtschaftsmacht. Frankfurter Allgemeine Zeitung. July 5*, U3.
Scharfstein, D. S. (1998). *Evidence on the dark side of internal capital markets*. NBER working paper Paper No. 6352.
Scharfstein, D. S. & Stein, J. C. (2000). The dark side of internal capital markets: Divisional rent-seeking and inefficient investment. *The Journal of Finance*, *55*(6), 2537–2564.
Schendel, D. (1992a). Introduction to the summer 1992 special issue on 'strategy process research'. *Strategic Management Journal*, *13*(Special Issue: Strategy Process: Managing Corporate Self-Renewal), 1–4.
Schendel, D. (1992b). Introduction to the winter 1992 special issues: 'Fundamental themes in strategy process research'. *Strategic Management Journal*, *13*(Special Issue: Fundamental Themes in Strategy Process Research), 1–3.
Schmidt, D. (2004). *Private equity-, stock- and mixed asset-portfolios: A bootstrap approach to determine performance characteristics, diversification benefits and optimal portfolio allocations*. Center for Financial Studies 2004/12.
Schoar, A. (2002). Effects of corporate diversification on productivity. *The Journal of Finance*, *57*(6), 2379–2403.
Scott, W. R. (2001). *Institutions and organizations*. Thousand Oaks, CA: Sage Publications.
Sender, H. (2007). Blackstone plan could reshape private equity – Listing would require public disclosures likely to intensify scrutiny. *The Wall Street Journal, March 19*, A1.
Sender, H., Berman, D. K., & Zuckerman, G. (2007). Debt crunch hits deals, deal makers and key IPO – KKR may find it hard to launch stock offer, let alone its financings. *The Wall Street Journal, July 27*, C1.
Seppelfricke, P. (2003). *Handbuch Aktien- und Unternehmensbewertung*. Stuttgart, Schaeffer-Poeschel.
Servaes, H. (1996). The value of diversification during the conglomerate merger wave. *The Journal of Finance*, *51*(4), 1201–1225.
Seth, A. & Easterwood, J. C. (1993). Strategic redirection in large management buyouts: The evidence from post-buyout restructuring activity. *Strategic Management Journal*, *14*(4), 251–273.
Sharpe, W. F. (1964). Capital asset prices: A theory of market equilibrium under conditions of risk. *The Journal of Finance*, *19*(3), 425–442.
Shaw, G., Brown, R., & Bromiley, P. (1998). Strategic stories: How 3M is rewriting business planning. *Harvard Business Review, May–June 1998*, 41–50.
Shin, H.-H. & Stulz, R. M. (1998). Are internal capital markets efficient? *The Quarterly Journal of Economics, May 1998*, 531–552.
Shivdasani, A. & Zak, A. (2007). The return of the recap: Achieving private equity benefits as a public company. *Journal of Applied Corporate Finance*, *19*(3), 32–41.
Shleifer, A. & Vishny, R. (1989). Management entrenchment: The case of manager-specific investments. *Journal of Financial Economics*, *25*(November), 123–139.
Shleifer, M. P. & Summers, L. (1988). Breach the trust in hostile takeovers. *Corporate takeovers: Causes and consequences* (pp. 33–56). A. Auerbach. Chicago: University of Chicago Press.
Silverman, B. S. (1999). Technological resources and the direction of corporate diversification: Toward an integration of the resource-based view and transaction cost economics. *Management Science*, *45*(8), 1109–1124.

Silverman, B. S. (2002). *Technological resources and the logic of corporate diversification*. London: Routledge.

Simmonds, P. G. (1990). The combined diversification breadth and mode dimensions and the performance of large diversified firms. *Strategic Management Journal, 11*(5), 399–410.

Singh, H. (1990). Management buyouts: Distinguishing characteristics and operating changes prior to public offering. *Strategic Management Journal, 11*(4), 111.

Sirmon, D. G., Hitt, M. A., & Ireland, R. D. (2007). Managing firm resources in dynamic environments to create value: Looking inside the black box. *Academy of Management Review, 32*(1), 273–292.

Slater, S. F. & Zwirlein, T. J. (1992). Shareholder value and investment strategy using the general portfolio model. *Journal of Management, 18*(4), 717–732.

Smart, S. B. & Waldfogel, J. (1993). Measuring the effect of restructuring on corporate performance: The case of management buyouts. *The Review of Economics and Statistics, 1993*, 503–511.

Smith, A. J. (1990a). Corporate ownership structure and performance. *Journal of Financial Economics, 27*, 143–164.

Smith, A. J. (1990b). The effects of leveraged buyouts. *Business Economics, 25*(2), 19–26.

Smith, K. V. & Schreiner, J. C. (1969). A portfolio analysis of conglomerate diversification. *The Journal of Finance, 24*(3), 413–427.

Smolka, K. M. (2006). *Eine Frage der Praeferenz. Financial Times Deutschland, Dossier Mischkonzerne, June 21*, 2–4.

Snow, C. C. & Hrebiniak, L. G. (1980). Strategy, distinctive competence, and organizational performance. *Administrative Science Quarterly, 25*(2), 317–336.

Spence, M. A. (1979). Investment strategy and growth in a new market. *The Bell Journal of Economics, 10*(1), 1–19.

Stake, R. E. (2005). Qualitative case studies. In N. K. Denzin & Y. S. Lincoln, *The sage handbook of qualitative research* (3rd ed.). Thousand Oaks: Sage Publications.

Stein, J. C. (1997). Internal capital markets and the competition for corporate resources. *The Journal of Finance, 52*(1), 111–133.

Stewart III, G. B. (1990). Remaking the public corporation from within. *Harvard Business Review, July–August 1990*, 126–137.

Stimpert, J. L. & Duhaime, I. M. (1997). Seeing the big picture: The influence of industry, diversification, and business strategy on performance. *The Academy of Management Journal, 40*(3), 560–583.

Stocker, F. (2007). *Gemeinsame Jagd auf die Großen. Welt am Sonntag, Finanzen, January 7*, 35.

Strauss, A. & Corbin, J. (1998). *Basics of qualitative research: Techniques and procedures for developing grounded theory* (2nd ed.) Thousand Oaks, CA: Sage Publications.

Stroemberg, P. (2008). The new demography of private equity. In A. Gurung & J. Lerner (Eds.), *Globalization of alternative investments: the global economic impact of private equity report 2008* (working papers, Vol. 1, pp. 3–42). Geneva: World Economic Forum.

Tannon, J. M. & Johnson, R. (2005). Transatlantic private equity: beyond a trillion dollar force. *The Journal of Private Equity, Summer 2005*.

Tanriverdi, H. & Venkatraman, N. (2005). Knowledge relatedness and the performance of multibusiness firms. *Strategic Management Journal, 26*(2), 97–119.

Teece, D. J. (1980). Economics of scope and the scope of the enterprise. *Journal of Economic Behavior and Organization, 1*, 223–247.

Teece, D. J. (1982). Towards an exonomic theory of the multiproduct firm. *Journal of Economic Behavior and Organization, 3*, 39–63.

Teitelbaum, R. (2007). The KKR way. *Bloomberg Markets, August 2007*, 36–45.

The Economist (2006). Private equity: Under the microscope. *The Economist, Finance and Economics, November 11*, 83–84.

Thompson Financial (2007). *Venture Expert, Thompson Financial*.

Thompson, S., Wright, M., & Robbie, K. (1992). Buy-outs, divestment, and leverage: Restructuring transactions and corporate governance. *Oxford Review of Economic Policy, 8*(3), 58–69.

Tobin, J. (1969). A general equilibrium approach to monetary theory. *Journal of Money, Credit and Banking, 1*(1), 15–29.

Torabzadeh, K. M. & Bertin, W. J. (1987). Leveraged buyouts and shareholder returns. *The Journal of Financial Research, 10*(4), 313–319.

Treynor, J. L. (1965). How to rate management of investment funds. *Harvard Business Review, January–February 1965*, 63–75.

Tyebjee, T. T. & Bruno, A. V. (1984). A model of venture capitalist investment activity. *Management Science, 30*(9), 1051–1066.

Ulbricht, N. & Weiner, C. (2005). *Worldscope meets Compustat: A comparison of financial databases*. Humboldt University Berlin, working paper. Berlin.

van Oijen, A. & Douma, S. (2000). Diversification strategy and the roles of the centre. *Long Range Planning, 33*(4), 560–578.

Vancil, R. F. & Lorange, P. (1975). Strategic planning in diversified companies. *Harvard Business Review, January–February 1975*, 81–90.

Varadarajan, P. (1986). Product diversity and firm performance: An empirical investigation. *Journal of Marketing, 50*(3), 43–57.

Varadarajan, P. & Ramanujam, V. (1987). Diversification and performance: A reexamination using a new two-dimensional conceptualization of diversity in firms. *The Academy of Management Journal, 30*(2), 380–393.

Varanasi, M. P. (2005). Round table: Diversification strategy and firm performance. *IIMB Management Review, September 2005*, 97–104.

Veliyath, R. (1999). Top management compensation and shareholder returns: Unravelling different models of the relationship. *Journal of Management Studies, 36*(January), 123–143.

Venkatraman, N. & Camillus, J. C. (1984). Exploring the concept of fit in strategic management. *Academy of Management Review, 9*(3), 513–525.

Villalonga, B. (2003). *Research roundtable discussion: The diversification discount*. Harvard Business School, case and teaching paper series 2003(April).

Villalonga, B. (2004a). Diversification discount of premium? New evidence from the business information tracking series. *The Journal of Finance, 54*(2), 479–506.

Villalonga, B. (2004b). Does diversification cause the diversification discount? *Financial Management, 33*(2), 5–27.

Waite, S. & M. Fridson (1989). Do leveraged buyouts pose big risks for the U.S. financial system? *Mergers and Acquisitions, March–April 1989*, 43–48.

Watsham, T. J. & Parramore, K. (1997). *Quantitative methods in finance*. London, Thomson Learning.

Weidig, T. & Mathonet, P.-Y. (2004). *The risk profiles of private equity*. EIF, working paper.

Weir, C., Laing, D., & Wright, M. (2005). Incentive effects, monitoring mechanisms and the market for corporate control: An analysis of the factors affecting public to private transactions in the UK. *Journal of Business Finance & Accounting, 32*(5), 909–943.

Weir, C. & Wright, M. (2006). Governance and takeovers: Are public-to-private transactions different from traditional acquisitions of listed corporations? *Accounting and Business Research, 36*(4), 289–307.

Welge, M. K. & Al-Laham, A. (2007). *Strategisches Management: Grundlagen-Prozess-Implementierung* (5th ed.) Wiesbaden: Gabler.

Welge, M. K., Al-Laham, A., & Kajüter, P. (2000). *Der Prozess des strategischen Managements – Ein Ueberblick ueber die empirische Strategieprozessforschung*. Wiesbaden: Gabler.

Wernerfelt, B. (1984). A resource-based view of the firm. *Strategic Management Journal, 5*(2), 171–180.

Wernerfelt, B. (1995). The resource-based view of the firm: Ten years after. *Strategic Management Journal, 16*(3), 171–174.

Wernerfelt, B. & Montgomery, C. A. (1986). What is an attractive industry? *Management Science, 32*(10), 1223–1230.

Wernerfelt, B. & Montgomery, C. A. (1988). Tobin's q and the importance of focus in firm performance. *The American Economic Review, 78*(1), 246–250.

West, R. R. (1967). Homemade diversification vs. corporate diversification. *The Journal of Financial and Quantitative Analysis, 2*(4), 417–420.

Weston, J. F., Smith, K. V., & Shrieves, R. E. (1972). Conglomerate performance using the capital asset pricing model. *The Review of Economics and Statistics, 54*(4), 357–363.

Whited, T. M. (2001). Is it inefficient investment that causes the diversification discount? *The Journal of Finance*, *56*(5), 1667–1691.

Wiersema, M. F. & Liebeskind, J. P. (1995). The effects of leveraged buyouts on corporate growth and diversification in large firms. *Strategic Management Journal 16*(6), 447–460.

Williamson, O. E. (1975). *Markets and hierarchies: Analysis and antitrust implications*. New York: Free Press.

Wollnik, M. (1977). Die explorative Verwendung systematischen Erfahrungswissens – Plaedoyer fuer einen aufgeklaerten Empirismus in der Betriebswirtschaftslehre. In R. Kohler (Ed.), *Empirische und handlungstheoretische Forschungskonzeptionen in der Betriebswirtschaftslehre* (pp. 37–64). Stuttgart: Poeschel.

Wright, M., Hoskisson, R. E., & Busenitz, L. W. (2001). Firm rebirth: Buyouts as facilitators of strategic growth and entrepreneurship. *Academy of Management Executive*, *15*(1), 111–125.

Wright, M. & Robbie, K. (1996). The investor-led buy-out: A new strategic option. *Long Range Planning*, *29*(5), 691.

Wright, M., Simons, T., Scholes, L., & Renneboog, L. (2006). Leveraged buyouts in the U.K. and Continental Europe: Retrospect and prospect. *Journal of Applied Corporate Finance*, *18*(3), 38–55.

Wrigley, L. (1970). *Division, autonomy and diversification*, doctoral dissertation. Boston, MA: Harvard Business School.

Wruck, K. H. (1989). Equity ownership concentration and firm value: Evidence from private equity financings. *Journal of Financial Economics*, *23*, 3–28.

Wruck, K. H. (1994). Financial policy, internal control, and performance: Sealed Air Corporation's leveraged special dividend. *Journal of Financial Economics*, *36*, 157–192.

Wruck, K. H. (2007). Reinvention of the market for corporate control. *The History, Impact, and Future of Private Equity, 27 November 2007*. American Enterprise Institute for Public Policy Research. Washington, DC

Yavitz, B. & Newman, W. H. (1982). What the corporation should provide its business units. *Journal of Business Strategy*, 2(1), 14–19.

Yin, R. K. (2003). *Case study research – Design and methods* (3rd ed.) Thousand Oaks, CA: Sage Publications.

Yip, G. S. (1982). Diversification entry: Internal development versus acquisition. *Strategic Management Journal*, *3*(4), 331–345.

Zahra, S. A. & Fescina, M. (1991). Will leveraged buyouts kill U.S. corporate research & development? *Academy of Management Executive* 5(4), 7.

Zimmermann, H., Bilo, S., Christophers, H., & Degosciu, M. (2005). *Risk, returns, and biases of listed private equity portfolios*. University of Basel, working paper. Basel.

Zong, L. (2005). Governance lessons from the private equity industry. *Journal of Private Equity, Winter 2005.*

About the Author

Daniel O. Klier is a strategy consultant with McKinsey & Company. He is specialized in growth strategies and business development for private equity clients, financial institutions, and real estate investors. He has worked on various international engagements across Europe, Asia and the Middle East.

Daniel holds a degree in business administration (lic.oec.hsg) from the University of St. Gallen (HSG) in Switzerland, where he developed particular expertise in the areas of strategic management and corporate finance. To complete his studies, he spent time at the London School of Economics (LSE). For his doctoral dissertation, Daniel worked with Professor Martin K. Welge from the Technical University of Dortmund and Professor Kathryn R. Harrigan from Columbia Business School.

Daniel was born on March 20, 1981 in Munich. His current residence is Berlin.

Breinigsville, PA USA
21 August 2009
222732BV00007B/46/P

9 783790 821727